UNIVERSITY OF MARY HARDIN-BAYLOR

TOWNSEND MEMORIAL LIBRARY
UNIVERSITY OF MARY HARDIN-BAYLOR
BELTON TEXAS 76513

D1221795

HOW THE BODY SHAPES THE MIND

TOWNSEND MEMORIAL LIBRARY
UNIVERSITY OF MARY HARDIN-BAYLOR
BELTON TEXAS 76513

How the Body
Shapes the Mind

SHAUN GALLAGHER

CLARENDON PRESS · OXFORD

OXFORD

UNIVERSITY PRESS

Great Clarendon Street, Oxford OX2 6DP

Oxford University Press is a department of the University of Oxford.
It furthers the University's objective of excellence in research, scholarship,
and education by publishing worldwide in

Oxford New York

Auckland Cape Town Dar es Salaam Hong Kong Karachi Kuala Lumpur
Madrid Melbourne Mexico City Nairobi New Delhi Shanghai Taipei Toronto

With offices in

Argentina Austria Brazil Chile Czech Republic France Greece
Guatemala Hungary Italy Japan South Korea Poland Portugal
Singapore Switzerland Thailand Turkey Ukraine Vietnam

Oxford is a registered trade mark of Oxford University Press
in the UK and in certain other countries

Published in the United States
by Oxford University Press Inc., New York

© Shaun Gallagher 2005

The moral rights of the author have been asserted
Database right Oxford University Press (maker)

First published 2005

All rights reserved. No part of this publication may be reproduced,
stored in a retrieval system, or transmitted, in any form or by any means,
without the prior permission in writing of Oxford University Press,
or as expressly permitted by law, or under terms agreed with the appropriate
reprographics rights organization. Enquiries concerning reproduction
outside the scope of the above should be sent to the Rights Department,
Oxford University Press, at the address above

You must not circulate this book in any other binding or cover
and you must impose this same condition on any acquirer

British Library Cataloguing in Publication Data

Data available

Library of Congress Cataloging in Publication Data

Data available

ISBN 0–19–927194–1

1 3 5 7 9 10 8 6 4 2

Typeset by Kolam Information Services Pvt. Ltd, Pondicherry, India
Printed in Great Britain on acid-free paper by
Biddles Ltd,
King's Lynn, Norfolk

TOWNSEND MEMORIAL LIBRARY
UNIVERSITY OF MARY HARDIN-BAYLOR
BELTON, TEXAS 76513

to MY MOTHER,

Bridget (McBride Coyle) Gallagher
from Ardbane, Donegal

and

in memory of MY FATHER

John (Andrew Simon) Gallagher
from Derryhassen, Donegal

Contents

List of Figures

List of Tables

Introduction

[I]t is not enough to say that the mind is embodied; one must say how.

(Edelman 1992: 15)

IN the beginning, that is, at the time of our birth, our human capacities for perception and behavior have already been shaped by our movement. Prenatal bodily movement has already been organized along the lines of our own human shape, in proprioceptive and cross-modal registrations, in ways that provide a capacity for experiencing a basic distinction between our own embodied existence and everything else. As a result, when we first open our eyes, not only can we see, but also our vision, imperfect as it is, is already attuned to those shapes that resemble our own shape. More precisely and quite literally, we can see our own possibilities in the faces of others. The infant, minutes after birth, is capable of imitating the gesture that it sees on the face of another person. It is thus capable of a certain kind of movement that foreshadows intentional action, and that propels it into a human world.

This starting point is already the result of complex processes that require explanations still being developed in sciences that range from genetics, to the neurosciences, to the behavioral sciences. Human life and the beginnings of the intelligent behavior that we can see in the infant are not only measured by their physical manifestations as bodily processes, they *are* those processes, and are constituted by them. Movement and the registration of that movement in a developing proprioceptive system (that is, a system that registers its own self-movement) contributes to the self-organizing development of neuronal structures responsible not only for motor action, but for the way we come to be conscious of ourselves, to communicate with others, and to live in the surrounding world. Across the Cartesian divide, movement prefigures the lines of intentionality, gesture formulates the contours of social cognition, and, in both the most general and most specific ways, embodiment shapes the mind.

These are themes that I explore in the studies that make up this book. They are topics that have been pursued in recent years by other authors who have helped to establish what is generally known as the embodied cognition approach (see e.g. Bermúdez, Marcel, and Eilan 1995; A. Clark 1997; Damasio 1994, 1999; Varela, Thompson, and Rosch 1991). The broad argument about the importance of embodiment for understanding cognition has already been made in numerous ways, and there is a growing consensus across a variety of disciplines that this basic fact is inescapable. Precisely because this insight has been developed across a variety of disciplines, however, there is still a need to develop a common vocabulary that is capable of integrating discussions of brain mechanisms in neuroscience, behavioral expressions in psychology, design concerns in artificial intelligence and robotics, and debates about embodied experience in the phenomenology and philosophy of mind. It is my aim in this book to contribute to the formulation of that common vocabulary and to develop a conceptual framework that will avoid both the overly reductionistic approaches that explain everything in terms of bottom-up neuronal mechanisms, and the inflationistic approaches that explain everything in terms of Cartesian, top-down cognitive states.

My explorations are philosophical in a way that is informed by empirical studies. They are motivated by two basic sets of questions that concern the structure of experience. The first set consists of questions about the *phenomenal* aspects of that structure, and specifically the relatively regular and constant phenomenal features that we find in the content of our experience. In regard to embodiment, I want to explore to what extent and in what way an awareness of my body enters into the content of my conscious experience? To what degree and in what situations am I, as an experiencing subject, aware or unaware of my own body? Does intentional action, for example, involve an explicit or implicit awareness of the body? No doubt these questions can be, and have been, phrased in different ways. Such questions, however, pertain to an important aspect of the structure of experience. If throughout conscious experience there is a constant reference to one's own body, even if this is a recessive or marginal awareness, then that reference constitutes a structural feature of the phenomenal field of consciousness, part of a framework that is likely to determine or influence all other aspects of experience.

The second set of questions focuses on aspects of the structure of consciousness that are more hidden, those that may be more difficult to get at because they happen *before we know it*. They do not normally enter into the phenomenal content of experience in an explicit way, and are often inaccessible to reflective consciousness. I use the term *prenoetic* to signify these hidden aspects. The basic question can be phrased in this general way: To what extent, and in what ways, are consciousness and cognitive (noetic or mental) processes, which include experiences related to perception, memory, imagination, belief, judgment, and so forth, shaped or structured *prenoetically* by the fact that they are embodied?

This question gets at a different issue than questions about phenomenal aspects of consciousness, which may or may not include an awareness or sense of the body. To ask about the prenoetic effects of embodiment is to ask about what happens behind the scenes of awareness, and about how the body anticipates and sets the stage for consciousness. More precisely, the question in this case is not about the apparent *structure* of consciousness, but about the *structuring* of consciousness, and the role that embodiment plays in the structuring process. How does the fact of embodiment, the fact that consciousness is embodied, *affect*, and perhaps *effect*, intentional experience? In any particular instance, for example, because of the fact of my embodiment, I necessarily perceive the world from a limited spatial perspective and within a seemingly amorphous framework of a particular emotive stance or mood. Such prenoetic constraints necessarily shape my experience, although they do not necessarily appear, in an explicit manner, as part of the phenomenal content that I experience.

The answers to these questions not only provide important insights into the nature of experience, they also tell us something about the nature of the human person, sometimes more abstractly referred to as the *self*. In some fashion, quite obviously, the human person is embodied in human form and matter. The human body, and the way it structures human experience, also shapes the human experience of self, and perhaps the very possibility of developing a sense of self. If the self is anything more than this, it is nonetheless and first of all this, an embodied self.

I have indicated here, in the briefest fashion, a collection of related problems involving consciousness, embodiment, and self. Within the setting of these problems I will also discuss a number of specialized issues, from the nature of movement and agency, to the operations of language, to questions of how we know other persons. Quite frequently in the following chapters the examination of pathological conditions will help us understand normal and everyday behavior. I will frequently call on disciplines such as psychology and neuroscience to help chart and navigate the philosophical regions involved. Thus the nature and scope of these problems call for some comment about the approach and methodology taken in this book.

In my view, there is no one methodology that will provide a full picture of the setting that we intend to explore. As a result I plan to borrow from already established insights provided by a number of different disciplines: developmental psychology, neuropsychology, the neurosciences, cognitive linguistics, phenomenology, and philosophy of mind. This, of course, is an extremely risky strategy, for I cannot claim proficiency in more than one of these fields, and certainly no one individual can be expert in all these areas. As I will explain, however, I have had a great deal of help, and in some sense, I am not entirely on my own.

The fact that I will be borrowing from many disciplines presents methodological difficulties as well as strategic dangers. Terminologies and conceptual frameworks vary across research fields. Indeed, the very definition of consciousness and even its usefulness as a theoretical concept have been matters of both inter- and intradisciplinary consternation and disagreement in both philosophy and the cognitive sciences. I cannot attempt to resolve all such problems, but I will touch on many of them. My approach involves the interpretation of a large amount of empirical data. The reader will have to judge to what extent my interpretations remain faithful to the scientific evidence and coherent across the various fields of research.

In constructing my interpretations I have not worked exclusively from either the bottom up or the top down. That is, my principle has not been to find the simplest and most basic experiences or physical events in order to construct a synthesis from such elements; nor has it been to start with the most complex phenomena and to analyze them into their basic constituents. I have not confined myself to working exclusively on the subpersonal level of cognitive mechanisms, nor exclusively in the realm of phenomenology. My project, as I have indicated, is neither reductionistic nor ontologically inflationary. Of course, when the theme of investigation is human nature and experience, I suspect there are hidden metaphysical assumptions about foundations and hierarchies in any approach, even in the most scientific and empirical ones. I have tried to avoid the worst of the foundational-hierarchical assumptions by taking an ontogenetic approach in several of the chapters. In other words, in many instances, I have tried to work *from the beginning onward*, rather than from the bottom up or the top down.

What constitutes a beginning, however, is relatively uncertain, and is neither the simplest nor the most complex of things. Different fields define the notion of a beginning in very different ways. One might, as a neurobiologist, begin with an evolutionary perspective. In that framework, for example, since movement can be taken as an important element in morphogenesis, one might try to discover how basic animal movement starts to shape the animal body, which simultaneously shapes what Aristotle would have called the animal soul. Thus, Gerald Edelman examines how anatomy and brain structure undergo 'continuous electrical and chemical change, driving and being driven by animal movement', and he discovers that animal movement itself is 'conditioned by animal shape and pattern, leading to behavior' (Edelman 1992). For my purposes this evolutionary perspective stays very much in the background, and although I do not deny the relevance of these insights (see Ch. 5), I define beginnings in the shorter term.

In several of the chapters, my point of departure includes considerations about ontogenesis and microgenesis. This approach, I think, does not assume, but discovers that experience is complex and holistic from its very beginning. A good example of this concerns the fact that perception is intermodal from the start, a fact that challenges traditional empiricist theories of perception, yet reaffirms a basic empiricist insight about the importance of experience (see Ch. 7). The idea that experience is holistic, however, does not mean that its explanation needs to be holistic, and to avoid the temptation to simply wave hands and declare everything to be connected in complex ways with everything else, I take care to avoid beginning with pre-established general principles. I try my best to avoid the existing and frequently conflicting assumptions that have marked the study of cognition in the last thirty years; for example, that everything can be explained in computational terms, or that everything is self-organizing. Rather, I look for domain-specific principles, ones that appear to work in a local context and are developmentally bound, and yet may be different from one developmental context to another. In many chapters I work my way through specific issues by working my way through specific problems and examples—case studies, or particular pathological symptoms, or a specific set of experiments—as a way to discern the principles that capture the import of embodiment. Although my intention is to construct a strong argument for the role of embodiment in the development and proper functioning of various aspects of cognition, my idea is not that one theory fits all or that every aspect of cognition is directly tied to embodiment.

Without being naive about the difficulties involved in such a strategy, I try to be careful in all these regards (staying close to the evidence, avoiding certain metaphysical assumptions, identifying the assumptions and approaches I do take) because in some limited contexts I will be forced to speculate. In these cases I want my speculations to remain close to the ground, and nicely tied to scientific evidence as much as possible.

A Vocabulary that Redefines the Terrain

A distinction divides up a conceptual space in a certain way; it does not necessarily divide up reality in the same way. The questions about phenomenal and hidden (prenoetic) structures signify a theoretical distinction that from a behavioral or existential perspective may seem too abstract. The distinction between phenomenal and prenoetic structures, however, is a relative one, and is not meant to signify two different ontological categories or classes of things that pertain to embodied consciousness. Furthermore, if one were tempted to take this distinction as signifying something along the lines of manifest versus latent, or conscious versus unconscious, one would be led in the wrong direction. It may be best to think of it as a functional distinction, so that the lines drawn between phenomenal structure and prenoetic structuring may differ from one context to the next.

In developing a picture of embodied consciousness and cognition I will draw directly from scientific traditions. Yet, even here, there are distinctions that are not as clear or as robust as we would like. Since distinctions that can be made clear conceptually may not remain so at the level of practical behavior, theoretical distinctions need to remain flexible enough to accommodate a certain degree of ambiguity; at the same time they need to be productive for theory and revealing of reality. A clear conceptual distinction between certain aspects of behavior can aid immensely in sorting out how these aspects interact in actual practice, even if in such interaction the aspects are not so clearly distinguished.

I intend to be cautious about how distinctions work between conceptual and practical contexts because at the very outset I will adopt one that is both controversial and, I will argue, productive—the distinction between *body image* and *body schema* (Ch. 1). Although these concepts have long been used in psychological studies of embodiment, they have also been criticized for being too ambiguous and even obscurant (for example, Poeck and Orgass 1971). Without denying that there is some *de facto* truth to this criticism, it is also the case that many of the problems with these concepts are due to the fact that researchers almost always fail to employ a systematic conceptual distinction between body image and body schema. I will argue that if the clear and proper distinction is made, these concepts carve up the conceptual space in a way that leads to a productive understanding of embodied consciousness. Along the way, this distinction will help to clarify not only perceptual experience and action, but also a variety of specific phenomena such as neonate imitation, phantom limbs, deafferentation, unilateral neglect, and the linguistic nature of gesture.

I will argue further that the vocabulary that can be developed around the conceptual distinction between body image and body schema, and specifically around the attempts to define their explanatory usefulness as well as their limitations, is one that is capable of integrating the first-person phenomenology and third-person science of embodied cognition. This distinction between first-person, subjective access to experience, and third-person, objective observation of physical and behavioral events is the most familiar way of defining the gap that seemingly has to be bridged. Whether we call it the explanatory gap, or the 'hard' problem, or the mind–body problem, it is a problem that is both methodological and epistemological. My approach, in contrast to reductionistic methods,[1] is to take the first-person perspective seriously. Often, however, approaches that do take first-person phenomenology seriously end up as a mere explication of correlations between physical processes and mental processes. Neither the cognitive neurosciences nor phenomenological approaches to consciousness, however, should be satisfied with simple *correlations* that might be established between brain processes described from a third-person perspective and phenomenal experience described from a first-person perspective. Such correlations do not constitute *explanations*, and indeed, such correlations are in part what need to be explained. At the same time, filling the explanatory gap is not a matter of bridging it with intermediate elements, for example, with theoretical models, causal mechanisms, or representations. We need to work with *what there is* and to understand such intermediaries for what they are—heuristic devices or theoretical models that may or may not be helpful. Rather than trying to locate or to construct an intermediary entity that would bridge the gap, the task, as I understand it, is to create a coherent and contextually rich background theory that supports and explicates the connections that actually exist among the elements of the embodied cognitive system. The vocabulary and conceptual framework that we need is not one that will build a bridge, but one that will redefine the terrain.

As an example (and at the risk of anticipating answers that are still to be worked out, and perhaps even begging all the questions—not an inappropriate procedure for an introduction, however), some of the vocabulary that we need to put to use in this project, and that relates directly to a discussion of embodiment, involves the notion of proprioception. Proprioception signifies one of the specific areas where the distinction between phenomenal consciousness and physical body gets redefined. Proprioception, however, is itself a complex phenomenon that is articulated in slightly different ways in different disciplines. On the one hand, neuroscientists may treat somatic proprioception as an entirely subpersonal, non-conscious function—the unconscious registration in the central nervous system of the body's own limb position. In this sense, it results in information about body posture and limb position, generated in physiological (mechanical) proprioceptors located throughout the body, reaching various parts of the brain, enabling control

---

[1] I include Dennett's (1991, 2003b) notion of heterophenomenology as one of the reductionistic approaches that I would avoid. It will be obvious in the following chapters that I do not accept his judgment about phenomenological approaches. 'First-person science of consciousness is a discipline with no methods, no data, no results, no future, no promise. It will remain a fantasy' (2002: 1). See Gallagher (1997, 2003a, forthcoming b) for my criticisms of heterophenomenology.

of movement without the subject being consciously aware of that information.[2] On the other hand, psychologists and philosophers sometimes treat somatic proprioception as a form of consciousness. One is said to be proprioceptively aware of one's own body, to consciously know where one's limbs are at any particular time as one moves through the world.[3] Thus proprioception can mean either non-conscious *information* or a form of conscious *awareness*. Conceptually, I try to keep these different senses apart by maintaining the distinction between proprioceptive *information* and proprioceptive *awareness*, respectively.[4] On the embodied experiential level, however, these two aspects of proprioception are fully integrated.

There are two further complications relevant to the concept of proprioception. First, the two proprioceptive aspects just mentioned, in their integrated functioning, form a standard, but narrow and specifically intracorporeal definition of somatic proprioception. Narrow, because proprioception is also taken in a much more general sense by Gibsonian psychologists. In this sense it means a certain aspect that belongs to any modality of perception (vision, touch, hearing, and so on) that delivers a corresponding sense of body position relative to the environment, or a corresponding sense of self, which Neisser (1988) terms the 'ecological self'. Thus, proprioception in this wider sense depends on integrating different modalities of sensory information concerning one's own body as a moving agent in the environment, with the intracorporeal information provided by an internally generated sense of posture and movement (Trevarthen 1986).

The second complication is a more philosophical one. It concerns the epistemological status of proprioceptive awareness. In most psychological discussions proprioception is considered to be a form of object-perception that identifies one's own body as its object. Indeed, in some cases, when proprioception is explicitly relied on, for example when subjects deprived of visual perception are asked to point to one of their own body parts, it seems to function in just this way. Is it also possible, however, that proprioceptive awareness functions as what Shoemaker (1984) calls a non-perceptual or non-observational self-awareness, which is a more direct and reliable form of awareness than object-perception? This question, to which I shall return, holds important implications for issues pertaining to self-consciousness and personal identity.

---

[2] For example, Sherrington (1953) often uses the term in this way. Since we have no awareness of neural events which 'register the tension at thousands of points they sample in the muscles, tendons, and ligaments of [a] limb', he maintains that 'I perceive no trace of all this [proprioceptive activity]' (p. 248). Sherrington, however, goes on to consider a proprioceptive awareness of movement. More recently, Fourneret and Jeannerod (1998) conducted experiments that showed subjects to be completely unaware of proprioceptive signals generated by their own movements.

[3] Thus O'Shaughnessy (1995) speaks of proprioceptive awareness. Sheets-Johnstone describes proprioception as follows: 'Proprioception refers generally to a sense of movement and position. It thus includes an awareness of movement and position through tactility as well as kinesthesia, that is, through surface as well as internal events, including also a sense of gravitational orientation through vestibular sensory organs. Kinesthesia refers specifically to a sense of movement through muscular effort' (1998, n. 13).

[4] This is a distinction clearly made in Bermúdez, Marcel, and Eilan (1995), and Bermúdez (1998).

From just these brief indications about the status of 'proprioception' one can see that it plays an important role in considerations about consciousness, embodiment, and self. As further indication of the direction taken in the following chapters, let me return to the idea that there is an essential relation between movement and cognition. Although movement is involved, at almost every turn, in considerations about perception and other acts of cognition, it is only rarely made the theme of philosophical investigation.[5] It is true that philosophers from Aristotle to Locke and Berkeley have indicated that a certain 'movement' in the soul, a successive flow structure in the mind, is responsible for structuring thought and for gaining regular connections among our experiences. But this is not the movement I mean. Rather, as I have already indicated, *bodily* movement is closely tied in various ways to perception and to other forms of cognition and emotion.[6] Indeed, there is now a large amount of evidence from a variety of studies and disciplines to show that the body, through its motor abilities, its actual movements, and its posture, informs and shapes cognition. Here are some examples.

• Visual perception involves the constant task of keeping the world relatively stable when many different features of the perceiving body may be in constant motion. From eye saccades and interocular motor adjustments to overall bodily balance, visual stability necessarily depends on motor control. For example, micro-saccadic eye movement helps to prevent the loss of visual object perception (Martinez-Conde, Macknik, and Hubel 2000).

• The shape and size of objects are perceived not simply in phenomenal terms (phenomenal size of an object depending on distance from the perceiver), but in pragmatic terms (as something I can grasp or manipulate). Phenomenally, the size and shape of an object may vary perspectivally or across distance; pragmatically, they remain invariant—the perceived object is something I am capable of picking up or it is not (Jeannerod 1994).

• There is good evidence to suggest that in certain cases, when we observe an object, even when we are not specifically required to reach for it or pick it up, 'canonical neurons' in the ventral premotor cortex (area F5) responsible for the motoric encoding of actions such as reaching and grasping are selectively activated (see Gallese 2000; Murata *et al.* 1997; Rizzolatti, Fogassi, and Gallese 2000). The visual observation of such objects automatically evokes the most suitable motor program required to interact with them, and the activation of motor preparation areas in the brain form part of what it means to perceive such objects.

• The development of perceptual and cognitive abilities is enhanced in correl-ation to a greater amount of crawling and mobility in infancy (Campos, Bertenthal,

---

[5] Recently, however, this subject has been addressed by two notable studies—Hurley (1999) and Sheets-Johnstone (1999*a*).

[6] The very onset of consciousness may be directly related to prenatal movement and accompanying proprioception. Still, I do not mean to endorse a motor theory of perception—a theory that would claim that mental states are produced by movement or muscle discharges related to interaction with objects. I want to treat movement as a *constraint on* rather than a *cause of* perception. For a review of motor theories of cognition, see Scheerer (1984).

and Kermoian 1992; see Thelen 1995), and more specific perceptual strategies develop only when infants are able to execute certain motor abilities (Bushnell and Boudreau 1993).[7] Recent studies in biodynamics show that movement and proprioception are intrinsically related to perception (Lockman and Thelen 1993).

• Both ontogenetic and phylogenetic studies suggest that motor-related neuronal processes and structures are integrally linked to sensory and emotive processes, and that much of this integration is organized by motor representations of the body (Panksepp 1998).

• Body posture can affect attention and certain kinds of judgment (Kinsbourne 1975). If subjects turn head and eyes to one side just prior to making a judgment, the direction of turning influences cognitive performance (ibid.). When subjects listen to a sentence with head and eyes turned right, their performance in cued recall is better than when they listened with head turned toward the left (Lempert and Kinsbourne 1982). In addition, trunk orientation induces directional biases in the ability to shift attention. The rotation of a subject's trunk to the left increases their response times to cued targets on the right and decreases their response times to cued targets on the left (Grubb and Reed 2002).

• The recent discovery of 'mirror neurons' in the premotor cortex, neurons that are activated either by the subject's own motor behavior *or* by the subject's visual observation of someone else's motor behavior, shows a direct and active link between the motor and sensory systems and has important implications for explaining how we understand other people (Di Pellegrino *et al.* 1992; Gallese *et al.* 1996; Rizzolatti *et al.* 1996).

There are many other studies that could be mentioned here, but my aim is not to give an exhaustive list; I simply want to provide a quick sense of what is in fact a small part of the terrain that we will be trying to remap in the following chapters, and a brief indication of how bodily movement and the motor system influence cognitive performance—how the body shapes the mind. It may even be possible to say that bodily movement, transformed onto the level of action, is the very thing that constitutes the self.[8]

---

[7] This is not to deny that the developmental relation between cognition and movement goes both ways. Thus, development of motor competence is essentially linked to the maturation of intrinsic and primitive recognitional abilities in early infancy to more explicit object recognition based on increased sensitivity to object properties (Bermúdez 1998; Russell 1996).

[8] Renaud Barbaras (1999, 2000) suggests a close connection between movement and perception and finds within this insight the beginnings of a radically non-traditional, non-metaphysical way of thinking of the self. I do not pursue this route here. It would entail giving up a certain concept of experience that I find useful for bridging the phenomenological tradition and discussions in cognitive science. I would note, however, that the connection between movement and perception is also found in metaphysical accounts of the self. For example, Fichte's concept of 'intellectual intuition' is not unrelated to these issues. He writes: 'I cannot take a step, move hand or foot without an intellectual intuition of my self-consciousness in these acts; only so do I know that *I* do it, only so do I distinguish my action, and myself therein, from the object of action before me. Whoever ascribes an activity to himself, appeals to this intuition' (1794: 38).

If, as indicated in these and many other studies, embodied movement contributes to the shaping of perception, emotional experience, memory, judgment, and the understanding of self and of others, then we need an account of embodiment that is sufficiently detailed, and that is articulated in a vocabulary that can integrate discussions across the cognitive sciences. The goal of this book is to begin to provide such an account and to remap the terrain that lies between phenomenology and cognitive neuroscience.

Acknowledgements

I mentioned that I am not entirely on my own in writing this book. A significant amount of the work found in this book is based on earlier studies that I co-authored with researchers in a variety of disciplines. Thus, besides the numerous sources that I cite, I have benefited a great deal from help provided by my co-authors and by a wide variety of people in different disciplines with whom I have discussed these matters.

The first chapter, 'The Terms of Embodiment', is an attempt to clarify a real muddle in the psychological literature, and to provide the first elements of a vocabulary that enables us to say how the mind is embodied. The distinction between *body image* and *body schema* that I propose here relies on a phenomenological analysis.[9] For me, however, phenomenology has never been 'pure' in the Husserlian sense. My efforts, following the path of Merleau-Ponty more than Husserl, have always been informed by extensive readings in psychology and neuroscience. Although the present book is a philosophical study and still has its roots in phenomenology, my attempts to understand the recent scientific discussions have, for me, redefined earlier phenomenological accounts. Thus, like several other authors, I have tried to pull phenomenology into the broader context of the cognitive sciences, creating, I think, an interdisciplinary approach that is both productive and mutually beneficial for the sciences and phenomenology (see Gallagher 1997; Gallagher and Varela 2001; Petitot *et al.* 1999; Varela 1996).

In my own case I was motivated to expand my understanding of the productive relationship between phenomenology and cognitive science by Anthony Marcel and his work in psychology. I was fortunate to be invited by him to an interdisciplinary workshop at King's College Research Centre at Cambridge University in 1992. The paper I presented there explored the effects of movement and posture on perceptual experience. Chapter 6 is a revised and extended version of that paper (Gallagher 1995). The King's College meeting was important for me because I met a number of people with whom I came to have a working relationship, and much of the present volume is the result of those collaborations.

---

[9] This analysis was first worked out in Gallagher (1986b).

One such collaboration was with Andrew Meltzoff, who conducted the original studies of neonate imitation (Meltzoff and Moore 1977). Sections of Chs. 3 and 4 are based on a paper we co-authored concerning neonate imitation, the body schema, and the phenomenon of phantom limbs in cases of congenital absence of limb (Gallagher and Meltzoff 1996). In Ch. 3, however, I introduce two qualifications to that previous work. First, I reformulate my understanding of the role played by the body image in neonate imitation. Second, I raise a question about the adequacy of explaining neonate imitation strictly in terms of proprioception, intermodal mechanisms, and an innate body schema. This question has important philosophical implications and is further explored in later chapters.

Subsequent to my work with Meltzoff, the late George Butterworth, a developmental psychologist at the University of Sussex, suggested a possible resolution to the problem of phantoms in congenital absence of limb. The details of this idea were worked out in a paper that focused on the contribution of prenatal movement to the development of the body schema (Gallagher et al. 1998). Parts of this study find their way into Ch. 4.

Another set of collaborations, this time with Jonathan Cole, can be traced to the King's College workshop. Chapter 2 is based on the case of Ian Waterman, a man who lost normal motor control due to a loss of proprioception and the sense of touch from the neck down (Gallagher and Cole 1995). I have given this chapter an apropos title, 'The Case of the Missing Schema'. The original study was written in part at Jonathan's home in the New Forest near Minstead, England, a town where one can find, among other things, such as a good pub, the gravesite of the author of classic detective fiction, Arthur Conan Doyle. The distinction between body image and body schema is used as a pivotal clue for investigating Ian's very rare condition. In Ch. 2 the case is reopened and the investigation expanded from the original paper, to show that the analysis of this case helps to define in more precise terms the conceptual distinction. It is further extended to include philosophical considerations about embodiment and the perception of space.

The case of Ian Waterman is also the basis for an investigation of the relationship between expression, social cognition, and embodiment in Ch. 5. Despite Ian's lack of proprioception and sense of touch from the neck down, and his resulting profound problems with movement, his hand gestures during conversation appear to be quite normal. This is puzzling since Ian employs a great deal of conscious control and concentration even to grasp and pick up a glass of water. Gestures are normally a form of non-conscious movement, and, one would think, normally governed by the non-conscious feedback of proprioceptive information that Ian lacks. Chapter 5 is based on empirical tests conducted with Ian at the Center for Gesture and Speech Research, David McNeill's psycholinguistics laboratory at the University of Chicago. Experiments there allowed us to confirm some remarkable hypotheses about the role embodiment and consciousness play in language production (Cole, Gallagher, and McNeill 2002). I explore some of the philosophical implications of this research here.

Most of the first part of this book, then, is based on my collaborations with others who are well versed in psychology and neuroscience. For me these have all been learning relationships and without my collaborators this book would surely not have been possible. Tony Marcel facilitated much of this work. A good part of my study and research was done at the Medical Research Council's Cognitive and Brain Science Unit (formerly the Applied Psychology Unit) in Cambridge where he invited me to be a Visiting Scientist. I was able to integrate various aspects of my work in a seminar I presented there, and my conversations with Tony, especially at that time, greatly helped me to clarify my interpretations. Certain elements of this first part were also tested out before a variety of conference and colloquium audiences at the Universities of Aarhus, Cambridge, Ghent, Huddersfield, Toronto, and Wales, at the Fetzer Institute, at CREA in Paris, at the Institut des sciences cognitives in Lyons, France, and at meetings of the American Psychological Association and various other societies and institutes in Europe and the United States.

In Part II I extend the results of the scientific and phenomenological studies developed in the first part into various philosophical problem areas that border on the cognitive sciences. These include questions about perception, the nature of self-consciousness, and our understanding of others.

Chapter 6 outlines a neo-Aristotelian, non-Cartesian approach to understanding the contributions made by embodiment to perception and other forms of cognition. It attempts to capture, in some detail, what I define as *prenoetic* factors—those embodied processes and performances that cannot be reduced to neurophysiology, but that necessarily happen before one knows anything in a cognitive manner.

Chapter 7 addresses a very old philosophical problem first formulated by William Molyneux in a letter to John Locke. Molyneux asked what appeared to be a simple question: whether a person who is congenitally blind and who later attains sight might then visually perceive the shape of objects. After three hundred years of discussion recent studies in developmental psychology and neuroscience suggest a definitive answer which is set out in terms of embodied, intermodal perception. My formulation of the solution to this problem was first presented at the New York State Philosophical Association's Creighton Club. Comments by Tamar Gendler, there, and by others at subsequent philosophy colloquia at Boston University, the University of Copenhagen, and at Molyneux's home university, Trinity College, Dublin, allowed me to further clarify my analysis.

The complex relationship between embodied action and cognition also offers insight into a variety of symptoms experienced by schizophrenics, specifically experiences of thought insertion, auditory hallucinations, and delusions of control. In Ch. 8 I explore both the phenomenology and the underlying cognitive mechanisms that appear to be involved in these symptoms. Beginning with a distinction between the sense of ownership and the sense of agency with respect to motor action, I consider whether such schizophrenic experiences can be fully explained on the subpersonal level. These considerations lead to an important insight into the basic and ubiquitous temporal structure that characterizes human experience across cognitive, emotional, and action dimensions. Insights into the temporal aspects of experience and movement also allow for a more dynamic view of body-schematic operations. Research for this chapter was supported by a grant from the National Endowment for the Humanities to participate at the Summer Institute on Mind, Self, and Psychopathology, directed by Jennifer Whiting and Louis Sass, at Cornell University in 1998. Earlier versions of this material were presented at the Joint Philosophy and Psychology Project on Consciousness and Self-Consciousness (University of Warwick) sponsored by the British Academy, at the seminar on *Exploration de l'expérience et pratique de la description phénoménologique* at the University of Paris, at the Conference on Phenomenological and Cognitive Approaches to Psychopathology, University of Copenhagen, and at the Gulbenkian Symposium on Science and Consciousness, Instituto Gulbenkian de Ciência, Lisbon, Portugal. I'm grateful for the helpful comments made by participants at these various meetings or in private correspondence; they include Timothy Bayne, José Bermúdez, Sarah Blakemore, John Campbell, Jean-Pierre Changeaux, Natalie Depraz, Naomi Eilan, Christopher Frith, Christof Hoerl, Marc Jeannerod, Teresa McCormack, Josef Parnas, Yves Rossetti, Louis Sass, Francisco Varela, and Dan Zahavi. Parts of this chapter were published in an earlier version (Gallagher 2000b). Chapter 8 is a substantially revised and expanded version.

Chapter 9 sets out an alternative approach to the standard views on theory of mind. I argue that our understanding of other persons is based on a form of interaction with others characteristic of 'primary intersubjectivity' (Trevarthen 1979) that is first and foremost embodied, and active from early infancy. Again, I have benefited from comments made by participants at colloquia at York University in Toronto, at the Danish Institute for Advanced Studies in the Humanities in Copenhagen, and at the British Society for Phenomenology in Oxford. An earlier version of this chapter appeared in the *Journal of Consciousness Studies* (Gallagher 2001a).

In the concluding chapter I summarize my arguments by drawing together what I take to be the important concepts that will enable theorists of embodied cognition to further their research. The conceptual framework that I have put forward is meant to hit its target at a behavioral level that is close to our ordinary human experience. Yet, at the same time that it remains true to a phenomenological description of experience, it remains open to empirical scientific explanation, especially from the perspectives of developmental psychology and cognitive neuroscience.

I must make the usual disclaimer. Despite all of the help I have received, responsibility for all mistakes and misdirections in the following chapters is mine. I do not hesitate to say that some of my colleagues may disagree with some of what I have set forth here. Still, this book could not have been written as it is without the conversations and correspondences that I've had with the people I mentioned above, and some others, including Ursula Bellugi, Per Aage Brandt, Peter Brugger, David Corina, Emma Crichton-Miller, Jean Decety, Helena De Preester, Frédérique de Vignemont, Chlöe Farrer, Vittorio Gallese, Todd Ganson, William Hirstein, Dina Lew, Laura Pedelty, Howard Poizner, Ian Robinson, Phillip Rochat, Beata

Stawarska, Evan Thompson, Gertrudis van de Vijver, and probably some people that I have not mentioned and to whom I apologize for my lapse of memory. Most especially, however, I thank Anthony Marcel, Andrew Meltzoff, Jonathan Cole, Francisco Varela, and Ian Waterman for their contributions to my education. As always, my own family supported me in untold ways, and generously tolerated my preoccupations and travels. My wife, Elaine, and my daughters Laura and Julia offered constant inspiration. Finally, I acknowledge the support of several institutions. Canisius College provided extensive financial support, and I have benefited greatly from a Summer Faculty Fellowship there in 1997, and a sabbatical in 1999. I am grateful to the National Endowment for the Humanities for a Summer Stipend in 1994 (#FT-40362–94) in support of my work on embodiment and self-consciousness, and again for support at the 1998 Cornell University NEH Summer Institute on Mind, Self, and Psychopathology. The University of Chicago and David McNeill's Center for Gesture and Speech Research funded my stay there. The excellent support and facilities provided me as Visiting Scientist at the Medical Research Council's Cognitive and Brain Science Unit in Cambridge gave me the opportunity to start the larger project of pulling all this together. Similar thanks go to the Danish National Research Foundation Center for Subjectivity Research and the research priority initiative on 'Body and Mind' at the University of Copenhagen, who hosted me as Visiting Professor and allowed me to finish.

PART I

Scientific and Phenomenological Investigations of Embodiment

1

The Terms of Embodiment

To what extent, and in what precise way, does one's body appear as part of one's perceptual field? To what extent, and in what precise way, does one's body constrain or shape the perceptual field? These are two different questions, both of them pertaining to the structure of perceptual consciousness.[1] They can be made more complex, more precise, or more general; they can also lead to other related questions. To begin, however, I want to start with just these two questions and propose a way of answering them. My approach will be developed at the intersection of three disciplines: phenomenology, psychology, and cognitive neuroscience.

Psychologists already have a relatively developed way of addressing the first question about the appearance of the human body in the perceptual field, or more generally, about the image that a person has of their own body. In most instances, this is referred to as a *body image*. The extensive literature on body image, however, is problematic. First, it is too wide-ranging. The concept is employed and applied in a great variety of fields, from neuroscience to philosophy, from the medical sciences to the athletic sciences, from psychoanalysis to aeronautical psychology and robotics. As often happens in such cases, a term can change meaning across fields and disciplines. Even within a particular discipline one can find subtle (and not so subtle) shifts in the meaning of the term 'body image'. Perhaps even more surprising is the fact that the term often shifts meaning within the works of a single author.

Problems about the meaning of the term 'body image' are also bound up with the use of another term, 'body schema'. This is not just a terminological problem, however. The terminological confusion tells of a more deep-seated conceptual confusion. Precisely such confusions, which can lead to problems involving experimental design and the interpretation of experimental results, motivate some authors to suggest that we ought to give up these terms, abandon them to history, and formulate alternative descriptions of embodiment. I argue here that it is important to retain these terms and to formulate a clear conceptual distinction

---

[1] The distinction I made in the Introduction, between phenomenal structure and prenoetic structure of experience, and which I develop in this chapter, is close to a distinction made by Galen Strawson between contents and operations of consciousness. '[O]ne is experientially in touch with a great pool of constancies and steady processes of change in one's environment including, notably, one's body (of which one is almost constantly aware, however thoughtlessly, both by external sense and by proprioception). If one does not reflect very hard, these constancies and steadinesses of development in the *contents* of one's consciousness may seem like fundamental characteristics of the *operation* of one's consciousness, although they are not' (1997: 423). The operations I want to explore, however, are prenoetic rather than noetic processes. The latter include perception, memory, judgment, etc. Prenoetic factors are those that shape noetic acts in implicit ways.

between them. It will be apparent in the following discussion that the distinction between body image and body schema cuts across a number of other distinctions, such as conscious/non-conscious, personal/subpersonal, explicit/tacit, and willed/automatic. The body image/body schema distinction, however, is not reducible to any one of these, and no other distinction seems to carve up the conceptual space in quite the right way.

With respect to the two questions I raised at the beginning of this chapter, I want to show that the distinction between body image and body schema can do some useful work despite the ambiguity involved in the historical use of these concepts. Each concept addresses a different sort of question. The concept of body image helps to answer the first question about the appearance of the body in the perceptual field; in contrast, the concept of body schema helps to answer the question about how the body shapes the perceptual field. So these terms and concepts, if properly clarified, provide a way to explicate the role embodiment plays in the structuring of consciousness.

Before turning to a brief review of the literature, it may be helpful to see an example of the ambiguity that currently characterizes these concepts. In an important reference work on cognitive psychology Parsons (1990: 46) defines the body image as a set of 'processes underlying the mental simulation of one's action and . . . not directly accessible to consciousness'. In this sense it operates as a non-conscious, subpersonal representation that depends on information provided by 'proprioceptive, kinesthetic, muscular, articular, postural, tactile, cutaneous, vestibular, equilibrium, visual, and auditory senses, as well as [information] from our sense of physical effort and from contact with objects and among our body parts'. The body image is also said to include information that contributes to a conscious, perceptual representation of the body, the 'mental simulation' itself, in which 'the apparent position of some parts affects the represented shape of others'. In his definition Parsons also refers to the concept of 'body schema' and uses the latter term interchangeably with 'body image'.

The definition offered by Parsons is actually quite consistent with the long history of inconsistent use of the terms 'body image' and/or 'body schema' in various scientific and philosophical literatures. The terms have been used interchangeably to signify, in an unclear and ambiguous manner, a group of related but not necessarily identical concepts. The result has been a conceptual confusion—an *aporia* that would inspire any philosopher. In part, the confusion turns on the question concerning the extent to which, and the manner in which, one's body is experienced as an intentional object of consciousness, as part of the perceptual field. Accordingly, Parsons' definition raises two issues that are consistently found to be unsettled in the literature. The first involves the shifting terminology between 'body image' and 'body schema', suggesting that these terms mean the same thing. The second issue involves conflicting claims about the body image as both a non-conscious representation and a conscious image. For example, Lackner (1988), who is cited by Parsons, associates the body image/body schema with a conscious perception of body surface and limb position. This is clearly not equivalent to what Parsons characterizes as an 'internal representation' of which we cannot be conscious.

Common Confusions in the Literature

Although many studies have long noted the terminological confusions and conceptual difficulties related to 'body image' and 'body schema' (e.g. Fisher and Cleveland 1958; Kolb 1959; Myers 1967; Poeck and Orgass 1971; Shontz 1969; Straus 1967, 1970) no consensus concerning terminology or precise definition has emerged. Furthermore, the terminological ambiguity leads to methodological and conceptual problems, as well as numerous inconsistencies in experimental results. These difficulties can be traced back to the early theoretical development of these concepts. Munk (1890) and Wernicke (1900), who were attempting to explain how the body maintains spatial orientation and organizes somatosensory signals despite constant movement, postulated the existence of 'images' stored in the sensorimotor cortex. Bonnier, as early as 1893, used the term 'schema' to signify a spatial quality related to awareness of the body (Bonnier 1905). Head and Holmes (1911–12), and Head (1920, 1926), however, are the most frequently cited sources in relation to the concept of body schema. They define it as a postural model of the body. Postural schemas actively organize and modify 'the impressions produced by incoming sensory impulses in such a way that the final sensation of position, or of locality, rises into consciousness charged with a relation to something that has happened before' (Head 1920: 606). According to Head, however, postural schemas are not conscious images; they are preconscious functions—generated and controlled by cortical representations, although not equivalent to these representations—which compare present posture to past posture. Schemas operate as a standard against which subsequent motor changes are measured, and they intervene in the organization of spatially oriented activities 'before the change of posture enters consciousness' (Head and Holmes 1911–12). Thus, Head and Holmes clearly distinguish body schema from a conscious image.[2]

A large amount of the historical confusion can be traced back to the work of Schilder (1923, 1935). Although he claims to be in agreement with Head, Schilder equates the postural model with the final, *conscious* sensation of position. That is, he equates the body schema, as defined by Head, with the image or representation of 'our own body which we form in our mind' (Schilder 1935: 11).[3] He calls this representation a 'body image' *or* 'body schema'. According to Schilder this image or

---

[2] In contrast to the schema, the body image, 'whether it be visual or motor, is not the fundamental standard against which all postural changes are measured' (Head and Holmes 1911–12: 187).

[3] Pick (1915a) had done the same thing. He adopted the term 'schema' from Head and Holmes, but equated it with a visual image of the body. More recently, Ramachandran and Blakeslee (1998) use the term 'body image', which they attribute to Head, to include both non-conscious processes of the parietal cortex *and* conscious experience associated, e.g., with phantom limbs.

schema is a conscious picture constructed not only from sensory impressions but also from unconscious libidinous elements and from socially formed images of the body. Schilder's definition, even as it extends the scope and import of the discussion, clearly shows a conflation of terms.

The image of the human body means the picture of our own body which we form in our mind, that is to say the way the body appears to ourselves.... We call it a schema of our body or bodily schema, or, following Head... postural model of the body. The body schema is the tri-dimensional image everybody has about himself. We may call it 'body-image'.

(Schilder 1935: 11)

Merleau-Ponty (1945), taking these concepts over into the context of phenomenological philosophy, was somewhat more careful. Following Head's concept, he consistently used the term *schema corporel* to signify a dynamic functioning of the body in its environment. The schema operates as a system of dynamic motor equivalents that belong to the realm of habit rather than conscious choice. Nonetheless, the schema works along with a marginal awareness of the body, and Merleau-Ponty often left the relation between the schema and the marginal awareness unexplained. To make matters worse, however, the term '*schema corporel*' was rendered 'body image' in the English translation of his work *The Phenomenology of Perception* (1962).

Terminological and conceptual confusions persist in the more recent literature. A renowned researcher on the psychology of body image, Seymour Fisher (1972: 113), for example, provides this influential definition of body image:

Body image can be considered synonymous with such terms as 'body concept' and 'body scheme'. Broadly speaking, the term pertains to how the individual perceives his own body. It does not imply that the individual's concept of his body is represented by a conscious image.... Body image... represents the manner in which a person has learned to organize and integrate his body experiences.

In their many empirical and theoretical studies Fisher and his colleagues use such terms as 'body schema', 'body image', 'body concept', and 'body perception' interchangeably. They even coin the phrase 'body image schema' (Fisher and Abercrombie 1958; Fisher and Cleveland 1957). Their studies often focus on a subject's perception of his/her own body in experimental situations where subjects are either explicitly asked about their own body, or indirectly tested about attitudes towards their own body (Fisher 1978; Fisher and Cleveland 1958). In this regard Fisher is not alone. The majority of psychological studies in this area concern the body image defined as involving perceptual or conceptual content, derived from or expressed as an explicit consciousness of the body (see e.g. Adame *et al.* 1991; Gardner and Moncrieff 1988).

Although I do not intend to review the entire literature here, the enduring confusion of these concepts in the research on embodiment can be seen in the following sample of studies.

• Kolb (1959: 89) defines body schema as a 'postural image', a 'perceptual image', or a 'basic model of the body as it functions outside of central consciousness'.

According to Kolb this schema, image, or model is dynamic; it 'modifies incoming sensory impulses'. He explains, however, that the body schema is only one aspect of the body image, and distinguishes another aspect he calls the 'body concept' or 'conceptual image'. The latter 'includes that which concerns the thoughts, feelings, and memories which evolve as the individual (ego) views his own body'. D. F. Clark (1984) and Toombs (1988) also classify the body schema as an aspect of the body image.

• Cumming (1988), however, does the reverse: the body image is considered an aspect of the body schema. Sims, in his textbook on psychopathology (1995), cites Cumming to distinguish between body schema and body experience, yet, in contrast to Cumming, defines the body schema as the aspect of the body image that signifies spatial characteristics of the body.

• Meuse (1996: 57), who invokes Head and Schilder, defines body image as 'an outwardly projected inward and mental structure', and body schema as 'the outward extension of the body reflected in an inward, mental map'.

• Yamadori (1997) considers the body schema a left-hemisphere mechanism that normally functions unconsciously, but is sometimes transformed into a conscious body image.

• There are also studies that equate the body image or schema with body position in objective space. Gibson (1966: 113), for example, defines the body percept, or body image, as 'a set of possible dispositions or poses—standing or lying—relative to the substratum and to gravity'.

• Straus (1970), following Gerstmann (1942), equates the body schema with a cortical representation, the neurophysiological map of body parts located in the somatosensory cortex. Yet Straus also defines it as 'the inner picture or model which one forms in one's mind of one's body.... It is a kind of inner diagram representing one's body as a whole, as well as its single parts according to their location, shape, size, structural and functional differentiation and spatial interrelation' (1970: 901–2).

• Berlucchi and Aglioti (1997) clearly distinguish between the underlying cortical representations responsible for corporeal awareness and the perceptual or mental representation of the body. In referring to the latter, however, they use the terms 'body image' and 'body schema' interchangeably.

• The terminological and conceptual confusion has drifted into the field of robotics and virtual reality as well. For example, Biocca (1997), citing the work of Fisher, uses the term 'body schema' interchangeably with 'body image' to signify a concept that includes (1) a mental model of the body that involves perceived shape and size, perceived relative location of the limbs and so forth, and (2) an adjustment mechanism related to visuomotor coordination.

Many of the conceptual ambiguities concerning body image and body schema revolve, in part, around the question of whether and to what extent an image or schema involves consciousness. This seems to be an underlying aporia. Head (1926), for example, holds that body schemas are 'outside of central consciousness' but that they provide information about posture and movement that sometimes 'rises into consciousness'. He distinguishes between the actual formation of body schemas which occurs 'on levels that are not associated with consciousness', and already formulated schemas that inform a consciousness of posture. Schilder (1935) contends that the schema or image is a conscious representation. Merleau-Ponty (1945) associates body schema with a 'global awareness' or 'marginal consciousness' of the body. Fisher (1972) states that the body image is not necessarily a conscious image and yet, in his empirical studies, draws conclusions about the body image based on experiments that require his subjects to direct their conscious attention to their own bodies (Fisher 1964, 1976).

I bring this short survey to a completion with reference to the author of a much more exhaustive survey. Tiemersma's (1989) review of the literature reflects both the extensive employment of these concepts across numerous disciplines (including psychology, medicine, developmental studies, psychopathology, phenomenology, and philosophy) and their ambiguous nature. Tiemersma (1982) himself suggests a consistent distinction between body image and body schema, but he then curiously uses the terms interchangeably, and in the end equates the body image to a sophisticated eidetic 'knowledge of the essential topological structure of the lived body in the world' (p. 249). On this view the body image is constituted at a very high level of ideational or conceptual activity.

In effect, across these various literatures, the schema or image of the body is alternately characterized as a physiological functioning, a conscious model or mental representation, an unconscious image, a manner of organizing bodily experiences, an artificially induced reflection, a collection of thoughts, feelings, and memories, a set of objectively defined physical positions, a neuronal map or cortical representation, and an ideational/conceptual activity. Although a good scientific understanding of embodiment involves conceptual complexity, it does not seem possible that the body schema/body image is at once or even at different times all of these things. The variety of proposals considered here suggests that, rather than one complex concept with a plurality of names, there is, over and above the terminological ambiguity, a basic conceptual confusion.

A number of theorists have recognized the ambiguity and confusion involved in these concepts. Shontz (1969) went so far as to suggest that definitions of these terms can only be arbitrary. There are even authors who remain satisfied with the ambiguous and amorphous character of these terms (Feldman 1975; Fisher 1970; Ham et al. 1983). Those who do criticize the lack of a clear conceptual understanding of these various notions sometimes go on to develop valuable suggestions about testing procedures and conceptual distinctions (Garner and Garfinkel 1981; Shontz 1974). Such clarifications, however, have been limited to considerations of the body image as a mental representation with perceptual, conceptual, and emotive or affective dimensions. Straus, who noted the 'vague terminology vacillating between body schema and body image' (1970: 137), suggested that the 'endeavors to clarify the concept of body schema only serve to awaken the suspicion that in the last analysis the schema is perhaps little more than a ghost (Schemen)' (1967: 108).

It has also been suggested that these concepts are simply inadequate for purposes of scientific explanation. Poeck and Orgass (1971) develop the most systematic and penetrating critique in this regard. They complain that the concept of body schema is ill-defined and 'difficult to reconcile with modern theories of central nervous functions' (p. 254). Furthermore they show that pathologies classified in terms of the body schema are too heterogeneous to be explained by this term.[4] Notably and understandably, part of their complaint is framed in terms of the tradition they are considering, that is, in terms that confuse body schema and body image. 'The body schema is interpreted as the knowledge or conscious awareness of the body . . . as an image . . . or cerebral representation of the body . . . or as a preconscious, physiological function' (p. 255). Poeck and Orgass specifically mention the question of the development (ontogenesis) of the body schema as one of the main areas in which theory has failed to provide good accounts. They conclude that the term 'body schema' does not have an unequivocal meaning and that it should be given up. At the same time, they confirm that there is some well-circumscribed function subserving the control of posture and movement, and that this needs to be explained, preferably in neurophysiological terms.

The objections raised by Poeck and Orgass, however, are *not* objections *in principle*. For the most part they express a large and justifiable complaint about conceptual misuse in the history of psychology. To meet their objections four things are required:

1. First, and most importantly, a conceptual clarification that will clear away the confusions found in the various literatures on body image and body schema;
2. an account of the ontogenetic development of the body schema and body image;
3. an explication that relates these concepts to recent developments in neuroscience;
4. a use of these concepts that is clarifying in systematic explanations of relevant pathological conditions.

The first part of this book shows how these requirements can be met. Requirements (2)–(4) are pursued in Chs. 2–4. In the remaining sections of the present chapter I address the first issue. I argue that the notions of body image and body schema, once properly clarified, can go some distance (although, as we will see, not the full distance) in helping to work out a conceptual framework and an appropriate vocabulary for understanding the roles played by embodiment in the constitution of cognition.

---

[4] Also see De Renzi (1991: 51): 'There have been attempts to attribute [various symptoms of spatial disorders] to the disruption of a common mechanism, identified as a hypothetical body image or scheme, but it is doubtful whether such a vaguely defined concept can provide a basis for interpreting symptoms dissimilar in nature and associated with different loci of lesion.' Similar and more general complaints about terminologies used in scientific considerations about pathologies of body awareness can be found as early as Pick (1915*b*).

A Conceptual Clarification

Body image and *body schema* refer to two different but closely related systems. The distinction in question is not an easy one to make because behaviorally the two systems interact and are highly coordinated in the context of intentional action. A conceptual distinction is nonetheless useful precisely in order to understand the complex dynamics of bodily movement and experience. Granted that a distinction between body image and body schema will not be adequate to explain all aspects of embodiment, we nonetheless need to draw some clear lines of demarcation between these concepts in order to begin to resolve certain problems and to see our way clearly into the ambiguity of embodied experience.

As a provisional characterization (to be elaborated in more detail), one can make the distinction in the following way. A *body image* consists of a system of perceptions, attitudes, and beliefs pertaining to one's own body. In contrast, a *body schema* is a system of sensory-motor capacities that function without awareness or the necessity of perceptual monitoring.[5] This conceptual distinction between body image and body schema is related respectively to the difference between having a perception of (or belief about) something and having a capacity to move (or an ability to do something). A body image involves more than occurrent perceptions, however. It can include mental representations, beliefs, and attitudes where the object of such intentional states (that object or matter of fact towards which they are directed, or that which they are about) is or concerns one's own body. The body schema, in contrast, involves certain motor capacities, abilities, and habits that both enable and constrain movement and the maintenance of posture. It continues to operate, and in many cases operates best, when the intentional object of perception is something other than one's own body. So the difference between body image and body schema is like the difference between a *perception* (or conscious monitoring) of movement and the actual *accomplishment* of movement, respectively. Obviously, however, a perception of one's own movement (or indeed someone else's movement) can be complexly interrelated to the accomplishment of one's own movement, although not all movement requires a body percept.

Importantly, this conceptual distinction has empirical support. It is possible, for example, to find cases in which a subject has an intact body image but a dysfunctional body schema, and vice versa. This kind of evidence is referred to in psychology as a double dissociation, and such dissociations constitute good support

---

[5] One can refer to *body schemas* in the plural. Head, for example, used the plural as well as the singular form of the noun. In the plural, body *schemas* (or schemata) refer to a collection of motor programs or motor habits that individually may be defined by a specific movement or posture, for example, the movement of hand to mouth. The motor schema, in this example, is more complex than it first might seem. Not only are the anatomical parts of hand and face involved, but also a large number of muscle systems throughout the body are activated for purposes of maintaining balance. One might refer to this entire complex organization of movement as 'a body schema', and consider that a subject is capable of many such complex patterns. When, in the following, I use the phrase 'body schema', it may refer to a particular schema or, more generally, to the larger system or collection of schemas.

for the real basis of a distinction. Evidence of an intact body schema in the absence of a completely intact body image can be found in some cases of unilateral neglect, a condition that often follows brain damage due to stroke. Denny-Brown and his colleagues report that a patient suffering from a neurologically caused persistent defect in perception related to the left side fails to notice the left side of her body; excludes it from her body percept. She fails to dress her left side or comb the hair on the left side of her left head. Yet there is no motor weakness on that side. Her gait is normal, although if her left slipper comes off while walking she fails to notice. Her left hand is held in a natural posture most of the time, and is used quite normally in movements that require the use of both hands, for example, buttoning a garment or tying a knot. For instance, she uses her left hand and thus relies on the motor ability of the neglected side, to dress the right side of her body (Denny-Brown, Meyer, and Horenstein 1952). Thus her body schema system is intact despite her problems with body image on the neglected side.

Dissociation of the opposite kind can be found in rare cases of deafferentation. Subjects who have lost tactile and proprioceptive input below the neck can control their movements only by cognitive intervention and visual guidance of their limbs. In effect they employ their body image (primarily a visual perception of the body) in a unique way to compensate for the impairment of their body schemas (see Cole 1995; Cole and Paillard 1995; Gallagher and Cole 1995). Such dissociations, then, provide some empirical reasons for thinking that there is a real and useful distinction to be made between body schema and body image. We will return to these cases in more detail in the next chapter when we consider the neuroscientific picture that underlies this distinction.

Some Phenomenological Details

The body image consists of a complex set of intentional states and dispositions—perceptions, beliefs, and attitudes—in which the intentional object is one's own body. This involves a form of reflexive or self-referential intentionality. Some studies involving body image (e.g. Cash and Brown 1987; Gardner and Moncrieff 1988; Powers *et al.* 1987) do make a distinction among three sorts of intentional contents:

1. *Body percept:* the subject's perceptual experience of his/her own body;
2. *Body concept:* the subject's conceptual understanding (including folk and/or scientific knowledge) of the body in general; and
3. *Body affect:* the subject's emotional attitude toward his/her own body.

Although (2) and (3) do not necessarily involve an occurrent conscious awareness, they are maintained as sets of beliefs, attitudes, or dispositions, and in that sense form part of an intentional system. In the remainder of this book, however, in our discussions of the body image, we focus primarily on the body percept.[6] Conceptual and emotional aspects of body image no doubt inform perception and are affected by various cultural and interpersonal factors. It is also the case, as I will suggest below, that the perceptual content of the body image originates in intersubjective perceptual experience. Furthermore, it is important to note that our beliefs and attitudes towards our bodies, even if non-conscious, will have an effect on how we perceive our bodies and the bodies of others. In this sense, the body image is not inert or simply an ideational product of cognitive acts; it plays an active role in shaping our perceptions.

In contrast to the body image, a body schema is not a set of perceptions, beliefs, or attitudes. Rather it is a system of sensory-motor functions that operate below the level of self-referential intentionality. It involves a set of tacit performances—preconscious, subpersonal processes that play a dynamic role in governing posture and movement. In most instances, movement and the maintenance of posture are accomplished by the *close to automatic* performances of a body schema, and for this very reason the normal adult subject, in order to move around the world, neither needs nor has a constant body percept. In this sense the body-in-action tends to efface itself in most of its purposive activities. To the extent that one does become aware of one's own body, by monitoring or directing perceptual attention to limb position, movement, or posture, then such awareness helps to constitute the perceptual aspect of a body image. Such awareness may then interact with a body schema in complex ways, but it is not equivalent to a body schema itself.

I said that a body schema operates in a *close to automatic* way. I do not mean by this that its operations are a matter of reflex. Movements controlled by a body schema can be precisely shaped by the intentional experience or goal-directed behavior of the subject. If I reach for a glass of water with the intention of drinking from it, my hand, completely outside my awareness, shapes itself in a precise way for picking up the glass. It takes on a certain form in conformity with my intention. It is important to note that although a body schema is not itself a form of consciousness, or in any way a cognitive operation, it can enter into and support (or in some cases, undermine) intentional activity, including cognition.

Thus, motor action is not completely automatic; it is often part of a voluntary, intentional project. When I jump to catch a ball in the context of a game, or when I walk across the room to greet someone, my actions may be explicitly willed and, at the same time, governed by my perception of objects or persons in the environment. My attention, however, and even my complete awareness in such cases, are centered on the ball or on the other person, and not on the precise accomplishment of locomotion. In such cases the body moves smoothly and in a coordinated fashion not because I have an image (a perception) of my bodily movement, but because of

---

[6] Denny-Brown and his colleagues rightly interpret the case of neglect cited above as a primary defect in the body percept that does not involve Head's notion of body schema. Noting the confusion of terms in Schilder, they use the term 'body image' to mean only a conceptual understanding of the body, which they show to be intact in their patient (Denny-Brown, Meyer, and Horenstein 1952: 463). Thus she is able properly to identify parts of her body or other bodies when asked. On our definition, however, in so far as this patient suffers from a defect of the body percept, it is a defect of body image.

the coordinated functioning of a body schema. In such movements a body schema contributes to and supports intentional action.

It is also the case, as I have already mentioned, that in some situations a body image or percept contributes to the control of movement. The visual, tactile, and proprioceptive attentiveness that I have of my body may help me to learn a new dance step, improve my tennis game, or imitate the novel movements of others. In perfecting my tennis serve, for example, I may, at first, consciously monitor and correct my movement. In another case, my movement along a narrow ledge above a deep precipice may involve a large amount of willed conscious control based on the perception of my limbs. Even in such cases the contribution made to the control of movement by my perceptual awareness of my body will always find its complement in capacities that are defined by the operations of a body schema that continues to function to maintain balance and enable movement. Such operations are always in excess of that of which I can be aware. Thus, a body schema is not reducible to a perception of the body; it is never equivalent to a body image.

Let us consider a little more closely the conscious awareness of one's own body. Is my body always intentionally present, that is, am I always conscious of my own body as an intentional object, or as part of an intentional state of affairs? The distinction between consciously *attending* to the body and being marginally *aware* of the body is important. It appears that sometimes we do attend specifically to some aspect or part of the body. In much of our everyday experience, and most of the time, however, our attention is directed away from the body, toward the environment or toward some project we are undertaking.

We all know that in normal conscious states our awareness of bodily sensation is limited—pushed aside by the fact that our attention is locked upon some social or situational issue. It is almost as if (as in the learning of a task) the functions of the body are on automatic pilot and do not usually have to be attended to consciously. (Crook 1987: 390–1)[7]

In cases where our attention is not directed toward the body, do we remain consciously *aware* of some aspect or part of the body? Some theorists argue that there is a constant awareness of the body that accompanies all movement and cognitive activity (e.g. Gurwitsch 1964; James 1890; Sheets-Johnstone 1998). Such awareness may vary by degree among individuals—some more aware, others, at times, not at all aware of their body. If I am solving a difficult mathematical problem, am I also and at the same time aware of the position of my legs or even of my grip on the pencil, or are these things so much on automatic pilot that I don't need to be aware of them?

To define a difference between body image and body schema, however, it is not necessary to determine to what extent we are conscious of our bodies. It suffices to say that sometimes we are attentive to or aware of our bodies; other times we are

[7] It has also been noted that 'for good adaptation and responsivity to the environment the conscious perceptive field is mostly occupied by external rather than internal stimuli to which the subject tends to respond.... When the subject focuses on his body, different components or images of body parts, of which the subject himself usually is unconscious, can emerge' (Ruggieri et al. 1983: 800).

not. A body image is inconstant, at least in this sense. Whether and to what degree body awareness is a constant feature of consciousness is not only a matter of individual differences, and differences in situation, but will also depend on precisely what one means by 'awareness'. Let us assume for now that when we are not perceptually attentive to the body, we still may have some degree of marginal awareness of it. I will look at this issue more closely in the following chapters. Although it may seem in some regards a minor detail, in philosophical contexts, where the very nature of intentionality, intentional action, and even free will and self-identity are at stake, it is a detail that can have profound implications.

On the one hand, as I have noted, conscious perception of my own body can be used to monitor and control my posture and movements. Ordinarily, however, I do not have to attend to putting one foot in front of another when I'm walking; I do not have to think through the action of reaching for something. I may be marginally aware that I am moving in certain ways, but it is not usually the center of my attention. And marginal awareness may not capture the whole movement. If I am marginally aware that I am reaching for something, I may not at all be aware of the fact that for the sake of balance my left leg has stretched in a certain way, or that my toes have curled against the floor. Posture and the majority of bodily movements operate in most cases without the help of bodily awareness.

On the other hand, in certain circumstances one's body will appear in the focus of attention, a present intentional object of consciousness. What kinds of circumstances push the body into the attentional field of consciousness? Such circumstances include voluntary reflection (as in medical examination, vain self-inspection, or even philosophical introspection). Many studies indicate that in addition to deliberate reflection on one's own body, the body manifests itself in consciousness in certain 'limit-situations', for example in fatigue, sexual excitement, experiences of pain or pleasure, sickness, certain pathologies, stress-situations, or physical challenges as in athletics or exercise (see Buytendijk 1974; Fisher 1976, 1978; Jaspers 1972; Mason 1961). Moreover, in such occurrences, the body can appear as thing-like, or object-like. In the case of fatigue or sickness, for example, it may appear as something 'in the way', a burden or annoyance, or impotent (Plugge 1967).

In any of these circumstances, from the philosophical to the pathological, when the body appears in the attentional field of consciousness the issue of ownership is usually already settled. The body image, as a reflexive intentional system, normally represents the body as *my own* body, as a personal body that belongs to me. This sense of ownership contributes to a sense of an overall personal self. The issue of ownership is complex, however, as some pathologies make clear. In unilateral neglect or in alien hand syndrome, for example, a subject can be alienated from a specific part of their body, and the patient may experience that part as if it were owned by someone else. In 'anarchic hand syndrome' (della Sala, Marchetti, and Spinnler 1994) the patient may have a sense of ownership for the body part, but no control over its action, and therefore no sense of agency for that action. In other cases (for example, in schizophrenia) the action itself is experienced as performed by the subject's own body, but the source of the action, an intention or command, seems to come from elsewhere or to belong to someone else (see Ch. 8).

The sense of ownership, however, does not require an explicit or observational consciousness of the body, an ideational, third-person stance in which I take my body as an object. Rather it may depend on a non-observational access that I have to my actions, an access that is most commonly associated with a first-person relationship to myself. In non-observational self-awareness I do not require the mediation of a perception or judgment to recognize myself as myself. I do not need to reflectively ascertain that my body is mine, or that it is *my* body that is in pain or that is experiencing pleasure. In normal experience, this knowledge is already built into the structure of experience. In some pathological cases, in contrast, the subject's relationship to his/her body is mediated by an observational judgment, and in some cases it is precisely a negative judgment about ownership. These are issues to which we return in later chapters.

To the extent that one attends to or becomes aware of one's own body in terms of becoming conscious of limb position, movement, or posture, then such an awareness helps to constitute the perceptual aspect of the body image. When that happens, when the body becomes the explicit object of attentional consciousness, it often appears as clearly differentiated from its environment. Body image boundaries tend to be relatively clearly defined (see Fisher 1964; Fisher and Cleveland 1958). Further, as one's conscious attention is directed towards one's body, there usually takes place a discrimination or isolation of the outstanding bodily feature defined by the circumstance. In such experience the body becomes consciously articulated into parts, although the isolated bodily feature or part continues to function only in relation to the rest of the body, which may not be the object of conscious attention.[8] Thus, a body image often involves a partial, abstract, and articulated representation of the body in so far as attention, thought, and emotional evaluation attend to only one part or area or aspect of the body at a time.

In the act of paying conscious attention to the body one does not have a consciousness of the body as a whole. Even a 'global awareness' is only an awareness of the general features or outlines of one's own body; it is not a consciousness of every part in holistic relation to every other part. Indeed, it is phenomenologically impossible to have a consciousness of some of the specific parts or functions of what is objectively one's own body—for example, certain internal organs, adrenal glands, or the reticular activating system. More precisely these are not parts or functions of 'my own' body, in a phenomenological or experiential sense. To consider these types of internal functions one must think of them in an objective fashion, as happening, but not as experienced, in one's body.

Consciousness of the body can involve various intentional acts. Not only do I perceive, I also remember, imagine, conceptualize, study, love, or hate my own

---

[8] For examples of this discriminating perception of the body in philosophical reflection see Husserl (1952: 159); for pathological cases see Goldfarb (1945); Jaspers (1972: 91 ff.); Minkowski (1933/1970: 321–2, 327); Schilder (1935: 97).

body. It is also possible that as a set of beliefs or attitudes about the body, the body image can involve inconsistencies or contradictions. I may know that illness and death are always a possibility, and yet sometimes still feel invincible. I may conceptually judge my body to be as strong as I would like it to be, but under different circumstances suffer from an emotional insecurity about my lack of bodily strength. Social and cultural factors clearly affect perceptual, conceptual, and emotional aspects of body image. Conscious feelings about one's body are sometimes straightforward and sometimes indirect and symbolic; they may be motivated by conscious or unconscious experience, and in many respects they are conditioned by cultural norms (see e.g. Bordo 1993; Schilder 1935; Weiss 1998). For example, I may be emotionally dissatisfied with the way my body looks because it does not match up to the cultural ideal of beauty or strength. Or I may be emotionally dissatisfied because of an altered and abnormal sense of body image, for example in cases of anorexia. The body image itself can operate as a complex phenomenon in such cases. It can, at the same time, be both the result of intentional (perceptual, conceptual, and emotional) experiences, and an operative determinant of such experiences. For example, my negative appraisal of a particular part of my body may, consciously or unconsciously, enter into my perceptual or emotional experience of the world.[9]

Some Implications for Experimental Design

It seems clear that not all aspects of the body image are consciously experienced at all times. Just as I am not constantly aware of, and certainly not constantly attentive to, all my beliefs about the world or about other people, I am not at all times aware of or attentive to all aspects of my body or all my beliefs about my body. This is an important consideration when psychologists design experiments that attempt to measure or define the body image. If there is not a constant and persistent attentive consciousness of the body, then certain ways that the body is made thematic in many studies of body image are open to question. Indeed, some methods employed in these studies might lead one to conclude that the phenomenon under study is an artifact of the experimental situation. Many experimental designs, whether they involve pathological or normal subjects, require the subject to reflect on and to describe his/her own body image. In general, any experimental situation that places the subject in a reflective attitude in order to ascertain

---

[9] Studies can be (and have been) conducted to investigate these various dimensions of body image. Many experiments have been designed to investigate how various subjects consciously perceive their bodies (e.g. Garner and Garfinkel 1981; Shontz 1969; Slade 1977). Others have asked about the cognitive understanding of various body parts (e.g. Gorman 1969; Wilf et al. 1983). Still others have focused on the emotional experience of the body in terms of, for example, satisfaction with one's own body (e.g. Calden, Lundy, and Schlafer 1959; Garner and Garfinkel 1981). Studies have also been designed to discover how the body image is constructed in personal experience, and how the body image enters into the person's perception of the world (see Fisher 1970).

something about prereflective experience is questionable. An act of reflection, and especially a directed reflection, can easily produce phenomena that are not necessarily contained within prereflective experience. While many authors claim that the body image is not necessarily a reflective conscious representation, many of these same authors proceed to draw conclusions about the body image on the basis of a conscious representation of the body induced within the experimental situation.[10]

Szmukler (1984), on methodological grounds, objected to having subjects view camera-distorted photographs of their bodies in order to choose which they preferred (see e.g. Allebeck, Hallberg, and Espmark 1976; Glucksman and Hirsch 1973; Touyz et al. 1984). Such procedures, according to Szmukler, called the subject's attention to what was being tested. Many body image tests for patients with anorexia nervosa are conducted in a manner such that patients are aware of what is being tested. Szmukler suggests that the results 'bear a closer relationship to [the subjects'] attitudes to treatment or the experimenter than to [the subjects'] perception of their bodies' (1984: 553; also see Garner and Garfinkel 1981).

It is also the case that one's conceptual understanding, and specifically one's own body concept can interfere with responses in testing other aspects of body image. In this regard Shontz notes that

measures of experience of the body are always obtained by way of the concepts the subject is capable of using. The subject is asked to draw, rate, or describe his experiences or his level of satisfaction with his body, but he can accommodate the experimenter only if the response language he is asked to employ is one he can use effectively.   (1969: 204)

Thus, experiments concerning body image sometimes depend on the sophistication of the subject's conceptual understanding of the body and the language employed to express that understanding. The language used within the experimental situation may in fact bias the subject's reports about their bodily experience. 'The results of [studies of body image] will be determined to a large extent by the nature of the system of response language chosen by the investigator' (Shontz 1969: 205). Other methodological difficulties noted in the literature include the question of the objective standard for measuring the accuracy of subjective estimates of body size, and the use of questionnaires (Gorman 1969; Shontz 1969).

Many difficulties and ambiguities encountered in the use of such methods are the result of confusing

1. the body as it can be scientifically and objectively measured;
2. the body as it is experienced by the subject; and

---

[10] Methods that seem to involve such reflective aspects include: (a) The administration of questionnaires that direct the subject's awareness to his/her own body, for example the Fisher Body Distortion Questionnaire (Fisher 1976), and the Body Focus Questionnaire (Feldman 1975; Fisher 1964; Fisher, Greenberg, and Reihman 1984; Ham et al. 1983). (b) The comparison of changes in body image reported by subjects while they observe their own mirror image through aniseikonic lenses (Fisher 1964), or in distorting mirrors (Traub and Orbach 1964). Similar situations are produced by asking subjects to estimate the accuracy of body image while introducing distortions via photographs or video camera, etc. (Freeman et al. 1984; Garner et al. 1976). (c) Asking subjects to rate their degrees of satisfaction with various parts of their bodies (Calden et al. 1959).

3. the body as it operates outside the subject's conscious awareness, although still having an effect on the subject's experience.

Many of the methodological difficulties can be resolved only when, on the theoretical side, clear conceptual distinctions and definitions are provided for these various categories.

A Negative Phenomenology of Movement

Some bodily operations that remain outside conscious attention, and even outside perceptual awareness, belong to the body schema. As I have indicated, a body schema is neither a perception, nor a conceptual understanding, nor an emotional apprehension of the body. As distinct from body image it involves a *prenoetic* performance of the body. A prenoetic performance is one that helps to structure consciousness, but does not explicitly show itself in the contents of consciousness. In just such performances the body acquires a certain organization or style in its relations with its environment. For example, it appropriates certain habitual postures and movements; it incorporates various significant parts of its environment into its own schema (Marivita and Iriki 2004). The carpenter's hammer becomes an operative extension of the carpenter's hand, or, as Head (1920) noted in commenting on the fashions of his day, a body schema can extend to the feather in a woman's hat. The system that is the body schema allows the body actively to integrate its own positions and responses and to deal with its environment without the requirement of a reflexive conscious monitoring directed at the body. It is a dynamic, operative performance of the body, rather than a consciousness, image, or conceptual model of it.

The body schema system, as the result of a variety of sensory inputs, prenoetically governs the postures that are taken up by the body in its environment. That a body schema operates in a prenoetic way means that it does not depend on a consciousness that targets or monitors bodily movement. This is not to say that it does not depend on consciousness at all. For certain motor programs to work properly, I need information about the environment, and this is most easily received by means of perception. If, in the middle of our conversation, for example, I decide to retrieve a book from across the room to show you something, I may be marginally conscious of some of the various movements I am making: rising from the chair, walking across the room, and reaching for the book. But my attention is not directed at the specific details of my motor behavior, nor am I even aware of all relevant aspects of my movement. Rather, I am thinking about the passage I want to show you; I am trying to pick out the book; I am perceptually aware of a piece of furniture I should try to avoid, and so forth. My consciousness of this environment and the location of things that I need to reach will guide my movement, and will help my body gear into that environment in the right way. In that sense, consciousness is essential for the proper operation of a body schema. But the fact that my posture undergoes a complete transformation, the fact that I put one foot in front of another in a specific way, the fact that my body maneuvers in a certain way around the furniture, the motor facts of my reaching and grasping, and so forth, are not the subject-matter of my consciousness.

In so far as I am conscious of what I am doing, the content of my consciousness is specified in its most pragmatic meaning. That is, if I were to formulate the content of my consciousness in this regard, it would not be in terms of operating or stretching muscles, bending or unbending limbs, turning or maintaining balance; it would not even be in terms of walking, reaching, standing, or sitting. Rather, in the context of an intentional project, if I were stopped and asked what I was doing, I would say something like 'I'm getting a book.' All the bodily movement entailed in that action remains phenomenologically hidden behind that description. I am aware of my bodily action not as bodily action *per se,* but as action at the level of my intentional project. Thus, prenoetic functions underpin and affect explicitly intentional experience, and they are subsumed into larger intentional activities. In this sense, detailed aspects of movement (such as the contraction of certain muscles), even if we are not aware of them (even if they are not explicitly intentional), are intentional in so far as they are part of a larger intentional action (see Anscombe 1957).

The body schema system takes measure of its environment in a pragmatic rather than objective fashion. Motor control takes its bearing from the intention of the agent, rather than from the level of muscle contractions or neuronal signals. For example, if I reach for a cup in order to drink from it, my grasp shapes itself, outside my awareness, according to my purpose. My grasp will in fact be different if I reach for the cup in order to pick it up and throw it, or if I reach for it in order to offer it to another person (Jeannerod 1997; Jeannerod and Gallagher 2002). This allows a subject who is immersed in conversation, for instance, to walk beneath a low-hanging tree branch without bumping her head; it enables her to maneuver around objects in her path without having to think about what she is doing or calculate the distance between her and the objects. In contrast to results obtained in body-image studies of estimation of body size, the issue of calculated objective measurement does not pertain to the body schema. For example, in studies of size estimation of one's own body, size is consistently overestimated relative to other objects (Gardner *et al.* 1989; Shontz 1969). If we depended solely on body image to get around— something that does occur in rare instances (see Ch. 2)—our movements would be inexact and awkward. Just consider, for example, the prospect of having to *think through* every step of walking across a room. In this sense, neither an account of body image, nor an objective, third-person account of bodily movement (that is, one that leaves out the notion of intention), is equivalent to an account of body schema and neither one fully represents the way in which the body functions in human experience.

The case of eyestrain illustrates how the body deals with its environment in a prenoetic way. In becoming conscious of eyestrain, a subject is first intentionally directed towards the environment rather than towards the body.

When the eyes become tired in reading, the reader does not perceive his fatigue first, but that the light is too weak or that the book is really boring or incomprehensible.... Patients do not primarily establish *which* bodily functions are disturbed, but they complain about the fact that 'nothing works right anymore,' 'the work does not succeed,' that the environment is 'irritating,' 'fatiguing'. (Buytendijk 1974: 62)

As a reader in this situation, I am not at first conscious of my posture, or of my eyes as they scan the pages. Rather, totally absorbed in my project, I begin to experience eyestrain as a series of changes in the things and states of affairs around me. Gradually the perceived environment begins to revise itself; the text seems more difficult, the lighting seems too dim, the body shifts itself closer to the desk, etc. In the end I discover the true problem—the fatigue, the headache. The eyes that have been reading have been anonymous eyes, doing their work without my reflective awareness of them. I was not conscious of my eyes at all. Now, however, my attention is directed to my eyes. They suddenly emerge out of prenoetic anonymity and become explicitly owned. My pain now becomes my present concern, and my body in general gets in the way of my reading comprehension.

When I am engaged in the world I do not perceive my body-schematic perform-ances. In the case of eyestrain I do not perceive that I shift my body closer to the desk. Such operations do not become apparent to consciousness until there is a reflection on my bodily situation brought on by pain, discomfort, fatigue, etc. When the body is 'in tune' with the environment, when events are smoothly ordered, when I am engaged in a task that holds conscious attention, then the body prenoetically performs on a behavioral level that is in excess of that of which I am conscious. In the example of eyestrain the body maneuvers to position itself closer to the text, the fingers guide the reading process over the difficult path of words, etc. The body does this without the reader's conscious decision or perceptual awareness of the body's behavioral performance. Perceptual attention is trained on the world and entrained by my projects. The body's mode of being in the perceiving act is more than to be perceived.

If for some reason the body-schematic performance fails, the body takes center stage in the perceptual field (see Ch. 2). A loss of balance, disequilibrium between body and environment, may motivate a spontaneous appearance of the body in attentive consciousness. Improved performance of the body schema, however, pushes the body into the recesses of awareness. The successful maintenance of posture, an equilibrium attained between body and environment, allows us to be more attentive to the world and our surroundings than to our body.

Complicating Issues

Even if we can establish a clean conceptual distinction between body image and body schema, things are not always so unambiguous on the behavioral level. As I've indicated, for example, body image sometimes has an effect on the postural or

COMPLICATING ISSUES 35

motor performances of body schemas. The dancer or the athlete who practices long and hard to make deliberate movements proficient so that movement is finally accomplished by the body without conscious reflection uses a consciousness of bodily movement to train body-schematic performance. Various experiments show that visual awareness of one's own body can correct or even override body-schematic functions (Gurfinkel and Levick 1991). For example, visual perception of wrist, elbow, or shoulder can recalibrate motor performance distorted by the effects of prismatic goggles (Paillard 1991*a*). Focused attention or the lack of it on specific parts of the body may alter postural or motor performance (e.g. Fisher 1970; Winer 1975).

Things are even more complex. Using Brian O'Shaughnessy's (1980, 1995) distinction between long- and short-term body images, we can say that certain long-term aspects of the body image (a long-standing sense of what my body looks like, or long-standing beliefs or attitudes, for example) can themselves function prenoetically. Certain established beliefs or dispositions concerning my body, even very basic ones concerning my human shape, may have an effect on my current body percept (short-term body image), and on the way that I move, and even on the way that I perceive the world. On the one hand, to the extent that the body image may be responsible for such non-conscious or tacit effects on movement, it ordinarily informs or has its effect through the body schema system. On the other hand, to the extent that we can become aware of what the body schema usually accomplishes prenoetically, this awareness becomes part of the body image.

These considerations suggest that establishing a conceptual distinction between body image and body schema is only the beginning of an explication of the role played by the body in action and cognition. They suggest that there are reciprocal interactions between prenoetic body schemas and cognitive experiences, including normal and abnormal consciousness of the body. Such behavioral relations between body image and body schema can be worked out in detail, however, only if the conceptual distinctions between them are first understood.

I suggested that the body image normally involves a personal-level experience of the body. I normally experience my body as *mine*. As already noted, however, there are pathologies in which this is not the case. In some cases of anosognosia, for example, when patients deny that their limbs are paralyzed, or in neglect, when they seem unaware of their limbs on one side, they also deny that the limbs are their own. The sense of ownership, or the failure of the sense of ownership, of a particular body part may be based on a failure of perceptual or sensory feedback (Kinsbourne 1995). Yet issues that involve the sense of ownership and the sense of agency for action are more complex than this. Ownership in part involves the issue of control. When I consciously decide to raise my hand, for example, and then do so with my perceptual attention focused on this action, intentional control over this movement is apparent and manifested in the body percept. Even in such intentional bodily movement, however, certain postural adjustments of the body that serve to maintain balance are not under conscious control. The vestibular system and various muscle groups make automatic adjustments of which I remain unaware, and in that sense control of bodily movement can never be made completely conscious. A sense of agency, however, is closely tied to body-schematic processes that subtend the initiation of movement. We will see in later chapters (Chs. 2 and 8) that problems with body schema can entail not only loss of motor control, but also a sense of depersonalization.

Another question that arises concerns the constitution of a veridical sense of embodiment. As I noted above, the body image often involves an abstract and partial representation of the body in so far as my perception, thought, and emotional evaluation attend to only one part or area or aspect of the body at a time. With respect to attention this has the status of a general law. Attention is always structured in terms of a figure on ground in which some figural aspect is maintained in attentional focus. In the case of the consciousness of one's own body, the limit of the perceptual field would be the whole body, and attentional focus would necessarily be less than that.[11] Thus, my body appears in consciousness with certain parts emphasized or singled out. For example, in the case of eyestrain, the aching area behind the eyes eventually becomes the focus of attention. In certain types of psychopathology (schizophrenia, depression) patients decidedly emphasize one type of sense experience over another—visual, tactile, kinesthetic, etc., and the body image is constructed accordingly. It is also possible that as a set of beliefs or attitudes about the body, the body image can involve inconsistencies or contradictions.

The body schema, on the other hand, functions in a more integrated and holistic way. A slight change in posture involves a global adjustment across a large number of muscle systems. For example, subsequent to isometric contraction, in a relaxed position, leg muscles begin to contract involuntarily causing extension of the knee joints. In this case, the scheme and degree of the extension is actually related to the posture of the head. If the head is turned on the vertical axis to the right, extension of the left knee joint is increased, and extension of the right knee joint is decreased. Moreover, this is not a fixed relation, for it depends on other postural factors. Inclination of the trunk in a forward direction, for example, reverses the reaction (Gurfinkel and Levick 1991). The holistic nature of the body schema can also be seen in the fact that various proprioceptive inputs originating in different parts of the body do not function in an isolated manner but add together, in a non-linear fashion, to modulate postural control. Extraocular (eye-muscle) proprioception, for example, contributes to overall (whole-body) postural regulation, as does proprio-ceptive input associated with neck and ankle muscles (Roll and Roll 1988; Roll, Roll, and Velay 1991). The body schema thus depends on a 'collaborative interaction of multiple afferent and efferent domains' (Lackner 1988: 293).

I suggested that when the body appears in consciousness, it normally appears as clearly differentiated from its environment. In experimental situations, body-image boundaries, for example, tend to be clearly defined. When I am immersed in experience, however, the limits of the body and environment are obscured.

---

[11] I thank Anthony Marcel for pointing this out to me.

In dance, for example, I may in some instances be conscious of precisely where my body stops and where my partner's body begins. In a certain movement, however, to maintain proper balance, my body has to take into postural-schematic account the moving extension of my partner, so that, one might say, the body schema includes information that goes beyond the narrow boundaries defined by body image. This extension of the body schema into its surrounding environment is reflected in its neural representations. Not only do bimodal premotor, parietal, and putaminal neuronal areas that represent a given limb or body area also respond to visual stimulation in the environmental space nearby, for some of these neurons the visual receptive field remains 'anchored' to the body part when it moves (Fogassi et al. 1996; Graziano and Gross 1998; Graziano et al. 1994). The body schema functions in an integrated way with its environment, even to the extent that it frequently incorporates into itself certain objects—the hammer in the carpenter's hand, the feather in the woman's hat, and so forth—pieces of the environment that would not be considered part of one's body image. Such extensions of the body schema are most often based on intentional usage of the tool or object (Marivita and Iriki 2004). In addition, it may be possible that certain prosthetic devices, such as artificial limbs, are incorporated into the body image over a period of constant use. So there is plasticity involved in both the body schema and the body image, and plastic changes in the body image may be generated through the operations of the body schema as it controls the interaction of body and environment. One might say that the body schema is not something entirely in-itself; through its posture and motor activity the body defines its behavioral space and environment under constraints defined by environmental affordances (Gibson 1979).

Conclusion

I began by suggesting that, despite a great deal of confusion and ambiguity in the established literature on body image and body schema, it is still possible to establish a conceptual distinction between these phenomena, and to employ them as part of a vocabulary that furthers an understanding of embodiment and its role in cognition and experience. I have also suggested that the employment of these concepts will not provide a full account of embodiment in this regard, and I have tried to indicate certain complexities that will constrain their use. We will learn much more about all these issues, and about both the potential and the limitations of these concepts, in the following chapters. For now, however, let me summarize what I take to be the essential aspects of the distinctions for which I have been arguing. I defined body image as a (sometimes conscious) system of perceptions, attitudes, beliefs, and dispositions pertaining to one's own body. It can be characterized as involving at least three aspects: body percept, body concept, and body affect. Body schema, in contrast, is a system of sensory-motor processes that constantly regulate posture and movement—processes that function without reflective awareness or the necessity of perceptual monitoring. Body schemas can also be thought of as a collection of sensory-motor interactions that individually define a specific movement or posture, including elementary (relatively defined) movements, such as the rotation of a wrist within a larger movement or the movement of hand to mouth.

If the body image is conceptually distinct from the body schema, then an account of the body image is not equivalent to an account of the body schema. I have suggested through a phenomenological analysis that the two concepts can be kept distinct, that the terminology does not have to be confused, and that such distinctions are clarifying rather than confusing.

Following this central distinction, we can outline several important facts.

- First, to the extent that I become perceptually aware of my body, as something in my peripheral field or as something attended to, then I have an occurrent body percept. Although I may not be conscious of certain beliefs or attitudes that I have concerning my body, in principle I should be able to bring such beliefs and attitudes to consciousness. In contrast, I have suggested that the body schema is always something in excess of that of which I can be conscious. Even if I become conscious of certain aspects of my posture and movement, the body schema continues to function in a non-conscious way, maintaining balance and enabling movement.

- Second, the body image normally involves a personal-level experience of the body that involves a sense of ownership for the body. The body schema, however, functions beneath the level of personal life. Even in pathologies where there is a failure in regard to a sense of ownership, the body schema may continue to function in its anonymous way, that is, in its ordinary, non-conscious way of dealing with its environment.

- Third, the body image involves an abstract and partial representation of the body in so far as one's perception, thought, and emotional evaluation can attend to only one part or area or aspect of the body at a time. Thus, one's body appears in consciousness with certain parts emphasized or singled out. The body schema, on the other hand, functions in a more integrated and holistic way. A slight change in posture involves a global adjustment across a large number of muscle systems.

- Fourth, the body, as it appears in consciousness, normally appears as clearly differentiated from its environment. In contrast, the body schema functions in an integrated way with its environment, even to the extent that it frequently incorporates into itself pieces of the environment that would not be considered part of one's body image.

- Fifth, consciousness of action tends to be specified in the pragmatic meaning of the intentional task, rather than in terms of a body percept that, depending on circumstances, might involve the perception of muscles stretching, limbs bending or unbending, walking, reaching, standing, or sitting. This means that the body is normally and to some degree experientially transparent, that it effaces itself in its projects. The prenoetic functions of the body schema tend to be subsumed into larger intentional activities. Body-schematic processes are ordered according to the intention of the actor rather than in terms of muscles or neuronal signals.

Although I began with a critique of the existing scientific literature, I do not mean to dismiss that entire literature. One may be able to find significant insights into the various issues that concern embodiment by carefully examining past studies of body image and body schema. Yet one needs to be careful about the terminological confusion to be found there. When the terms 'body schema' and 'body image' are used in many studies, they do not necessarily signify the concepts that we have delineated above. Furthermore, the conceptual distinctions that we have outlined are based more on phenomenology than on a study of empirical function, and they do not tell us in precise terms what the body schema is or how it functions. For that we need to turn to empirical studies.

We need to examine empirical studies for another reason. Justifiable objections have been raised against the use of the concepts of body image and body schema (by Poeck and Orgass 1971, among others). We begin to answer these objections only by making a clear conceptual distinction between these concepts. We still need to show that these concepts can do justice to the complexities of embodied cognition, or, at least, acknowledging their limitations, we need to show that they can carry us some distance in this direction, and how they can contribute to a more developed vocabulary of embodiment. To complete this task we need to continue our analysis by proceeding to

1. show how a consistent distinction between body image and body schema can further our understanding of embodiment;
2. provide a developmental account of the body schema and body image;
3. examine these phenomena in light of recent neuroscientific findings; and
4. show how these concepts are useful and clarifying for systematic explanations of pathological conditions.

2

The Case of the Missing Schema

PHENOMENOLOGY runs into certain natural limitations when it comes up against non-phenomenal processes. In some sense the body schema poses such a limitation. In the previous chapter I worked out a description of the characteristics of the body schema by means of a contrast to the body image—a negative phenomenology, so to speak. If, as I propose, the body schema is an important aspect of embodiment, and if we want to explore this aspect further, we need to take a different approach. In this respect the examination of certain pathological cases will be helpful.

I mentioned one such pathology in the previous chapter: unilateral (personal) neglect. Stroke patients sometimes fail to perceive or attend to one side of their body. Such problems are the result of brain lesions in the hemisphere opposite (contralateral) to the neglected side. A lesion in the right parietal lobe, for example, may cause neglect of the left side of the body. In cases such as this, the left side of the body is excluded from the body image—it is ignored, denied, and sometimes disowned as something that does not belong to the patient. The patient may deny that the left arm or leg belongs to him/her.[1] In some cases, despite this problem with body image, body schemas may remain intact and operational. Thus Denny-Brown's patient was able to use the neglected side of her body to dress herself.[2]

The patient, an elderly woman, 'religious and fastidious in her manners showed unusual behaviors after a right parietal lobe lesion: she modestly adjusted her clothing on the right while parts of the left side of the body were heedlessly exposed' (Melzack 1989: 5; citing Denny-Brown et al. 1952). The patient, however, was still capable of using her left arm and hand to make the adjustments and to dress herself. More generally, patients who do not suffer paralysis on the neglected side may still be able to *use* that side to dress, walk, eat, and so forth. In such cases motor activity on the neglected side is governed by an intact body schema which is sufficient to the task. Dressing, for example, involves complex spatial and motor skills. Despite the fact that garments constantly change spatial orientation in the course of the procedure, subjects normally perform the required motions in a close

---

[1] Such cases may involve affective as well as perceptual and representational aspects of the body image. For example, a stroke victim may say not only that the affected arm doesn't look or feel like her arm, but that, when she comes to be aware of it, she doesn't like the arm being there. In one case the subject states: 'I think it's ugly, and I wish it would go away' (see Pribram 1999: 23).

[2] Not all cases of neglect involve an intact body schema. Coslett (1998) offers experimental evidence to show that in some cases body-schematic functions are disrupted. Such disruptions also result in problems with body image. The experiments conducted by Coslett were complicated, however, by the fact that his subjects tested positive for left hemispatial neglect in line bisection and cancellation tasks, and not simply personal neglect of the body.

to automatic way. Even if they are fastidious in attending to their appearance, they normally do not have to attend to their movements in order to maintain balance and to put on their clothes in a more or less efficient manner. The patient described by Denny-Brown shows that even without cognitive recognition of a certain aspect of the body, a sophisticated motor use of that aspect is still possible.

Ogden (1996: 109) describes a slightly different case. A neglect patient, Janet, is 'reluctant to dress the left side of her body' and she lets her left leg hang over the edge of the bed. Janet has been diagnosed with *motor neglect* or akinesia, which involves deficits that seem to be associated with the body schema. Patients with this condition show an inability to initiate an action on the neglected side (Heilman *et al.* 1987). Despite appearances, however, Janet is not hemiplegic. In fact, she suffers from an attention problem, and it is her body image that is deficient for the neglected side. Although she will not spontaneously move her neglected left arm, she is still able to use that arm if its movement is directed to the right side, ipsilateral to the brain lesion. Patients such as this may unconsciously use their left arm to brush a fly from their face, or be able to use it with concentrated effort. Janet, for example, sometimes uses both legs to walk. Other times, she hops on her right leg.

In a case described by Pribram, the subject uses her neglected arm but is unaware of it. She reports that she takes classical guitar lessons, but doesn't feel the strings or frets. 'I don't know where my fingers are nor what they are doing, but still I play' (Pribram 1999: 23). In such cases, awareness of the arm is seriously impaired, but purposive movement is still possible.

Similar observations about intact body schemas have been made in tests of hand grip conducted with unilateral neglect patients. Despite neglect of the left hand, for instance, a subject made to pick up an object with the left hand shows completely normal hand grip for the task (Milner 1998). That is, the hand reaches and shapes itself in the appropriate fashion for picking up the particular object—the details of such motor action being quite different for different objects, a fork rather than a cup, for instance, and for different purposive actions, throwing rather than drinking. Normal manual grip relative to different objects is neither the result of conscious decision nor controlled by mechanisms that involve body awareness. At a subpersonal, non-conscious level visual information about the target object informs the motor system and the hand is automatically shaped for the best grip relative to the subject's purpose (see e.g. Jeannerod 1997). Thus, even in cases where the hand is not integrated into the subject's body image (as in unilateral neglect), motor programs are sufficiently intact to accomplish the action. There is also evidence that some impairments in the reaching behavior of neglect patients are due to problems with visual representation rather than to body-schematic functions.[3]

Such cases of neglect, then, indicate a clear dissociation of body image and body schema. This is not meant to be explanatory for neglect, which, in any case, is not a

---

[3] Jackson *et al.* (2000) show that impairments in the reaching behavior of neglect patients are visual rather than motor. Specifically, when the target to be reached is defined visually the reach of the neglected limb is significantly curved. In contrast, when the target is defined proprioceptively, the reach is closer to normal.

single or clearly defined disorder. Problems with body image in neglect cases probably involve more basic difficulties with perception or attention (see Kinsbourne 1987). It is also the case that distortions or disruptions of body image coexisting with normally functioning body schemas can be found in other types of disorders,[4] some of which have etiologies very different from neglect. Anorexia nervosa is a clear example. Dissociations are less clear in other pathologies. In cases of apraxia (disorders of skilled movement), for example, it is often not clear whether the disturbance of motor skill is due to failure of motor memory or a failure of spatial orientation. Together with an intermodal relation between vision and proprioception these functions are important for the proper functioning of body schemas, but may also contribute to the phenomenon of body image (see below).[5] The complexities and etiological differences involved in these different pathologies suggest that, although the distinction between body image and body schema can do some useful work in defining and clarifying these problems, we need to look deeper into how these aspects of embodiment work.

In this chapter I want to explore in some detail the phenomenon of deafferentation, a condition that goes in the opposite direction to cases of neglect. The specific condition is so rarely diagnosed that it has no official name. At the time of writing, only a handful of cases have been documented in the medical literature. The behavioral symptoms are caused by a large nerve fiber neuropathy. In this case, the large mylenated nerve fibers that run throughout the body below the neck have been demyelinated and damaged from an autoimmune reaction, resulting in deafferentation, specifically, the loss of the sense of touch and proprioception from the neck down. Jonathan Cole and I (Gallagher and Cole 1995) have suggested that in such cases patients have, to varying extents, lost their body schema, and if they are to regain control over their movements they are required to develop an extremely

---

[4] Paillard, Michel, and Stelmach (1983) offer a related example of intact body schema and problematic body image. A patient suffers from a deafferented forearm following a parietal lesion. When blindfolded, the patient is unable perceptually to detect the presence or location of tactile stimulation on the forearm, although she is quite able to point to the place of stimulation automatically with her intact hand. Information available at a non-conscious level allows for the automatic localization without perceptual awareness, that is, without the ability to specify the stimulus in terms of a conscious body percept. One might think of this as the motor equivalent of blindsight, as Paillard suggests. Paillard (1997, 1999), following the same distinction between body image and body schema outlined in the previous chapter (he cites Gallagher 1986 and Gallagher and Cole 1995), suggests that this case represents one half of a double dissociation. For the other half he cites the case of GL, a subject who, like IW discussed below, has lost proprioception and the sense of touch for most of her body. Also see Paillard (1991b).

[5] The complexity of cases that involve disordered relations between body image and body schema often extends to associated perceptual or cognitive problems, as in anorexia. These may include problems of self-reference. Korsakoff's psychosis is a condition associated with distinct patterns of neural damage in the diencephalon or temporal lobes, often the result of alcoholism. It involves a complex of symptoms that include disorders of peripheral nerves, short-term memory loss, and what seems to be confabulation and falsification of memory. According to Rosenfield (1992) it also involves a problem in temporal perception caused by a disorder in the mechanisms that provide feedback from the body to the limbic system. Rosenfield writes: 'When brain damage destroys specific aspects of self-reference, it alters the structure of consciousness. . . . [The patient's] injury meant that he could sustain a sense of body image for only about twenty seconds, too brief a span for him to establish a sense of time. His self-consciousness, his self-awareness, was thus deeply altered' (p. 85).

high-functioning body image to make up for the loss. Where unilateral neglect provides one side of a double dissociation between body image and body schema, these cases of deafferentation provide the other side, namely, an intact body image, but a missing body schema.

A close examination of deafferentation will not only deepen our understanding of the distinction between body image and body schema, and how they function, but will also help to show how these two systems are normally interrelated on a behavioral level. It will also take us some distance toward answering our questions about the relations between cognition and embodiment.

A Case History

The case[6] we will examine has been well documented by Jonathan Cole (1995). His patient, Ian Waterman, sometimes referred to as IW in the literature, suffers from an acute sensory neuropathy in which large fibers below the neck have been damaged due to illness.[7] As a result he has no sense of touch and no proprioception below the neck. Ian is still capable of movement and he experiences hot, cold, pain, and muscle fatigue, but he has no proprioceptive sense of posture or limb location. Proprioception is the bodily sense that allows us to know how our body and limbs are positioned. If a person with normal proprioception is asked to sit, close his eyes, and point to his knee, it is proprioception that allows him to successfully guide his hand and find his knee. If I ask Ian to sit, close his eyes, and point to his knee, he has some difficulty. If, in this situation, I move either his knee or his arm, he is unable to point to his knee since, without vision or proprioception, he does not know where either his knee or his hand are located. He would assume that they were in exactly the same location as when he last saw them and he would move his hand so as to point to where he remembers his knee to have been.

Prior to the neuropathy Ian had normal posture and was capable of normal movement. At the onset of his illness Ian's initial experience was the complete loss of postural and motor control. He could not sit up or stand or move his limbs in any controllable way. For the first three months, even with a visual perception of the location of his limbs, he could not control his movement. In the course of the following two years, while in a rehabilitation hospital, he gained enough motor control so that he could feed himself, write, and walk. He went on to master everyday motor tasks involved in personal care, housekeeping, and those movements required for gainful employment in an office setting. Today Ian's movement

---

[6] Although I will focus on one particular case here, IW, the discussion applies to several other cases with which I am familiar. See e.g. Cole and Paillard (1995) for a discussion of GL.

[7] This happened in 1971 when Ian was 19. The onset of the neuropathy was acute following an illness documented at the time as infectious mononucleosis. Neurophysiological tests confirm the loss of large myelinated fibers below the neck (Cole and Katifi 1991).

appears close to normal. He runs his own business and pursues the hobby of outdoor photography.

Because of the loss of proprioception and tactile sense, however, Ian still does not know, without visual perception, where his limbs are or what posture he maintains. In order to maintain motor control he must conceptualize his movements and keep certain parts of his body in his visual field. His movement requires constant visual and mental concentration. In darkness he is unable to control movement; when he walks he cannot daydream but must concentrate on his movement constantly. When he writes he needs to concentrate on both his body posture and on holding the pen. Maintaining posture is, for him, a task rather than an automatic process. Ian learned through trial and error the amount of force needed to pick up and hold an egg without breaking it. If his attention is directed toward a different activity while he holds an egg, his hand either crushes the egg or drops it.

As I indicated in the previous chapter, in a majority of situations the normal adult maintains posture or moves without consciously monitoring motor activity. Posture and movement are usually close to automatic; they tend to take care of themselves, outside attentive regard. One's body, in such cases, effaces itself as one is geared into a particular intentional goal, and this effacement is possible because of the normal functioning of a body schema. In terms of the distinction between body image and schema, Ian has lost major aspects of his body schema, and thereby the possibility of normally unattended movement. He is forced to compensate for that loss by depending on his body image in a way that normal subjects do not. As we will see, Ian's body image is itself modified in important respects. For him, control over posture and movement is achieved by a partial and imperfect functional substitution of body image for body schema.

At the earliest stage of his illness he had no control over his movements and was unable to put intention into action. There was, one might say, a disconnection of will from the specifics of movement. If Ian decided to move his arm in a certain direction, and then tried to carry out the intended movement, the arm and other parts of his body would move in unpredictable ways. Without support, Ian was unable to maintain anything other than a prone posture. He had no knowledge of limb position unless he saw the limb. But even with vision, he had no control over his movement. Because of the absence of proprioceptive and tactile feedback his entire body schema system failed.

That proprioception is a major source of information for the maintenance of posture and the governance of movement—that is, for the normal functioning of the body schema—is clear from Ian's experience. But proprioception is not the only possible source for the required information. Ian, as a result of extreme effort and hard work, recovered control over his movement and regained a close to normal life. It is important to understand that he did not do this by recovering proprioceptive sense. In strict physiological terms, he has never recovered from the original problem. His neuropathy has not been repaired. He has been able to address the motor problem on a behavioral level, however, by rebuilding a partial and very minimal body schema and by using body image to help control movement. This case, in terms of the body image/body schema distinction, is just the opposite to neglect. If the neglect patient is capable of controlled movement even on the neglected side because of an intact body schema, Ian, who is unable to depend on a body schema, must employ his body image to guide his movement. In complete contrast to neglect, Ian is required to pay an inordinately high degree of attention to his body.

Just the Facts

As indicated in the previous chapter, I am using the term 'body schema' to signify a certain collection of sensory-motor functions responsible for maintaining posture and governing movement. The body-schema system might best be conceived as consisting of three functional aspects. The first is responsible for the processing of new information about posture and movement. This information is constantly being provided by a number of inputs, including proprioception. A second aspect involves output, and can be characterized as a set of motor programs or motor habits, movement patterns that are either innate or learned. The final aspect consists of certain intermodal capacities that allow for communication between proprioception and other sense modalities.

1. Proprioception and Other Inputs

The body works to maintain posture or govern movement on the basis of information received from numerous sources. Besides somatic proprioceptive information from kinetic, muscular, articular, and cutaneous sources, contributions also originate in vestibular and equilibrial functions. Visual sense is also a source of information vital to posture and movement. Visual sense, in this regard, can be distinguished as (a) visual exteroception, specifically, direct visual perception of the location and movements of limbs (see e.g. Crook 1987); and (b) visual proprioception and visual kinesthesis (Gibson 1979; Jouen 1988; Neisser 1976). Direct visual perception of one's own body helps to constitute the perceptual aspect of the body image. Normally it does not play a major role in motor and postural control, but for Ian Waterman it is the primary source of information about his body. Visual proprioception and visual kinesthesis are more directly related to the body schema and involve the tacit processing of visual information about the body's movement in relation to the environment. In this regard such processes contribute to balance. They are, in Gibson's term, *ecological* in that they provide information about the environment and about how the experiencing organism moves through that environment. Working together with the vestibular system, they help to distinguish between movements made by objects in the environment and one's own movements. They can override vestibular information, however, and lead to a mistaken sense of movement. For example, when you are sitting on a train waiting for it to move and the train next to it begins to move, visual proprioception will provide a sense that you are moving. On the basis of such ecological information, outside conscious awareness, adjustments in posture are made in order to compensate for changes in the optical flow that accompany movement in the visual environment (Assaiante, Amblard, and Carblanc 1988; Brandt 1988; Lee and Lishman 1975). Closely connected to vision, extraocular muscles, responsible for eye movement, also provide proprioceptive information that contributes to head stabilization and whole-body posture (Roll and Roll 1988; Roll, Roll, and Velay 1991). The visual and vestibular systems are highly integrated with somatic proprioception very early in development.[8]

Proprioception, in the ordinary (non-visual) sense of somatic (mechanical) information about joint position and limb extension, is normally the major source of information concerning present bodily position and posture. Even in this sense, however, the term 'proprioception' is used in a variety of ways. O'Shaughnessy (1995), for example, defines proprioception as a form of direct awareness that contributes to the knowledge, representation, or image of our body. Without visual perception of one's body, for example, one can still sense limb position on the basis of proprioceptive awareness. One can still find one's knee with one's eyes closed. If I ask you to do so, I am asking you to use proprioceptive awareness in an explicitly reflective and what O'Shaughnessy calls 'involuted' way. To be precise, however, one usually does not have to 'find' one's knee, in the sense of distinguishing it among some set of things or picking it out of a collection of objects. One already knows where one's knee is because of ongoing pre-reflective proprioceptive awareness. For this reason, even if proprioceptive awareness is a pre-reflective pragmatic awareness that does not take the body as an object, it contributes a certain spatial structure to the perceptual body image. This fact raises an important question with respect to Ian Waterman's ability to move, act, and perceive within an egocentric frame of reference. I return to this question in the final section of this chapter.

In contrast to the notion of proprioceptive *awareness* (PA), in the neurological tradition proprioceptive *information* (PI) is defined as a non-conscious process—the result of physiological stimuli activating certain proprioceptors, but not consciously experienced by the subject. On this view, proprioceptive information, generated at peripheral proprioceptors and registered at strategic sites in the brain, but below the threshold of consciousness, operates as part of the system that constitutes the body schema. This aspect of proprioception is not something we can be directly aware of.

For our purposes it is important to maintain a clear distinction between PA, which can be either a reflective (involuted) or pre-reflective awareness of

---

[8] Jouen and Gapenne (1995) trace the development of and the interaction among the vestibular, proprioceptive, oculomotor, and visual-proprioceptive systems. The vestibular system, which is fully mature at birth, provides information about movement and spatial orientation of head and body, and contributes to the regulation of postural and motor activity at a subcortical level. Intermodal hard-wired connections run from secondary-order vestibular neurons to oculomotor and spinal levels, and represent 'a major brainstem integration center for the perception of self-motion and for the regulation of postural and occulomotor activities involved in body spatial orientation' (p. 283).

movement, and PI, which informs the body schema system and the non-conscious performance of movement.[9] Somatic proprioception is thus twofold, and serves a twofold function. Ian, however, has neither aspect of somatic proprioception, and this affects both his body image and body schema, but in different ways.

Normally, information from proprioceptive, vestibular, and other sources constantly updates the body about posture and whatever stage of movement it is in. Of these various sources, Ian still has input from the vestibular system, and visual proprioception. He has a grossly impoverished sense of physical effort, which is of no use in movement control (Cole and Sedgwick 1992). He has lost tactile and proprioceptive information, so there is no kinesthetic, cutaneous, muscular, or articular input. He depends heavily on visual perception of his limbs and visual proprioception in order to control his movement. To maintain balanced posture, for example, he has learned to designate a stationary object in the environment as a reference point that he keeps within his visual field. Deprived of vision, in a darkened room, Ian is not able to maintain posture. Without sight he loses both visual inspection of his body and visual fixation on an external point.

It is clear that Ian makes up for his loss of somatic proprioception with a high reliance on visual perception and visual proprioception to provide a running account of limb position and postural balance. Since his muscles still work and he has a 'crude' sense of effort in this connection, he is able to tense his muscles and freeze in position.[10] He can do this in an articulated manner, so, for example, he is able to maintain posture in legs and trunk while working with his hands. All of this—use of visual perception, freezing of position, and movement of limbs—takes concentrated effort. Whereas in the normal subject all of this takes place without conscious effort, prenoetically, and certainly without thinking about it, in Ian, conscious effort—the conscious processing of information about body and environment—is what informs, updates, and coordinates his postural and motor processes.

2. Motor Programs and Motor Images

Motor programs, a repertoire of motor schemas, are, on the behavioral level, flexible and corrigible patterns. Some are entirely learned; others, which may be innate, are elaborated through experience and practice. Examples of behavior guided by motor programs include swallowing, reaching, grasping, walking, and writing. We normally learn to ride a bicycle or to swim, for instance, by attending to

[9] This distinction is nicely worked out in the 'Introduction' to Bermúdez, Marcel, and Eilan (1995: 14). Phillips (1985) insists on the distinction between the *performance* of movement and the proprioceptive *awareness* of movement. He points out, *contra* Sherrington, that 'the fact that the same receptors supply the information that is necessary for the automatic governing of movement as well as that necessary for the perception of his own movements by a conscious perceiver does not seem to justify the indiscriminate application of the term "muscle sense" to these two functions, the one conscious, the other not "amenable to introspection" ' (p. 43).

[10] This sense of effort is likely to be based on A-delta fibers, and this is very different from control subjects (see Cole and Sedgwick 1992; Cole *et al.* 1995).

the task; but subsequently we ride or swim without any thought of motor action. Not all motor programs or schemas persist indefinitely and in order to maintain them they need to be refreshed by use.

Motor programs or schemas have been conceptualized in neuroscience as a way to describe complex patterns of movement that are generated by complex patterns of neuronal activation in the premotor and motor areas, and other related areas of the cortex (e.g. Arbib 1985; Arbib and Hesse 1986; Jeannerod 1997). On the behavioral level, a motor schema corresponds to an elemental aspect (e.g. the rotation of my wrist) of a larger, more complex movement (reaching to grasp a cup). On the neurological level, a motor schema corresponds to the specific neuronal activity required for that elemental aspect of movement. At this level, motor schemas combine to form more complex 'representations' of intentional actions. Ian had built up a set of motor schemas over the course of nineteen years prior to his illness. Although it is likely that these cortical representations were not destroyed by the loss of proprioception and touch, they were no longer accessible when he lost proprioceptive feedback.

There are at least two ways to explain the effects of Ian's lack of proprioceptive information on motor programs. The first involves the problem of updating and gaining access to programs that continue to exist. When, for example, one buttons one's shirt, one accesses a motor program that carries the action through without the need of attention on how exactly to move one's fingers. I can hold a conversation even while I am dressing. The movement guided by the motor program is for the most part automatic. Normally this is possible because proprioceptive information updates the motor process with regard to finger location and movement. If the process is not kept updated in this manner, however, if proprioception fails to register the present motor state, or fails to provide the proper cues, then either the motor program cannot be accessed, even if it remains theoretically intact, or it must be accessed in an alternative way.[11] The loss of proprioceptive information, which would, in normal circumstances, keep the system updated with regard to present posture and limb position, puts Ian in this type of situation—his motor system doesn't know where it is in the movement process. Motor programs can stay in the process only if the system can register its present motor state.

A second possible explanation involves the retention or lack of retention of motor schemas. Like non-motor habits, when motor programs are not used, they fade and cease to exist (Head 1920). Because of the lack of proprioceptive updating, Ian may have been unable to put all his motor programs to use, and it remains unclear to

[11] Volpe, LeDoux, and Gazzaniga (1979) have suggested that simple motor programs can proceed effectively without proprioceptive feedback. Their subjects, following cortical damage, suffered deafferentation limited to one arm. When provided with tactile cues on relevant areas of the unaffected arm they could sometimes initiate motor programs that were accurate but not finely controlled. These subjects are quite different from Ian in that they have lost sensation as a result of cortical damage. Are they accessing motor programs using touch as a cue? Ian, of course, does not have touch. Does Ian use visual information to initiate motor programs? When motor programs are activated the relevant movement is in large part automatic. For Ian, it is not clear that his instrumental movements ever reach the stage of being automatic. See below for comments on his locomotive movement.

what extent such patterns continue to exist, or to what extent Ian can establish new motor schemas. Observation of Ian's movements, and his own phenomenological report, indicate that very little of his motor activity is governed by automatic motor programs. Although it is probable that he was able to recover as well as he has because he had already learned normal patterns of movement prior to his illness, this does not mean that his movements are the same as they were before. His movements have been re-engineered in a way that does not depend on motor programs. Or, better expressed, his movements are constantly being re-engineered because, for the most part, he cannot depend on motor programs.

Still, not all aspects of his movements in walking are under his volitional control the whole time. His recoveries in writing and walking, for instance, have probably depended on his ability to delegate some aspects of the motor act to a rudimentary, close to automatic, schematic level. On the first explanation, this may indicate some minimal access to intact motor programs (Bernett et al. 1989) based on visual input rather than on proprioception. It would be consistent with the second explanation to say, not that his movements are based partially on relearned or re-established motor programs, but that the conscious control of movement becomes less exacting with practice. For example, when he relearnt to walk it required all his concentration. Now he estimates that walking over a flat, well-lit surface takes about 50–70 per cent of his attention, though walking over an uneven surface still requires close to 100 per cent. Thus, Ian's success in recovering useful movement function has depended primarily on his finite mental concentration, and, to a much lesser degree on reaccessing or relearning motor programs which are, so far, poorly understood in terms of how we access them.

To what extent might the kind of updating provided by the visual perception of one's own limbs supply information that would allow access to or activation of motor schemas? Normally vision is directed at various objects in the environment that I want to interact with. Information derived from visual perception of the environment certainly plays a role in launching motor programs and allowing for adjustments in the ongoing movement. But this requires a coordination with proprioceptive information about body position. To begin to reach for something I need to know not only where the object is (via vision), but where my hand is (normally, via proprioception). Vision is not designed to take the place of somatic proprioception. Control of intentional movement does not normally travel from body image to body schema except in abstract, self-conscious, or imaginatively practiced movement. Outside a practical situation, when, for example, one is thinking philosophically about the nature of the will, one might abstractly command one's arm to raise itself in order to demonstrate the relation between will and movement. Even in that case one would be hard pressed to say exactly how one translates conscious will into movement. But in most everyday circumstances, volitional movement means reaching to grasp something, or pointing to something, and the focus is on the *something*, not on the motor act of reaching or grasping or pointing. These movements tend to follow along automatically from the intention. In Ian, however, focused visual attention had to be realigned toward the actual motor accomplishment. In reaching to grasp, for example, he has to see not only the target object, but also his hand. On the basis of what he sees, he needs to think about how to shape his hand in order to pick up the object. This realignment of vision involves important changes in the neurological picture. In terms of neurological processes, visually guided movement (that is, movement guided by visual perception of objects in the environment) normally activates the dorsal stream and feeds into the motor system for launch of a motor program. Ian's visual control of movement, in contrast, activates the ventral stream and orbito-frontal cortex (areas responsible for cognitive and (roughly) non-motor visual tasks).[12] One result of the realignment toward visual and cognitive control of movement is that Ian demonstrates articulated movement that is different from normal. His need to attend to his movement alters the way in which he produces a movement across phenomenological, neurological, and behavioral dimensions.

A good way to explain how Ian controls his movement using vision and cognition is to appeal to the concept of motor images. Ian reports that he quite often imagines a specific movement in order to accomplish it. There is a good neurological basis to support this phenomenological strategy. Many of the same brain areas that are activated when a subject executes a movement are also activated when the subject imagines herself moving. Neuronal patterns responsible for generating a motor image of an action are in large part the same neuronal patterns that are activated in the case of observing action and in performing action (see Decety and Summerville 2003; Grezes and Decety 2001). In an experimental situation a subject may be asked to execute an action or to imagine herself executing an action. Neuroimaging shows a significant overlap between action execution and imagined execution in the supplementary motor area (SMA), the dorsal premotor cortex, the supramarginal gyrus, and the superior parietal lobe. If many of the same brain areas responsible for organizing the details of motor action are activated in the generation of a motor image, it is likely that Ian is able to enlist those areas to control movement through a combination of vision and motor imagery.

3. Cross-modal Communication

In Ian's case vision was not enough *at first* to gain control over his movement. There are two related reasons for this. First, just as the loss of proprioceptive *information*

---

[12] This is based on unpublished PET experiments (Cole, private correspondence). When Ian makes a movement that he does not see, the inferior parietal and cerebellar areas are activated. Ian and six controls performed a simple sequential left-side finger-thumb apposition task. PET scans were taken under two conditions: movement with on-line visual feedback via a video display, and movement with vision of the still hand (no visual feedback of movement). In the first condition, in Ian, a wide number of areas (not activated by controls) were activated in the right pre-visual and bilateral cerebellar areas suggesting greater dependence (relative to controls) on visual feedback for supervision of movement. In the second condition, movement with no visual feedback, the right prefrontal, the right inferior parietal cortex, and the bilateral cerebellum (both visual and motor areas) are activated. This indicates a top-down, cognitively planned control of movement. Activation of the right inferior parietal cortex in the latter condition suggests that in some regards Ian takes a third-person perspective toward his body (see Ruby and Decety 2001).

impairs the body schema and disrupts the control of posture and movement, so the loss of proprioceptive *awareness* results in an impoverishment of, or possibly the restructuring of, the perceptual aspect of the body image. Although he was able to see his body, Ian did not have immediate control over his posture or movement. Seeing one's own arm move is somewhat different from both seeing and feeling it move. Second, due to the absence of proprioception another important part of the body-schema system, a capacity for specific kinds of intermodal communication, failed. As a result, Ian lost not only the kind of automatic movements that allow normal subjects to walk without seeing or thinking of their legs; he lost controlled voluntary movement.

Even in those instances when a person uses the body image to guide movement, this does not happen without the non-conscious operations of the body schema. In the early stage of Ian's illness his body image was not up to the task of compensating for the missing proprioceptive information that usually supports body-schematic functions. Even with vision and thought he could not control motility. With the loss of proprioception, Ian's body image was also impaired. This impairment had experiential consequences, for example, the felt sense of his own body *as his own* and as under his control had disappeared. More than this, however, it had consequences for the actual control mechanisms for movement. There is normally an intermodal communication between proprioception and vision, and this is missing in Ian. For example, I am able to imitate the bodily movement of another person without drawing up a theory of how to do it, because what I see automatically gets translated into a proprioceptive sense of how to move. The possibility of intermodal translation between vision and proprioception, an innate feature of our sensory-motor system (see Ch. 3), allows visual perception to inform and coordinate movement. It is also possible for visual perception to correct proprioceptive distortions or illusions (Gurfinkel and Levick 1991; Ramachandran and Rogers-Ramachandran 1996; Ramachandran, Rogers-Ramachandran, and Cobb 1995). In Ian, however, the 'language' of proprioception, an important part of the inter-modal code, was missing. If vision were to take over the work of proprioception, that is, if it were constantly to update information on present posture and move-ment, then it would have to learn to communicate with and drive motor processes more directly than it normally did through intermodal means.

Although it is uncertain how vision can control ongoing movement without proprioceptive feedback, the realignment toward visual and cognitive control of movement results in some clear differences from normal motor control. In addition to the PET studies mentioned above, such differences in Ian have been ascertained through the technique of Transcranial Magnetic Stimulation of the brain which makes it possible to stimulate the motor system in humans at both cortical and subcortical levels. This technique involves a painless procedure in which a magnetic flux, discharged through a coil placed over the scalp, produces a magnetic field within the brain. This discharges the neurons that are close to their threshold for activation, and leads to a muscle twitch (see e.g. Rothwell *et al.* 1987). At low intensities of stimulation only neurons close to their discharge potential are activated. Magnetic stimulation can be used, therefore, to investigate those cells that are close to that level. In the motor system this procedure allows study of those neurons related to the neural basis of attention to movement. In the normal subject magnetic stimulation of a specific motor area of the brain will produce a small twitch movement in an arm or leg. If a magnetic pulse is superimposed at the time the subject is in the process of making a movement, then a much larger twitch is produced. In addition, the threshold to produce the twitch falls dramatically when the person is beginning a movement on his own.

Cole *et al.* (1995), using this technique, demonstrated that Ian has a more focused command of movement. Ian was asked to move his thumb while an appropriately directed magnetic pulse was superimposed. His focusing of command onto movement of the thumb was far more accurately limited to the thumb than in control subjects. In control subjects thumb movement facilitated other movements when magnetic pulse was superimposed; this was not the case with Ian. Clearly his need to attend to his movement alters the way in which he produces a movement even at the cortical level.

In these types of experiments, imagined movement also lowers threshold and promotes a larger twitch. Ian was asked to *imagine* moving his thumb while a magnetic stimulation was superimposed. Under these conditions Ian is still able to reduce the threshold for producing a movement in the thumb muscle alone, in contrast to control subjects who are unable to limit the effect to the thumb muscle (ibid.). Thus, in Ian's progression from will to motor control, his voluntary control is more focused, and, compared to control subjects, there is less difference between a real movement and an imagined movement.

In place of the missing body schema processes, we might say that Ian has substituted a virtual body schema—a set of cognitively driven motor processes. This virtual schema seems to function only within the framework of a body image that is consciously and continually maintained. If he is denied access to a visual awareness of his body's position in the perceptual field, or denied the ability to think about his body, then, without the framework of the body image, the virtual body schema ceases to function—it cannot stand on its own. What is the exact nature of the body image that Ian uses to control his posture and movement? To what extent is his conscious effort a matter of visual attention, or simply keeping certain body parts within the visual field? To what extent does it consist of a set of judgments— i.e., thoughtful judgments about what his body is doing?

According to Ian's own phenomenological reports, when he is moving he does not think about certain muscle groups, but simply that he will move an arm or finger. Normally when he is making a coordinated movement he will both see and think of the coordinated moving part, e.g. the arm reaching to grasp. It appears that he does not think about muscle operations themselves, nor did he do so even when he was relearning to move. His conscious effort in moving essentially consists of a set of motor images and judgments; he then monitors the movement with vision and uses the visual feedback to maintain movement and to stay on target. This means that for intentional action the cognitive load is greater for Ian. A normal subject needs only to think 'I'll take a drink from this glass', and as this is being acted upon, she can anticipate her next activity. Not only must Ian think 'I'll take a drink from this glass'; he must think 'I'll reach this hand, and as I reach I'll lean this way to keep balance, and shape my hand in this precise way and make a final adjustment as I grasp the glass'.

There is some evidence that Ian has automated some of this process in his locomotive movement.[13] One way to conceive of this is to say that he has re-established access to some motor programs learned prior to his illness; but this is minimal or unlikely for reasons already indicated. Alternatively, he may have established some set of learned motor strategies (habitual motor images) monitored at the level of the body image—a set of sequential motor steps that he can follow without an inordinate or debilitating amount of attention. Some evidence for this view can be found in Ian's performance on the 'Star of David' experiment. Asked to trace the edges of the Star of David with their finger while viewing it inverted through a mirror, normal subjects find it difficult or impossible to turn the corners because of the conflict between proprioceptive information, not affected by the mirror, and visual information, which is affected. One would expect Ian to have no trouble tracing the edges, because in his case there could be no proprioceptive interference with visual guidance. Another deafferented subject, GL, who suffers from a similar loss of proprioception, was able to do the task effortlessly the first time.[14] Ian, however, was much more like control subjects in that when he came to a point on the star there was a conflict. This cannot be due to proprioceptive interference, since he has no proprioception. One hypothesis is that the interference comes from internal sequential motor images that Ian generates cognitively without proprioceptive feedback.[15] On the basis of such motor image sequences Ian is able to maintain simple repetitive movement for up to a minute. When required to concentrate on a simple subtraction problem (subtracting serial 4s or 7s from 100), however, the performance of repetitive movement deteriorates within seconds. To alter a repetitive movement Ian requires visual feedback (Cole and Sedgwick 1992).

[13] There is some phasic activation and relaxation of calf muscles in relation to gait cycle. These are not under visual control and may therefore be non-conscious (Bernett et al. 1989). Ian himself reports that walking on flat surfaces takes approximately half the concentration required initially.

[14] Both Ian and GL lost touch and proprioception, Ian from the collarline down, GL from about mouth level down. Ian has normal position sense for the neck, but GL has no sensation from her neck muscles or in the lower part of her mouth and face. Both subjects have maintained vestibular information, information about head position and movement in the gravitational field. Ian may be more able to focus attention on motor planning and may thus be able to construct motor images, due to the fact that he has a more stable head and neck posture than GL. One result is that while Ian walks, GL remains in a wheelchair. See Cole and Paillard (1995).

[15] Ian's case may throw some light on the way we normally construct motor representations. For example, how do we know how to hit a golf ball first time? Feedback will not tell us. We need to launch a motor act constructed internally, based on an image. By looking at Ian's capacity to do this without feedback we can begin to reflect on how we do this ourselves. For this reason, Ian has drawn the attention of NASA scientists who are interested in training astronauts to use robotic arms in weightless conditions where proprioception functions differently than in the Earth's gravitational field (see e.g. Cole, Sacks, and Waterman 2000).

There is also evidence for the retention, over a period of more than thirty years, of certain coordinated 'reflex' motor actions, although they are of no use to Ian in controlling movement. If one removes a drink from a tray held by someone else the arm of the subject carrying the tray will move upwards as the drink is taken off. The upward movement does not happen, however, if it is the holder of the tray who removes the drink. This 'waiter's illusion' depends on a reflex motor program, and still occurs in deafferented subjects (Forget and Lamarre 1995). A few other coordinated actions have been found, though none are of any use to deafferented subjects. Ian does not automatically withdraw his hand from pain. A simple fall can be serious for him, because he has to think about how to put his arms out to break the fall, and he can only do so slowly.

In control subjects coordination between limbs and body is apparent in simple tasks such as raising an arm. As one raises an arm a variety of muscles in other parts of the body adjust themselves in order to keep the head and the rest of the body balanced. This is an automatic and holistic function on the level of the body schema. In contrast, when Ian moves his arm when standing he has to think about his center of gravity and he must produce opposing movements to keep his balance. In raising his hand he does not know how far it has gone without visual feedback. So, in order to raise it safely he has first to assess how free and safe the space is in front of him, and how safe his body position is to allow an alteration in the center of gravity relative to raising the arm. If he wants accuracy in this movement, he requires visual perception of the arm.

We learn from this case that mental control of movement is limited in four ways. First, there are attentional limitations: Ian cannot attend to all aspects of movement. Second, his rate of movement is slower than normal. The fact that movement is driven consciously slows motility down. Third, the overall duration of motor activity is relatively short because of the mental effort or energy required. Finally, complex single movements (such as walking across rough ground), and combined or compound movements (walking and carrying an egg) take more energy.

Thus, a body image based primarily on visual perception can substitute for a body schema based primarily on proprioception, but it does so inadequately. Visual feedback involves delays that are too great to allow for normal motor activity. Ian also has to simplify movements in order to focus his command of them. Ian has learned to make gross compensatory adjustments somewhat quickly after, or along with, the movement of a limb. Still, his movements appear somewhat stiff and slow and could not be mistaken for normal. Some aspects of his movement may benefit from acquired strategies concerning the adjustment of certain muscles in particular movements. To the extent that any of this is a matter of habit, even a habitual behavior of consciously adjusting certain muscles in any particular movement, such habitual behavior would help to constitute the virtual (image-dependent) body schema. Ian, however, insists that once a motor behavior has been performed it does not mean that it requires less concentration subsequently. His rehabilitation necessitated huge increases in his attentional abilities.

The cognitive demands of this activity cannot be overestimated, for other deafferented subjects have not managed such a functional recovery. Anything that might upset his perceptual or cognitive processes has an affect on his movements. A head cold renders Ian unable to do anything and he takes to his bed. In this case his visual perception may be fairly unaffected, but he finds it difficult to focus his conscious and attentive will, and movement becomes more than he can deal with.

Within this set of limitations, Ian has reinvented movement. A partial and virtual body schema is instituted on the basis of vision and of some limited information that normally serves the body schema—visual proprioception, and vestibular information, and less so, a sense of physical effort. In the case of the normal body schema, however, this information is processed automatically within a framework that includes the larger role of proprioception. This system allows the normal subject to control movement (once learned, as in infancy or in practice) relatively effortlessly and for the most part without conscious attention or awareness. In Ian's case the partial and virtual body schema depends on a consciously maintained body image which is constantly sustained through visual perception (attention to body parts or awareness of the body in the visual field) and through a set of judgments about position.

A Body of Evidence

Some of the limits encountered in a purely phenomenological account of the distinction between body image and body schema can be overcome by the study of the right pathological cases. Whereas certain cases of neglect can be characterized roughly as cases in which body-schema processes can work even in the absence of an intact body image, cases of deafferentation show that the body image can be employed to make up for a lack in the body schema. Such cases also tell us more about the contrasting characteristics that define the differences between body image and body schema. Specifically, they help to verify and explicate certain issues that were outlined in the phenomenological analysis—issues pertaining to non-conscious functioning, ownership and agency, partial versus holistic embodiment, and integration with the environment.

1.   Non-conscious Functioning

Normal somatic proprioception, understood as contributing to the prenoetic performance of body schemas, grants a degree of motoric freedom to the normal subject that is limited in deafferented patients like Ian. With respect to moving around the world, the normal and healthy subject can in large measure forget about her body in the normal routine of the day. The body takes care of itself, and in doing so, it enables the subject to attend, with relative ease, to other practical aspects of life. To the extent that the body effaces itself, it grants to the subject a freedom to think of other things. The fact that Ian, who lacks proprioception, is forced to think about his bodily movements and his posture much of the time demonstrates the degree to which, in the normal subject, this is not the case. Just to the degree to which body schemas function non-consciously without the intervention of a body image, the latter remains an accessory with regard to posture and movement. Of course, this is not to deny that the body image may serve other important functions in this regard. Indeed, in terms of learning and developing some of the habitual operations of the body schema, one requires a certain perceptual awareness of one's body.

2. *Ownership and Agency*

Ian's case presents a more complex picture with regard to the sense of body ownership and the sense of agency for movement. It suggests that both the body schema and body image play an important role in underwriting a sense of embodied self. The notion of agency refers to the initiation or source of the act. It involves a sense of generating or being the willful initiator of an action. In the normal phenomenology of voluntary or willed action, the sense of agency and the sense of ownership coincide and are indistinguishable (although it is quite possible to distinguish them in the case of *involuntary* action—see Ch. 8). Intentional movement is accompanied, if not by an explicitly conscious sense of volition, then at least by the lack of a sense of helplessness or want of control. A sense of agency is built into intentional movement and is noticed when it goes missing. If your arm suddenly begins to move on its own, without your intentional control, you are very likely to think, ruling out reflex movement, that someone else is moving it, and it would be quite surprising if that were not the case. If one loses control over motor activity, one also loses a sense of agency (or gains a sense of helplessness).

Initially Ian was unable to control his movements and over the first few days after onset of his condition he felt a loss of embodiment or an alienation from his body. This supports the view that volition or control is an important invariant in the sense of selfhood (Stern 1985). As soon as he was able to see his body and its movements properly, however, even though he had not attained motor control over them, the sense of disembodiment diminished. Ian's experience is consistent with the idea that the body image is an important source for the sense of ownership. This is especially the case in regard to the visual sense (Cole, Sacks, and Waterman 2000). Visual attention to bodily movement 'suffices to identify a body part as existing and being (conceptually) one's own' (Kinsbourne 1995: 217). For Ian, body ownership was re-established very quickly. Yet, because his intentions to move were imperfectly fulfilled his sense of agency continued to be deficient. As he gained more precise control of movement, using a body image framework, his sense of agency was gradually re-established.

That his sense of agency is now well established can be seen in the Transcranial Magnetic Stimulation study cited above (Cole 1995). Ian was asked to imagine a small movement with the thumb. A magnetic stimulation was superimposed upon this, leading to an actual movement. Without visual feedback he had no idea that the actual movement had occurred. But when he was allowed to watch his fingers and was asked to imagine moving his thumb, he was surprised at the actual movement and insisted that *he* did not do it. He has a very good sense of when he generates movement and when he does not.

Ian's control over movement and his sense of agency were regained by exploiting aspects of his body image. This suggests that the sense of agency is not specifically tied to proprioceptive feedback, which Ian lacks. This idea is reinforced by experimental research on normal subjects. These studies suggest that control of one's action, and the sense of agency that comes along with it, are based not on sensory (proprioceptive or visual) feedback from movement itself, or from peripheral effort associated with such movement, but on processes that precede action and translate intention into movement (Fourneret and Jeannerod 1998; Marcel 2003). One's initial awareness of a spontaneous voluntary action is coordinated with pre-action motor commands relating to the effectors to be used (Haggard and Eimer 1999; Haggard and Magno 1999). That is, although the content of experience may be the intended action, the sense that I am generating the action can be traced to processes that lie between intention and performance (Gallagher and Marcel 1999). Ian has intentions from which he must generate pre-action motor commands. Despite the fact that he was required to learn new strategies involving motor images to generate these commands, the very fact of their generation contributes to a sense of agency for his actions. That Ian felt alienated from his body in the original condition where he lacked control over his movements suggests that the fulfillment of such commands also plays a role in a sense of agency for movement. We will have occasion to explore these issues further in Ch. 8.

3.   *Partial versus Holistic Embodiment*

The various limitations involved in the conscious control of movement based on body image support the idea that the body image involves an abstract and partial perception of the body. Conscious attention can focus on only one part or area of the body at a time. One cannot attend to all aspects of bodily movement, and if one is forced to control movement by means of the body image, motility is slowed. The more complex the movement, that is, the more aspects of simultaneous bodily adjustments that require monitoring, the more difficult it is to perform. The more that Ian can make his movements automatic through the use of learned motor strategies, and so the less attention that is required for movement, the easier and more natural it seems. In effect, movement appears relatively more coordinated and holistic to the degree that motor decisions have been made close to automatic, and less attention is required. In Ian, however, this degree is still far from normal, and the slightly stiff and deliberate character of his movements makes them appear less than holistically integrated.

4.   *Integration with the Environment*

The proper functioning of a body schema provides a higher degree of integration between body and environment, incorporating elements that are not part of the objective body or necessarily reflected in the body image. Ian approaches this kind of integration in only one circumstance: driving a car. In the experience of driving, the automobile can seem to be an extension of the body—the car's movements are easily and often unattentively under one's control. Thus, an experienced driver does not need to think about or be explicitly attentive to the details of driving or the car's movements. In some instances, for example, one can arrive at one's destination without a recollection of the actual details of the drive—the driving body has been on automatic pilot so to speak.[16] Ian drives and enjoys it. It seems effortless to him in comparison to walking. He reports that it is easier for him to drive 300 or 400 miles than to stop and refuel. Driving actually allows him to relax his attention to his bodily movement. Ian maintains his posture by 'freezing' in place. He needs only to keep his hands within the visual field (his controls are all manual), and he is assisted in a high degree by visual proprioception which facilitates automatic control in the case of driving (Lee and Aronson 1974). Ian has to think hard about walking, but not as hard for driving.

The interior of the automobile is also a much safer environment for Ian than most others. He requires a well-defined personal space surrounding him to avoid the danger of unexpected movements by others. An unexpected touch or bump can easily upset his balance. Thus, in most circumstances, personal boundaries are maintained visually; he is, in a high degree, conscious of his body as clearly differentiated from its environment, and he constantly monitors the positions of his limbs relative to external objects and the position of other people.

What implications do these observations have for our questions about the structure of consciousness? To whatever extent proprioceptive *awareness* contributes to the content of the phenomenal and marginal structure of consciousness, or to whatever extent proprioceptive *information* (as an important part of a body-schema system) allows our conscious experience to be free of attention directed toward the body, a loss of proprioception can mean a change in the structure of consciousness and self-consciousness. Thus, as Oliver Sacks remarks, the loss of proprioception in Ian 'shows how such a peripheral disorder can have the profoundest "central" effects on what Gerald Edelman called the "primary consciousness" of a person: his ability to experience his body as continuous, as "owned", as controlled, as *his*. We see that a disorder of touch and proprioception, itself unconscious, becomes, at the highest level, a "disease of consciousness" ' (Foreword, Cole 1995: p. xiii). Such a disordering of consciousness runs deeper than simply the changes that play out on the level of phenomenal content or with respect to aspects of the phenomenal body (body percept, body image). In such a disorder changes to the *noetic structure* of consciousness itself occur. A feature that is more or less kept in the wings in the ordinary theater of consciousness comes close to center stage in Ian. If in ordinary

---

[16] This does not mean that the driver has been unconscious or has paid no conscious attention to driving. Rather, for the efficiency of the ongoing processes of the perceptual-motor system, such experience is not stored in long-term memory. In effect, in driving a car, and in many other tasks, it is much more efficient (and less dangerous) that we quickly forget what we have just done and focus on what is present and just about to occur (see Gallagher 2001d for discussion).

experience embodiment frames our approach to the world, in Ian the frame begins to occlude the picture. Jonathan Cole suggests that in contrast to Sacks's patient, 'the disembodied lady' (Sacks 1985), Ian may be considered super-embodied. He is so constantly conscious of his body that it reorients the attentional structure of his consciousness.

Framed by the Body

Further changes involve an important restructuring of consciousness in regard to the spatial aspects of perceptual experience. In other words, at stake here is not only how I experience my body, but how I experience the surrounding world. The body is the source of spatiality, as Merleau-Ponty remarks: 'far from my body's being for me no more than a fragment of space, there would be no space at all for me if I had no body' (1962: 102). Ian Waterman's condition reminds us that, remarkably, in normal experience there is no phenomenal division between motor space, proprioceptive space, and perceptual space. Rather, conscious experience is normally of an intermodally seamless spatial system. Various contributions to this unitary spatiality can become dissociated in experimental or unusual circumstances. For example in mirror drawing, when I try to trace over the Star of David visually guided by a mirror image, my proprioceptive directions come into conflict with my visual directions, and I find it extremely difficult to accomplish the task without studied calculation about how to move.

Without exception, perceptions that involve a differential spatial order (for example, vision, touch, and audition) do so in terms of an egocentric (body-centered, perspectival) spatial framework. Indeed, this is so because there is no disembodied perception. An egocentric (body-centered) frame of reference contrasts to an allocentric (object-centered, non-perspectival) framework—that is, a frame of reference that takes its bearing from an object other than the perceiver. One of the important functions of the body in the context of perception and action is to provide the basis for an egocentric spatial frame of reference. Indeed, this egocentric framework is required for the very possibility of action, and for the general structure of perceptual experience. The fact that perception and action are perspectivally spatial (for example, the book appears to my right or to my left, or in the center of my perceptual field), is a fact that depends precisely on the spatiality of the perceiving and acting body. This is expressed in a judgment made by Poincaré, that the notion of space derives from 'a system of axes invariably bound to our body'. John Campbell (1994) suggests that Ian Waterman represents an exception to this rule. He suggests that Ian's perceptions and actions are organized in an allocentric frame of reference. In his purely visually guided action Ian uses a fixed point in the environment as a benchmark for his movements; he judges the position of his arm and the distance he needs to move it by reference to an objectively fixed point. Thus, Campbell suggests,

It does not seem to be an unintelligible hypothesis that in action the subject may be using only an allocentric frame of reference, one centered on his fixed point, and that there is no immediate use of any body-centered frame of reference.... Would the existence of an allocentric frame of reference, one not centered on the subject and that need not be immediately used to guide action, show that there is an objective level of thought that resists empiricist-pragmatist criticism of the Poincaré type?

(Campbell, 1994: 21)

In part this suggestion depends on the precise details of how normal intentional action and the egocentric spatial framework are related to embodiment. O'Shaughnessy (1980), consistent with Poincaré's rule, claims that proprioceptive-tactile awareness of one's body constitutes a necessary condition for intentional action. He argues that since action is always mediated by the body, one cannot perform an action without a direct, albeit pre-attentive awareness of the body that is physically responsible for the performance. He differentiates, however, the pre-attentive, proprioceptive body awareness required for action from a visual perception (or more generally, object-perception) of one's own body. In contrast to proprioceptive awareness, visual perception of the body is less direct, more attentive, and involves something closer to propositional attitudes that can be integrated into conceptual or belief systems (pp. 215 ff.).

If the spatiality of action and the visual perception of the world are egocentrically organized by an implicit reference to our bodily framework, the awareness that is the basis for that implicit reference cannot itself be based on the egocentric framework of visual perception without the threat of infinite regress. As Bermúdez (1995: 388) puts it: 'If information about the location and orientation of the body is acquired sense-perceptually, then . . . it needs to be mapped onto information about the location and orientation of the body.' To avoid the infinite regress one requires an experiential reference to one's body, a form of body awareness that is built into the structures of perception and action, but that is not itself perspectival or egocentric (see Gallagher 2003b). Why does proprioceptive awareness eliminate the infinite regress? Because proprioceptive awareness, even as it contributes to the establishment of an egocentric spatial framework for perception, operates in a non-perspectival, intra-corporeal spatial framework that is quite different from the egocentric structure of action and exteroceptive perception (see Ch. 6 for arguments in support of this point).

The issues raised here are informed by a long history of discussion that can be traced from at least the time of Berkeley, through the writings of such philosophers as Thomas Reid, Thomas Brown, and John Stuart Mill, as well as Poincaré. Not unlike these thinkers, O'Shaughnessy maintains that, on its own, *visual* perception of one's own body seems inadequate as a source of the egocentric orientation required for intentional action.

A similar account of intentional action is given by Sheets-Johnstone (1998). She claims that movement constantly generates a qualitative, proprioceptive, and kinesthetic consciousness of our bodies. Built into any movement there is a felt sense of one's movement, and, as a result, movement-generated qualia constitute a constant bodily awareness. These qualia can be precise enough to enable us to distinguish between such kinetic bodily feelings as smoothness and clumsiness, swiftness and slowness, brusqueness and gentleness, in what Sheets-Johnstone calls 'bodily-felt distinctions'. Such distinctions, she argues, are essential for intentional action. Indeed, kinesthetic and proprioceptive qualia are claimed to be the *sine qua non* of agency, so that a creature who had to depend solely on visual perception of the body would not be in any real sense an agent. An agent is such, precisely in so far as she or he is aware of what Brown (1820) had called 'the bodily frame'.[17]

Sheets-Johnstone argues against claims about action and our visual access to movement made by Dennett—claims that seem to suppress the role of the body in action. Dennett's agent, Sheets-Johnstone explains, 'would suffer not only from having to have in sight at all times all parts of his/her body in order to see where they were and what they were doing. His agent, being oblivious of [motor-generated] qualia, could in no way build up practices in the manner Dennett suggests, for the build up of such practices depends upon kinesthesia and kinesthetic memory, i.e. upon an awareness of the spatio-temporal and energy dynamics of one's movement.' Sheets-Johnstone carries this to the following conclusion: 'An agent devoid of kinesthesia in fact belongs to no known natural species. Agents—those having the power to act—necessarily have a kinesthetic sense of their own movement' (1998: 274).

Consistent with Campbell's suggestion, it appears that objections might be raised against the accounts of both O'Shaughnessy and Sheets-Johnstone by citing the case of Ian Waterman. Ian, not unlike Dennett's agent, seemingly represents the precise counter-example to the necessary conditions for intentional action claimed by both these theorists. On O'Shaughnessy's theory, since Waterman lacks direct proprioceptive and tactile awareness of his body and guides his movement by visual perception, he would be trapped in a practical infinite regress, and thus be incapable of intentional action. As Bermúdez (1995) rightly points out, this is manifestly not the case. Ian leads a normal life and is quite capable of intentional action. Moreover, he does this by relying in part on a visual perception of his body and in part on an attentive regard to his movements, precisely those aspects of experience that both O'Shaughnessy and Sheets-Johnstone rule out as necessary, and certainly as sufficient, conditions.

Bermúdez (1995), like Cole (1995), recognizes the importance of the direct (proprioceptive) bodily awareness that Ian possessed prior to the neuropathy, and uses this fact to circumvent what O'Shaughnessy had considered an infinite regress. Bermúdez argues that Ian has retained a long-term body image from those years of direct body awareness, and is able to map his current visual awareness onto that body image, thereby avoiding the infinite regress.

---

[17] Brown (1820: 505). The bodily frame, constituted by muscular sense, was, for Brown, equivalent to a certain perceptual aspect of the body image. The tacit experience of the bodily frame provided the egocentric framework necessary for the perception of spatial extension. My thanks to Todd Ganson for alerting me to Brown's text.

Although it is clear that Ian relies on a body image to control his actions, it is not clear how this would avoid the infinite regress. Could a long-term body image be based, as Bermúdez suggests, on a direct body awareness like proprioception? Proprioceptive memory is extremely short term, more of the order of working memory, and it is precisely this fact that allows us to move on in our actions and our perceptions of the world, without getting caught up in the details of our previous movement. One might also suspect that if Ian had retained a long-term body image that in some fashion included a direct, proprioceptive awareness of his body, he very likely would have suffered from the presence of a phantom, at least some time since the neuropathy. Cole notes that this is not the case (p. 136). Thus, it is difficult to believe that Ian, who is now so dependent on vision for motor control, has retained a long-term body image for over thirty years without it becoming somewhat conceptual or propositional. As such, this is a body image based on the kind of object-perception that O'Shaughnessy had discounted as basic to action. In any case, the explanation of how Ian could have retained the kind of direct proprioceptive experience required over the long term without making it a conceptual construct is lacking.

One might suggest that only an experientially occurrent body image, or what O'Shaughnessy calls a 'short-term body image', involves the kind of direct information required. In Ian, however, independently of vision, a short-term body image is close to non-existent. He has direct awareness of pain, muscle fatigue, and temperature, but these are sensory experiences that are not themselves intrinsically spatial. In the normal subject one might think of habitual posture or motor programs. But, as Cole indicates, these are precisely the things that Ian lost through the neuropathy. Indeed, he has even lost the ability to form new motor programs as they are ordinarily understood.

If, then, there is no proprioceptive awareness of the body in the form of a long-term body image available to Ian, is there any way to avoid the infinite regress that seems implied by his dependence on visual perception? At this point one might be tempted to turn to Campbell's thesis that in his actions Ian may be using an allocentric frame of reference and that in his case there is no immediate use of a body-centered perspectival frame of reference. Is it possible, however, that Ian, or anyone else, could live a close-to-normal life with movement confined to a completely allocentric frame of reference? Indeed, is it not logically necessary that specifications for intentional bodily action are in an egocentric frame of reference, since they specify movements in space from the body's points of origin? For practical commensurability with spatial targets, bodily disposition needs to be represented in egocentric coordinates (Gallagher and Marcel 1999). Consistent with this logic, Cole (1995) reports that Ian does rely on an egocentric sense of space that organizes his perception and his action.

The problem is to explain how Ian can have an egocentric frame of reference that does not trap him in a practical infinite regress, if he does not have proprioception in the short term, or a long-term body image that maintains a direct, non-conceptual spatial sense of his own body. I want to suggest a solution to the infinite regress problem in the case of Ian Waterman, and thereby affirm the idea that an egocentric frame of reference is essential for intentional action even for him. Ian has a perfectly good prenoetic anchor for the constitution of an egocentric frame of reference, namely, the movement of his body *from the neck up*. He does have proprioceptive information from his neck. If his deafferentation were even slightly higher up, at chin level, for example, Ian would be capable of a much more limited range of movements (Cole and Paillard 1995). Also, the importance of extraocular muscles that are undergoing constant modification in the performance of vision, along with vestibular information essential for the maintenance of balance—both of these aspects intact in Ian—should not be underestimated. In normal subjects extraocular eye muscles are essentially integrated with a more holistic body schema, and their constant modifications work to coordinate balance and movement.[18] Visual proprioception also contributes to the constitution of Ian's motor control system. In this respect peripheral vision is quite important for maintaining postural stability (as shown in developmental studies),[19] and Ian's well-developed peripheral vision is extremely sensitive to movement.

There is, in the most general sense of the term, a 'proprioception' of the face, head, and neck that still operates as a control area for Ian's movement and action. Indeed, for him to be able to use an external focal point to maintain his balance and his orientation, he must be able to relate that external point to something that is implicitly egocentric and tied into his personal system of balance and spatial perspective. Even though direct links with the rest of his body are severed, Ian's visual perception of his own body is mapped onto the direct and occurrent performance of vestibular and proprioceptive systems associated with his neck, head, and face. This performance, in turn, is linked in complex ways to oculomotor and visual-proprioceptive performances.

There is something of an ecological circle here with regard to vision and the function of extraocular muscles. Movement of the eyes in vision feeds back (in the form of efferent copy) through extraocular channels to coordinate balance and movement.[20] This feedback loop helps to establish that when Ian's eyes move to take in the visual field, *he*, rather than the world, is moving. This circle, however, is not the makings of an infinite regress of the sort O'Shaughnessy wants to avoid; rather it is a self-organizing circle not unlike the one found between vision and movement in normal subjects. For Ian Waterman, I suggest, it is an important part

---

[18] This can be seen, for example, in experiments using vibration techniques that show the links between extraocular eye muscles, postural muscles in other parts of the body, and balance (Roll and Roll 1988).

[19] Pope (1984) showed that slight movement in the peripheral visual field is sufficient to cause a complete loss of stability in infants. Infants too young to sit up by themselves and incapable of independent locomotion do make compensatory postural adjustments in response to optic flow (Butterworth and Hicks 1977; Jouen 1986).

[20] We will have opportunity to discuss this in more detail in Ch. 5. For example, Ian is able to use different signals from his visuo-oculomotor system to improve accuracy of arm movements (Blouin *et al.* 1996).

of the anchor that allows him to use the visual perception of his body to reinvent movement.

These considerations suggest some qualifications on Merleau-Ponty's claim that 'for the normal person every movement is, indissolubly, movement and consciousness of movement' (1962: 110). For Ian and those who have lost proprioception, movement precisely coincides with the consciousness of movement. More generally, there is an open circuit of communication between one's intentional life of contextualized plans and actions and one's motor abilities. But when an agent with normal proprioception is engaged in such actions, she does not ordinarily consciously plan her movements *per se*; one does not take movement itself to be the project, or even part of the project (Gallagher and Marcel 1999). That my movements are not blind does not mean that they are phenomenally visible to me. Rather, my movements and motor abilities subtend my intentions. Conscious experience is normally, in this regard, out ahead of movement, directed at the environment; it does not have to hang back to make sure my body is moving in the right direction. In normal behavior, movement underpins and supports intentional activity, but does not itself require reflexive conscious attention. In another regard, it is best to say that action is faster than consciousness—at least, it is faster than the kind of consciousness one would require to monitor action (see Jeannerod and Gallagher 2002). In contrast to Ian's action, normal grasping action shapes the hand before we become aware of it. If we needed consciously to monitor the shape of our grasp, as Ian does, action would have to slow down to the speed of consciousness. The general rule is that conscious experience is itself constrained and shaped by my prenoetic motility, but consciousness does not *directly* shape movement. This is most clearly demonstrated, in the negative, in cases where movement, instead of remaining under the non-conscious control of the body schema, must be made the phenomenal object of consciousness if it is to be controlled at all.[21]

---

[21] My remarks here are directly relevant to recent discussions about the possibility of free will. I return to this issue in the final chapter.

3

The Earliest Senses of Self and Others

I TURN now to questions about development. In sorting out the relations between consciousness and embodiment, one may be inclined to see a certain complication arising with respect to developmental issues. Even if we say that embodiment constrains consciousness in certain ways that involve concepts such as body image and body schema, one may think that at some point in individual development this is not true. Prior to the development of a body image or a body schema in a small child, for example, perhaps something like a less embodied consciousness exists. Less embodied may even mean less structured, along the lines of William James's famous description of the infant's experience as a 'blooming, buzzing confusion' (James 1890). It is not unusual to find proponents of the view that conscious experience is in some way the developmental source for both the body image and the body schema. Indeed, as we will see, this is the traditional view in both psychology and philosophy.

An empiricist, for example, might hold that a body *image* is generated only on the basis of the prolonged perceptual experience that one has of one's own body. Conceptual and emotional aspects of the body image, and the structural aspects that the body image brings with it, are obviously traceable to certain early and originary experiences that the child may have in tactile, visual, and other sensations of the body. It might also be thought that a body *schema* develops only through the conscious experience of movement. Much as we learn habits through practice, we learn to control our movements through the practiced experience of movement. This seems to be the case in examples we referred to before, such as in the learning of a new dance movement. It seems more obviously true of learning to crawl and to walk. On this view, then, conscious experience is at the origin of such things as body image and body schema. Thus, a certain kind of consciousness, primitive and perhaps disorganized, would predate the consciousness that is shaped and structured by embodiment.

This traditional view assumes that the newborn infant has no body image or body schema, and that such mechanisms are acquired through prolonged experience in infancy and early childhood. This idea has been worked out in a number of ways and in a variety of contexts in scientific and philosophical discussions. Up until about thirty or forty years ago this position was the almost unanimous consensus among developmental theorists. At that time, however, on several fronts, new evidence was developed in support of a more nativist position. The idea that body schemas may in fact be innate was put forward, for example, in studies of phantom limb in cases of congenital absence of limb (Weinstein and Sersen

1961). In the 1970s, in studies of neonate imitation (Meltzoff and Moore 1977), further evidence was provided to show that certain elements of what previously were understood to be learned motor behaviors were in fact already present in the newborn.

To define in more precise terms the relations between consciousness, embodiment, and self it will be helpful to review the assumptions and the evidence associated with the two positions: the traditional and strongly empiricist view, and the more recently defended nativist view. In this chapter, after reviewing the traditional standpoint, I focus on studies of neonate imitation and their implications for the development of a sense of self in early infancy. In the next chapter I return to the question of phantom limbs in cases of congenital absence of limb.

The Traditional View

Throughout most of the past century, the received doctrine had been that the body schema is an acquired phenomenon, built up in experience, the product of development. Given the confusions in the literature about body image and body schema (reviewed in Ch. 1), however, we need to be careful about interpreting claims about either of these concepts. Nevertheless, on the issue of whether the body schema or body image is acquired or innate, the traditional view is the same for either of these concepts. As I have already noted, there are very few theorists who clearly distinguish between body image and body schema. The two theorists I will select to represent the traditional view, however, do, at some juncture of their work, make the proper distinction.

Marianne Simmel (1958, 1962, 1966) is a developmental psychologist who does recognize a distinction between Head's notion of body schema and Schilder's notion of body image; at least she does so when she sets out to define these concepts. For Simmel, it seems, there is no question that the body image is something that comes relatively late in development, through an organization of touch and vision. Furthermore, concerning the body schema, Simmel claims that it is 'built up as a function of the individual's experience, i.e., it owes its existence to the individual's capacity and opportunity to learn. This means that at some early time in the development of the human organism the schema has not yet been formed, while later . . . it is present and is characterized by considerable differentiation and stability' (1958: 499). Following Head's terminology, she claims that the 'postural schema' depends 'primarily on a history of postural-tactile inputs' (1966: 93).

Although Simmel is an exception in regard to making a careful distinction between body image and body schema, she is in full agreement with traditional developmental psychology in her judgments about their dependence on experience. We can see this again in Merleau-Ponty (1962), a philosopher greatly influenced by his study of developmental psychology and by the psychologists and psychological research he cited, including the work of Piaget, Wallon, Guillaume, and Lhermitte. In discussions that range across a number of cognitive and existential issues, he made good use of the concept of body schema (*schema corporel*). From developmental psychology he learned and accepted the view that the body schema is a product of development. Although he conceives of the body schema as an *anterior condition of possibility*, a dynamic force of integration that cannot be reduced to the sum 'of associations established during experience', still, in terms of development, the operations of the body schema are '"learnt" from the time of global reactions of the whole body to tactile stimuli in the baby...' (pp. 101, 122 n.). The body schema functions *as if* it were an 'innate complex' (p. 84), that is, as strongly and pervasively as if it were innate, but, as an acquired habit with a developmental history, it is not actually innate.

This view has important implications for how one considers the conscious experience of the young infant. Merleau-Ponty, following Wallon, believed that experience begins by being interoceptive, and that the newborn is without external perceptual ability (1964: 121). James's 'blooming, buzzing confusion' does not attain order until between the third and sixth month of life when a collaboration takes place between the interoceptive and exteroceptive domains—a collaboration that simply does not exist at the beginning of life (1962: 121). On this view, one reason for the lack of any organized exteroceptive perception is precisely the absence of a 'minimal bodily equilibrium', an equilibrium that must be sorted out between a developing body schema and the initial and still very primitive stages of a body image. For Merleau-Ponty, motor experience and perceptual experience are dialectically or reciprocally linked. The mature operation of a body schema depends on a developed perceptual knowledge of one's own body; and the organized perception of one's own body, and then of the external world, depends on a proper functioning of the body schema. 'Up to that moment perception is impossible.... The operation of a postural schema—that is, a global consciousness of my body's position in space, with the corrective reflexes that impose themselves at each moment, the global consciousness of the spatiality of my body—all this is necessary for perception (Wallon)' (Merleau-Ponty 1964: 122). The infant does not yet have a body schema, according to Merleau-Ponty, Wallon, and others, because of a certain lack of neurological development. The myelination of nerve fibers responsible for proprioception, which is said to become operative between the third and sixth month of infancy, and is later in some limbs than in others (feet vs. hands; left hand vs. right hand), was thought to be required for the full and proper functioning of relevant parts of the nervous system.[1] The development of the body schema, it was thought, can happen only after these physical conditions are met and, thus, only in a fragmentary way at first. Motor schemas are then gradually integrated, and in a reciprocal system with external perception and sensory inputs, they become 'precise, restructured, and mature little by little' (p. 123).

[1] Windle (1971: 71) notes: 'The theory that initiation and maturation of function of the nervous system depends upon formation of myelin sheaths has had proponents for many years.... Nevertheless much well-organized activity of animal fetuses is present before there is any myelin.'

Merleau-Ponty does not make an explicit conceptual distinction between body image and body schema, yet he is much more careful and consistent than the psychological literature is on this point. He argues that on an existential level there is a continuous development between the schema and the image, that they are elements of a unified system, but that on the level of the lived experience of the body there is an 'indistinction' between these elements. Nonetheless, on the conceptual or analytical level he is careful not to confuse them. For example, it is quite clear that Merleau-Ponty, citing the notion of a postural schema described by Head (1920), names and identifies the body schema as an anterior condition of possibility for perception. In the context of developmental psychology, however, Merleau-Ponty links the emergence of the body schema with the early development of body image, that is, the development of a conscious awareness in which the 'child takes notice of his own body'. At a later stage the mirror or specular image, which can involve a conscious objectification of the body, provides a way of further developing the body image (pp. 121–5). This kind of explicit and visual knowledge of one's own body seemingly allows for a more cohesive body schema.

Simmel and Merleau-Ponty are good representatives of the traditional view that both body schema and body image are acquired through experience. This view then defines what is possible and what is not possible in a number of different instances. We have seen in brief outline what it implies about the conscious experience of the infant: conscious experience is disorganized; exteroceptive perception is at first impossible. It also implies certain other limitations. Consider, for example, the capacity for imitation—an important capacity directly related to questions about perception, social recognition, the ability to understand another person, and the origins of a sense of self.

On this issue we will let Piaget represent the traditional view. The question is about a certain kind of imitation called 'invisible imitation'. Piaget defines invisible imitation as the child's imitation of another person's movements using parts of the child's body that are invisible to the child. For example, if a child does not see its own face, is it possible for the child to imitate the gesture that appears on another person's face? Piaget's answer is that at a certain point in development it is possible; but in early infancy it is not. The reason it is not possible for infants is that invisible imitation requires the operation of a relatively mature body schema. Thus, according to Piaget (and Guillaume (1943), as well as most other classical theorists of development), invisible imitation is not possible prior to 8–12 months of age.

The intellectual mechanisms of the [child under 8 months] will not allow him to imitate movements he sees made by others when the corresponding movements of his own body are known to him only tactually or kinesthetically, and not visually (as, for instance, putting out his tongue). . . . Thus since the child cannot see his own face, there will be no imitation of movements of the face at this stage. . . . For imitation of such movements to be possible, there must be co-ordination of visual schemas with tactilo-kinesthetic schemas . . .

(Piaget 1962: 19, 45)

Piaget's reasoning here involves two issues that are essentially related. First, for invisible imitation to be possible the child must have developed the proper body schemas that define her specific motor capacities and to which she can relate or coordinate the visible movement or gesture of the other person. Piaget's traditional view on invisible imitation is completely consistent with the idea that body schemas are not sufficiently developed in early infancy, from which it follows that imitation dependent on such schemas would not be possible until their acquisition at 8–12 months of age. Thus invisible imitation is absolutely out of the question for a neonate. Second, there must be some mechanism that allows for the translation between what the infant sees and what movements the infant is capable of. The traditional view on this issue, going back as far as John Locke's original statements on sense perception (1690), is that different sense modalities (vision, touch, and proprioception, for instance) are not naturally intermodal, and that prolonged experience is required to be able to translate between vision and tactilo-kinesthetic sensation. (We examine this issue in more detail in Ch. 7.) Piaget's claim that the child's intellectual mechanisms are not sufficiently developed to perform the imitation suggests that the child still needs to learn to relate sense experiences (vision and proprioception) that are not naturally related.

Merleau-Ponty follows Guillaume and Piaget in regard to these issues. To imitate, he contends,

it would be necessary for me to translate my visual image of the other's [gesture] into a motor language. The child would have to set his facial muscles in motion in such a way as to reproduce [the visible gesture of the other]. . . . If my body is to appropriate the conducts given to me visually and make them its own, it must itself be given to me not as a mass of utterly private sensations but instead by what has been called a 'postural' or 'corporeal schema'.   (1964: 116–17.)

Since Merleau-Ponty also holds that exteroceptive perception is unorganized in early infancy, precisely because the body schema is not there to organize interoceptive experience sufficiently, the infant under 3 months of age would seemingly have a difficult time even seeing the face of the other person. Even beyond 3 months, when the infant could distinguish facial features of the other person, it has little or no familiarity with its own face, and has little or no control over moving that face, since motor schemas are not yet in place. As a result, the young infant could not even begin to imitate the facial gesture of the other person. Merleau-Ponty observes that this kind of imitation is possible only by 15 months (1962: 352).

Neonate Imitation

In complete contrast to this traditional view, studies on imitation in infants conducted by Meltzoff and Moore (1977, 1983) show that invisible imitation does occur in newborns. Their experiments, and others that replicate and extend their results (see Meltzoff and Moore 1994 for summary), show that newborn infants less than an hour old can indeed imitate facial gestures. A review of several of their experiments will help to clarify the results and their relevance to the issues of body schema, body image, and intermodal perception.

Body Schema

In one experiment (Meltzoff and Moore 1983) forty normal and alert newborn infants ranging in age from less than 1 hour to 71 hours were tested. The experimenter presented each infant with a mouth-opening gesture over a period of 4 minutes, alternating in 20-second intervals between the mouth opening and a passive facial appearance. The same procedure was then followed using tongue protrusion as the target gesture (see Fig. 3.1). The study showed a clear and statistically significant result in terms of both the frequency and duration of the infants' response gestures, demonstrating that normal and alert newborn infants systematically imitate adult gestures of mouth opening and tongue protrusion. Notably, even the youngest infant in the study, 42 minutes old at the time of the test, showed a strong imitation effect. Other experiments have extended the range of

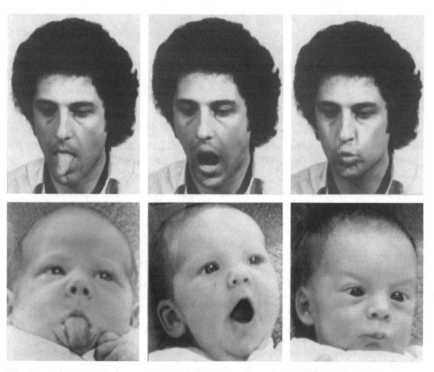

FIG. 3.1.   Photographs from videotaped recordings of 2–3-week-old infants imitating tongue protrusion, mouth opening, and lip protrusion. *Source:* Meltzoff and Moore (1977).

gestures that young infants imitate to a wider set, including lip protrusion, sequential finger movement, head movements, smile, frown, and surprised expressions.[2]

In a second experiment (Meltzoff and Moore 1989), forty normal and alert newborn infants, all of them less than 72 hours old (the youngest at 13.37 hours) were tested. Each infant was shown tongue protrusions and head movements (full rotations of the head clockwise in the frontal plane) in experimental conditions similar to the first experiment. As in the first experiment, infants systematically matched the adult display shown to them. There were a significantly greater number of infant tongue protrusions when they were shown the tongue-protrusion gesture than when shown the head movement, and vice versa. The data were analyzed to discriminate between head movement that simply tracked the displayed head movement, that is, counter-clockwise movement of the infant's head which tracked the experimenter's clockwise movement ('perceptual tethering'), and genuine imitation (infant's clockwise head movement) which anatomically matched the presented movement. Infants produced more clockwise head movements in the passive-face intervals following the head-movement displays than in the passive-face intervals following tongue-protrusion display. Infants were also able to track the experimenter's head movement without moving their own heads, and then, subsequently, match the head movement.

These two experiments were modeled on an original study (Meltzoff and Moore 1977) which showed some form of memory to be involved in early imitation. In this study, infants between the ages of 16 and 21 days imitated facial gestures after a delay. This involved putting a pacifier in the infant's mouth as the infant was shown a facial gesture. After the presentation of the facial gesture was complete, the pacifier was removed and the infant imitated the gesture. Thus, imitative responses were delayed and only allowed when the gesture had vanished from the perceptual field.

Even in circumstances of longer delays (of 24 hours) infants clearly remember and imitate gestures. In a fourth experiment Meltzoff and Moore (1994) tested forty normal and alert 6-week-old infants. An adult experimenter displayed either a passive face or one of three target gestures: mouth opening, tongue protrusion at midline, or tongue protrusion to the side. Tests with the same infants occurred over three days and were divided into five time periods: three involving immediate imitation, and two 'memory periods' involving imitation at a delay of 24 hours. The experiment showed not only immediate imitation, as in previous experiments, but also imitation after a delay of 24 hours. After 24 hours the infant saw the identical person they had seen the day before, but now presenting a passive face (instead of demonstrating the gesture). If the earlier display gesture had been tongue protrusion, the infant, 24 hours later, would produce significantly more tongue protrusions during the memory period. A second important finding of this study was that infants improve their gestural performance over time. Their first

---

[2] Meltzoff and Moore (1977) showed that 16- to 21-day-old infants imitated three facial gestures (lip protrusion, mouth opening, and tongue protrusion) as well as sequential finger movement (opening and closing the hand by moving the fingers in a serial fashion). Field et al. (1982) demonstrated that 2-day-old infants could imitate the smiling, frowning, or surprised expressions of adult models.

attempts at imitation do not necessarily replicate the seen gesture with a high degree of accuracy. When tongue protrusion is displayed, infants quickly activate the tongue; but they improve their motor accuracy over successive efforts.

The findings of imitation under these experimental conditions rule out 'reflexes' or release mechanisms as potential mediators of this activity. Reflexes and release mechanisms are highly specific—that is, narrowly circumscribed to limited stimuli. One cannot have a reflex or release mechanism for imitation in general. As a result, the range of behaviors displayed by infants would require the unlikely postulate of distinct reflexes or release mechanisms for each kind of imitative behavior: tongue protrusion, tongue protrusion to one side, mouth openings, smile, frown, etc. While it may not be difficult to imagine how evolution might provide for a reflex smile, it is difficult to understand why it would furnish a reflex for angular tongue protrusion (Fig. 3.2). Furthermore, the data from the third and fourth experiments indicate that neonate imitative behavior involves memory and representation, since imitation can happen even after a delay. The fourth experiment also shows that infants improve or correct their imitative response over time. Neither delayed response nor improvement in response is compatible with a simple reflex or release mechanism.

If we follow the logic expressed by the proponents of the traditional view, namely, that imitation requires a developed body schema, then the studies on newborn imitation suggest that there is at least a primitive body schema from the very beginning. This would be a schema sufficiently developed at birth to account for the ability to move one's body in appropriate ways in response to environmental, and especially interpersonal, stimuli—an innate body schema sufficiently developed to account for the possibility of invisible imitation.[3] (Here I use the word

FIG. 3.2.   Six-week-old infants imitating angular tongue protrusion. *Source*: Meltzoff and Moore (1994).

---

[3] The traditional view that no body schema exists at birth was probably based on what appears to be the disorganized movement of infants' limbs and the disappearance of certain motor patterns in early infancy. Careful observation of infant movement, however, reveals more coordination than previously thought (see e.g. Butterworth and Hopkins 1988; Lew and Butterworth 1995). I discuss this point in the next chapter. Other factors, including weight of limbs and gravity, can explain why certain responses (e.g. the stepping response) seem to disappear in early infancy (Thelen 1985; Thelen and Fisher 1982). Thelen and colleagues have also demonstrated that mature motor schemas for walking movements exist in infants and are operative when infants are offered the proper postural support (Thelen 1986; Thelen, Ulrich, and Niles 1987).

'innate' to mean, literally, 'something existing prior to birth'. The question of prenatal development will be discussed in the next chapter.)

Body Image

If the evidence from neonate imitation makes it possible to speak of an innate body schema, this motivates a further question. Is it also possible to speak of an innate body image? Gallagher and Meltzoff (1996) suggested that some primitive percep- tual element of the body image seems to be required for the infant to have awareness of its own face. For example, without awareness of its face it would be difficult to explain how the infant could improve its imitative performance. It is clear, however, that newborns do not have a visual perception of their own face and that furthermore they are not in a position to have conceptual or emotional aspects of a developed body image. The neonate, however, does have, in the most general sense, a proprioceptive awareness of its own face. I want to suggest that this proprioceptive awareness is a tacit, pre-reflective awareness that constitutes the very beginning of a primitive body image. It is in the intermodal and intersubjective interaction between proprioception and the vision of the other's face that one's body image originates. The body image, then, is *not* innate, although the capacity to develop a body image can be exercised from birth.

As I have indicated earlier, proprioception can be understood as having a twofold function. First, it consists of non-conscious, physiological *information* that updates the motor system with respect to the body's posture and movement. Proprioceptive information (PI) is processed on the subpersonal, non-conscious physiological level that subtends and operates as the basis for proprioceptive *awareness* (PA), a self- referential, but normally pre-reflective, awareness of one's own body. PI, as we indicated, contributes to the body-schematic control of posture and movement, and plays an essential role in the operations of body schemas. The physiological processing of PI always involves more than PA. If I jump to catch a ball, I am not aware of the 'calibrations' that register in and between proprioceptors and neural structures and that allow me to maintain balance among a number of muscle groups; nor am I necessarily aware of the actual muscle adjustments. The calibra- tions and adjustments are carried out without the mediation of PA. Postural control and movement are normally governed by the more automatic processes of the body schema, and the majority of normal adult movements do not require anything like an explicit monitoring, although PA may be used to monitor and assist motor activity in certain instances.

To be proprioceptively aware of one's body does not involve making one's body an object of perception, although this might happen in the case of an involuted, reflective use of proprioception. Proprioceptive-kinesthetic awareness is usually a pre-reflective (non-observational) awareness that allows the body to remain experi- entially transparent to the agent who is acting. It provides a sense that one is moving or doing something, not in terms that are explicitly about body parts, but in terms closer to the goal of the action. The infant does not have to deliberate about which of its body parts to move in order to accomplish the imitation. It does not have to identify its mouth or tongue *as* a mouth or tongue, or even as the correct body part to move. There is no comparative calculation that matches the visually perceived face with another perceptual object that happens to be the perceiver's own face. The nature of embodied action, and proprioception, is such that the infant cannot make a mistake by attempting to imitate the facial gesture with its hand or foot.

The infant and the adult are similar in this respect. The pre-reflective awareness that one has of one's body in the normal performance of intentional action (let us call this 'performative awareness') does not involve a process in which one has to identify a particular body or body part as one's own. If my intentional action is defined by the project of building a bookcase, I may set out on the task by first making an inventory of materials and tools that I require. In making that inventory I do not count my body or body parts. I do not say, 'I have a hammer, I have a saw, I have an arm.' In the process of building the case I need to keep track of the hammer and the saw, but do I need to keep track of my hands? Perhaps I do in some limited sense under certain conditions. I may deliberate about where the best hand-position on the board might be when I'm cutting it, and I may want to be careful about where my hand is placed when the electric saw is running. But in this process of being careful about where I put my hands, I never have to identify my hands as such. I never have to ask 'Are *these* my hands?' or 'Where *are* my hands so I know where to put them?' I do not even have to keep track of them in the peripheral field. Yet it would not be incorrect to say that I am aware that my hands and the rest of my body are performing the work. This performative awareness that I have of my body is tied to my embodied capabilities for movement and action. I am aware of what I can do with my hands (and I am aware of an object in the environment in terms of how I can manipulate it), but I am not aware of my hands as objects to manipulate. And my knowledge of what I can do with my hands is *in my body*, not in a reflective or intellectual attitude that I might take toward my hand. The infant already knows how to grasp, and is performatively aware of its hand *in* the grasping. In the case of imitation, the performative awareness that the infant has of its face and hands is awareness *in* the imitating action. It is not like the perceptual awareness that I have of an object, but an awareness that comes along with knowing that I can do certain things.

The studies of infant imitation suggest that the infant has both a primitive body schema (a system that works non-consciously to allow the infant to control and coordinate its imitative movements), and some degree of proprioceptive performative awareness. Together they provide the infant with a sense of its own capabilities. The infant, faced with novel motor and gestural activities, has the capacity to act out what it sees in the face of the adult—it recognizes what it sees as one of its own capabilities. Proprioceptive performative awareness allows it to correct and improve its imitative performance. The infant knows, pre-reflectively, in the very act of gesturing, whether the gesture is on target or not. Conclusions like these are entailed by the experimental data that show, not just that infants imitate, but that they correct their imitations, and that they are able to imitate novel gestures (for example, tongue protrusion to the side).

Perceptual Intermodality

How is it possible for a visual perception of someone else's face to guide the performance of the infant's own face? What mechanisms allow for this possibility in the neonate? Meltzoff, Moore, and their colleagues have proposed a model that involves an intermodal sensory system that enables the infant to recognize a structural equivalence between itself and the other person. In support of this idea their experiments show that there is an early relation between vision and touch as well as between the sound of speech and the particular lip movements that cause them.[4] Meltzoff and Moore (1997) propose a psychological-cognitive model, a set of theoretical black boxes representing 'comparison function', 'act equivalence', 'recognition of my own capability', and so forth. Here I want to suggest some neurophysiological structures that might help to fill in the black boxes in this cognitive model. For the infant to be able to imitate a displayed facial gesture, it must be able to translate a visual display into its own motor behavior. In an intermodal system, proprioception and vision are already in communication with each other. In certain cases, what I see automatically gets translated into a proprioceptive sense of how to move. On this basis, visual perception can help to inform and coordinate movement and can correct proprioceptive distortions or illusions.[5]

The dual nature of proprioception, as both non-conscious, physiological information (PI) and pre-reflective performative awareness (PA), may help to explain how intermodal communication between vision and proprioception is at the same time a communication between sensory and motor aspects of behavior. There are two interrelated processes involved here:

1. intermodal communication between vision and PA;
2. communication between sensory systems (which include vision and PA) and the motor system (which includes PI).

On the physiological level PI and PA depend on the same proprioceptors, and in some cases the same central neural structures. These mechanisms generate the information necessary for both the automatic governing of movement and

---

[4] See Meltzoff (1993). Meltzoff and Moore (1995) provide a detailed analysis of the nature and limits of infantile intermodality.

[5] Here are several examples. One can experimentally induce a phantom limb only when vision is excluded. Once the subject sees the position of his real limb, the proprioceptive phantom immediately merges with it (Gurfinkel and Levick 1991). One can also correct proprioceptive and nocioceptive sensations associated with a phantom by creating a visual illusion of the phantom using mirrors (Ramachandran and Rogers-Ramachandran 1996). Adjustments made to the visual system (for example, by wearing wedge-prism glasses), can recalibrate proprioception and the body schematic system, as well as the egocentric spatial framework of perception. This recalibration in hemispatial neglect patients happens quickly and has relatively lasting effects (Rossetti et al. 1998).

the sensation of one's own movements (Phillips 1985). Since PI and PA depend on and are constituted by the same physiological mechanisms it would not be unreasonable to suggest an immediate connection, a close interactive coordination, between proprioceptive information, which updates motor action at the level of the body schema, and proprioceptive awareness, as a pre-reflective, performative accompaniment to that action. Although it is likely that body schemas and PA are constituted on, or share, the same information, it would not be accurate to claim an identity between PI and PA, since the latter is not present in all cases where PI informs movement. Furthermore, for the occurrence of PA, as a form of consciousness, it is likely that certain central processes are involved beyond what is needed for the registration of PI and motor control.

Somatic proprioception (PI and PA) and vision are intermodally linked in several ways, and these linkages are part of a more general link between sensory and motor activities. For example, and quite relevant to the possibility of neonate imitation, both proprioception and vision are integrated with vestibular information about head motion and orientation. The vestibular nucleus, a relatively large midbrain structure, serves as a complicated integrative site where first-order information about head position is integrated with whole-body proprioceptive information from joint receptors and oculomotor information about eye movement. This integrated multimodal information projects to the thalamus, informing connections that project to cortical areas responsible for control of head movement. Vestibular neurons in the parietal lobe respond to vestibular stimulation, but also to somatosensory and optokinetic stimuli, and more generally there is cortical integration of information concerning self-motion, spatial orientation, and visuomotor functions (Guldin, Akbarian, and Grüsser 1992; Jouen and Gapenne 1995).

Importantly, these structures, which contribute to the generation of a primary, performative self-awareness, are mature at birth.[6] Thus in the case of neonate imitation, the imitating subject depends on a complex background of embodied processes, a body-schema system involving visual, proprioceptive, and vestibular information. In the foreground, what the infant sees gets translated into a proprioceptive awareness of her own relevant body parts; and PI allows her to move those parts so that her proprioceptive awareness matches up to what she sees. This intermodal *intra*-corporeal communication, then, is the basis for an *inter*-corporeal communication and has profound implications for the child's relations with others (see Ch. 9).

---

[6] Vestibular structures can be identified as early as 6 weeks' gestation. By 14 weeks' vestibular receptors, which appear similar to those of adults, develop. By birth the vestibular system is entirely formed and functional, with myelination comparable to that observed in adults. There is direct behavioral evidence that the vestibular system functions in neonates. Vestibular stimulation during body tilting and head rotation results in compensatory eye adjustments in the newborn. Connections between vestibular stimulation and whole-body posture are also in evidence in newborns (but not in premature infants). Vestibular adjustments are made in response to changes in optic flow (visual proprioception). Visual structures in the brainstem, which involve the coding of direction and self-motion, are mature at birth. See Jouen and Gapenne (1995) for details and summary.

Recent studies in neuroscience suggest that there are specific neurophysiological mechanisms that can account for the intermodal connections between visual perception and motor behavior. These are mechanisms that operate prenoetically, as general conditions of possibility for motor stability and control (outlined in the previous paragraph), but are also directly related to the possibility of imitation. Indeed, some of these studies suggest that what psychologists refer to as the mirror stage in later childhood, and consider to be important for the development of a mature body image and the onset of self-recognition, may in fact be prefigured in what one might call an earlier and interior mirror process. I refer here to what neuroscientists now describe as processes that involve mirror neurons (Gallese 1998; Gallese *et al.* 1996; Rizzolatti *et al.* 1996). Mirror neurons link up motor processes with visual ones in ways that are directly relevant to the possibility of imitation.

Mirror neurons were discovered in the premotor cortex of the macaque monkey. There is now good evidence that they also exist in area F5 of the ventral premotor cortex and Broca's area in the human (Fadiga *et al.* 1995; Grafton *et al.* 1996; Rizzolatti *et al.* 1996). Mirror neurons respond *both* when a subject *performs* a particular (goal-directed) action involving arm, hand, or mouth *and* when the subject *observes* such actions being done by another subject. This class of neurons thus constitutes an intermodal link between the visual perception of action or dynamic expression, and the *intra*subjective, proprioceptive sense of one's own capabilities. Their functioning clearly helps to account for the communication between proprioception and vision, and between specific movements and the visual perception of those movements in others. In principle there is no reason to think that mirror neurons do not function at birth.[7] In this regard, the following reasonable hypothesis can be formulated: when the neonate sees another person perform a specific motor act, for instance a tongue protrusion, the visual stimulus initiates the firing of the same mirror neurons that are involved in the infant's own performance of that motor act. Although precise experiments that would verify this hypothesis have not been carried out, this kind of mechanism would go a long way toward accounting for the capabilities for imitation we see in neonates. At a neurophysiological level, it is likely that numerous intermodal mechanisms allow for the prenoetic communication between proprioception and vision, or more generally, between movement, proprioceptive awareness, and perception (see Ch. 9 for further discussion).

---

[7] The fact that at birth mirror neurons may be unmyelinated would not prevent them from functioning. The lack of myelination would simply slow their activation. Imitation involves more than mirror neurons, however. For recent attempts to identify the neurological substrate for imitation, see Blakemore and Decety (2001); Chaminade, Meltzoff, and Decety (2002); Decety *et al.* (2002), and Iacoboni *et al.* (1999).

A Primary Embodied Self

Body schemas may in fact develop and mature over the course of childhood, but, in certain important aspects they have an innate status; they exist prenatally and are sufficiently developed at birth to allow for neonate imitation. Since the visual perception and proprioceptive awareness involved in such imitation are in fact instances of conscious experience, then consciousness from the very beginning is structured by embodiment in certain ways. Moreover, if proprioceptive awareness is a form of self-consciousness, then some primitive and primary sense of embodied self is operative at least from the very beginning of postnatal life.

Claims that self-consciousness is involved in neonatal imitation, and indeed, even the claim that consciousness is involved in the process, are not uncontroversial. I want to make two points in regard to these issues. The first pertains to the appropriate strategies for deciding the issues. The second has to do with what we can conclude even if we cannot decide the issue at this time.

First, to decide these claims I would argue for the following strategies. The question seems to be whether we want to call the responses involved in neonate imitation conscious responses or non-conscious responses.[8] On some definitions of consciousness, self-consciousness is a necessary element of what it means to be conscious. On this view, if the child is not self-conscious of what it is doing when it imitates, one would have to say the child is reacting unconsciously. Lots of things happen in the brain to enable imitative responses, but that does not necessarily mean that the neonate is conscious of what it is doing. Whatever judgments we make on the basis of behavioral evidence—that the infant is capable of seeing and remembering what it sees, and that the response looks very much like a conscious response—some theorists would still argue that such considerations are just not good enough to show that there is indeed consciousness involved.

The other option, then, is to look at the neurological evidence to see whether sufficient mechanisms are in place that would allow us to say that consciousness is possible in such cases. Of course that strategy pushes us back to the more fundamental question of the neural correlates of consciousness. If, however, we could resolve that issue, and if we could find in the neonate's brain sufficiently developed mechanisms for consciousness, and if such neurological evidence seems consistent with behavioral observation, I suggest that would be sufficient evidence to warrant the reasonable claim that the neonate is conscious of what it is doing when it imitates. If there is a better way to make judgments about this sort of question I do not know what it is.

---

[8] Several theorists (Kinsbourne 2002; and Bennett Bertenthal at the University of Chicago (private correspondence)) have recently proposed the idea that neonate imitation may be the result of motor priming and the lack of any inhibitory mechanisms in the newborn human to prevent the reaction. This explanation would not require the infant to be self-consciously aware of what it was doing. The testing that would confirm this hypothesis, however, has not yet been carried out. I'll return to this suggestion below.

Second, if the evidence from both the neurological and behavioral side turns out to be inconclusive on this point (that is, if it can be interpreted either way), then given evolutionary explanations of why we have consciousness, or what consciousness does for us, it seems justifiable to say that consciousness would itself be a good mechanism to enable this sort of behavior, and that the infant is conscious at birth. If, on the other hand, it turns out that the neurological evidence is simply not there to support the claim of consciousness, then the neonate responses, involving both perception and memory, might be non-conscious responses, a case of motor priming. Even in that case, however, one can still claim what I want to press as the main point, namely, that whenever consciousness begins, it will already be informed by embodiment and the processes that involve motor schemas and proprioception. This fact stands, regardless of the timing of the onset of consciousness.

This fact is not unimportant for the related issues of a sense of self and the perception of others. For traditional theorists, problems concerning the perception of others and of self are postponed in ontogenetic time until the child is at least 6 months of age (e.g. Merleau-Ponty 1964). In more recent cognitive approaches such problems are discussed in relation to the development of a child's theory of mind between approximately 3 to 5 years, or, at the earliest, 18 months (Gopnik and Meltzoff 1997). The studies of neonate imitation, however, suggest that we ought to look at these issues within the framework of earlier experience (see Ch. 9). Does this difference in time-frame make any difference for the nature of the experience of self and others?

When, in both philosophical and psychological traditions, the sense of self is conceived as developing in a relatively later time-frame it is frequently discussed in terms that are explicitly related to cognitive development. Such cognitive models of the self clearly imply that personal identity or a sense of self may be primarily and for the most part a psychological phenomenon (e.g. Shoemaker 1984). In contrast, if a sense of self is operative earlier, and specifically, if we can find a sense of self already involved in neonatal behavior, the concept of self starts out closer to an embodied sense than to a cognitive or psychological understanding.

One way to approach this issue is to further consider the notion of intermodal communication between vision and proprioception. Vision seems to direct the child outward, toward the world and other people; proprioception, as the word itself signifies, is more concerned with a sense of self. The central problem in this context was already stated by Merleau-Ponty. For invisible imitation to be possible 'it would be necessary for me to *translate* my visual image of the other's [gesture] into [my own] motor language' (1964: 116, emphasis added). On this view, the central problem is a translation problem, and the *sine qua non* of translation is that there be, metaphorically speaking, two languages—in this case a visual language and a motor/proprioceptive one. Would a difference in time-frame (e.g. 0 versus 6 months) make an important difference in the translation problem?

According to Merleau-Ponty,

the different sensory domains (sight, touch, and the sense of movement in the joints) which are involved in the perception of my body do not present themselves to me as so many absolutely distinct regions. Even if, in the child's first and second years, the translation of one [modality] into the language of [other modalities] is imprecise and incomplete, they all have in common a *certain style* of action. . . . Understood in this way, the experience I have of my own body could be transferred to another . . . giving rise to what Wallon calls a 'postural impregnation' of my own body by the conducts I witness.   (1964: 117–18)

This suggests that the intermodal translation among my own senses provides me with a way to understand a person other than myself. Several things should be noted here. First, Merleau-Ponty (consistent with the traditional view) thought that the translation process was an imprecise one even in very late infancy and early childhood. Second, Wallon and Merleau-Ponty thought that 'postural impregnation' only occurred relatively late in infant development (between 12 and 24 months). Furthermore, for Merleau-Ponty, the translation process between visual and proprioceptive senses is accomplished in my own body first (visual and tactile experiences of my own limbs, for example, becoming coordinated with proprioceptive experience of them), and only then is 'transferable' to my relations with others. In this sense, the awareness 'of one's own body is ahead of the recognition of the other' (p. 121). This indicates something like a development 'from the inside out', that is, from the body outward, so that one can start to perceive the world and others only after a minimum bodily equilibrium is established. On this view, the immaturity of body equilibrium prevents, blocks, or acts as a brake on perceptual and intersubjective development. This view is also consistent with the idea that in early infancy external perception is not possible, or if possible is chaotic and not correlated to interoceptivity.

    In contrast, the studies on newborn imitation indicate that the intermodal translation is operative from the very beginning. More precisely, and strictly speaking, no 'translation' or transfer is necessary because it is already accomplished in the embodied perception itself, and is already intersubjective. An intermodal code already reaches across the child's relations with others. Infants already apprehend, with quickly improving precision, the equivalencies between the visible body transformations of others and their own invisible body transformations which they experience proprioceptively. The concept of an intermodal code means that the visual and motor systems speak the same 'language' right from birth.[9] It is not, as the traditional view would have it, a matter of gradually developing a translation process between initially independent spaces—a visual space, a lived proprioceptive space—that function independently and are coordinated with growth and experience. Rather, information picked up by the separate sense organs are represented with relative precision within a common 'space' that is already intermodal (Meltzoff

---

[9] The same claim is made with respect to vestibular processes: 'inputs representing head velocity that originate from the vestibular system must have the same coding dimension as the visual signal representing visual motion' (Jouen and Gapenne 1995: 288).

1990a, 1993; Meltzoff and Gopnik 1993; Meltzoff and Moore 1995). This is a space that is quite likely instantiated within a complex set of neuronal systems, including vestibular, proprioceptive, and visual systems, with integrated connections made by intermodal neurons, including, for example, mirror neurons. This is a framework already organized in a 'somatocentric' fashion, already sketched out for consciousness in operations that are deeply embodied.

From early infancy, then, my visual experience of the other person communicates in a code that is related to the self. What I see of the other's motor behavior is reflected and played out in terms of my own possibilities. This communication is organized on the basis of an innate system that does not necessarily give priority to my own body awareness over and against my perception of the other. Quite literally, in any particular instance, it may be the other's movement that triggers my own proprioceptive awareness. There exists in the newborn infant a natural intermodal coupling between self and other, one that does not involve a confused experience. Rather than confusion, a self-organizing collaboration between visual perception and proprioception, between sensory and motor systems, and between the self and the other is operational from the very beginning. Body schemas, working systematically with proprioceptive awareness, constitute a proprioceptive self that is *always already* 'coupled' with the other.

With the notion of an innate intermodal system of body schema, proprioceptive experience, and perception it is possible to propose a solution to a problem that many philosophers have attempted to answer—the problem of how we know others, the problem of intersubjectivity. Basically stated the question is, 'How do I know that the other body that I perceive is indeed another person who, like me, is conscious?' Let us examine briefly a phenomenological approach to this problem (for a more developed account, see Ch. 9).

Edmund Husserl (1970: §§ 50–4) proposed an answer that depends on the experiencing subject making an analogy (not a thought-out inference but an 'analogizing apprehension') between herself and the other person on the basis of the similarity between the subject's own body and the body of the other. On one reading, this theory depends upon a comparison or analogy between body images—the perceptual image I have of my body and the perceptual image I have of the other's body. This analogy involves what Husserl calls an 'ap-presentation', that is, a move beyond mere bodily appearance toward the other person's interior life.

As Husserl himself realized, there are several problems with this account that need to be sorted out.[10] First, the nature of the proposed analogy remains unclear. Husserl contends that the analogizing apprehension is not an act of inference, but a conscious act that 'transfers' to present experience an already instituted meaning gained in previous experience. He traces this possibility of transferral back to what he calls a 'primal instituting' in early childhood, which involves a specific instance of a more general form of perceptual association called 'pairing' (1970). Thus Husserl

---

[10] Husserl wrote extensively about intersubjectivity. Here I am focusing on one account, which is the one he published, and yet perhaps the least satisfactory. For more on Husserl's accounts, see Gallagher (forthcoming c).

argues that the analogizing apprehension that allows us to perceive the body of another *as* the body of *another person*, comes to be built into perception in an implicit way through experience. In this case the analogizing apprehension seems to be part of the experiential structure of mature consciousness (part of the way our consciousness functions), but not something of which we are explicitly conscious.

This idea, which depends on the notion of prior experience involving associative pairing, leads on to a second problem. Husserl explains 'primal instituting' and 'pairing' by claiming that my own living body is always present for me, and that I perceive a *similarity* between it and other bodies. It has frequently been objected, however, that since I experience my own body in a way that is not similar to my perception of the other's body, the analogizing apprehension must in some way transcend the non-similarity involved.[11] Neither the solution nor the objection to it is clear on precisely what aspect of the other person's body we perceive in such instances—whether it is the *appearance* of the other's body, the *movement, action,* or *behavior* of the other, or certain *stylistic aspects* of the other's actions that are expressive of intention or emotion. In this respect we need a more precise account of what it is that we experience and how we can transcend that experience toward an understanding of the other as other.

Husserl's theory might be reformulated in the following way. If an analogizing process is involved, then the analogy would really have to be made from my own body, operating as a coordinated system (of body schema and proprioceptive experience), to the visual image of the other's body. But this restatement remains imprecise on two counts. First, the previous objection might be reformulated: we are still talking of two different types of experience—proprioception and visual perception. The proprioceptive experience of my own body is still very different from the visual perception I have of the other body. So, rather than speaking of an *analogy* made between two bodies, one might speak, as Merleau-Ponty does, of an intermodal *translation* that is also a bridge to apprehending the other person. But, on Merleau-Ponty's account, to the extent that the translation process is viewed as something entirely learned through experience, the intentional transgression of the other would be delayed for one to two years after birth. In contrast, the conception of an innate, intermodal visual-proprioceptive / sensory-motor linkage suggests that the link to the other person is immediate; *experientially,* and not just objectively, we are born into a world of others.

Second, it is not precisely the *image* of the other's body, in the sense of the other's objective appearance or the way the other body looks, that forms the exteroceptive moment of this relation. The newborn infant does not attend to the outward appearance of the other, but rather attends to the *action* and *expression* of the

[11] This has been a frequent objection in the phenomenological literature against what was called the 'argument by inference from analogy' (see e.g. Gurwitsch 1931/1978; Scheler 1954; Schutz 1932, 1966). The objection runs as follows: the way my body is experienced by me (e.g. more through kinesthetic-proprioception than through exteroceptive or visual perception) is quite different from the way the body of another person is perceived by me (exclusively through exteroception). But this objection is questionable: if intermodal perception is operative from the very beginning of life, what I see is automatically registered in a code that is common to other sense modalities, including proprioception.

other. Some time later in development the child comes to interpret the other person's intention through their actions. On this point Merleau-Ponty makes some progress: 'Thus it is in [the other's] conduct, in the manner in which the other deals with the world, that I will be able to discover his consciousness.' The other presents me with 'themes of possible activity for my own body' (1964: 117). Understanding another person is dependent more on perceived intentional action and expression than on analogies made on the basis of appearance, shape, or image of the other person's body. The infant does not perceive the other person as an object so much as it senses at a behavioral and motor level, that the expression of another is one the infant itself can make.[12]

Studies of newborn imitation also suggest an important modification in the conception of early experience, which Merleau-Ponty describes as the 'pre-communication phase'. According to this description, which Merleau-Ponty adopts from a wide variety of theorists who have espoused it, including Guillaume, Wallon, Gestalt psychologists, phenomenologists, and psychoanalysts, for the infant, 'there is not one individual over against another but rather an anonymous collectivity, an undifferentiated group life' (p. 119). Wallon calls this 'syncretic sociability'. 'Syncretism here is the indistinction between me and the other, a confusion at the core of a situation that is common to us both' (p. 120). On this view there seems to be, in the infant's phenomenal experience, a complete lack of differentiation between itself and the other person. A transformation begins only when the infant starts to acquire a body schema, and the syncretism is totally overturned when the child acquires a body image (some time between 6 months and the mirror stage at 18 months).

The studies of newborn imitation, however, not only demonstrate that imitation of actions, conducts, and gestures is possible from the very beginning, and that the intermodal system that makes this possible is innate; they also indicate that the original indifferentiation is never complete. The first exclusively *visual* notion of self may be tied to the later mirror stage, or a later form of imitation (Campbell 1995; Meltzoff 1990a). However, self-recognition in the mirror is only one measure, one aspect of a broader concept of self. The phenomenon of newborn imitation suggests that much earlier there is a primary notion of self, what we might call a proprio-ceptive self—a sense of self that involves a sense of one's motor possibilities, body postures, and body powers, rather than one's visual features. The newborn infant's ability to imitate others, and its ability to correct its movement, which implies a recognition of the difference between its own gesture and the other's gesture, indicates a rudimentary differentiation between self and non-self. This may be

---

[12] For further studies on infants recognizing people by their actions and not merely by their static perceptual features, see Meltzoff and Moore (1994, 1995). For an account of how infants learn the affordances of objects through observing the conduct of others with those objects, see Meltzoff (1988a, 1988b, 1990b), and Gopnik and Meltzoff (1997). These studies are consistent with experiments on mirror neurons that show neuronal activity is correlated with behavior at the level of actions (e.g. grasping) rather than motoric elements (e.g. muscle contractions) (see Gallese and Goldman 1998; Jeannerod 1997; also see Ch. 9).

a bare framework of the self that is based on an innate system of embodiment. But it serves to introduce a disruptive moment into the supposed indifferentiation of the earliest hours, and at the very least, a rudimentary differentiation between self and non-self, so that one's earliest experiences include a sense of self and of others.

The concept of a proprioceptive self suggested here is quite consistent with what Neisser (1988, 1991) calls an *ecological self* and a primitive self-awareness that is based on both visual proprioception and a sense of movement and action. The account provided here complements and supports Neisser's suggestions that there are connections between ecological aspects of self and interpersonal aspects of self and that there is not a complete lack of differentiation between self and non-self at birth.[13]

An Open Philosophical Question

By working through these various aspects of embodiment—body schema, body image, proprioception, intermodal communication, ecological self-awareness—have we set forth an adequate explanation of neonate imitation and a primary self? I want to leave this as an open and unresolved question to which I will return in Ch. 5, and again in Ch. 9. I am motivated to pose this question by the large claim I made in the opening paragraph of the Introduction to this book. There I suggested that the newborn human infant can see its own possibilities in the faces of other people, and is thus capable of a certain kind of movement that foreshadows intentional action, and that propels it into a human world. Taking *human* as something more than a biological category, do we have enough of an explanation here that would account for the human nature of the self that comes into the world?

The philosophical import of this question may be apparent. It can be seen clearly in claims made by some philosophers concerning the moral status of young children. According to some philosophers (Dennett 1976; Frankfurt 1971), young children do not have the moral status of personhood because they lack self-consciousness. Others have argued that there is no morally significant difference between a fetus and a neonate (Gillon 1985; Singer 1979; Sumner 1981), a position that leaves open the question of infanticide as a moral possibility. Would it be sufficient to respond that there is an ecological self-awareness, or a primitive self-consciousness implied in neonate imitation, and to explain this in terms of a proprioceptive awareness (see e.g. Bermúdez 1996)? Would it be enough to outline a theory of self-consciousness based on the elements:

1. a proprioceptive awareness of one's body;
2. a differentiation between self and other;

---

[13] Jouen and Gapenne also draw this conclusion from their studies of intermodal relations between vestibular and visual systems: 'Our results clearly show that some of the major characteristics of global postural reactions that allow discrimination of the self from the environment are present from birth' (1995: 297).

3. a recognition that the other is of the same sort as oneself (see e.g. Bermúdez 1996; Gallagher 1996)?

All these elements of primitive self-consciousness are implied by neonate imitation. But would they be sufficient to answer the moral question? Raising this question here is simply meant to highlight the importance of asking whether our explanation of neonate imitation (primarily in terms of sensory-motor mechanisms) is adequate. I will propose later (Ch. 5) that another element—an innate capacity for expression—is important for establishing the primary embodied self as a human self.

4

Pursuing a Phantom

In the previous chapters we explored some relations between consciousness, movement, and proprioception. It is important to push the developmental question further and to ask when and where these relations are established. What is the earliest relation between movement and consciousness? I return, in this chapter, to an issue related to the innate status of the body schema—the issue of phantom limb in cases of congenital absence of limb (aplasia). The logic internal to this issue will be familiar, for it is the same logic that had been debated in the context of the question about the possibility of neonate imitation. On the one hand, according to what we will again call the traditional view, if a body schema is something that is acquired only over the course of experience (in the first 8–12 months of life) then an aplasic phantom is just as impossible as neonate imitation. On the other hand, if a body schema is innate in the right way, then it should be quite possible to find cases of aplasic phantoms. Now despite the fact that there is good evidence for an innate body schema to be found in the examination of neonate imitation, much of the evidence cited for an innate body schema in discussions of aplasic phantoms is problematic. Indeed, the evidence that is cited to support the idea of an innate body *schema* in this context misses the mark because it actually pertains to the notion of body *image*.

Two issues, therefore, are in need of clarification. First, if there is an innate body schema system, as studies of neonate imitation indicate, what role does it play in explaining the aplasic phantom? Second, what precisely does it mean for the body schema to be 'innate'? In other words, what are the precise developmental details that lead to the existence of a body schema at birth? The issue of a prenatal development of body schemas is of interest because it helps to explain the earliest relation between movement and consciousness.

A Scientific Dispute Concerning Aplasic Phantom Limbs

In 1961 a scientific debate about the status of phantom limbs began. The focus of the debate concerned whether phantoms exist in cases of the congenital absence of a limb or following early (prior to age 6) amputations. The psychological and neurological literature stretching from the early twentieth century to the early 1960s indicated that in cases of aplasia and in most cases of early amputation no phantoms develop. This was the established scientific doctrine and it was the view held in the overwhelming majority of studies up until the early 1960s (e.g. Bailey and Moersch 1941; Bonnier 1905; Browder and Gallagher 1948; Gerstmann 1927; Head 1920; Kolb 1954; Lhermitte 1939; Pick 1915a; Simmel 1962, 1966; White and Sweet 1955). Indeed, it is still cited as the correct view in more recent literature (Dennett 1978: 207 n.; Meuse 1996).

Simmel (1961) reaffirms this tradition, offering evidence that seems to support the contention that phantoms for congenitally missing limbs do not exist. Making the traditional assumption that the phantom limb is a phenomenon of the body schema [image],[1] Simmel also makes clear what is at stake in this observation, namely, the view that a body schema is acquired or is built up in experienced (proprioceptive, kinesthetic, and tactile) sensations. On the assumption that a body schema is simply not present at birth, then a person who lacks an extremity at birth and has therefore received no sensations from the missing limb should not experience a phantom (Simmel 1958). The studies conducted by Simmel confirmed this view. There is no phantom in aplasia because the limb in question is never experienced, and thus is never incorporated into a body schema or body image.

This view of the phantom was also expressed by Merleau-Ponty in connection with his acceptance of the received doctrine that the body schema is a product of development. For the very same reasons that the traditional view implied the impossibility of neonate imitation, it also implied the impossibility of aplasic phantoms. On this view, the existence of a phantom limb in the case of amputation is based on a history of sensory inputs to the now missing limb, and the continuation of sensory inputs at the stump. Sensory impulses, which are organized in a coherent fashion by a developed body schema, 'establish and maintain [the phantom's] place, prevent it from being abolished, and cause it still to count in the organism'. Sense experience organized by a body schema is the *sine qua non* by which we 'build up the phantom' (Merleau-Ponty 1962: 86). Since, in the case of aplasia, the missing limb is never the subject of sensory impulses, there can be no aplasic phantom, that is, the missing limb is not incorporated into a body schema or body image.

A challenge to the traditional consensus about the development of a body schema and the impossibility of aplasic phantom limbs started to take shape in 1961. Weinstein and Sersen (1961) cited evidence that directly challenged the received doctrine. They found, in a study of thirty cases of aplasia, that 17 per cent of the subjects experienced a phantom limb. Even this small percentage, they reasoned, would be enough to indicate that phantoms do not require prior stimulation of the missing part. 'The fact that phantoms can exist for limbs which

[1] Again, we need to be aware of the ambiguity and confusion about these terms as found in the traditional literature (see Ch. 1). Across the traditional discussion of phantom limbs the terminology varies between body image and body schema. I use the construction 'body schema [image]' to indicate precisely those points where the tradition is unclear. As I pointed out in Ch. 3, Simmel is one of the few psychologists who does acknowledge a theoretical distinction between body schema and body image. She and many of the authors who discuss the aplasic phantom attribute it to the body schema. Part of the problem to be sorted out, however, is whether they really mean body schema or body image as I have defined these terms in Ch. 1.

themselves never existed indicates that some native factor must be responsible, at least in part, for the existence of the phantoms' (p. 910). In more precise terms, similar to the evidence concerning neonate imitation, the evidence for aplasic phantoms raises the possibility that the basic framework of a body schema is innate. Subsequent studies (Melzack 1989; Poeck 1963, 1964; Scatena 1990; Vetter and Weinstein 1967; Weinstein, Sersen, and Vetter 1964) supported the thesis of an innate body schema based on a built-in neural substrate. This implies a body schema system from the very beginning, but one that is also open to modification by multimodal sensory experiences throughout the lifetime of the organism (for summary of cases involved in these studies, see Table 4.1).

TABLE 4.1.   *Summary of data from four studies of aplasic phantoms*

Case	AO	AS	Prosthesis	Missing part	Description of phantom
Weinstein and Sersen 1961					
1	m	8	no	LA starting $1\frac{3}{4}$ in. below E w/ malformed digit at center of stump	full length w/ hand
2	?	7	yes R & L since $3\frac{1}{2}$	Both arms and congenitally abnormal legs L = 6 in. long; R = 4 in.	no leg phantoms bilateral arm phantoms present only when prosthesis worn
3	7	9	yes since 5 yrs	L forearm	1 in. extended below stump only when no prosthesis is worn
4	5–6	10	yes (cosmetic)	$\frac{2}{3}$ of L forearm stump $4\frac{1}{2}$ in. below E	slightly shorter than other full limb
Poeck 1964					
1	6	11	no	both forearms and hands	normal hands about 15 cm. below stumps but no forearms
Weinstein, Sersen, and Vetter 1964					
1	7	7		RA above E	entire arm, but shorter than other
2	m	10		R hand	entire hand
4	m	10		L hand	entire hand
5	5–6	13		L & R A above E	2 in. beyond L stump; lasted only 1 yr.
7	m	8		RA below E	entire hand, shorter length
8	m	8		LA above E	5 fingers at stump
9	m	11		LA above E	entire limb
10	m	5		LA below E	palm and middle finger
14	m	10		LA below E, R below W L & R below knee	L wrist, thumb, and palm no leg phantom

(Continues)

Case	AO	AS	Prosthesis	Missing part	Description of phantom
15	?	12		LA above E; RA above E R leg above knee	R & L arms, no hands, R thigh only
17	4	11		L & R arms above E	entire LA
18	12	12		LA below E; RA above E	LA, 2–3 in. beyond stump
Saadah and Melzack 1994					
1	16	18	yes	LA below E	full length w/ hand and fingers (onset in connection with injury)

Note: AO = Age at Onset; m=as long as they can remember; AS=Age at time of Study; L=Left; R=Right; A=Arm; E=Elbow; W=Wrist.

Source: based on Gallagher et al. 1998.

Phantom Limb: Image or Schema?

The theorists and experimenters on both sides of this debate, that is whether they defended the notion of an *acquired* schema [image] or an *innate* schema [image], failed to use these concepts with precision in their investigations of aplasic phantom limbs. This lack of precision qualifies their conclusions in an essential way. Simmel (1958, 1962, 1966), for example, who, as previously noted, is one of the few psychologists to recognize an explicit distinction between Head's notion of body schema and Schilder's notion of body image, nonetheless goes on to confuse the two concepts in her discussion of aplasic phantoms. She claims that the aplasic phantom is not part of a body *schema*, although she contends that the non-aplasic (post-amputation) phantom is precisely that. The body schema's relative resistance to alteration accounts for the non-aplasic phantom. Yet, the evidence cited in her study actually suggests that the phantom is part of a body *image*—what Katz (1993: 151) terms the 'phantom limb percept'. Simmel's data, based on interviews in which subjects were explicitly asked to describe their perceived phantom, show that the phantom is an 'experiential representation' which patients consciously 'feel' (as itchy or painful, for example), and that it has a cognitive status, dependent on intellectual maturity. Thus, Simmel *defines* the phantom as part of a body schema, but *describes* it as part of a body image.

On the other side of the controversy too, in studies that claim to show evidence for an innate body schema, the evidence cited actually points to the existence of a body image developing some time after birth. The procedures used by Weinstein and Sersen (1961) involve, for example, asking the child to indicate kinesthetic sensations associated with the phantom limb, or to estimate the length of the phantom. Such questions require the child to focus perceptual attention on the phantom. In effect, they test for a phantom limb percept. The descriptions supplied in their case studies of aplasic phantoms, for example, descriptions of the perceptual appearance of the phantom—long, short, wrinkled, etc.—also indicate an image-based phenomenon rather than a schematic process. Similar procedures have been used by other researchers. Poeck (1964) and his patients describe 'the conscious presence of a phantom' which appears or disappears under certain circumstances. Scatena (1990) refers to phantom phenomena as 'perceptual events'. Melzack (1984, 1990), who rejects the explanation of the phantom in terms of the body schema in favor of the concept of neural matrix, describes it as involving perceptual awareness.

We need to sort things out a little better than this. Following our distinction between body image and body schema, it should be possible to make more precise sense out of the aplasic phantom. Even if the evidence provided in studies since 1961 indicates that the aplasic phantom is part of a body image (and more generally it can be noted that most analyses of post-amputation phantoms treat the phantoms as perceptual phenomena),[2] the question is still open: is it also part of a body schema? First, let us consider two items that seem to reinforce the idea that aplasic phantoms do *not* have the status of a body schema. These considerations will help us to understand what sort of evidence is appropriate to establish a connection between aplasic phantom and body schema.

One clear kind of evidence that a *non-aplasic* (post-amputation) phantom is an aspect of a body-schema system (and not solely part of the body image) is described in numerous studies and is sometimes referred to as a form of 'forgetting' (Melzack 1990; Merleau-Ponty 1962; Poeck 1964; Simmel 1966). In some cases of phantom limb after amputation, although the subject clearly knows about and acknowledges the loss, he seems to act as if unaware of the loss and in certain instances of motor behavior relies on the phantom as one would on the real limb. For example, an amputee who attempts to walk with his phantom leg is surprised when he falls. Poeck (1964: 272) reports this type of incident in a 50-year-old woman who lost her right thumb when she was 5 years old. 'Every time she handles an object with her right hand, she tries to grasp it as if the missing member were still present. Even today, it is only when her grip fails that she becomes consciously aware of her defect.' The phenomenon of forgetting suggests that the missing limb continues to function schematically in motor behavior for an indefinite time. It continues to play a part in the organization of instrumental or locomotive actions. Its absence is not taken into account.

Does this continued functioning depend on a vivid representation or percept of the missing limb? This is a view expressed by numerous theorists (e.g. Aglioti, Bonazzi, and Cortese 1994; Melzack 1990); they suggest that the vividness of the phantom (in effect an aspect of the body image) accounts for such incidents of forgetting. This would need to be an unusually complex combination of awareness and forgetting, however. Against a background of conscious acknowledgement concerning the missing limb, the subject would have to have a vivid awareness of

---

[2] Phantom limbs are usually understood to be part of the body image, and phenomenological descriptions are offered as the best way to understand them. Thus Halligan, Zeman, and Berger (1999) write: 'We stand to learn most from phantoms if we attend closely to patients' subjective reports.'

the phantom, not as a phantom, but as a present and workable member. The forgetting in this case would be a forgetting that this vividly present limb is nothing more than a phantom. It would involve a basic and complex contradiction in the body image: not simply a perceptual presence alongside a conceptual acknowledgement of absence, which is in some regards the mark of a phantom, but this, together with a forgetting of the conceptual acknowledgement.

A more parsimonious explanation is possible, however. The phenomenon of forgetting is actually a normal part of normal motor action. Movement in general, and specifically the continued functioning of a phantom part in movement, does not depend on a vivid representation or percept of the body, or specifically of the missing limb. Rather, forgetting is normal and possible precisely because motor behavior does not ordinarily require that my limbs be included in my perceptual awareness. I step out to walk, or I reach out to grasp something, not by making my limbs vividly present; nothing in such cases depends on their vivid presence. Smooth movement, successful walking, reaching, and grasping depend on a certain experiential transparency of the body. This transparency is possible because, thanks to the coordinated processes of body schemas, movement usually takes care of itself. If I am aware of my body in the motor act, my awareness is a pre-reflective, performative awareness rather than a vivid perceptual presence. On this account, forgetting is explained in the normal workings of body schemas, and the inference is that the phantom, precisely in this regard, is an element of the body schema.

In incidents of forgetting after amputation, missing (phantom) parts of the body remain operative within motor schemas, and not just as part of a body image. Significantly, however, although incidents of forgetting are frequently reported following amputation, no incidents of forgetting have been reported in subjects with aplasic phantoms.

Does the fact that aplasics do not exhibit the phenomenon of forgetting imply that the aplasic phantom does *not* operate as part of a body schema? Although it seems clear that aplasic patients do experience certain perceptual (kinesthetic) aspects of phantom limbs, it remains uncertain whether schema-related experience with an actual limb at some point of one's life is a necessary condition for such errors as 'forgetting one doesn't have it' to occur. The fact that aplasics do not report the forgetting phenomenon raises the possibility that the aplasic phantom is not part of a body schema, although it is very likely part of a body image. In the literature on aplasic phantoms, however, these issues remain unstated, and certainly unresolved. We return to them shortly.

A second item that seems to reinforce the idea that aplasic phantoms do *not* have the status of a body schema is the fact that in the majority of cases of aplasic phantoms the onset of the phantom takes place relatively late (see Table 4.1). In cases where specific ages are provided, the age of onset ranges from 4 to 30 years, with the majority of subjects experiencing the onset of the phantom between the ages of 5 and 8 years. For example, Poeck (1964) reports that an 11-year-old girl born with congenital absence of forearms and hands did not experience phantoms until 6 years of age. In a study of eighteen cases of aplasia with phantoms reported, five of the subjects developed phantoms at the age of 7 years or older, with one of them developing a phantom only at age 12 years (Weinstein, Sersen, and Vetter 1964). One patient born with her left forearm and hand missing began to feel a painful phantom with her first menstruation at the age of 14 years (Sohn 1914). Saadah and Melzack (1994) report the onset of phantoms following minor surgery or injury to the congenitally absent limb site, at ages 6, 16, 26, and 30 years respectively in four subjects with congenital limb deficiencies.

The lateness of onset in cases of aplasic phantoms contrasts to cases of phantoms following amputation. In children 4–5 years old, phantoms follow amputations almost immediately (see Weinstein, Sersen, and Vetter 1964: cases 21, 22, and 30; and Poeck 1964: cases 2 and 3). The earliest *report* of a phantom was made by a 3-year-old girl whose legs were amputated at age $1\frac{1}{2}$ years (Simmel 1962: case 454). This difference seems puzzling, and a complete account of the aplasic phantom would need to include an explanation of it. To understand this delay it is important first to understand whether we are dealing with a phenomenon that is part of a body image only, or whether it is also an element of a body schema.

If the aplasic phantom is part of the body image alone, then the explanation for the delayed onset may be purely psychological. It may involve stress- or anxiety-related or emotionally motivated change in the body image (Katz 1993). It has been suggested that purely perceptual processes may generate a phantom in the aplasic case. Subjects may project the phantom limb into their own body image on the basis of their constant perception of other humans who have the full complement of limbs because so much else about their bodies is perceived to be the same. This possibility of an extreme intermodal learning, an incorporation of significant aspects of others into the embodied self, is not unrelated to the mechanisms that underpin neonate imitation, but would seemingly depend on a set of experiences that could only be fulfilled later in childhood. More speculative explanations are sometimes given in the psychoanalytic literature, some going so far as to attribute the phantom limb to 'cultural phenomena of denial' (Meuse 1996).

Notice that according to the psychological and social-psychological accounts there would be nothing innate about the aplasic phantom. Its origin would depend on the experience of other persons or certain social factors that would motivate its development only relatively later in life. Thus, just in case the aplasic phantom is an element of the body image alone, its relatively late onset would be evidence against the innate status claimed for it by various researchers since 1961. If, however, it is possible to show that the aplasic phantom is part of a system of body schemas, a different explanation of the delayed onset must be offered—one that would preserve the idea of an innate schema as the basis for the aplasic phantom.

The evidence cited in the above studies suggests that the aplasic phantom is an element of the body *image* that develops relatively late. Clearly on this evidence the inference made by several of the researchers, namely that the body *schema* is innate, is not logically justified. Of course, as I have indicated in the previous chapter, studies of neonate imitation do provide good evidence for an innate body schema.

This motivates us to seek a better explanation of the aplasic phantom—an explanation that would be consistent with the findings from studies of neonate imitation.

Indeed, the data on aplasic phantoms are not inconsistent with the idea that a body schema system exists at birth. Furthermore, although there are no data to support it, there is no inconsistency with the idea of an earlier onset of aplasic phantoms. It is quite possible that, as in some cases with phantoms after amputation, aplasic phantoms gradually disappear as the schema and/or image undergo adjustment and development. Since this could happen relatively early in the case of aplasic phantoms, it would not be impossible that most subjects simply do not recall a phantom when interviewed later. This, and not the traditional doctrine that denies the existence of a body schema and body image at birth, may be the basis for the data reported in the studies—specifically that most subjects do not report a phantom in cases of aplasia.

It is also possible, in regard to the lateness of onset and lateness of report of aplasic phantoms documented in the post-1961 studies, that reports of aplasic phantom limbs may be limited by the subject's abilities to reflect and verbally express such experience. This is something that many children may not be able to do prior to 4 years old. Ability to report may be complicated especially because there would be a contradictory representation of a limb being proprioceptively present and simultaneously perceptually (for example, visually) absent. Conflicts between proprioception and vision are often resolved in favor of vision (positively in some cases, see e.g. Ramachandran and Hirstein 1998). This sort of conflict between proprioception and visual perception may well be a problem for children less than about 4 years old (an age at which much empirical research on children's 'theory of mind' indicates there are substantial intellectual changes).

Neither the absence of memory for a phantom that disappeared, nor the lack of linguistic ability to report the phantom are inconsistent with the suggestion that in many cases phantoms later appear (or *ex hypothesis*, reappear) temporarily, and for various reasons, due to stress, anxiety, or physical stimulation. So, even if there is an innate basis for aplasic phantoms, it is still possible for the phantom to disappear earlier than memory can recall, and for it to reappear at later ages along with reports of aplasic phantoms. Some of the various possibilities are summarized in Table 4.2.

In summary, the early studies of aplasics concluded not only that aplasic phantoms do not exist, but are actually impossible because no body schema exists at birth. The more recent data on aplasics indicate that aplasic phantoms do exist, and it is sometimes inferred on this basis that this is evidence for an innate body schema. None of the studies, however, clearly differentiates between body image and body schema, and the evidence cited in these studies supports the idea that the aplasic phantom has the status of body image rather than body schema. Furthermore, the evidence that shows the aplasic phantom to be part of a body image also shows late onset. Although this is not inconsistent with an innate mechanism, it certainly does not suggest an innate mechanism. What does this tell us about the innate status of the body schema or body image? The most conservative position is

TABLE 4.2. *Possible explanations for the delay in onset or delay in report of aplasic phantom*

Aplasic phantom as part of:	Cause of onset	Time of onset	Cause of late or no report	Status (acquired or innate)
Body image	Psychological	Later childhood	Late onset	Acquired
Body image	Physical trauma	Later childhood	Late onset	Acquired
Body image or schema	Part of innate system	Prenatal but early disappearance	Inadequate memory	Innate
Body image or schema	Part of innate system	Prenatal	Inadequate language	Innate
Body image or schema	Part of innate system	Prenatal but early disappearance	Reappearance due to psychological or physical trauma	Innate

that no firm conclusions can be reached on the basis of the data supplied by this research.

Is there a way to resolve the uncertainty about aplasic phantoms and show that they are indeed elements of a body schema? I suggest that it is possible to pursue a different course through more broad-ranging developmental, behavioral, and especially neurological evidence. This different approach supports the idea that an aplasic phantom would be part of an innate system of body schemas. It also provides some indication of the early involvement of movement in the onset of consciousness.

Hand–Mouth Coordination in the Fetus and Neonate

In ontogenesis we should not be surprised by a certain priority of movement. Although a good part of brain development involves a genetic blueprint that predetermines the patterns of growth, self-organizing movement plays an important role in stimulating and promoting normal growth. Reflex movement in the embryo begins around week 7 gestational age and grows in complexity in the 8th week (Flower 1985). The actual development of embryonic neural tissue depends, in part, on fetal movement, and on components that are important for the attainment of postural balance. The principle is 'movement influences morphology' (Edelman 1992; Sheets-Johnstone 1998). Proprioceptors in the muscles (muscle spindles) which will ultimately be responsible for a sense of position and movement first appear at 9 weeks gestational age (Humphrey 1964); spontaneous and repetitious movements follow shortly (De Vries, Visser, and Prechtl 1982). The development of semicircular ear canals that, as part of the vestibular system, later provide a sense of balance begins as early as the 4th month of gestation (Jouen and Gapenne

1995). Even as the cortical plate begins to form early connections are made with the brainstem (Flower 1985), and later neural development of the motor cortex and other cortical and subcortical areas continue to be stimulated by fetal movement (Sheets-Johnstone 1998).

Consider a certain kind of movement that emerges in early fetal development. Ultrasonic scanning of fetuses shows that movement of the hand to the mouth occurs between fifty and one hundred times an hour from 12–15 weeks gestational age (DeVries, Visser, and Prechtl 1984).[3] This suggests that hand-to-mouth movement may be an aspect of an early, centrally organized coordination that eventually comes to be controlled proprioceptively. This kind of prenatal movement may in fact be precisely the movement that helps to generate or facilitate the development of body schemas. That is, quite consistent with the traditional hypothesis, it may be movement (motor experience) that one requires for the formation of a body schema. The only difference is that this movement occurs much earlier, and by implication, body schemas develop much earlier than the traditional account permits, that is, in the fetus rather than in the 6–8-month-old infant. But we are getting ahead of ourselves here. Let us take a closer look at this kind of movement.

Fortunately, for purposes of investigation, there is some continuity between this very early movement and postnatal movement. Spontaneous movements such as whole-body flexions or more localized limb movements occur in human neonates until approximately the third month of life. These movements are very similar to fetal spontaneous movements[4] and are generally thought to reflect the relative motor immaturity of humans at birth compared to other mammals (Hopkins and Prechtl 1984; Prechtl and Hopkins 1986). Butterworth and his colleagues, however, have discovered relatively organized movements of hand to mouth (similar to the fetal movement mentioned above) embedded within these spontaneous movements. They suggest this as evidence for an innate coordination between the hand and the perioral region (Butterworth and Hopkins 1988; Lew and Butterworth 1995).

It turns out that in young infants who are midway between feeding times approximately one-third of all arm movements resulting in contact with any part of the head lead to contact with the mouth, either directly (14%) or following contact with other parts of the face (18%). Moreover, a significant percentage of the arm movements that result in contact with the mouth are associated with an open or opening mouth posture, compared with those landing on other parts of the face. Important here is the fact that in such movements the mouth 'anticipates' arrival of the hand. Since the eyes are no more likely to be open than closed when the hand finds the mouth directly, there is no evidence that this motor behavior is guided by vision. Butterworth has also tested to rule out the possibility that these movements are the result of reflex responses such as the Babkin reflex where the infant's mouth

---

[3] The ultrasonic scans were sufficiently fine-grained to show jaw openings, yawns, and even movements of the tongue.

[4] De Vries *et al.* (1984: 48) states: 'There was a striking similarity between prenatal and postnatal movements, although the latter sometimes appeared abrupt because of the effect of gravity.'

opens when the palm is pressed. Nor is any instance of the rooting reflex observed in relation to these movements.

When the infant is hungry, the mouth more frequently opens in anticipation of arrival of the hand than when the infant has been fed.[5] This suggests that hand–mouth coordination in the fetus and the neonate may be an early form of orally targeted reaching linked to the appetitive system. An additional link between hand, mouth, and feeding occurs in the suckling posture, where the hands are brought in a fisted posture to either side of the mouth and nipple (Casaer 1979).[6] This behavioral evidence of an early link between the hand, mouth, and appetitive system is supported by neuroanatomical and single-cell recording evidence in primates.

There is a network of substantial and specific interconnections in the primate between regions in the orbital and medial prefrontal cortex which receive gustatory inputs from cortical and subcortical areas, as well as inputs from regions of the somatosensory cortex that represent the hand, arm, and face. There are also projections from the ventral premotor cortex to these same prefrontal areas (Carmichael and Price 1995). Rizzolatti *et al.* (1988) identified neurons in the prefrontal cortex (ventral area 6) that fire in relation to movements that can be described as 'grasping with the hand and/or mouth'. This neuronal activity occurs only when these kinds of movements are directed at food items, however. It is also the case that stimulation of ventral premotor cortex elicits both oral and hand movements in owl monkeys (Preuss, Stepniewska, and Kaas 1996). This is consistent with the observation that the area of ventral premotor cortex plays a role in hand-to-mouth movements (for review see Jackson and Husain 1996).

The number of such neural convergences motivates Carmichael and Price (1995) to postulate a network in the prefrontal cortex (especially area 13l) that involves hand–mouth coordination and is dedicated to feeding behavior. For example, in the orbital and medial prefrontal cortex (especially in area 12m), neural projections from somatosensory areas responsible for representation of hand, arm, face, mouth, and tongue meet up with projections from premotor areas. In area 13l, projections from somatosensory representations of mouth and tongue converge with imputs from premotor areas (for example, premotor area 6va which contains a neural representation of the mouth and hand and is connected with the perioral regions of the motor cortex), the gustatory cortex and related subcortical structures.

The complexity of this network makes it difficult to pin down all the neuronal details. It seems clear, however, that such a network can constitute the innate neural basis for a specific body schema, the behavioral evidence for which we see in fetal and neonate hand–mouth coordination.

---

[5] In early infancy, sucking on the hand is more frequent before feeding than after (Feldman and Brody 1978). Lew and Butterworth (1995) found that the strong relationship between movements that landed on the mouth and open mouth postures held only when the baby is hungry.

[6] Blass *et al.* (1989) and Rochat, Blass, and Hoffemeyer (1988) found that a few drops of sucrose solution placed on the tongues of neonates produced suckling posture-like effects, where, in the absence of the breast, sucking on the hand occurred.

Implications for the Aplasic Phantom

The notion of an innate motor schema in connection with hand–mouth coordination is consistent with two hypotheses, both of which can help to explain the aplasic phantom as a product of innate mechanisms.

Hypothesis 1. Where a functional system is disrupted by failure of limb formation, the system may generate a phantom because a specific movement coordination is represented within a neural matrix.[7] One needs to think of the hand–mouth coordination as having two related elements: the hand movement and the mouth movement. Remember that the mouth opens to anticipate the arrival of the hand. In the case of a missing limb, it is not just that the intact body part involved in the coordination, for example the mouth and perioral region in the hand–mouth coordination, is neurally represented. In so far as the motor coordination or schema itself is represented, there must be some implicit representation of the 'other end' of the coordination. Even if the arm and hand are not there, a circuit or a defined schema (involving some definite tendency of arm movement) would require that both sides of the circuit be neurally defined.

If this is the case, then, under certain conditions, a stimulation of the mouth would be sufficient to activate the joint mouth–limb neural system. The virtual limb (the phantom) could thus come into existence when the coordination is activated. A singular representation of the coordinated schema or action pattern incorporates both ends of the movement, the mouth and the hand, even when there is no hand. Touching the mouth, or perhaps less proximally, the stimulation of gustatory needs, activates the circuit that includes the missing limb ordinarily responsible for feedback in the specific motor program.

This account depends on an innate body schema, in this case a specific coordination or motor capacity. This first hypothesis, of course, does not require that the 12–15-week-old fetus be conscious of the movement. The coordinated movement, even in the neonate, can function without the necessity of perceptual monitoring and probably starts in the fetus prior to any possibility of perceptual monitoring. Still, it is likely that at some point in development a proprioceptive accompaniment develops along with the movement. The enactment of the motor schema would, at some ontogenetic point, cause proprioceptive information to be transmitted to the brain, and eventually this would generate a proprioceptive sense of movement. More generally it would not be unreasonable to say that movement precedes the awareness of movement but contributes to the generation of that awareness (in the form of proprioceptive awareness) when the system is sufficiently developed to allow for it. Awareness of movement may in fact be ontogenetically the first instance of phenomenal consciousness (I return to this point in the last section). In this specific case the proprioceptive sense of hand–mouth-coordinated movement may form the initial aspect of an experienced phantom.

[7] This hypothesis was first suggested by George Butterworth (see Gallagher *et al.* 1998). The view summarized here is consistent with Melzack's concept of an innate neural matrix (Melzack 1989, 1990).

In the non-aplasic case, hand–mouth coordination is an automatic movement. In the case of aplasia the same movement pattern may be initiated, but without the reinforcement of completed movement the neural representation of the coordinated action pattern may deteriorate, although it may not completely disappear. Furthermore, in the case of the aplasic limb, the proprioceptive experience that develops along with the initiated coordinated movement finds no fulfillment or reinforcement in the modality of touch (contact of mouth with hand). If there is a proprioceptive sense of hand–mouth motility, without the hand there is no tactile reinforcement of that experience. Lacking such reinforcement, it is possible that the neural matrix underlying the schema begins to reshape itself even *in utero*. Depending on individual differences and circumstances, the phantom may disappear or be reactivated, much as behavioral studies indicate (Table 4.1).

Of course, I have simplified the story a good deal. Given the complexity of the neural matrix distributed across a variety of both cortical and subcortical areas, and given the likelihood of a large number of specific motor schemas associated with different kinds of hand movements, the phantom hand may be activated in a variety of circumstances (not just oral or gustatory stimulation).

We should not overlook the fact that this account also suggests a precursor to the phenomenon of 'forgetting'. As we mentioned, in the case of post-amputation phantoms, some subjects 'forget' and attempt to use their missing parts in motor activity. Remember too that there are two explanations for the phenomenon of forgetting. According to one view, forgetting is caused by a vivid representation or percept of the missing limb (Aglioti, Bonazzi, and Cortese 1994; Melzack 1990). The subject is so conscious of the phantom limb, she 'forgets' that it is not actually there and attempts to use it in her motor activity. According to a second view, the phenomenon of forgetting implies that the missing limb continues to function transparently as part of a body schema (Gallagher and Meltzoff 1996). Forgetting is possible precisely because motor behavior does not ordinarily require that one's limbs be the objects of one's perception. Rather, motor behavior tends to follow practiced or genetically predetermined motor programs that integrate with intentional action. Support for this second view can be found in the suggestion that hand–mouth coordination exists even in the case of a congenital absence of arm. According to Hypothesis 1, activation of the appropriate motor schema causes an anticipatory opening of the mouth for reception of a hand that is not there. One might say that the mouth 'forgets' that the hand is not there. This would be a 'forgetting' that is the result, not of a perceived presence or literal forgetting, but of the working of a predetermined and innate motor schema. In this sense, it is not so much that the subject forgets, but that the schema remembers.

The first hypothesis is also consistent with recent research on neural plasticity in cases of phantoms after amputations. Ramachandran and his colleagues (Ramachandran, Rogers-Ramachandran, and Stewart 1992; Yang *et al.* 1994; also see Halligan *et al.* 1993) investigated the plasticity of the somatosensory cortical representation of the body. Their studies demonstrate that after amputation of a limb, neural structures correlated with both the amputated part and other body parts change. The neural structure associated with the amputated part may deteriorate but not totally disappear. More specifically, short- and/or long-term mechanisms responsible for neural plasticity may be set in motion. In the short term, synaptic remodeling, the formation of new synaptic contacts or the activation of pre-existing but inactive or inhibited connections may take place. In the longer term, neural structures in the somatosensory cortex responsible for representing other parts of the body (for example, the face) may invade the neighboring area which had been responsible for representing the now missing limb—some form of neuronal deterioration having taken place in that area. Activation of the expanded face-representing neural map may also reactivate the indigenous limb-representing neurons and thus cause the phantom experience. Thus, as several studies have shown, amputation may cause a disinhibition or unmasking of pre-existing synaptic connections that allow for the simultaneous transmission of information from the face to both the hand and the face area of the cortex or thalamus (Kaas 2000; Pons *et al.* 1991; Ramachandran, Rogers-Ramachandran, and Stewart 1992; also see Kew *et al.* 1997).

To the extent that the innate neural framework in the somatosensory cortex responsible for body awareness is modified, the phantom gradually fades from the body image. Still, stimulation of body parts associated with the invading neural structures can cause activity in the deteriorated neural structure and sensation in the corresponding (phantom) part. Modality-specific stimulation of parts of the body other than the stump (for example, stimulation applied to the face) can produce similar modality-specific sensations (for example, of temperature and movement) in the phantom part (e.g. the phantom hand) in a percentage of cases (Ramachandran, Rogers-Ramachandran, and Stewart 1992). The plasticity described in Ramachandran's work on phantoms after amputation could be extended theoretically to the case of aplasic phantoms. The second hypothesis concerning aplasic phantoms follows more directly from this work on neural reorganization.

Hypothesis 2. In the developing cortex some aspects of the missing arm and hand come to be neurally represented simply on the basis of genetic instructions—that is, in development that takes place independent of actual arm movement (see e.g. Rakic 1995). If, in aplasia, the arm itself does not develop, the corresponding developing neural representations are not reinforced by movement or tactile experience as they need to be for normal and full development (see e.g. Shatz 1990). Lacking experiential reinforcement they deteriorate to some degree, and are displaced or dominated by neighboring neurons, stimulation of which can generate phantom limb experience.

To develop this second hypothesis more fully, two qualifications need to be added. First, there are several reasons to think that the neural matrix responsible for phantom phenomena is more distributed than studies that focus solely on the somatosensory cortex indicate. It is likely that neural reorganization takes place not just in the somatosensory cortex, but in other cortical and subcortical areas. With respect to cortical reorganization in areas other than the contralateral somatosensory cortex, there is evidence for post-amputation reorganization in the motor cortex (Karl *et al.* 2001; Ojemann and Silbergeld 1995) and in various bilateral cerebral structures (Knecht *et al.* 1995). Concerning the role of subcortical mechanisms, the evidence from ultrasonic scanning of hand–mouth coordination behavior *in utero* suggests that some relevant neuronal substrate must develop and be in place by 12–15 weeks gestational age, which is well prior to the completion of cortical formation (Rakic 1995).

The neurobiological evidence from primate studies (cited above) indicates that neural representations of hand and mouth are extant in a number of networked cortical areas and that this network includes correlated projections from subcortical (limbic and thalamic) areas (see e.g. Garraghty and Kaas 1991; Jones and Pons 1998). The beginnings of the formation of these complex connections can be seen as early as 8 weeks gestational age (approximately 54 post-ovulatory days) with the formation of thalamocortical and corticothalamic fibers, the development of neopallium fibers that run between areas that will become cortex, and the developing subcortical formations such as the basal ganglia, cerebellum, and brainstem, all responsible for motor coordination (O'Rahilly and Müller 1994). Thus it is likely that neural reorganization (or the effects of some limited reorganization), rather than remaining localized in one specific area, follows the distributed lines of this extended matrix. There are numerous cortical areas (at least seven in the parietal, frontal, and temporal cortexes (Merzenich and Kaas 1980)) and subcortical areas in which somatic representation occurs (the cerebellum, for instance, has its own sensory and motor representations of the body). Neural reorganization in one area does not necessarily imply reorganization in another, although reorganization in one may have an effect on the others ('relayed plasticity'), and by varying degrees. Higher degrees of alteration, however, can be more 'dramatic' in higher stations of the somatosensory cortex (Kaas 1991).

Second, it is important to note that in the developmental context the mechanisms responsible for neural reorganization are most probably more efficient and somewhat different from the case of the adult. This difference may account for the fact that a smaller percentage of aplasics actually experience a phantom (17 per cent in Weinstein and Sersen's original study) compared to approximately 85 per cent of subjects following amputation (Jensen *et al.* 1984). In the adult, following amputation, neuronal reoganization most likely occurs first, and quite quickly, via synaptic remodeling; and in the long term, neuronal deterioration, branching, and reorganization can happen. In contrast, in the developing fetus of 12–15 weeks, when hand–mouth correlation becomes manifest, cortical genesis is still in its beginning phase, and dendritic branching and synaptogenesis are minimal (maximal dendritic growth occurring at 18–24 weeks). Neural representation of arm and hand, and the motor program responsible for hand–mouth coordination are, in the case of aplasia, mainly genetically determined, and the lack of experiential reinforcement would already initiate (or at least set the stage for) changes in developing organization.

The developing brain is also far more plastic than the adult brain. In effect, in the case of the aplasic, there is less to undo or redo, and possibly more efficient mechanisms to do it. In the developing brain of the aplasic subject, mechanisms that involve the retraction of collateral axons that project to a variety of brain systems may be modified in those areas that would have been responsible for the aplasic limb. Later synaptic development also tends to adjust to compensate for unusual circumstances in both cortical and subcortical areas (Sarnat 1992). Given that the developing brain is more plastic, and that there is less to undo or restructure, both these mechanisms (synaptic formation, rather than synaptic remodeling, and neuronal branching) are likely to do a more efficient job than in the adult brain. If the neural matrix responsible for the phantom more efficiently redesigns itself, the phantom is less likely to manifest itself in the aplasic subject. And this corresponds to the behavioral data.

Some Additional Considerations

On the first hypothesis, the aplasic phantom hand is based on the existence of a neural circuitry for the innate motor schema responsible for hand–mouth coordination (which may be part of a complex developing network dedicated to feeding behavior). The missing hand comes to be represented as the 'other end' of that circuit. Implicit in the representation of the motor possibilities of the mouth, there must be a representation of the missing limb as well—enough, at least, so it 'closes the circuit' (by opening the mouth in anticipation) and completes the coordinated mouth-limb schema. Activating the circuit generates a virtual or phantom limb.

On the second hypothesis, the phantom is based on mechanisms that involve a reorganization of the neural representation of the missing limb in a complex neuromatrix, an alteration that may be most clearly expressed in the somatosensory cortex. A neural substrate of the missing limb, to some degree displaced in developmental organization, may continue to exist, and phantom experience may be the result of stimulated restructured synaptic connections and/or neural structures that have settled in a cortical area originally meant to represent the absent limb.

The two hypotheses concerning aplasic phantoms are not inconsistent. Indeed, one can see them as complementary rather than alternative hypotheses. The first hypothesis, which makes reference to neural representations and networks in prefrontal, premotor, and motor cortexes, as well as subcortical structures, takes its starting point from the idea of innate motor schemas. It explains the role played by specific motor schemas, such as that involved in hand–mouth coordination, in the formation of a phantom limb. This explanation may be extended to account for the proprioceptive experience of the limb and possibly to what emerges as sensory (especially kinesthetic) aspects of the body image, their eventual dissolution, and possible reappearance. The second hypothesis, which makes reference to neural reorganization, expressed most dramatically by changes in the somatosensory cortex, but likely to be part of or involve a more extended neuromatrix, corresponds more closely to aspects of sensory phantom experience associated with the body image (kinesthetic and tactile sensations, etc). On this explanation, given the timing of development, we can understand why aplasic phantoms manifest themselves as part of the body image less frequently than phantoms after amputation. The possibility of an innate basis for the aplasic phantom is not inconsistent with the fact that some subjects do not experience or even remember a phantom (because it has disappeared very early) or the fact that some subjects experience the onset of an aplasic phantom relatively late.

According to both hypotheses, one can speak of an innate neural substrate for the aplasic phantom and indicate in relatively precise neurological terms the structures responsible for various features of the phantom and their developmental history. Peter Brugger (private correspondence) has furthered these considerations by suggesting that mirror neurons may also play a role in the generation of aplasic phantoms. Since the same mirror neurons fire either when the subject *sees* a specific action such as grasping or movement of hand to mouth performed by another person or when the subject *performs* the action herself, observation of another's actions may activate the body-schematic representation of one's own limb-action. If, in such circumstances, the limb involved in that representation is congenitally missing, neural circuits may be activated nonetheless, thereby causing the phantom. This suggestion is quite consistent with our combined hypotheses since it would require precisely the kinds of innate neural structures, and innate body schema, discussed above.

Brugger also notes that aplasic phantoms of the upper limbs are much more frequently reported than those of lower limbs. This may be accounted for by a reporting bias: arms may be more perceptually central than legs, or the hand–mouth coordination schema may have high survival significance. The presence of a hand–mouth coordination schema, however, is obviously not sufficient to account for aplasic phantoms in general since one can experience an aplasic phantom for a lower limb, as indicated in Brugger's own studies of congenital aplasia in a female without arms and legs (Brugger *et al.* 2000; Kollias *et al.* 1998; Müri *et al.* 1998). One possible answer to this is the more general proposal that there are numerous coordination schemas at work in the body, and that some such schemas could account for activation of the lower phantoms.

This proposal, however, sets a problem that is not easy to resolve: what kind of coordination schema can be found in relation to lower limbs? This turns out to be an interesting but difficult question about which to speculate. There seems to be no obvious, analogous innate coordination schema, like hand–mouth, for the case of leg phantoms. There is found in infants a well-known innate stepping movement that anticipates the species-typical walking posture. This schema is derived from a motor synergy observable from the fetal period. Although this synergy may be similar to the hand–mouth relation in some regard, it is dissimilar in that it is not obviously an intracorporeal or bipolar (body part to body part) relation.

Curiously, however, it has been noted that in some amputees stimulation in the genital area leads to phantom leg phenomena. For this to be the basis of a good explanation of an appropriate synergy (a coordinated pattern of activity serving some functional purpose) one would need to come up with a functional link between genitals and legs and/or feet analogous to the one between hand and mouth. Needless to say, there are several interesting possibilities, none of which is singularly convincing.[8] One explanation runs from neuroanatomy to unusual function. Ramachandran points out that representations of feet and genitals are located next to each other on the cortical somatosensory strip (S1). This and the fact that some amputees report sensations in a phantom leg or foot during sexual intercourse or genital stimulation suggest to Ramachandran not only an explanation for phantom activation, but also for foot fetishes (Ramachandran and Blakeslee 1998).

George Butterworth (personal communication) suggested a different explanation which focuses on a biologically contingent situation. He pointed out that Leonardo da Vinci's anatomical drawings of the fetus in the womb shows the fetus in the typical legs-crossed position, with feet close to or touching the genital area (Fig. 4.1). In his mirror writing Leonardo notes 'Il pissiare puto', that is, the posture

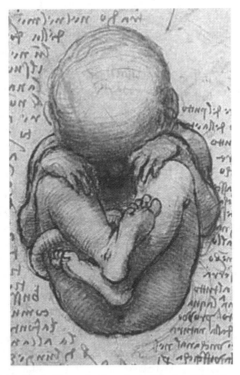

FIG. 4.1.   Leonardo da Vinci, *Views of a Fetus in the Womb*, c.1510–12.

[8] The following considerations have benefited from suggestions made by Peter Brugger, who originally suggested this problem, Jonathan Cole, and especially the late George Butterworth. Christopher Frith has indicated to me that he finds none of it convincing.

is intended to stop the fetus from urinating. Setting aside Leonardo's specific suggestion about function, it is true that typical fetal posture for the later part of pregnancy may set up a postural synergy between the genitals and feet, both of which are highly sensitive areas. Indeed, it may be the proximity of feet and genitals during this important developmental period that explains why representations for genitals and feet lie close together on S1. To speculate again about a functional explanation of the foot-genital connection, and revising Leonardo's suggestion, one might think of typical squatting posture or the natural posture for sitting without a chair.

On the other hand, the apposition of feet and genitals may simply be fortuitous, the result of womb size. By 21 weeks the fetus is tightly packaged in the womb, typically with legs crossed and flexed. So, one simple explanation might be that the posture is an intra-uterine adaptation, specifically to ensure that the fetus fits. Perhaps, however, rather than an adaptation that is forced by the restricted amount of space available, it is one that anticipates its environment since the fetus at 44 days often has its ankles crossed while there is still plenty of room for stretching the legs, which also happens.

It is also the case that there are other intracorporeal relations that seem more fortuitous than essential for postural or motor synergies. The claim cannot be that all phantoms necessarily have a body schema component since some phantoms have no apparent connection with motor programs. Thus, 25 per cent of women who undergo mastectomy experience a phantom breast when the pinna region of the ear lobe (on the same side as the mastectomy) is stimulated (Aglioti, Cortese, and Franchini 1994). This finding suggests the two regions might share neighboring neural representations on the sensory homunculus in the brain (Halligan, Zeman, and Berger 1999). Finally, the fact of penile phantoms suggests that sensation, of itself (without motor or postural purpose), can be a determinant of a phantom occurrence (restricted to body image rather than involving body schema) since, on most phenomenological accounts, the penis is not controlled by a particularly accurate motor program, compared, for example, with the hands.

Such singularly unconvincing speculations aside, however, it can be easily maintained that in the case of aplasic phantom legs it is still likely that an innate body schema is involved. The schema, however, need not be a coordination schema in the sense of the hand–mouth synergy. If Brugger's suggestion about mirror neurons is correct, and on the reasonable hypothesis that the mirror neuron system is more widespread than currently shown, then any body schema that involves the legs could be activated and could in turn activate the phantom. Of course the body schema for walking is in some part a learned rather than an innate one. Nonetheless, it is possible that someone born without legs, upon seeing someone else walk, activates (via mirror neurons) the body schema associated with the innate stepping movement that anticipates the species-typical walking movements.

The Onset of Consciousness

I conclude this chapter by following up on the suggestion that the development of proprioception in association with movement is especially important in sorting out the ontogenetic relations between embodied movement and the onset of consciousness. This also addresses the open philosophical question mentioned in the previous chapter. Specifically, proprioceptive awareness of movement may be the very first kind of consciousness to emerge in the developing nervous system. There is good evidence that proprioceptive awareness develops prenatally (Butterworth 1995; Butterworth and Hopkins 1977; Butterworth and Pope 1983).

But is proprioceptive awareness really a form of consciousness? Some theorists insist that consciousness involves self-consciousness, and they mean that if someone is conscious they know that they are conscious. As John Locke famously put it, it is 'impossible for anyone to perceive without perceiving that he does perceive. When we see, hear, smell, taste, feel, meditate, or will anything, we know that we do so' (1694: p. II. ch. 27. § 11). This could be understood as a relatively advanced form of consciousness in so far as it seems to involve a conceptual understanding, and on this supposition newborn infants would not be self-conscious (Dennett 1976; Frankfurt 1971).

Yet many people would accept the idea that some animals as well as human infants are conscious, but that they do not necessarily have a conceptual understanding that they are conscious. Even for theorists who insist on defining consciousness as involving an aspect of self-consciousness, one can argue that in some minimal and primary sense, proprioceptive awareness, by definition, involves a primitive, primary, pre-reflectively phenomenal, and non-conceptual self-consciousness, since proprioceptive awareness is an awareness of one's own body.

Consider, first, a hypothetical state of consciousness that does not have a pre-reflective self-consciousness as part of its structure. In that case, if proprioceptive awareness were such a consciousness, it would be possible for me to be proprioceptively aware of my body, but not as my own body. This would involve a structure similar to a situation in which I am aware that someone, X, is acting in a certain way, but I do not know that X is myself. This can happen in certain cases when I perceive X in an objective way, 'from the outside', but not when the awareness is based on proprioception, which is an awareness 'from the inside'. There are good arguments to be made that, for just this reason, proprioception provides a kind of information about oneself that is immune to error in regard to misidentifying oneself (see Cassam 1995; Gallagher 2003b). This suggests that proprioceptive awareness is necessarily structured as a pre-reflective *self*-consciousness—that when I am proprioceptively aware of a body, I am necessarily aware of only my own body, and necessarily aware of it *as* my own.

For proprioception to operate in this way, however, that is, to have proprioceptive awareness function as a consciousness that is pre-reflectively self-conscious—as a mode of consciousness in the proper, even if still primitive, sense—I think that one further element is necessary. Moreover, it would be difficult to think of proprioception without this element. Specifically, proprioceptive-kinesthetic awareness functions only as part of an ecological structure, and to the extent that it does, it contributes to an experiential differentiation between self and non-self. Movement never happens outside some environment. This involves several things.

1. Exteroceptive sense modalities (such as touch or vision) provide, as a subject moves, information about both the environment and the moving subject (tactile and visual proprioception).
2. Such information comes into a complex intermodal relationship with somatic proprioception to form a coordinated and intermodal sensory feedback.
3. That sensory feedback coordinates with efferent copies of motor commands in the nervous system, verifying that it is the subject who is moving rather than the environment.

Just to the extent that proprioception contributes to this sense that the subject, rather than the environment, is moving, it contributes to the differentiation between self and non-self.

We have already seen how proprioceptive awareness and a primitive differentiation between self and non-self function in an intermodal way with vision in the case of neonate imitation. This proprioceptive structure, including the differentiation between self and non-self, is likely to exist prenatally in the late-term fetus, at least in a primitive form, along with the sense of touch. The non-self or the *other*, in this case, is not clearly experienced as another person, as in the case of neonatal imitation. The important part of the primitive differentiation that constitutes consciousness as self-consciousness, however, does not necessitate that the perceiver perceives the other as another person, but only that it can distinguish itself ecologically from the non-self (see Gallagher 1996).

Consciousness, as it emerges ontogenetically, consists of a proprioceptive awareness that is already embedded in an ecological framework, and is in intermodal communication with another exteroceptive sense (touch). It is already structured as a pre-reflective, non-conceptual self-consciousness, and involves an experiential differentiation between self and non-self.

5

The Body in Gesture

LANGUAGE is a modality of the human body. It is generated out of movement. As Merleau-Ponty expressed it, 'the body converts a certain motor essence into vocal form' (1962: 181). Some theorists go so far as to claim that the propositional and metaphorical structures of language and thought are shaped by the non-propositional movements and movement patterns of the body (see M. Johnson 1987; Lakoff 1987; Lakoff and Johnson 1980; also see Boden 1982; Talmy 1988; Thelen 1995; and Turner 1991). In this chapter I raise a set of questions about the precise role played by embodiment in the generation of language. Specifically, can we say that part of what it takes to generate a linguistic act (a gesture or a speech act) depends on the body schema? Or is language something that transcends embodiment? If so, in what sense, and how? This set of questions will also take us back to an unresolved issue concerning neonate imitation. Is it possible that in our explanation of what makes neonate imitation possible (Ch. 3) we have made the concepts of body schema and proprioception carry too much weight? Is there some other element that we need to consider to work out a more adequate account of neonate imitation?

To the degree that embodiment shapes language, one could conceive of the translation of embodied spatial frameworks into linguistic form, through the medium of gesture (see McNeill 1992: 263–4). One could imagine gesture as the origin of language, and spoken language gradually emerging from embodied movement, a special kind of oral motility. Speech on this view would be a sophisticated movement of the body. If there is some truth to this, it is not the complete truth. In addition, one needs to understand how gesture comes about, and whether it is generated out of instrumental or locomotive movement. In so far as instrumental and locomotive movements can be purely solipsistic—simply for one's own sake—it would be necessary to show how a kind of non-solipsistic or intersubjective movement, including the expressive movement of gesture and language, might be generated from them.

In Ch. 2 I mentioned the case of a woman who suffers from left unilateral neglect but is still able to use her left hand and limbs to dress herself and to walk. Let us consider now, briefly, a case of unilateral neglect that extends not only to the left side of the subject's body, but to the entire left perceptual field (hemispatial neglect). In this case the subject neglects everything left of his visual midline, as well as the left side of his body. A subject like this does not refer to things in his left hemispace; he seems not to see or attend to anything left of center. He also has difficulty with spatial tasks in left hemispace, so, for example, he may be unable to map out a room or properly describe the layout of objects in place. In some cases the subject ignores the left side of objects even if they are within right hemispace.

There are people who are afflicted with hemispatial neglect who are also deaf. Like other neglect patients, these subjects are unable to describe spatial layouts, and by all conventional tests, they ignore the left side of their perceptual field. One might expect that subjects in this category who also communicate using sign language are likely to have an additional problem. In American Sign Language (ASL), for example, certain syntactical constructs depend on the use of spatial location. When an object is introduced into ASL discourse it is often assigned a spatial location in a signer's personal (egocentric) space around his body so that the precise location can be returned to as a way of executing anaphoric reference. One would expect that hemispatial neglect would disrupt the accomplishment of this important aspect of ASL. Yet these subjects have little or no trouble discursively assigning or referencing objects in their left hemispace.[1] Moreover, these same subjects are capable of understanding ASL presented by others, even if the signs are presented to the subject's left visual field (Bellugi and Klima 1997). In these cases the linguistic acts are seemingly able to transcend the pathological limitations that affect embodied perception. How is that possible?

Here is a rough neurological explanation. It is well known that language ability is a left-hemisphere (LH) phenomenon (in right-handed persons), and it turns out that damage to the right hemisphere (RH) of the sort that causes left unilateral neglect leaves language intact even with respect to the visual-spatial aspects of sign language. The ability to use the neglected space required for relatively coherent ASL appears to be correlated with LH language processes, so that severe spatial deficits among subjects with RH damage do not affect the spatial elements required for producing or understanding ASL (Bellugi and Klima 1997).

Is the ability to use aspects of an embodied spatial framework that are not otherwise available for the neglect patient a purely linguistic ability? It might be possible to argue that such ability is not in itself linguistic but primarily related to a body schema function that is simply co-opted by the linguistic system. Recall that some neglect patients are quite able to use their neglected limbs for instrumental and locomotive movements and in that respect maintain body-schematic capability. Perhaps a pragmatic (but not representational) spatial framework linked to body-schematic functions is spared and put to use in communicative circumstances when

---

[1] Bellugi and Klima (1997); Corina, Kritchevsky, and Bellugi (1996); Marcel (1992). To be clear, such patients do not use their left (neglected) hand to sign. Nor do they generally form gestures with their left hand, except in some cases where the gesture is bimanual (Laura Pedelty (private correspondence) indicates one rare exception, and several instances of bimanual gestures). In many cases, however, for purposes of ASL reference, the right hand will cross over to the left side. In one subject studied by Bellugi and Klima, for example, the right hand crosses over to the left (neglected) side. Thus, 'he used the left side as well as the right in producing signs, and even used the left side of his signing space for establishing nominals and verb agreement' (1997: 181). This was also the case with a patient with neglect and a dense hemiplegia on the left side (Corina, Kritchevsky, and Bellugi 1996). My thanks to Ursula Bellugi, David Corina, Anthony Marcel, Laura Pedelty, and Howard Poizner for helpful communications on this issue.

damage is confined to certain regions of the RH (and when it does not cause hemiplegia). At least one recent theorist argues that the body schema system is located in the LH (Yamadori 1997), and if that were so it would be unaffected by a lesion in the RH. Part of the solution, then, might refer us back to the fact that in some cases of left unilateral neglect without hemiplegia body schemas involving the left side seem to be intact. Thus, the woman who suffers from left unilateral neglect was still able to use her left hand and limbs for instrumental and locomotive movements, to dress herself and to walk, despite major problems with body image. Perhaps signing ability, in so far as it requires certain non-representational, pragmatic aspects of a spatial framework, involves just that body schema system. In that case, the use of sign language, and more generally, linguistic movement of any kind, may be linked to the same kind of movement controlled by motor programs for reaching, grasping, etc. This idea is consistent with a *motor theory* of gesture—a kind of theory that my colleagues and I have argued against, however.[2]

Jurgen Streeck (1996) and Sotaro Kita (2000) have independently advanced a motor theory of gesture. On their view, gestures are virtual actions, that is, instrumental actions without actual objects, and they involve the same neural pathways as those involved in real actions. Thus Kita suggests that gestures as virtual actions are equivalent to (or analogically equivalent to) instrumental actions. A gesture is something like a re-enactment that reproduces the original instrumental action in a virtual (imaginary) space. LeBaron and Streeck (2000: 137) assert that when the hands are used in both gesture and instrumental action, the same motor system is involved.

Moreover, the speaker's hands know how to do things other than gesticulation, and it seems unlikely that the skills that the hands bring to bear on their symbolic tasks are entirely separate from those that they have acquired while handling things. Rather, the patterns that are at hand when there is a need to gesture appear to be made from the same fabric as those that are required in instrumental action. And this 'producer's knowledge', too, is socially and culturally shared.

So gesture is the original action once again, but in an analog form, and this time in the virtual, communicative environment. Accordingly, gesture is something like a motor supplement to linguistic practice; not an intrinsic part of language, but something added to speech to help it along.

To test out this theory, and to see why it is wrong, it will be helpful to take another look at the case of Ian Waterman. In Ch. 2, I suggested that in some

---

[2] David McNeill, Jonathan Cole, and I have argued against a pure motor theory of gesture based on experiments with Ian Waterman summarized below (see Cole *et al.* 1998; Cole, Gallagher, and McNeill 2002; Gallagher, Cole, and McNeill 2001, 2002). If a motor theory was indeed a viable explanation, then we would expect to see more use of the left hand in sign formation in some of these subjects who still retain body-schematic functions for the neglected side. As I've noted, however, this rarely happens. This may or may not depend on the sample of subjects who were studied. It is also to be noted that sign-language is different from less formally structured gesture in various ways. Furthermore, in some cases stroke can eliminate sign-language while motorically equivalent gestural movements remain intact. For a good review of the evidence concerning distinctions between sign-language and more general spatial-motor functions, see Hickok, Bellugi, and Klima (1998).

respects Ian's loss of body schema involves a contrasting condition to unilateral neglect. In some unilateral neglect patients the schema system is still intact despite a major problem with body image. In Ian the body schema is not intact. Given his great difficulty controlling movement, one might predict that, consistent with the motor theory of gesture, Ian would not be capable of gesture, or at least, would show some deficiency in his use of gestures.

Recall that Ian suffers from an acute sensory neuropathy in which large fibers below the neck have been damaged as a result of illness. Although he has no sense of touch and no proprioception below the neck, and so no sense of posture or limb location, he is still capable of movement. In order to maintain motor control, however, he must think about his movements and keep certain parts of his body in his visual field. His movement requires constant visual and mental concentration. He is unable to control movement when in darkness. When he writes, his attention is divided among his overall body posture, his movement of the pen, and the thought he is putting on paper. Maintaining posture is, for him, an activity rather than an automatic process.

One would expect that Ian's motor difficulties would carry over to gesture. Indeed, several behavioral scientists, upon first hearing about his condition, were surprised to learn that Ian does gesture. Even more surprising, Ian's gestures appear to be normal, unlike the slightly rigid appearance of his gait.[3] The fact that Ian's gestures appear to be normal is surprising because normal gestures, like many movements in normal subjects, are not usually thought out or under conscious control. Gestures are not automatic movements, but neither are they movements of which we are fully aware. When I am in conversation with someone, my attention is not ordinarily focused on how my hands are moving. I do not monitor my gestures; I do not consciously control them. I may not even be aware that I am gesturing. In fact, if someone calls my attention to the fact that I am using gestures, it is very possible that in becoming aware of them their timing or their integration with my speech will be thrown off and they will appear more like affectations than integral parts of my speech acts. If Ian controls his gestures in the same way that he controls his other movements, then one might expect that they would not resemble normal gestures. The question naturally arises whether they are indeed normal, or whether, perhaps, Ian has just practiced his basic conversational hand gestures to the point where they look natural.

[3] Informal observations confirm that this is also the case with two other deafferented subjects. CF, who suffered a similar deafferentation as Ian Waterman, but relatively later in life, is confined to a wheelchair and has much greater difficulty with movement than Ian. His difficulties apply to both instrumental movement (e.g. buttoning his shirt) and locomotive movement (e.g. walking). He is nonetheless able to gesture freely during conversation, and his gestures appear to be close to normal. GL, who suffered deafferentation from the chin down, is also confined to a wheelchair and has similar difficulties with motor control. She also appears to have close to normal gestures during conversation.

Experiments on Gesture

To address this question Jonathan Cole, David McNeill, and I designed and conducted a series of experiments with Ian at the Center for Gesture and Speech Research, McNeill's lab at the University of Chicago. McNeill (1992) has developed an exhaustive analysis of gestures that involves classification of different types, a microanalysis of how gestures are formed, and a precise computerized technique for measuring the timing of gestures *vis-à-vis* speech.

When Ian lost control of his movement at the onset of his neuropathy he also lost the ability to gesture. It is not at all clear how we should think of his loss of gesture during this early stage of his illness. There are a number of possible explanations. One, consistent with the motor theory of gesture, is that gestures are part of the same system as all other motor programs. Gestural movement is the same kind of movement involved in instrumental and locomotive actions, so the loss of proprioceptive input will naturally disrupt control of gestures. On this view, gestures could be re-established only under conscious control. Another possibility is that even if gestures are primarily linguistic in nature, the control of gestural movement requires (as a necessary condition) either an intact motor system (a body-schema system) or some other form of motor control (for example, Ian's use of vision to substitute for proprioceptive feedback). In other words, even if gesture is not a form of instrumental or locomotive movement, gesture nonetheless may use or build upon the system that controls such movement. A third possibility is that gestures require good postural support—something that Ian did not have in the first months of his illness (Cole 1995). On this view it was only when he was able to maintain a stable posture that gestures returned. This would not necessarily entail that the control system for instrumental or locomotive movement is a necessary condition for gesture, although postural control would be.

When Ian regained control of his posture and movements, he also regained his ability to gesture. From all appearances, however, his gestures seem to take care of themselves, approaching something like spontaneous movement. These spontaneous gestures are relatively small movements made in an environment in which Ian feels safe. He does have to expend cognitive effort to make larger gestures, like an extended arm movement, which might require him to brace his body to maintain posture. He also uses vision to make precise gestures that require some targeting, for example, two hands coming together or a hand up to the head.

At McNeill's lab we systematically observed Ian's gestures under three conditions (Cole *et al.* 1998; Cole, Gallagher, and McNeill 2002; Gallagher, Cole, and McNeill 2001):

- first, while narrating from memory the story of an animated color cartoon that he was previously shown, both with and without vision of his hands;
- second, as his gaze was monitored with an eye-tracking device, while describing the route that he had followed to enter the lab building; and

- third, while conversing with the experimenters when vision of his hands was occluded.

Narration

During the narration task, with his hands within his visual field, Ian made numerous meaningful gestures well synchronized with his co-expressive speech, confirming that he had the ability to produce gestures. His gestures looked essentially identical to non-neuropathic performance, and further computerized analysis of videos confirmed this.

To discover whether Ian controlled his gestures using visual feedback, a blind was placed in such a way as to block his view of his hands (Fig. 5.1). Asked again to narrate the cartoon story, however, Ian did not gesture at all; his hands remained clasped in his lap. He explained this lack of gesture as a decision he made not to gesture because he was not sure of the space his hands were in and whether it would be safe to move them. Since Ian has no sense of touch, he cannot tell whether his hands are hitting something unless he sees them. He often places them in his lap and uses the sensations of warmth to locate them without vision.

When we assured him that it was safe to move his hands and again placed him in the blind situation, and, without cueing either form or timing, requested him to gesture, Ian did gesture. Once he allowed his gestures to get under way, they seemed to have a mind of their own. They did not appear to be under his attentional control, and they were consistent with normal measurements in terms of timing, relative to his speech acts, and shape. In this blind condition he was able to perform

FIG. 5.1.   Ian Waterman under the blind.

gestures similar to those seen without the blind, his meaningful hand movements synchronized with co-expressive speech. In this case, the gestures were smaller and showed some slight loss of coordination of the two hands. Despite these differences, Ian evidently had not lost the ability to perform and integrate gestures with speech in the absence of vision.

That the timing of his gestures *vis-à-vis* his speech acts (measured on a scale of hundreds of msecs.) remains intact can be explained by appealing to three factors. *Prosodic feedback* in speech provides a target for hand motion peak. This partly explains Ian's ability to synchronize speech and gesture around discursive points for maximal contextual emphasis. *Semiotic feedback*, that is, the fact that manual and speech modes of semiotic representation express the same underlying idea unit, keeps the two modes moving together. The co-expressiveness of the two modes (gesture and speech) contribute to their synchronization. Finally, *pragmatic feedback* relating to the communicative situation, the meter or cadence of the conversation, which may also involve response gestures made by one's interlocutor, may offer important cues for maintaining synchronization.

The spatial organization of Ian's gestures is especially important. *Morphokinetic* aspects of movement, that is, those aspects of movement having to do with shape or form regardless of spatial location, can be distinguished from *topokinetic* aspects, those that have to do with precision in regard to spatial location and accurate movement to targeted external points (Cole and Paillard 1995). Instrumental movement depends to a high degree on topokinetic precision. To pick up a glass or catch a ball I need to be able to move my hand to a target position in the surrounding space. In most instances gesture requires morphokinetic accuracy, but not a high degree of topokinetic accuracy. That is, it needs to be shaped in the right way to communicate meaning, but there are very few topokinetic constraints placed on gesture. Under the blind condition Ian would not be able to perform instrumental movements requiring sustained spatial accuracy. His sense of topo-kinetic space is highly degraded without visual guidance, and the topokinetic aspects of his gestures show a good deal of inaccuracy, in contrast to controls. For example, if he is signifying a square by drawing it in the air, the shapes that he makes for the square will be morphokinetically correct, but his fingers may fail to meet up at the beginning and end of the process of sketching the square (e.g. as in Fig. 5.2). Despite this topokinetic inaccuracy, he can make movements in space with some degree of accuracy to differentiate meanings; for example, to the right for one meaning, to the left for a contrasting meaning.

Is the difference between morphokinetic and topokinetic movement sufficient to explain Ian's ability to perform gestures? That is, is he better at gestures simply because they do not require a high degree of topokinetic accuracy? Ian's perform-ance in the blind condition suggests that something more is involved. Try this experiment. Sit at a table with your hand placed underneath it, out of view. Make a fist and then extend your index finger. Curl it back into the fist and then extend it again. The mechanisms that allow you to tell when your finger is extended or not, or even that you have made a fist, simply do not work for Ian. If you can imagine not

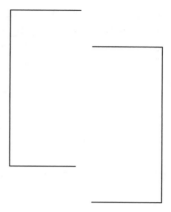

FIG. 5.2.   Morphokinetic accuracy with topokinetic inaccuracy

knowing whether your finger is extended or curled, then you can start to imagine the difficulty involved in attaining even morphokinetic accuracy when you are deprived of both proprioceptive and visual feedback. Yet Ian's gestures reflected, with a significant degree of morphokinetic precision, the meaning he was attempting to convey, suggesting that meaning itself plays a part in how those gestures are shaped and how his hands move in gesture. Ian's gestures are also precisely synchronized with the verb phrases he uses to describe various events.

One other difference is to be noted. McNeill (1992) distinguishes between two perspectives from which gestures can be made within a narrative. (1) Character viewpoint (CV) gestures: these are gestures made as if from the perspective of the character being described. (2) Observer viewpoint (OV) gestures: gestures made from the perspective of the narrator. When Ian makes gestures that are within his visual field, he makes both CV and OV gestures. Under the blind, however, CV gestures disappear. CV gestures have meaning as mimicry. In effect, they are the re-enactments that reproduce the original instrumental actions of someone else in a virtual (imaginary) space, as discussed in the motor theory of gesture. In so far as they involve the reproduction of instrumental actions they are based on a kind of action that requires topokinetic control, for which Ian requires visual guidance.

In summary, under the blind, Ian's gestures were normal in their morphokinetic properties and in regard to timing vis-à-vis speech acts. They are degraded with regard to topokinetic precision, and this prevents the formation of CV gestures that are related to instrumental action.

Monitored Gaze

In a second test, Ian was equipped with an eye-tracking device—an apparatus worn on the head (permitting free movement) that continuously pinpoints the locus of the gaze and superimposes this onto a video of the scene (Fig. 5.3). We asked Ian to

00:03:46;03

FIG. 5.3.   Ian Waterman with eye-tracking device.

describe, with the aid of maps and floor plans, how he had arrived at the lab that morning. While recounting his journey and arrival most of his gestures involved pointing at the map or floor plan, with his gaze directed at the same place as he was pointing. At numerous times, however, while making well-formed, synchronous, and large gestures, his gaze shifted to his interlocutor who was seated approximately 90 degrees to his side. When he broke off his deictic indexing at these moments, he performed non-deictic metaphoric gestures, and his gaze on these occasions shifted totally away from his hands. Several times the gaze-tracking cross-hairs zeroed in on the interlocutor's face while Ian's gestures remained in perfect synchrony with his speech and were semantically appropriate for non-deictic comments—normal gestures in every way.

On these occasions it would have been difficult for Ian to have guided his gestural movements with peripheral vision. That these gestures were relatively large ones suggests that visual guidance is not required for size of gesture, although it is possible that some cognitive control of posture is required.

Conversation

Ian himself believes that some of his gestures, like his other movements, are under his conscious control. In conversation he explained how he makes gestures to 'add drama' and to help him get his ideas across when words seem insufficient. His sense is that he selects gestures from a pre-established repertoire, organizes and arranges them in a sequence, and in general follows a deliberate, self-aware procedure of gesture-building. There is some reason to think that in this case Ian's phenomenology does not reflect what is actually happening.

At one point during the conversation Ian displayed how he deliberately manufactures gestures. His demonstration actually provided a good example of a transition from a normal meaning-controlled gesture to a more self-conscious intention-controlled gesture. The conversation took place when his hands were visually occluded; and he was unable visually to monitor his movement. The gestures during the conversation were all metaphoric; thus formulation of meaning was the primary factor. It was striking to see the change of character of the gestures as Ian began to make them on purpose, as part of his display of what he believes he normally does. The displayed gestures appeared to be self-consciously constructed and quite different from the series of spontaneous gestures that had preceded the display, which clearly were not deliberate performances. Subsequent analysis showed that spontaneous gestures were small, quick, and well synchronized with fluent, non-drawled speech; they appeared unwitting and thus quite normal in their meaning and timing. The displayed and deliberately constructed gestures were slow and large in comparison, and the speech accompanying them was drawled to make the words and gestures coincide. In this regard Ian is not different from normal. A normal subject who focused his attention on his gestures instead of on the meaning expressed by the gestures would also manifest this sort of self-conscious construction of gesture.

Two Interpretations: Motor and Communication Theories of Gesture

There are two possible interpretations of Ian's performance in these experiments. First, it is possible that Ian's gestures are to some extent under his conscious control, in the same way as his instrumental and locomotive movements are. Some of Ian's locomotive control (some aspects of his walking, for example) have become automated, through repetition, becoming part of a habitual, perceptual-motor practice. Thus, although Ian consciously monitors his walking, some of what started out to be the exclusive conscious center of attention (much as it is in the case of a toddler still learning to walk) has become much more peripheral, and perhaps non-conscious. This is consistent with Ian's reports that walking, especially on flat and familiar surfaces, requires little monitoring. With respect to gestures, it is consistent with

- Ian's report that he consciously decided to practice gesturing after his illness,
- his report that he still consciously initiates the gesture, and
- the observation that certain aspects of his current gesturing appear to be automated in the same way as his walking.

On this first interpretation, consistent with a motor theory of gesture, we would be led to the conclusion that gesturing is primarily a matter of movement, falling within the domain of sensory-motor behavior. Ian, an exceptional case with respect to sensory-motor control, would have consciously to monitor his speech and his gesticulation to keep them in synchrony. Although this seems unlike the normal case where there is usually no conscious monitoring of gesture, it would imply that in the normal case gestural movement, like instrumental and locomotive movement, comes under the control of the body schema system. Because Ian has lost most of his body-schema functions, he is required to take up those functions on the level of the body image. Gestural movement is simply one of those functions that he controls in that way, and in that sense, his gestures would not be formed in the normal way.

There are three problems with this interpretation. First, consciously controlled gestures are different from normal in launch and timing. But even under the blind Ian's gestures are normal in this regard. Second, at one point Ian is clearly unaware of his gestures—which continue to be normal for timing and morphokinesis;[4] and this contrasts with his conscious gesturing when he attempts to explain how he gestures. Finally, according to the motor theory of gesture, Ian would have difficulty with gesture in the same way that he has difficulty with instrumental action requiring accuracy in Cartesian space. Since Ian can perform gestures normally and fluently under conditions in which instrumental action would be difficult or impossible for him, namely, without visual feedback, gestural movement and instrumental movement cannot be the same with regard to control mechanisms.

The important distinction to be made here is between (1) instrumental action (which, along with locomotive action, is a kind of motor action with which Ian has problems) and (2) expressive or communicative action—action with meaning mapped onto it. The hypothesis put forward by Streeck and Kita's motor theory claims that gesture belongs to the same class of instrumental movements as reaching, grasping, and so forth. The experiments with Ian suggest an alternative hypothesis: that gesture is not a form of instrumental action but a form of expressive action; not a reproduction of an original instrumental behavior, but a different kind of action altogether. Character-viewpoint gestures have some relation to instrumental action, but we should think of them as gestural movements that have instrumental actions embedded or represented within them. This would be different from saying that they are instrumental movements in the service of the communicative act. Gesture is not a form of instrumental action that takes place within a virtual or narrative space. Rather, gesture is an action that helps to *create* the narrative space that is shared in the communicative situation. This suggests that

---

[4] At one point during conversation in the blind condition Ian's hands began to form gestures that were clearly outside his awareness. This was made clear because during the first 20 seconds of the conversation he performed a string of gestures (fourteen in all) and then said, revealingly, 'and I'm starting to use my hands now' while continuing to gesture. His gestures were non-exceptional during the 20 seconds when they were outside his awareness, and they looked and timed with speech exactly as all other non-conscious gestures did.

it is part of and is controlled by a linguistic/communicative system rather than a motor system.

Ian's capacity for gesture under non-feedback conditions, where he is incapable of making accurate instrumental movements in a seamless and complex progression, suggests that communicative action involves a direct mapping of meaning onto space and motion, and that gestures are not reducible to instrumental actions. The fact that Ian's gestures can be decoupled from visual monitoring and can be performed without sensory feedback of any kind, and yet remain relatively accurate in time and form, suggests that gestural movements are controlled by a system that is in some measure independent from the system that controls the same muscles in instrumental actions. Gestures may share the final motor pathway to the spinal level, but is it possible that the control of that pathway is different at a higher level of the neuroaxis? (I return to this issue below.) The evidence for this goes beyond issues pertaining to the accuracy of timing and form, to the fact that gestural programs appear to unfold with speech in a way that is not reflectively controlled, and thus, in a way not seen in Ian's instrumental acts. It seems clear that control of gestures cannot be a matter of body-schematic processes, since Ian, who has lost body-schema functions, is still capable of normal gesture. It is also clear, from the experiments in the blind situation, that gestural movement goes beyond Ian's practice of controlling his movement by means of conscious visual control, that is, by means of his body image.

A second interpretation is that Ian's gesturing is close to normal. That is, that Ian's gesturing is not consciously controlled, but is much more integrated with linguistic behavior, and controlled by factors that go beyond ordinary sensory-motor control. This interpretation is consistent with

- the fact that the timing of Ian's gestures is normal, that is, normally integrated with his speech acts, something which is unlikely to be the case if gestures were under conscious control, and
- the fact that even under blind conditions, his gestures are normal with regard to their morphokinetic properties.

This interpretation also allows for the possibility that gestures are controlled neither by the body image in Ian's case, nor by the body schema in the normal case. It suggests that the control of gestural movement is primarily and essentially tied to linguistic and communicative processes. I will refer to this as the *communicative theory of gesture*.

According to the communicative theory of gesture, gesture is essentially language and functions primarily in communicative contexts. It is not a motor supplement to language, or something added on to speech to enhance meaning. This theory of gesture is best expressed by David McNeill, who claims that 'gesture and language are one system'.

[G]estures are movements that occur only during speech, are synchronized with linguistic units, are parallel in semantic and pragmatic functions to the synchronized linguistic units, perform text functions like speech, dissolve like speech in aphasia, and develop together with speech in children. Because of these similarities, a strong case can be made for regarding gestures and speech as part of a common psychological structure.   (McNeill 1992: 351)

The claim made in the communicative theory of gesture is not that Ian has *no* conscious control over his gestures. The kind of conscious control that he has may be seen in the first experiment when, in the blind condition, he refrained from gesturing at first. Ian explained that he did not gesture because he was unsure of the space under the blind and he was concerned about the 'safety' involved in his movements. Just in such situations a certain kind of conscious control is introduced. Ian can consciously inhibit gestures in those cases where he does not feel safe in gesturing. He has, one might say, a veto power over gesture. This is not the same as saying that Ian consciously initiates gesture. In situations when the precise nature of the surrounding environment is unknown, for the sake of safety Ian simply does not allow the gesture to get started, he inhibits his natural tendency to gesture. Otherwise gesturing starts and continues without his conscious monitoring. In this regard, Ian is absolutely normal. Think of yourself in a tight position next to a very hot stove. If your gestures would take you too close to that stovetop it is likely that you would carry on your conversation without gestures.[5]

None of this is inconsistent with the fact that we sometimes deliberate about a gesture and intentionally control it. In such cases, however, gesture is still controlled differently from instrumental actions directed at objects. The experiments with Ian provide two instances that show this. First, in the circumstance of displaying how he makes gestures (in the third experiment), by consciously deciding to present the meaning slowly, as a display, Ian needed to control both the speech and gesture, in unison, by stretching out the presentation of meaning that was passing through each of them. That is, he was able to control both his speech-making and his gesture-making by presenting an idea slowly. It is important to keep in mind, however, that these displayed gestures were created without proprioceptive or visual feedback of any kind. Whatever conscious control Ian had over the

---

[5] As I indicated, Ian's gestures disappeared during the first few months following the onset of his illness, when he was still trying to gain control over his movements. There may be a variety of ways to explain this. Ian was extremely cautious about moving at all. He didn't know precisely what to expect at first since a minor movement might end up (or end him up) in an unexpected position. In such circumstances, it is not unlikely that one would exercise one's veto power over gesture. Also, to some extent, gesture depends upon a stable posture. If one is walking a tightrope and trying to maintain balance, one might very well speak, but one would probably not gesture. It might be the case that Ian had to re-establish control over movement and posture before gesture could be brought back. Ian reports that he had to practice gesture in order to recover it. What does this mean precisely? Does it mean that (1) he did not know how to make a gesture and he had to reinvent it? That is, he knew what a gesture was but could not accomplish it unless he planned out the whole thing—in that case, reinventing the motor elements of the gesture. Or (2) he knew how to make a gesture but had to practice doing it because of motor and postural instability. That is, for example, when he made a gesture he consciously had to practice adjusting his posture to maintain balance. This second option might *seem* very much like reinventing and practicing gesture (and being conscious of the gestural movement)—but in some sense it would be practicing precisely the other kind of motor control. It is difficult to discriminate between these possibilities in retrospect. What is clear is that the constraints on locomotive and instrumental movement were very different after the neuropathy, and in that motor context Ian had to do some reinvention with respect to gesture.

presentation, it was neither visual nor proprioceptive control. It is the case, however, that even in displaying a gesture, Ian is still involved in a communicative performance. His deliberate slowing down of speech and gesture in unison, if anything, reinforces the point of the communicative interpretation: gestures are controlled by a linguistic or communicative system in a way that is different from the control of instrumental or locomotive actions. Gestures, whether deliberately formed or not, always involve the mapping of meaning onto a linguistic space.

Second, as noted, at least at one point during conversation in the blind condition Ian's hands began to form gestures that, according to his own report, were clearly outside his awareness. During this time his gestures were non-exceptional, and they looked and timed with speech exactly as all other gestures did.

On the communicative theory, gesture is not a motor supplement to speech. Nor is it subordinate to speech, but is semantically and performatively coordinated with it. The conversion of 'a certain motor essence' into gesture, suggested by Merleau-Ponty, is not a conversion that allows for gesture simply to remain part of movement. Ian Waterman shows us that gesture is in a different class of actions than instrumental or locomotive actions. For Ian, self-organizing motility breaks down. Yet, the self-organizing intentionality of language remains intact, and gesture, temporarily disrupted by Ian's illness, re-establishes itself to a higher degree than his capacity for instrumental or locomotive movement.[6] According to the communicative interpretation the reason gesture can be re-established with such proficiency is that gesture, as a movement concerned with the construction of *significance* rather than with *doing* something, is organized primarily by the linguistic-communicative context.

Further evidence that puts pressure on the motor theory of gesture, but both supports and qualifies the communicative theory, may be found in studies of gesture in two other groups: those with congenital absence of limbs, and those with congenital blindness. Ramachandran and Blakeslee (1998) report the case of a subject with congenital absence of limbs, Mirabel, an individual born without arms who reports a remarkable, vivid experience of gestures with phantom limbs:

Dr: 'How do you know that you have phantom limbs?'
M: 'Well, because as I'm talking to you, they are gesticulating. They point to objects when I point to things. . . . When I walk, doctor, my phantom arms don't swing like normal arms, like your arms. They stay frozen on the side like this' (her stumps hanging straight down). 'But when I talk, my phantoms gesticulate. In fact, they're moving now as I speak.'

Mirabel suggests here that her phantoms are not active in locomotive action, although they clearly are in communicative contexts that involve gesture. Peter Brugger (private correspondence; see Brugger *et al.* 2000) has worked with a subject, AZ, a 44-year-old female, born without arms or legs. Like Ramachandran's patient she appears to use her phantom arms and hands for gesturing, but not for

---

[6] As noted above, this is also the case for other deafferented subjects.

instrumental action. In fact, AZ has upper arms, and they gesticulate 'wildly' as she talks, so that the phantoms seem to be moving in coordination with the stumps. The gesticulation of the stumps appears wild only because what one sees is an incomplete gesture, and the least important part of it—that is, one does not see the hands.

The experiments with Ian Waterman suggest that gesture is possible without either proprioceptive or visual feedback. Of course Ian had experienced motor feedback prior to the neuropathy, and except in the experimental blind condition, continues to have visual perception of his body. The fact that aplasics gesture with phantom limbs may also suggest that gesturing does not depend on specific peripheral feedback. This is a complex question, however. The possibility of gesture in cases of aplasic phantoms does not entirely rule out the involvement of innate mechanisms associated with a body schema (Ch. 4).

The idea that gesturing is primarily part of a communicative process, however, is qualified by observations of subjects who are congenitally blind. Iverson and Goldin-Meadow (1998) report on a study of congenitally blind children and adolescents who gesture despite the fact that they never have had a visual model. All the blind speakers who were studied produced gestures that could not be differentiated from sighted speakers. Moreover, gestures were used even in situations where blind subjects were communicating to other blind subjects. The experimenters clearly distinguished between gestures and instrumental action that involved the manipulation or the exploration of objects. This raises two questions. First, is gesture an entirely learned behavior? Even if certain aspects of gestures are culturally determined, the fact that congenitally blind subjects use gestures (and even use them to communicate with other blind subjects) suggests that *the fact of gesturing* is more a fact of nature than of nurture.

Second, and perhaps more to the point, what are gestures for? Are they strictly for communication? If congenitally blind subjects use gestures in communicative activities even with other blind subjects, and thus in cases where, unseen, they accomplish nothing for the communicative process, why do they make them? The experiment with Ian Waterman pushes this one step further. Under the blind, and without sensory feedback, Ian has no explicit or external awareness of his produced gestures. Sometimes he is clearly unconscious that he is making them. In this case, what does he gain from his gestures? Merleau-Ponty tells us that language *accomplishes* thought. It seems quite possible, then, that gesture, as language, assists in that accomplishment. Even if we are not explicitly aware of our gestures, and even in circumstances where they contribute nothing to the communicative process, they may contribute implicitly to the shaping of our cognition.[7] Ian, as well as persons who are congenitally blind, and persons with aplasic phantoms, provide good

---

[7] The question here is not about access to gestures, but about the cognitive effects gestures might have even if we have no conscious access to them. This is an extremely difficult question to answer if we think of cognition (thought) as a completely internal process that happens in a disembodied mind. It may be, however, that certain aspects of what we call the mind just are in fact nothing other than what we tend to call expression, that is, occurrent linguistic practices ('internal speech'), gesture, and expressive movement.

evidence for that idea. Gesture as language may serve communication with others, but it may at the same time accomplish something within ourselves, capturing or generating meaning that shapes our thought.[8]

These two aspects of gesture, its *inter*-subjective (communicative) and *intra*-subjective (cognitive) functions, may be difficult to pry apart. The intra-subjective function of gesture brings us back full circle to the idea that embodied movement shapes cognition. These empirical studies also make it clear that one does not have to be conscious of embodied functions for them effectively to accomplish thought. Gesture and language work in a prenoetic manner.

An Integrative Theory of Gesture

The empirical studies and our considerations here lead to a clarification of the precise way that gesture and language remain embodied. On the one hand, the type of movement that gesture involves is irreducible to movement controlled exclusively by body-schema or body-image processes. We can thus distinguish between four different types of movement: reflex, locomotive, instrumental, and expressive movement (Table 5.1).

Gesture, as it is activated in the communicative setting, is an expressive movement that is not consciously thought out beforehand. It contributes to the accomplishment of thought; it enables communication. In these regards it seems to transcend its purely motor aspects. 'Gestures are not just movements and can never be fully explained in purely kinesic terms. They are not just arms waving in the air, but *symbols that exhibit meanings* in their own right' (McNeill 1992: 105). The

TABLE 5.1. *Four types of movement*

Type of movement	Examples	Primary control
Reflex	Babkin reflex, sneeze	automatic motor programs
Locomotive	walking, sitting	body schema (body image in IW)
Instrumental	reaching, grasping	body schema (body image in IW)
Expressive	pointing, gesturing	cognitive-semantic and communication

[8] Goldin-Meadow (1999) reviews a number of studies that support the idea that gestural movement shapes thought. She summarizes these results: 'Gesture helps speakers retrieve words from memory. Gesture reduces cognitive burden, thereby freeing up effort that can be allocated to other tasks. For example, pointing improves young children's performance on counting tasks particularly if the pointing is done by the children themselves. As another example, gesturing while explaining a math task improves performance on a simultaneously performed word recall task. Gesturing thus appears to increase resources available to the speaker, perhaps by shifting the burden from verbal to spatial memory. [...] Gesture may also provide a route through which learners can access new thoughts. For example, children participating in science lessons frequently use gesture to foreshadow the ideas they themselves eventually articulate in speech, perhaps needing to express those ideas in a manual medium before articulating them in words.'

thing that makes gesture more than movement is the fact that gesture is language, or, as McNeill suggests, 'gesture and language are one system' (p. 2). On the other hand, and it would be wrong to lose track of this, gesture is nonetheless movement. Gesture and language remain embodied in some important ways.

Thus, a fuller explanation of gesture is to be found in a theory that integrates, in very specific ways, the insights gained in both motor and communicative approaches. Normally, one requirement for gesture is that there be some knowledge in the system concerning the location of the hands relative to each other and relative to the rest of the body. Topokinetic properties of gestures depend on position feedback that is not linguistic. In the normal case proprioception provides the feedback necessary for locating our hands, even with our eyes closed. For Ian Waterman vision provides the feedback that he requires to know where his body parts are. Lacking proprioception and vision, Ian is, for the most part, unable to locate his hands except by memory—he thinks they are wherever he last saw them. With sustained subsequent movement, without visual feedback, he loses track of them. One can see this under the experimental blind condition. The topokinetic aspects of the gesture start to go off track and eventually the positions of Ian's hands are lost to him. This starts to interfere with other aspects of gesture, such as its morphokinetic properties.

The case of Ian Waterman helps to define an *integrative theory of gesture*—one that integrates aspects of motor and communicative theories of gesture in a very precise way. Specifically, an integrative theory understands gesture to be, first, *embodied* (constrained and enabled by motoric possibilities); second, *communicative* (pragmatically intersubjective); and third, *cognitive* (contributing to the accomplishment of thought, shaping the mind). To make this more precise, we can distinguish several different aspects of gesturing, and identify the different roles played by motor, communicative, and cognitive processes.

- *Initiation of gesture* is generally unconscious and tied to cognitive and communicative requirements, but in some cases conscious control exercises veto power over gestural movement.
- *Launching and timing* is integrated with communicative and cognitive factors; tied to semantics and the pragmatics of the situation.
- *Morphokinesis* is integrated with communicative and cognitive factors tied to semantics.
- *Topokinesis* is dependent primarily on body-schematic processes and proprioception in the normal case.

The term 'cognitive factor' does not imply conscious control. The empirical studies we have cited make it clear that one does not consciously control the timing or morphokinesis of gesture. More generally, we do not have to be conscious of embodied functions for them to effectively accomplish thought. Gesture and language shape cognition in a prenoetic manner.

So, on the one hand, with respect to launching, timing, and morphokinesis, communicative and cognitive processes win out. And to the extent that communicative and cognitive factors govern gesture, it is irreducible to pure movement. On the other hand, however, gesture is not something that transcends the body in any complete sense. It is inevitably constrained by the requirements of motor control. Specifically, gestures do not stay on track for very long without some form of motor feedback that allows the system to know where the hands are in relation to each other and to the body.

When Ian lost proprioceptive feedback he was unable to update or to access the central motor programs responsible for controlled movement. In the absence of proprioceptive feedback, however, central motor programs may continue to exist.[9]

It is possible that links centrally made between a cognitive-linguistic system and hand movement may be involved in gestural control, both normally and in Ian. Such links may be analogous to those that exist between the visuo-oculomotor system and arm movements. For example, in experiments that involve eye-tracking, the latency of onset of smooth pursuit of a moving target by the eyes is shorter, and the velocity of smooth eye-tracking higher (before saccadic movements) when the visual target is moved by the subject's hand, than if the target is moved by an external device. This is the case for control subjects and for Ian and another deafferented subject (Vercher et al. 1996). This suggests a non-conscious and proprioception-independent connection or coordination at the level of central motor commands for hand and eye movement. In another experiment the relative extent to which Ian was able to use different signals from his visuo-oculomotor system to improve accuracy of arm movements was shown (Blouin et al. 1996). Ian was asked to track a visual target eccentrically to the left with his eyes and then move his unseen arm to the same place. He was able to do this better if the eyes were moved to the target in a short saccade than if he moved his eyes slowly or, with eyes still, judged the eccentricity by movement of the target across his visual field. This suggests that he can calibrate arm movement from eye-movement command, though, again, not at a conscious level.

These examples demonstrate that Ian is able to use motor command in one domain to improve motor performance in another. In the first experiment arm movement improved eye-tracking and in the second, eye movement improved the accuracy of arm reach. Such visuo-oculomotor experiments provide evidence of a cross-domain and non-conscious interaction between motor programs. Language generation and cognition might constrain or enable the control of gestural move-ment in a similar manner (Jonathan Cole, private communication). As Ian speaks and gestures, brain regions responsible for the generation of language and thought may be contributing to control of gestural movement by enabling access to motor programs that underpin his gesture stream. There is good evidence from

---

[9] See Ch. 2. Again, this is difficult to ascertain. Without feedback most motor programs seem not to work. It is possible that they degrade with time. It is also possible, however, that they do not disappear completely. Ian reports that movements were easier to relearn if they were well established before the neuropathy. Even if such programs continue to exist they may not be able to be accessed in the absence of proprioception. The fact that the mechanical constraints of movement are also different complicates the issue. See Gallagher and Cole (1995) for further discussion.

neurophysiology and neuropsychology to suggest the establishment of such relations between language centers and motor areas in the human brain (see the next section below). Consistent with the experiments on eye-tracking and arm movement, it may be possible that language circumvents, in some degree (although not entirely), the purely motoric/proprioceptive aspects of feedback and access to motor programs. It is possible that the semantic, communicative (pragmatic), and cognitive aspects of gesture provide sufficient feedback to sustain control of gestural movement in regard to timing and morphokinesis. Nonetheless, to the extent that gesture depends on a link to motor programs it is still constrained at the mechanical or bottom end, or more precisely, in those aspects that normally depend on the body schema. In addition, in Ian there are specific engineering problems pertaining to postural readiness and the changed mechanics of movement and that are reflected as constraints on gesture.[10] Here some version of the motor theory is inescapable. Gesture is not purely a cognitive-communicative phenomenon; it requires motor control, and is thus embodied in a very basic way.

There is thus a certain tension between the semantic-pragmatic aspects of language and embodied movement. For example, McNeill (1992: 19) indicates that the method used by the gesture to convey meaning is 'fundamentally different from that of [spoken] language'. Although gesture and speech are performed in a constant and synchronized temporal relation, with gesture slightly anticipating speech (p. 25), gesture has a temporal structure different from linear forms of speech or written text. Gesture (considered from the point of view of semantics) is close to instantaneous and expresses an image analogically by being spatial and thus involving the order of simultaneity. Speech (or written text) is linear and segmented, distributing across a successive structure the meaning of something, which might be a relatively momentary event. Yet it is also clear that, despite the simultaneity involved in a gestural image, gesture involves a development of successive stages, and this is due to the fact that it involves movement and not just semantics. The same can be said for speech, since at some level speech is itself an embodied gesticulation.[11] McNeill has explicated the microgenesis of speech and gesture from a primitive stage or 'growth point' through the kinesic stroke where they coincide semantically, pragmatically, and motorically (p. 246).

Like movement, gesture is a prenoetic performance. Merleau-Ponty reminds us: 'What we have said earlier about the "representation of movement" must be repeated concerning the verbal image: I do not need to visualize external space and my own body in order to move one within the other.' Of course, Ian Waterman is a rare exception to this. Ian does have to visualize external space and his own body in order to move one within the other. But this is not the case for his gesturing.

---

[10] My thanks to Jonathan Cole for making these points clear to me (private correspondence).

[11] Speech actually is a phonetic gesticulation. 'The spoken word is a genuine gesture, and it contains its meaning in the same way as the gesture contains its' (Merleau-Ponty 1962: 183). Vocal gesticulation is 'a contraction of the throat, a sibilant emission of air between the tongue and teeth, a certain way of bringing the body into play suddenly allows itself to be invested with a *figurative significance* which is conveyed outside us' (p. 194).

Merleau-Ponty continues: 'In the same way I do not need to visualize the word in order to know and pronounce it. It is enough that I possess its articulatory and acoustic style as one of the modulations, one of the possible uses of my body' (1962: 180). In the case of instrumental or locomotive movement, this self-organizing intentionality depends on the implicit workings of the body schema. For Ian Waterman this particular self-organizing motility breaks down. Yet the self-organizing intentionality of language, including gesture, remains intact. This can only mean, as we have tried to make clear, that the movement on which language depends, that is, expressive movement, is different from the movement organized primarily by body schemas.

In any particular case, the system that guides the movement of gesture and language includes the particular semantic and pragmatic contexts of cognition and communication. The difference between reaching out to pick up a glass (instrumental action normally controlled by body schema, or in Ian's case, by the body image) and formulating a gesture to signify the action of picking up a glass, will depend to some extent on the fact that the gesture serves an entirely different function than the actual grasping—a cognitive and possibly a communicative function that requires the generation and expression of meaning. The gesture may for just that reason differ in its mechanical recipe from the instrumental action. The meaning and the communicative situation call forth the gesture; the relevant feedback for that gesture will not be proprioceptive or body schematic, but cognitive and linguistic. Ian Waterman, who, in a blind and aproprioceptive condition, is unable to locate his hands, nonetheless expresses and creates meaning with them, because they are moving in synchrony with this vocal expression, and are parallel with his semantic and pragmatic intentions.

The body materializes language by means of movement that is already expressive. Like language itself, expressive movement must be both natural and conventional, shaped by innate mechanisms that allow for the onset of communicative behavior, and by cultural determinants that define different languages and linguistic practices.[12] Although speech and gesture depend on movement as a necessary condition, they nonetheless *transcend* motility and move us into a semantic space that is also a pragmatic, intersubjective, intercorporeal space. Language, in so far as it involves an 'open and indefinite power of giving significance' transforms and transcends the natural powers of the body (Merleau-Ponty 1962: 194), without leaving the body behind.[13] Thus, language is irreducible to either the purely noetic

---

[12] Gesture is less conventional than speech, and less constrained by the rules that spoken language must follow. McNeill points out that because gestures 'are unregulated, integrating them with [spoken] language allows free play to idiosyncratic imagination in the midst [of] an act of social standardization. . . . The gesture is the injection of personality into language' (1992: 251).

[13] Gesture transcends movement and the body. We mean this in the same sense as Merleau-Ponty indicated: 'The use a man is to make of his body is transcendent in relation to that body as a mere biological entity. . . . Behaviour creates meanings which are transcendent in relation to the anatomical apparatus, and yet immanent to the behaviour as such, since it communicates itself and is understood' (1962: 189). And again, 'the human body is defined in terms of its property of appropriating, in an indefinite series of discontinuous acts, significant cores which transcend and transfigure its natural powers. This act of transcendence is first encountered in the acquisition of a pattern of behavior, then

or the purely motoric, even though it shapes thought and depends upon motor ability. Although, as Merleau-Ponty suggests, the body 'lends itself' to gesture (p. 183) gesture is never a mere motor phenomenon; it draws the body into psychological and communicative orders defined by their own pragmatic rules. Meaning overflows the movement that is involved in gesture and speech, and, just so far, language transcends embodiment at the same time that it depends on it.

Expressive Movement From the Beginning?

In terms of evolution, did language originate in instrumental movement? This idea would be quite consistent with a motor theory of gesture and language (see e.g. Allot 1992). Is it possible to infer an answer to this question from the biological adaptations that must have accompanied its evolutionary development, adaptations that are still observable? If language organizes an evolutionarily unique system of action control, then comparisons of the language specialization areas in the human nervous system and homologous areas in primates may provide some guidance. Can we say that evolution co-opted the brain areas for linear action control in such a way that manual gestures and the articulatory actions of speech were brought into a single framework of neuro-motor programming?

Consider that, in terms of brain anatomy Broca's area in the human is homologous with areas of the premotor cortex in the primate. We indicated above that there is good evidence from neurophysiology and neuropsychology to suggest the establishment of relations between language centers and motor areas in the human brain (Iverson and Thelen 1999). These relations are explicated in terms of a common brain mechanism responsible for timing of sequential movement and linguistic performance (Ojemann 1984), and the activation of supplementary motor cortex and premotor regions along with the cerebellum and Broca's area in the production of language and movement. There is evidence that Broca's area, a well-known language area of the brain, plays an important role in the generation of coherent sequencing of movement (Iverson and Thelen 1999).

Even in the primate, however, there is behavioral evidence for expressive movement. Animal communication is gestural. It is well known that primates are very sensitive to perceived posture in others, including the posture of humans who work with them. They read meaning into posture and movement; the movement of others, for them, is expressive. The neurophysiological possibility of such expressive movement is understandable if we keep in mind that some of the areas of the brain

in the mute communication of gesture ...' (p. 193). An interesting observation in this respect has been made by Jonathan Cole (2004: 303 n. 1). Some tetraplegics who may have very little instrumental use of their arms and hands, 'have expansive use of their arms and shoulder in gesture of which they are hardly aware. Language seems to need embodied expression and will use whatever parts that move.' He goes on to note that Christopher Reeve recovered a gestural move in his left index finger before consciously driven movement.

responsible for it—premotor cortex in primates, and the premotor cortex and Broca's area in humans—contain mirror neurons and other neural areas of shared representations. Such neural activations correspond to meaning that is intersubjective in the literal sense—it is meaning that is simultaneously shared in the modalities of observation (of others) and action capability (of my own). More generally, the brain areas responsible for planning my own action are the same ones activated during the observation, imaginative simulation, or imitation of the action of others (see Decety and Sommerville 2003; Grezes and Decety 2001; Ruby and Decety 2001). These areas also partially overlap with language production.

Gestures would have been, and still are, both products and active producers of this brain organization. Across evolutionary time-frames, the links between movement, language, and thought would have influenced the structure of the human brain itself.

These are suggestive, but inconclusive observations. We can make similarly inconclusive but suggestive observations if we think about neonate imitation in terms of these issues. We have seen (in Ch. 3) that neonate imitation is not reflex movement. It is clearly not locomotive or instrumental movement either. Imitation of facial gesture is expressive movement; indeed, it is a gesture itself. It is certainly expressive movement from the viewpoint of the person who perceives it. Is it expressive movement from the point of view of the neonate? Following the insight of Merleau-Ponty, we have suggested that gesture helps to accomplish thought. The wrong way to think of expressive movement is to think of it as necessarily expressing something that is internal and already formed—a belief, or thought, or idea. 'What, then, does language [or gesture or expressive action] express, if it does not express thoughts? It presents or rather it *is* the subject's taking up of a position in the world of his meanings' (Merleau-Ponty 1962: 193). In the case of the neonate, we do not have to posit some prior internal cognition that the infant is attempting to express or externalize through imitation. The infant has seen something, a facial gesture, and it is expressing what it has seen by taking up the capacity it has for that expressive movement on its own face. Whether neonate imitation is an instance of a priming effect or something closer to intentional action, it brings the infant into a direct relation with another person and starts them on a course of social interaction. At the earliest stages, the adult's responses to the infant may be what brings the infant into this interaction. By 4–6 weeks, however, imitation is definitely a two-way social interaction in which the child is actively engaged (Rochat 2002)—imitation is a social-communicative (and fully embodied) expression for the infant.

This brings us back to the unresolved question posed in Ch. 3. Do we have a complete explanation of neonate imitation if we frame it exclusively in terms of an innate body schema, and the accompanying sensory-motor concepts of proprioception, intermodal mechanisms, etc.? If imitation is expressive movement, then an explanation limited to terms of an innate body schema is inadequate for an account of imitative behavior. Unless the neonate's gestural imitation remains semantically empty and purely mechanical, the requirements are not fully specified in terms of a motor theory of gesture, or a motor theory of social cognition—theories that reflect what some neuroscientists call 'motor chauvinism'.[14] To the extent that we have shown that expressive movement is not reducible to those forms of movement controlled by body-schematic processes, even if it is embodied and normally requires some limited aspect of body-schematic control, then we are led to conclude that perhaps the greater part of the explanation of neonate imitation is yet to be developed. It would seem that, in conformity with the integrative theory of gesture, neonate imitation of facial gesture also depends on some innate (evolution-prepared) expressive component. Furthermore, expressive movement is expressive only on one condition: that there is already intersubjectivity.

The question we left open concerns the *human* nature of the newborn infant, which is to say, it concerns *human nature*. Even if it were possible to have both a biological embodiment, in the form of a complete human body, and a set of gestures framed for the solipsistic shaping of a mind, without other human persons the system would fall short of being a human person. We return to this issue once more in Ch. 9. For now we can say this. If expressive movement in the form of language transcends the body (to some degree, but not in full), it also returns to the body in the sense that it makes the body move in certain ways. The relation between embodiment and language, however, is a self-reciprocating, self-organizing one only if there is another person. The body generates a gestural expression. It is, however, another person who moves, motivates, and mediates this process. To say that language moves my body is already to say that other people move me.

---

[14] Wolpert, Grahramani, and Flanagan (2001: 487, 493) write: 'From the motor chauvinist's point of view the entire purpose of the human brain is to produce movement. Movement is the only way we have of interacting with the world. All communication, including speech, sign language, gestures and writing, is mediated via the motor system. [...] It could be that the same computational processes underlie action, the perception of action, and social cognition. [...] Although the behavior of others in response to our actions is more noisy and non-linear than the response of our arm to a motor command, computationally they are not fundamentally different.' For a critical discussion of this view from the integrative point of view, see Gallagher, Cole, and McNeill (2002).

PART II

Excursions in Philosophy and Pathology

6

Prenoetic Constraints on Perception and Action

IN the first part of this book, by working my way through a variety of problems and issues that involve developmental, neurological, pathological, and phenomenological dimensions, I have tried to specify and justify some of the terms that can contribute to a conceptual framework rich enough to capture the details of the body's role in shaping consciousness and cognitive experience. The terms of this conceptual framework include innate body schemas, body image, proprioceptive and ecological dimensions of experience, intermodal transformations, senses of ownership and agency, the phenomenal structure of consciousness, and prenoetic performances that affect all these dimensions. The basic idea is that a full picture of human cognition can be drawn only by exposing the details of the various prenoetic processes that constitute the body's contribution to the shaping of experience. One can get to these details neither through phenomenology alone, nor through neuroscientific studies alone, nor through cognitive and behavioral approaches alone. A combined deployment of all these disciplines, however, begins to outline a picture of embodied cognition that is rich and demanding of further investigation.

In pursuing this project a number of things have been clarified.

1. Evidence from both phenomenological and empirical studies supports the distinction between body image and body schema, and this distinction, although limited, is nonetheless useful for specifying details of phenomenal structure and prenoetic processes.
2. Evidence found in developmental studies supports the idea that various aspects of this framework are innate.
3. Evidence found in neurological and pathological studies ties this framework to both specific and global brain processes and complex neuronal structures that have to do with sensory-motor processing, action, imitation, the observation of others, and so on.
4. The details of these multidisciplinary studies can be coordinated in a way that helps to explain a variety of normal and pathological phenomena.

Finally, although much of the discussion has been guided by the scientific and phenomenological literatures, along the way I have raised a number of philosophical issues that touch on the nature of the human person, the structure of consciousness and its onset, the nature of language, and so on.

In the following chapters I will further explore and define this conceptual framework and its implications for some traditional philosophical problems concerning perception, self-reference, and the knowledge of others. I begin, in this chapter, with the mind–body problem, and with specific reference to problems of perception and action.

One important mark of the contemporary cognitive sciences is the explicit and nearly universal rejection of Cartesian dualism. Yet it seems that Cartesianism is not so easy to escape, and often, implicitly, the idea that the body has little to do with cognition continues to haunt all claims to the contrary. In the neurosciences, for instance, it is only recently that one is able to find acknowledgement and explanation of the role played by the body as a whole in the cognitive operations of the brain.[1] More generally, strategies for avoiding mind–body dualism include reducing mental events to brain processes, and replacing intentional explanations with neurophysiological accounts. In such reductionist approaches, however, it is often the case that the body itself is regarded as reducible to brain processes. In some cases the body is reduced to its representation in the somatosensory cortex, or is considered important only to the extent that it provides the raw sensory input required for cognitive computations. In other cases, the body is first treated as an intentional object, an image, a mental representation, and then reduced to neural computations. This elimination of the body in favor of the brain is not so un-Cartesian. Descartes proposed, in his *Meditations*, what is today a commonly accepted view, that 'the mind is not immediately affected by all parts of the body, but only by the brain' (1641: Med. 6. par. 20).

Functionalism, of course, is a major strategy that refuses to attribute to the human body an essential role in cognition. In so far as cognition is reducible to computations, and computations can, in principle, run on silicon-based hardware, nothing like a human body seems to be required for cognition. Cognitive processes can be understood in full abstraction from their physiological embodiment. Indeed, one of the most striking and influential images provided by functionalist philosophy is the image of the brain in the vat (see e.g. Dennett 1981). A disembodied brain, sustained in a chemical bath, seems perfectly capable of experience and cognition as long as the correct neurons are stimulated. On this view, neither body nor environment is required; or at most, for experience to remain close to human experience, one needs only a phantom body in a virtual environment, constituted in neural connections. This image is surprisingly influential even for opponents of functionalism. Thus, Searle, who takes an anti-functionalist view, nonetheless, in championing neurobiology above all else, appeals to the same brain-in-the-vat image.

Even if I am a brain in a vat—that is, even if all of my perceptions and actions in the world are hallucinations, and the conditions of satisfaction of all my externally referring Intentional

---

[1] This chapter is based on a paper I wrote for a workshop at King's College Research Centre at Cambridge University in 1992. At that time I wrote 'In the neurosciences it is difficult to find any acknowledgment or explanation of the role played by the body as a whole in the cognitive operations of the brain' (see Gallagher 1995). Varela, Thompson, and Rosch (1991) had just appeared. Since that time, however, a number of other important works have been published. They include Clark (1997), Damasio (1994), Hurley (1999), and Sheets-Johnstone (1999).

states are, in fact, unsatisfied—nonetheless, I do have the Intentional content that I have, and thus I necessarily have exactly the same Background that I would have if I were not a brain in a vat and had that particular Intentional content. *That* I have a certain set of Intentional states and *that* I have a Background do not logically require that I be in fact in certain relations to the world around me... (1983: 154)

That is, to have the conceptual and even the cultural and skill-based 'Background' necessary for meaningful cognition, the input to neuronal processes need not be embodied, and need not even be reflective of the physical or social environment that normally surrounds and interacts with a human body. Thus, Searle strongly asserts: 'Each of our beliefs must be possible for a being who is a brain in a vat because each of us is precisely a brain in a vat; the vat is a skull and the "messages" coming in are coming in by way of impacts on the nervous system' (1983: 230). According to this picture it would seem that the nervous system holds no special relation to a uniquely human body (see Meijsing (2003) for further discussion of this issue).

In the field of neuroscience, Damasio is one theorist who has recently attempted to provide a corrective to just this Cartesianism. He argues that 'The mind is embodied, in the full sense of the term, not just embrained' (1994: 118). Yet for Damasio, the details of this embodiment are worked out in terms that either inflate the body to the level of ideas in a phenomenologically untenable way, or reduce it to neuronal processes. Body image plays an essential role in his analysis of feeling, for example. Feeling, according to Damasio, depends in some fashion on consciously monitoring one's own body, of experiencing 'what your body is doing *while* thoughts and specific contents roll by'. Changes in bodily states are translated into 'particular mental images that have activated a specific brain system', and feeling an emotion is just the experience of such changes juxtaposed to mental images. 'In other words, a feeling depends on the juxtaposition of an image of the body proper to an image of something else, such as the visual image of a face or the auditory image of a melody' (p. 145). Images, in turn, are reducible to the activation of neurons.

Regardless of how one works out the details of this emphasis on embodiment, there are philosophers still today who are skeptical of the very idea that considerations of embodiment have much to do with cognition. Shoemaker, for example, in the context of his analysis of personal identity, considers the idea that biological embodiment could play an essential role in the constitution of the person to be a 'radical supposition' which he is hesitant to accept (1999: 306). The only thing that gives him pause from ruling it out entirely is the scientific evidence that he finds summarized by Damasio, and this evidence is explicated exclusively in terms of the brain. 'The apparatus of rationality, traditionally presumed to be neocortical, does not seem to work without that of biological regulation, traditionally presumed to be *sub*cortical' (Damasio 1994: 128; cited by Shoemaker 1999: 301). Even in philosophers who acknowledge the importance of a biological approach to such issues, one cannot always be sure that they would admit the 'radical supposition'. Olson, for example, is led to just the opposite conclusion—that 'the notion of a human body is best left out of philosophy, or at least out of discussions of personal identity' (Olson 1997: 150).

There are important exceptions to this theoretical elimination of the body. Merleau-Ponty was ahead of his time in this regard. Several cognitive psychologists, too, have maintained that the body plays an irreducible role in cognition. Neisser (1987), for example, suggests that cognitive schemata often begin their development as meaningful structures at the level of our bodily movements through space, in an interaction between an organism and its environment (also see Medin and Watten-maker 1987; and Piaget 1971). In a very similar vein Johnson (1987: 5) proposes that 'propositional content is possible only by virtue of a complex web of nonproposi-tional schematic structures that emerge from our bodily experience'. Varela, Thompson, and Rosch (1991) and Clark (1997) provide detailed support for this view, maintaining that cognition depends on experience that is informed by a body with various perceptual and motor capacities. In contrast to cognitive approaches that focus on just the brain, 'excluding as "peripheral" the roles of the rest of the body and the local environment' (Clark 1997: p. xii), studies of embodied and situated cognition shift the focus to the body understood as embedded within physical and social environments and situations that motivate thought and action.

The studies presented in the first part of this book support the idea that embodiment plays a central role in structuring experience, cognition, and action. I have tried to show that in the phenomenological and empirical details of experi-ence, the body both shows and hides itself in irreducible ways, and that in these performances it has a structuring effect on experience. In this chapter I explore further the details of how embodiment shapes perception and action. Perceptual experience is generally accepted to be fundamental to other modes of cognition and action. In developmental studies, for example, a close connection between the development of perception and the child's understanding of perceptual content informs a further development of cognitive attitudes such as belief (Gopnik and Meltzoff 1997). Philosophers of mind emphasize that perceptually based mental events are not only foundational for the acquisition of further knowledge and for the development and functioning of other cognitive states, but that, by their internal content-based coherence they provide a foundation for an overall unified subjective experience (see e.g. Bermúdez 1998). Studies of memory, so important for all forms of cognitive activity, suggest that memory is clearly formed along the lines of perceptual experience. Strong claims made by phenomenologists in this regard are supported by experimental evidence. Marbach (1993), for example, following Husserl, contends that episodic memory involves a re-enactment of perception. This is substantiated by findings that neural activity associated with memory occurs in 'the same early sensory cortices where the firing patterns corresponding to perceptual representations once occurred' (Damasio 1994: 101). This idea, which is reminiscent of Tulving's (1983) notion of 'ecphory', is further supported by evidence of neurological differences involved in illusory versus veridical memory, the latter associated with perceptual areas (Schacter et al. 1996).

If perception is basic to other forms of cognition, then to show how the body shapes perception is to outline a framework for building a more general understanding of embodied cognition. The way we understand the basic details of perception will have far-reaching theoretical consequences. In this regard there are certain approaches that correctly emphasize the importance of embodiment for perception, but that are nonetheless mistaken in the details of their analysis. Thus, on some psychological and neuroscientific accounts, normal object perception is misconstrued as complicated by a simultaneous perception of the body. For example, Damasio's 'juxtaposition' of an image of the body proper with images of perceived objects is meant to emphasize the body's contribution to the emotional background of perception. Similarly, Gibsonian psychology contends that the body is proprioceptively co-*perceived* in every objective perception. This idea also finds its way into philosophical analyses that argue for the importance of nonconceptual, embodied content (e.g. Bermúdez 1998). It is possible to show, however, that to understand ecological, proprioceptive, or nonconceptual awareness as an instance of perception in the strict sense of object-perception, or as a juxtaposed co-perception, results in a certain kind of infinite regress.

We can see this by briefly considering the fact that one of the important functions of the body in the contexts of perception and action is to provide the basis for an egocentric (or body-centered) spatial frame of reference (see e.g. Cassam 1995; Evans 1982). Indeed, as we learned in Ch. 2, this egocentric framework is required for the very possibility of action, and for the general structure of perceptual experience. The fact that perception is perspectivally spatial is a fact that depends precisely on an implicit reference to the spatiality of the perceiving body. If one accepts the premise that sense perception of the world is spatially organized by an implicit reference to our bodily framework, the awareness that is the basis for that implicit reference cannot depend on perceptual awareness without the threat of infinite regress.[2] To avoid the infinite regress one requires a pre-reflective bodily awareness that is built into the structures of perception and action, but that is not itself egocentric (see Gallagher 2003b).

Certain phenomenological descriptions avoid this infinite regress. On a Husserlian view, for example, kinesthetic-proprioceptive awareness provides a non-perceptual accompaniment to perception. Kinesthetic experience plays a role in structuring the spatial nature of perception by pragmatically defining the body as the unperceived center of a perspectival (egological) spatial framework necessary for both perceptual coherence and action (Gallagher 1986a; Husserl 1973; Zahavi 1999). More specifically, proprioceptive awareness is not itself a perception of the body as an object; for if it were, it would require an ordering system, a spatial frame of reference, that was independent of the body. Generally speaking, the

---

[2] Bermúdez (1995a: 388) is one of many who point this out: 'If information about the location and orientation of the body is acquired sense-perceptually, then ... it needs to be mapped onto information about the location and orientation of the body.' Similar arguments occur in Sartre (1956) and in Merleau-Ponty (1962). The argument is also implicit in Shoemaker (1984, 1994). Also see Zahavi (1999) for discussion.

proprioceptive spatiality of the body is not framed by anything other than the body itself. In other words, proprioception is a non-perspectival awareness of the body.

For example, we can ask about the distance and direction of a perceived object in terms of how far away it is, and in what direction. But these spatial parameters are meaningful only in relation to a frame of reference that has an origin. This does not apply to proprioception.[3] Proprioceptive awareness does not organize the differential spatial order of the body around an origin. Whereas one can say that this book is closer to me than that book over there, one cannot say that my foot is closer to me than my hand. Thus, whereas perception organizes spatial distributions around an egocentric frame of reference that is implicitly indexed to the perceiving body, somatic proprioception reflects the contours of my body, but not from a perspective of another perceiver.[4] Proprioception operates within a non-relative, non-perspectival, intra-corporeal spatial framework that is different from both egocentric and allocentric frameworks. Neither proprioception nor kinesthesia offers a perceptual perspective on my body. If they did, they would require a second body, or perhaps a homunculus that would act as an index. Our pre-reflective, kinesthetic-proprioceptive experience thus plays a role in the organization of perception, but in a way that does not require the body itself to be a perceptual object.

Intentionality and the Body Schema

To further this analysis we need to address the following question: What constraints are placed by the *perceiving* body on perception in general, and on the conscious experience of one's own body in particular? The human body is found on both sides of the intentional relation. On one side the body can be the object or content of intentional consciousness. I perceive (or remember, imagine, conceptualize, study, love, hate) my own body as an intentional object, as a body image, a mental construct or representation. This fosters a set of beliefs or feelings about the body. The body as it functions on the hither side of the intentional relation, however, is perhaps more important for our considerations. In its *prenoetic* roles the body functions to make perception possible and to constrain intentional

---

[3] Bermúdez (1998: 153) points out: 'In contrast with vision, audition, and the other canonically exteroceptive modalities, there are certain spatial notions that do not seem to be applicable to somatic proprioception'. Specifically he mentions distance and direction.

[4] Although it is possible to say that bodily sensation A is to the left of bodily sensation B, or that sensation A is farther away from sensation B than is sensation C, this spatiality is not reducible to the perceptual spatial framework. Left, right, center, and distance are spatial parameters that are completely relative in *perceptual* experience. What is to my right may be to your left. And what is to my right now will be to my left if I turn 180 degrees. But intra-bodily parameters are absolute in proprioception. What is proprioceptively on the right side of my body is just so, whether my right side is located to your left, or whether I turn. If I move my left hand to touch my right shoulder, it does not become a second right hand. If sensation A is just this distance from sensation B, I cannot make them closer on the proprioceptive map even if I contort my body to make them objectively closer.

consciousness in various ways. Here are included operations of body schemas—the body's non-conscious, sub-intentional appropriation of postures and movements, its incorporation of various significant parts of the environment into its own organization.

Although, as I have indicated, body schemas involve complex neurological components, I want to argue that they are not reducible to neurological functioning. Neurological accounts of the human body, which are usually called upon in this context, do not adequately capture the schematic operations in which the body acquires a specific organization or style in its relations with a particular physical and social environment. Nor is body posture, for example, equivalent to represented position in objective space; rather it involves a prenoetic spatiality that is never fully represented in consciousness or captured by objective measurement. Importantly, even if the operations of a body schema cannot be reduced to objective physiological description, or inflated to conscious image, it does not seem possible to work backward from intentional contents to neurophysiological processes, or forward from neurophysiological processes to intentional contents without finding indirect evidence of the operations of body schemas. The effects of these operations reach across this distinction.

By focusing on the performances of body schemas we can deepen our understanding of how the body contributes to the determination of perceptual consciousness, and in particular, the perceptual experience of the body which helps to form the body image. To view the performances of body schemas as continually and persistently constraining intentional experience would not be inconsistent with, and may contribute to, the already noted approaches taken in cognitive psychology (Neisser 1987), semantic theory (Johnson 1987), and phenomenology (Varela, Thompson, and Rosch 1991). If the body itself is doing the perceiving, then such prenoetic operations provide specific conditions that shape perceptual consciousness. The body and its natural environment work together to deliver an already formed meaning to consciousness. As Merleau-Ponty puts it: 'there is a logic of the world to which my body in its entirety conforms, and through which things of intersensory significance become possible for us [. . .] To have a body is to possess a universal setting, a schema of all types of perceptual unfolding' (1962: 326).

Consider the following fact. In the act of reading, our eyes depend more on scanning the tops rather than the bottoms of the printed lines (Johnson 1987—one can easily test this out: cover the top half of a line of print and try to read it; then cover the bottom half of a similar line of print and try to read it). This is not something readers are aware of; it is something their visual system does prenoetically, for the sake of efficient and quick reading. Body schemas operate in a similar way. Returning to the case of eyestrain, for example, the body begins to make automatic postural and motor adjustments prior to the subject's becoming aware of the oncoming headache. A subject who is absorbed in the act of reading is not explicitly conscious of the body's adjustments, which may include squinting and moving closer to the text. The body performs these functions, coping with the demands made upon it in this environment, without the subject's reflective awareness. Yet such prenoetic adjustments will determine perceptual content in important ways. In the case of eyestrain, body schema adjustments may motivate the subject first to fix on the environment or the text as problematic; the lighting seems too dim; the book becomes difficult or boring. Postural adjustments may allow the subject to continue reading by keeping her attention directed away from her body.

Perceiving subjects move through a space that is already pragmatically organized by the construction, the very shape, of the body. This space is neither isotropic nor absolute; it is defined relative to the perceiving body. Uexküll (1926) long ago suggested that perceptual systems, and therefore perceived environments vary with body design across species. The world perceived by the frog is quite different from the world perceived by the human. Even within a specific body design, optimal modes of perception vary with sense modality and with pragmatic purpose. Where must an object be located within my perceptual field to afford an optimal perception? It depends on the sense modality with which I perceive, and on the purpose of my perception. The perceived world is contoured by the capacities of my perceiving body, a body that is human and able to see relatively far, but can only touch or grasp something that is relatively close. If, as phenomenologists sometimes suggest, 'objectivity' is constituted as the correlate of all the possible subjective ways of gaining perceptual access to the thing, and this is prescribed in advance by the structure of the perceptual field (see e.g. Petit 1999), this field, in turn, is prescribed in relation to the perceiving body, the design of its sense organs and its capacity for movement.

Evidence of the prenoetic functioning of body schemata can be found within the intentional realm itself, specifically, within the content of various kinds of perceptual experience. To see, for example, is not only *to see something*, as Husserl's principle of intentionality would indicate, but also to see *from somewhere*, that is, under conditions defined by the position and postural situation of the perceiving body. In the normal situation, to see is also to see with binocular vision, that is, to see something under conditions defined by certain physical possibilities of the body and its sense organs. The visual field appears spread out in a continuous, although variable, horizon or visual distribution. Within this setting, and always relative to the perceiving body, some things appear closer than others; some things are to the right, others to the left; some are in front, others to the rear. Things appear in a body-centered spatial gestalt, organized in terms of foreground and background. The world appears only partially and in egocentric perspective; things show themselves only one profile at a time. All of these features are built into perceptual meaning in the form of prenoetically determined presuppositions and horizons. Teachers often say to young students: 'Now sit up straight and pay attention.' There is some truth in the teacher's coaxing. Perception and attention cannot be uncoupled from the body's postural attitudes. Consider the experiments conducted by Kinsbourne and others on the effects of body posture on judgment and attention (Grubb and Reed 2002; Kinsbourne 1975; Lempert and Kinsbourne 1982), which show that the lateral position of head and eyes or whole body influences cognitive performance. When subjects listen to a sentence with head and eyes turned right, for example, their performance in cued recall is better than when they listen with head turned toward the left. Trunk rotation to the left increases response times to cued targets on the right and decreases response times to cued targets on the left. The conditions placed on perception by the body, and the various postures that it takes, help us to organize the perceptual world in a meaningful way.

These conditions are both constraining and enabling factors produced in the ecological interaction between body and environment, or as Merleau-Ponty puts it, in a logic that is shared by the body and the world. What Gibson (1979) calls 'affordances', for example, or what Neisser explains as 'the possibility of actions that we have not actually undertaken' (1987: 12), are defined as such for intentional consciousness only on the basis of possibilities projected by body schemas. The floor affords walking, the chair affords sitting, the mountain affords climbing, and so forth, only in conjunction with the possibilities of particular postural models. All such features afforded by the environment, and evidenced in the implicit structure of perceptual meaning, are predicated on the prenoetic functioning of body schemas.[5]

Postural and motor adjustments of the body schema, as prenoetic, tend to remain 'behind the scene', operating *a tergo*. When I perceive, I do not perceive my body making the schematic adjustments that both enable and shape perceiving. They do not appear as explicit parts of the perceptual meaning, although implicitly they help to structure such meaning. For this reason, body posture is not reducible to objective position. The body projects a pragmatic and egocentric spatial framework that does not correspond precisely to objective (allocentric) spatial measurements. Body schemas enable us to find our way in space; to walk without bumping into things; to run without tripping and falling; to locate targets; to perceive depth, distance, and direction; to throw and to catch a ball with accuracy. Indeed, such things happen despite and independently of an established discrepancy between the conscious size estimation of one's own body and the size estimation of other objects (Shontz 1969). In other words, body awareness, or the body image, does not normally interfere with the performance of the body schema.[6]

We can also note that the perceiving body provides a coherence to consciousness across simple perceptual events. If, for example, we are concerned to define a unity of consciousness across time in a way that will account for the identity of a single, relatively continuous consciousness, we can appeal to a certain coherency produced by the fact that it is one body doing the perceiving. It is not that in consciousness all the various contents of experience cohere with each other in some thematic fashion.

[5] Here I am focusing on only one side of the body–environment relation. The environment too plays an important part in defining the operations of the body schema. It is well established, for example, that perceptual experience affects the performance of the body schema. Gibson's (1979) concept of visual kinesthesis means that to some extent the postural schema is tuned in to its environment so that bodily motion is partially specified by experiential transformations of the environment. Also see Neisser (1976).

[6] As we have already noted, this does not mean that the body image cannot affect the body schema. For example, in cases of learning dance or athletic movements, focusing attention on specific body parts can alter the established postural schema.

Rather, a structural coherency across all perceptually based experiences (including certain types of memory, imagination, and intention) is founded on the continuity of the prenoetic body, which is their point of origin. This does not depend on the embodied point of origin becoming part of the explicit content of perception, in the form of a body image or explicit marker that is constantly linked or juxtaposed with other contents. Rather, the spatial framework, definable in terms of the body schema, as well as other prenoetic aspects of embodiment and emotional dispositions (see below), are implicitly reflected in the meaning of the perceptual world. The fact that the perceiving body takes a single path through space-time resonates in the content of the perceptually based experiences associated with that body. Such experiences reflect a point of view, a spatial perspective on the world, which is at the same time richly contextualized by emotion and other prenoetic factors of embodiment.

The body *actively organizes* its sense experience and its movement in relation to pragmatic concerns. In this regard, prenoetic operations of the body schema are not reducible to physiological function, even if physiological events are necessary conditions for such operations. How the body reacts to a particular environment, even if it reacts in an automatic fashion, is not a matter of simple mechanics or reflex. The perceiver's pragmatic circumstances and intentional activities elicit appropriate movements and determine whether physiological events are integrated into, for example, a thermal experience rather than a tactile experience. When I touch something, the intention of my touch can determine, not just my conscious focus, but how my body will react. The fact that I may feel the object as hot rather than as smooth, for example, will depend not only on the objective temperature of the object, but on my purposes. Thus physiological processes are not passively produced by incoming stimuli. Rather, my body *meets* stimulation and organizes it within the framework of my own pragmatic schemata. A stimulus, 'when it strikes a sensory organ which is not "attuned" to it', does not reach perceptual consciousness (Merleau-Ponty 1962: 75). Although a good deal of the attuning process remains non-conscious, the intentional interests of the subject, in part, help to define that attunement.

More stimuli than are required for conscious purposes are registered on the physiological level. But only those values relevant to an intentional project may be elicited and translated to the level of consciousness (see Marcel 1983). To the extent to which the prenoetic functions of the body play a role in producing the postural balance for an intentional action or the adjustment of sense organs for a perceptual act, it is always selective among what is physiologically possible. For example, my body is capable, physiologically, of many different movements. But in any particular context I produce a *specific* movement. When in the context of a game I jump to catch a ball, that action cannot be fully explained by the physiological activity of my body. The pragmatic concern of playing the game motivates the action. The physical environment, the size and shape of the ball, along with the effects of all my previous practice (or lack thereof), and even the rules of the game as they are habitually expressed in the practiced movements of my body, may define how I jump to make the catch. Without a certain amount of selectivity, built up by practice and the cultivation of habitual movements, the body might move in any one of multiple ways, since the possibilities allowed by physiology are much greater than the particular movements necessary to catch the ball in the proper way. Thus the body schema is much more selectively attuned to its environment than what physiology on its own will specify. To explain this selectivity, or what Rosenbaum *et al.* (1993) call 'soft constraints', one needs more than physiology.

Cognitive constructionists speak of feed-forward mechanisms in this context (see e.g. Weimer 1979). It is often pointed out that sensory impulses from the retina can effect but not completely specify activity in the visual cortex. 'On the average, as much as 80 percent of what we "see" may be a tacit construction "fed forward" from the superior colliculus, the hypothalamus, the reticular formation, and the visual cortex itself' (Mahoney 1991: 101). Maturana and Varela (1987) generalize this feed-forward model to apply to all aspects of the central nervous system. Such mechanisms, however, are not reducible to neurophysiological processes accomplishable by a brain in a vat. Feed-forward or selective mechanisms, even if they are specifiable in strict neurophysiological terms, are ultimately the result of interactive relations between the brain, as one important part of the body, and the body as a whole, within a specific environment. We need to consider the brain as part of a holistic system.

Thus, not only have neuroscientists demonstrated that neural paths and cortical connections develop and are constantly transformed on the basis of sensory and motor experiences (for review, see Kandel and Hawkins 1992; Shatz 1992), developmental psychologists have shown that just such sensory and motor experiences (for example, localization of a particular sound or reaching for a particular object) depend on postural adjustments (Neisser 1976). The brain, thanks to its plasticity, is shaped in part by the body's movement. It is also clear that the organization and functioning of the brain depend on certain 'adjustment reactions' that take place throughout the body (Gellhorn 1943; Mason 1961). Precisely because the brain, in its neurophysiological performances, does not originate, but at best can only mediate, the various performances of the body as a whole, along with the individual's linguistic, cultural, historical, and personal experience, what is fed forward to define the body's perceptual attunement can neither be reduced to physiology nor inflated to conscious control.

Empirical Support

The various prenoetic performances of the body, such as those that can be expressed as performances of body schemas, thus place constraints on perceptual experience and action. Although there is evidence for these constraints manifested in the structure and shape of intentional experience, they cannot be completely apprehended in a phenomenological model. Neither can they be fully captured by neuroscience. Further evidence for such constraints, however, can be found in recent psychological studies of perception and action. These studies indicate that changes in various aspects of body schemas have an effect on the way subjects perceive their own bodies. More generally, changes in body schemas also affect spatial perception, the perception of objects, and intentional action. Consider these conclusions drawn from a variety of studies.

1. Changes and anomalies in posture, motility, physical ability and other behavioral aspects associated with body schemas and prenoetic functions of the body, imposed by abnormality, disease, or illness (for example, obesity, rheumatoid arthritis, multiple sclerosis), or by temporary physical changes (like pregnancy), have an effect on the perceptual, cognitive, and/or emotive aspects of body image. For example, degeneration of bodily functions and changes in motility lead to decreases in the senses both of body integrity and of strong body boundaries (Gardner et al. 1988; Halligan and Reznikoff 1985; Keltikangas-Jarvinen 1987; Powers et al. 1987). Such changes also affect the way one perceives and moves around one's environment. Certain items or spaces in the physical environment that may now pose threats or inconveniences to such patients are perceived as such, and constrain movement accordingly, whereas before that was not the case.

2. Exercise, dance, and other practices that affect motility and postural schemas can have an effect on the emotive evaluation of one's own body image (Adame et al. 1991; Dasch 1978; Davis and Cowles 1991; Skrinar et al. 1986). In these studies, subjects who improve in neuromuscular coordination, strength, and endurance, or who experience increased coordination, balance, agility, and improved posture through exercise, gain a perception of body competence and achieve a higher degree of satisfaction with their own bodies and motor capacities. Thus changes in the control of movement associated with exercise alter the way that subjects emotionally relate to and perceive their bodies. It is not difficult to imagine that such positive effects can change one's attitude toward and perception of the surrounding world in ways that may be diametrically opposed to the patients discussed in (1).

3. Changes in muscular tone involve specific adjustments to body schemas. In cases of increased muscular tone, interpreted as a sign of a higher degree of preparedness to action or readiness for external response, body-perception scores decrease, corresponding to a low awareness of one's own body. A decrease in muscular tone is correlated with an increase in body-perception scores (Ruggieri et al. 1983; Sabatini, Ruggieri, and Milizia 1984). Thus changes in muscular schemata correlate with changes in the subject's bodily awareness and perceptual awareness of the environment. These studies also suggest that prenoetic body adjustments allow the perceiver to direct attention to external rather than internal stimuli. More generally, to the extent that the body makes its adaptations to the environment prenoetically, and thereby remains in the perceptual background, cognitive attention can be focused elsewhere in any variety of intentions.

4. Retardation in the development of body schemas, caused, for example, by an absence of early crawling experience in the infant, has a negative effect on the development of spatial perception. Studies by Joseph Campos and his colleagues have demonstrated that crawling and locomotor experiences in infancy have an effect on the perception and evaluation of spatial heights (Campos, Bertenthal, and Kermoian 1992). Self-produced locomotion also plays a role in the development of visual attention to changes in the environment (Bertenthal and Campos 1990) and strategies for perceptually searching for objects (Kermoian and Campos 1988). Crawling experience and locomotion facilitate the development of body schemas. The longer the subjects have been moving in these ways and the more developed their body schemas, the better their spatial perception. In broader terms, 'the process of crawling provides a state of eye-hand coordination, vestibular processing, improvement of balance and equilibrium, spatial awareness, tactile input, kinesthetic awareness, and social maturation' (McEwan, Dihoff, and Brosvic 1991: 75).

5. Experimental alterations of the postural schema (for example, by asymmetrical body tension induced by experimental tilting of the body) lead to perceptual shifts in external vertical and horizontal planes (Bauermeister 1964; Wapner and Werner 1965). Like the studies by Campos and his colleagues, these studies show that changes in body schemas result in changes in external space perception. Merleau-Ponty refers to related studies of spatial perception, in situations where the apparent external vertical is tilted. Such studies show that perceptual orientation is not made on the basis of a consciousness of my body as a thing in objective space. Rather, visual perception is reoriented in terms of a body schema, a set of motor equivalencies that allow the body to reorder perception according to 'a system of possible actions' (1962: 248–50).

6. Several studies indicate that proprioceptive adjustments of the body schema help to resolve perceptual conflicts. Adaptation in the realm of visual experience involves changes in proprioceptive information. For example, perceptually adapting to 180-degree rotation of the retinal image is facilitated by 'changes in the position sense for various parts of the body' (Harris 1965: 419). In experiments in which visual information comes into conflict with proprioceptive input, for example, where an object is viewed through a reducing lens while in tactile contact with the body, adjustments take place in the interpretation of proprioception so that the body schema accommodates vision (Rock and Harris 1967). Studies such as these lead Shontz to conclude that 'body schemata themselves are not fixed photographs of bodily structure but are active, changing processes' (1969: 162). These types of effects have been exploited in medical and therapeutic settings using prism glasses and virtual reality technology to address a variety of pathologies (see Gallagher 2001c; Riva 1994, 1995; Rossetti et al. 1998; Vallar et al. 1993; Wann et al. 1998).

7. Vision not only contributes to a proprioceptive sense of posture and balance (e.g. Jouen 1988), but it is also the case that posture and balance contribute in a reciprocal fashion to how we visually perceive the surrounding environment.

Experimental studies indicate that there is a 'close linkage between eye posture or [eye] movements and the spatial organization of the whole-body posture' (Roll and Roll 1988: 159). Thus vibration of extraocular eye muscles results in body sways and shifts in balance. But also, vibration-induced proprioceptive patterns that change the posture of the whole body are interpreted as changes in the perceived environment. Under experimental conditions where the subject is limited to monocular vision of a small luminous target in darkness, 'a directional shift of the visual target was elicited by vibration applied to neck muscles...and, more surprisingly, to ankle postural muscles'. That is, a change in the apparent posture of the head or whole body induced by vibrations is 'interpreted by the stationary subject in darkness as if it were an upward displacement of the target' (Roll and Roll 1988: 162). It follows that alterations in proprioceptive information, that is, information closely connected to the organization of body schemas, lead to changes in visual perception.

In all of these cases, changes or distortions introduced at the level of the prenoetic body or body schema result in changes or distortions in perceptual consciousness or motor behavior. But this simply reflects the general rule. In all cases, prenoetic performances of the body schema influence intentionality. They operate as constraining and enabling factors that limit and define the possibilities of intentional consciousness.

Neo-Aristotelian Neurobiology

The Cartesian divide between mind and body had its roots in the more ancient Neoplatonic tradition. Plato himself, of course, would never have thought to explain ideas in terms of the body. There is a wonderful encounter at the beginning of Plato's *Republic* when Socrates, looking for a free meal, visits the house of Cephalus. Cephalus is an older man, and in the conversation he voices agreement with Sophocles who praises the virtue of old age because there are fewer temptations of the flesh to distract him from thinking about the really important things in life. In effect, women (let us assume) no longer turn him on sexually. Is this virtue or testosterone depletion (hypogonadism)? As males age, their systems produce less testosterone and some (10% at age 40) begin to experience a drop in libido. The drop in hormonal levels actually causes a perceptual change. What we might call the Cephalus effect literally changes the way that a male visually experiences women. Women will simply not be seen as sexually attractive—sexual qualia will literally drop out of the visual modality (and perhaps other sensory modalities). A certain dimension of meaning is eliminated; or at best, it is transformed into a purely intellectual and abstract sense that there is such a thing as sexual attraction. Cephalus, who now enjoys conversation better than sex, is glad to be rid of it; others may not be. Although Plato sees the connection to old age, for him it is not so much a question of an aging body, but of maturing wisdom. Socrates, by the way, never does get his dinner—something that would minister to his body; rather, he gets multiple courses of conversation.

There is, however, another tradition that may predate Plato, but that certainly had its best expression in Aristotle's philosophy. In contrast to Plato, Aristotle defined the soul as the *form* of the body, where the word 'form' is frequently (but not always[7]) a translation of the Greek term *morphe*, meaning shape. In a most basic sense Aristotle's understanding of the soul, including its rational abilities, requires that it depend on the shape of the body. The human soul is essentially tied to the human shape. On Aristotelian principles, the instantiation of the human soul in another animal form (or, in a computer that lacks human shape) is simply impossible. I do not intend to focus on Aristotle's own well-known analysis, or on the various theological, ethical, and philosophical problems this theory entails for ideas of reincarnation, eternal life, cloning, or functionalist thought experiments concerning teleportation of mental information. Rather, I want to pursue an understanding of the implications of this Aristotelian idea by examining its reflection in evolutionary and neuroethological observations.

Much of what I want to say here is an extension of Erwin Straus's remarks on the upright posture (Straus 1966). He notes that the upright posture is distinctive for the human species, and that this has far-reaching consequences, not only with respect to perceptual abilities, but also in regard to moral values and judgments. The phrase 'to be upright' has a moral connotation and, as Straus suggests, this may signal more than just a metaphorical expression.[8] His more general claim is that 'the shape and function of the human body are determined in almost every detail by, and for, the upright posture' (p. 138); and in Aristotelian terms this means that the upright posture is an essential aspect of what makes us human.

Here is an incomplete inventory of those aspects of human life that are related to or dependent on attaining the upright posture.

1. *Human anatomy and skeletal structure*: the shape and structure of the human foot, ankle, knee, hip, and vertebral column, as well as the proportions of limbs, demand a specific musculature and nervous system design. All these aspects enable the upright posture, but are also shaped by the attainment of the upright posture, which in turn permits the specifically human development of shoulders, arms, hands, skull, and face. With these changes what counts as the world is redefined. New capabilities, new affordances (in Gibson's sense of the term) appear.[9]

---

[7] Aristotle (*De Anima* 412[b] 10) also used the words *eidos, ousia, logos,* and *ti en einai* in his definition of the soul as the form of the body. To put *morphe* ahead of these other characterizations of the soul is to suggest a controversial interpretation of Aristotle that most scholars would not accept. I do not intend this as a scholarly interpretation of Aristotle, but a provocative *neo*-Aristotelian reading.

[8] Straus's analysis is much more detailed across social and political dimensions than we need to consider here. His essay anticipates in some detail much of what Johnson (1987) and Lakoff and Johnson (1980) explicate.

[9] These capabilities are first of all motor; but they extend to the most abstract and rational capacities for cognition, such as counting and the development of mathematics (see Sheets-Johnstone 1990: 76 ff.).

2. *Developmental conditions*: Attaining the upright posture is delayed in humans and requires the infant to learn it and, in opposition to gravity, struggle for it. This depends on a basic level of consciousness, namely, wakefulness. Fall asleep and you fall down. Posture and movement start to shape this basic wakefulness even prior to standing; movement, including early crawling behavior, influences the development of perception and cognition (Campos, Bertenthal, and Kermoian 1992). The change of posture that comes with standing and walking equally affects what we can see and to what we can attend.

3. *Independence*: With the upright posture we gain distance and independence. Distance from the ground; distance from things; independence from other people. In standing, the range of vision is extended, and accordingly, the environmental horizon is widened and distanced. The spatial frameworks for perception and action are redefined. Things are less close, less encountered as one crawls among them; they are confronted, as signified in the German word for 'object', *Gegenstand*: standing over and against. Standing frees the hands for gnostic touching, manipulation, carrying, tool use, and for pointing (a social gesture), all of which transcend grasping. At the same time, these functional changes introduce complexities into a brain structure that is being redesigned for rational thought (Paillard 2000). Standing also brings us 'face to face' with each other, and this profoundly transforms sexuality from strict animality to something human.[10]

4. *Sensory systems*: With the upright posture the olfactory sense declines in importance; seeing (the sense of distance) becomes primary. We are able to see far ahead of where we are currently located. Distal sight grants foresight and allows for planning. Olfactory mechanisms shrink and no longer dominate facial structure. Since our hands are liberated for more proficient grasping and catching, our mouths are liberated for other purposes. The upright posture thus transforms the jaw structure (along with dietary possibilities), with less need for massive musculature and the skeletal infrastructure it requires. This allows for the development of the more subtle phonetic muscles.

The transformation of the facial structure coordinates with the expansion and remodeling of brain structure and nervous system. Along with language and a larger, more developed cortex comes the rationality that makes us human and that allows us to conceive and speak of our own soul.

The establishment of human shape, then, is not neutral with respect to how we perceive the world or how we act in it. If we think of perception as something that happens only in the brain, we ignore the contribution of embodiment to sensory 'pre-processing'. Studies of comparative anatomy show the specifics of this pre-processing. With respect to auditory sensation, for example, the shape and location of the ears determine directional information by amplifying or filtering specific inputs (Chiel and Beer 1997). The motor system produces movement that, rather than fully determined at brain-level, is re-engineered by the design of muscle

---

[10] On the close relationship between upright posture, sexuality, brain size, and the development of language, see Sheets-Johnstone (1990).

and tendons, their degrees of flexibility, their geometric relationships to other muscles and joints, and their prior history of activation (Zajac 1993). Movement, for the most part, is not centrally planned; it is based on a competitive system that requires what Andy Clark terms 'soft assembly'. The nervous system must learn 'to modulate parameters (such as stiffness [of limb or joint]) which will then *interact* with intrinsic bodily and environmental constraints so as to yield desired outcomes' (Clark 1997: 45). The very design of the body imposes such constraints on the nervous system and the way it works. 'The nervous system cannot process information that is not transduced by the periphery, nor can it command movements that are physically impossible for that periphery' (Chiel and Beer 1997: 554). This suggests that at the most basic levels of perception and action the hypothetical experience of a brain-in-the-vat would be essentially different from an embodied brain.

The shape of the body is not the only aspect of embodiment that constrains and enables perception and action. Many bodily systems that operate below the threshold of consciousness in an automatic way are not irrelevant to perception, even if they are not directly involved in the production of perceptual experience. To the extent that these systems and operations have an effect on perception, they fall into the category of prenoetic factors that ought to be considered in any full explanation of cognitive life. For example, internal autonomic adjustments play a role in the perceiver's ability to attend to or concentrate on perceived objects without the distraction caused by changing environmental conditions. In dealing with temperature fluctuations, for example, the body at first copes without the help of consciousness. It 'interprets' environmental changes and regulates its own functions (metabolism, heart rate, blood pressure, respiratory volume, adrenalin levels, etc.). As a result, when the experiencing subject eventually becomes aware that she is too cold or too hot, the intentional meaning of that feeling will have already been conditioned by the body's prenoetic performance, and will have already affected perception. Similar performances of the body can be described in cases involving stress, pain, hunger, fatigue, lability, and so forth. Physiological baroreceptor processes, involving higher or lower blood pressure respectively, can raise or lower sensory thresholds, and shorten or prolong stimulus impact, depending on a variety of complex homeostatic factors (Sandman 1986). Sandman and his colleagues performed a variety of experiments that showed similar influences of lowered and elevated heart rates on cognitive and behavioral performances (summarized in Table 6.1). The background of occurrent perception and action is provided and delineated in part by such prenoetic functions.

Thus, in many instances, although these kinds of prenoetic processes remain open to purely physiological description, and are well described in such terms, it is also the case that such processes may (1) be caused by one's perceptual experience, and in turn (2) 'color' or bias one's perceptual experience and behavior. Such processes may not motivate specific action, but the behavior that one is engaged in, as well as one's perceptual experience, may take on a certain feeling because of them. Buytendijk (1974), for example, suggests that each environment calls forth

TABLE 6.1. *Relationship between heart rate, brain, and behavior*

Lowered heart rate	Elevated heart rate
Slower reaction time for cognitive tasks	Faster reaction time for cognitive tasks
Faster reaction time for attentional tasks	Slower reaction time for attentional tasks
Decreased perceptual thresholds	Increased perceptual thresholds
Enhanced ERP	Attenuated ERP
Lower resistance to persuasion	Higher resistance to persuasion

Note: ERP is event-related potentials of the brain, electrical activity recorded from the scalp, time-locked to specific stimuli.

Source: Adapted from Sandman (1986), summarizing the results from experiments by McCanne and Sandman (1974, 1976); Cacioppo, Sandman, and Walker (1978); and Petty and Cacioppo (1977).

appropriately specified heart, kidney, stomach (and so forth) processes and appropriately specified bodily regulations, adaptations, and emotional reactions.

In the *working-body* the 'technique' of heart action, for instance, is changed with respect to the automatic self-regulation of circulation and respiration. This can be ascertained and analyzed. These changes, however, are mutually connected with a pathic tuning of the body to the lived interior and exterior sensations and with the characteristic of availability which is brought forth in work from its ground in the completely unconscious impersonal and prepersonal level.   (Buytendjik 1974: 46–7)

Along these same lines Sheets-Johnstone (1999*b*) has called attention to the work of Edmund Jacobson (1970), who developed evidence to support the idea that neuro-muscular activity is an integral part of mental activity. This view is supported further by the experimental work of Sperry (1952), and recent dynamic systems theory (Kelso 1995). So even the most recessed of prenoetic processes are not unefficacious with regard to behavior and perception. In some cases they may have a negative or limiting influence. They could include, for instance, processes that involve physiological tensions, throbbings, and rhythms that accompany normal, untroubled respiration, blood-flow, and heartbeat. Indeed, it is better to say that such prenoetic processes accompany and are implicit in every kind of behavior and consciousness so that they define what is possible for behavior and consciousness but in such a way that they remain non-conscious, anonymous, and for the most part, normal.

On one view these processes are just physiological ones. One might ask: How are they related to perception if they are not sensations or in some way felt by consciousness? The point is, however, that these processes do have an effect on consciousness and the way that we experience the world. They condition, constrain, and color perception. They involve the attunement of the body to the environment, as well as the homeostasis of the body itself. If that tuning were upset, if a certain process connected with respiration, for example, failed, then one's perception of the world would be different in some way. To the extent that some change in consciousness would result, however, these processes are more than *purely* physiological; they are prenoetic processes that shape consciousness in important ways.

Such effects are not fully explainable in terms of what happens in the brain, or even in the whole nervous system. The neurophysiological components of such embodied processes are part of a much larger system that involves the entire body interacting with its environment. How I experience the world depends, in some degree, on how hot or how cold it is in my part of the world, and how my body is reacting to environmental temperature. How I experience the world depends, to some extent, on how much food I have in my stomach, and on certain hormonal levels existing in different parts of my body, and so forth. These are not only objective, physical facts; they are facticities to which my body reacts and with which it copes. Much of the reacting and coping may be describable in terms of neurophysiological functions, but neither the fact of the matter, nor the facticity of embodiment, is fully reducible to or identical with the firing of neurons.

We must add to all of this that there is an emerging interdisciplinary consensus about the importance of emotions in cognition. Damasio (1994, 1999), emphasizing the effect of emotion on experience, discusses muscular-visceral-endocrine adjustments that are non-conscious but that nonetheless shape our conscious experience. As he suggests, 'to perceive an object, visually or otherwise, the organism requires both specialized sensory signals *and* signals from the adjustment of the body, which are necessary for perception to occur' (1999: 147). Bodily adjustments across such visceral and emotional dimensions are not just 'optional accompaniments', but essential to the accomplishment of perceptual experience. Varela and Depraz (2000), following the emphasis placed on affect in Husserl's later analyses, reiterate the inseparability of lived body, affect, and cognition. Complementing such phenomenological analyses, Panksepp (1998) has detailed a dynamic neurobiology of affect. He shows how subcortical systems responsible for primitive emotional and motivational states interact with neural schemas of bodily action plans, reiterate their signals at various cortical levels, and resonate into experienced feelings. Such 'somatic markers' (as Damasio calls them, although we should understood these as prenoetic factors rather than mental images) introduce important emotional constraints on perception and cognitive experience.

Studies of pathologies such as Capgras and Cottard Delusions, which involve a failure of affective mechanisms, suggest that affect does not merely color or bias perception in certain ways but is at least partly constitutive of perceptual experience and creates a bodily framework within which perception and cognition operate (Ratcliffe 2004). It is not that perception predates emotional reaction, but that affect already shapes perception (Stone and Young 1997: 358). In the same way, it is not that a man sees a woman and then decides whether she is sexy; vision is already sexually informed. Cephalus's problem (or virtue if you value platonic relationships) is that his perception is impoverished.[11]

---

[11] Testosterone depletion is only part of the larger testosterone story. Prenatal levels of testosterone influence the development of the right side of the brain and affect visual acuity in the judgment of speed and distance (Manning 2002). There is also some speculation that high prenatal testosterone levels may contribute to the development of autism (Lutchmaya, Baron-Cohen, and Raggatt 2002).

I will not summarize any further the growing body of evidence about the integration of bodily posture, muscle tension, 'corporeal tonicities', movement, emotion, and cognition (evidence from ethology, dynamic systems theory, and phenomenology is well summarized by Sheets-Johnstone (1999b)). It is already clear enough from these considerations that the Aristotelian idea of the soul as the form of the body, explicated through a variety of contemporary philosophical and scientific investigations, offers an important counterpoint to the Platonic, Cartesian, and functionalist-computational traditions. The very shape of the human body, its lived mechanics, its endogenous processes, and its interactions with the environment work in dynamic unity with the human nervous system to define necessary constraints on human experience.

What implications do these considerations hold for the cognitive sciences? If the body as a whole significantly affects cognitive functions, then neither the privileging of physiology over intentionality, or vice versa, nor the development of a discourse that strictly correlates physiological functions with intentional meanings will be adequate as a complete model of cognitive behavior. If one reduces the prenoetic performances of the body to neurophysiology, or inflates them to an intentional body image, certain aspects of embodiment that place important constraints on cognitive life are overlooked. To the extent that some cognitive scientists still persist in approaches that refuse to recognize the complications introduced by the various roles of the human body in cognition, their models run the risk of remaining abstract and disembodied.

7

Neurons and Neonates: Reflections on the Molyneux Problem

A CENTRAL tenet of empiricist philosophy is that experience, in the sense of relatively prolonged exercise or practice of the sense organs, educates perception. On this view, human perception is not something that happens automatically in the first instance, or in the first moments of life; it takes time and exposure to the natural environment to develop properly. This idea has informed many attempts to solve a long-standing problem first raised by William Molyneux in a letter to John Locke over three hundred years ago. The question framed by Molyneux has been called the central question of eighteenth-century epistemology and psychology (Cassirer 1951). Although explicit discussions of the Molyneux problem decreased in number in the nineteenth century, and fell off even more in the twentieth century, the issues that it originally raised continue to be of interest, not only to contemporary philosophers of mind, but to psychologists and cognitive neuroscientists. Indeed, I want to suggest that recent findings in developmental psychology and in neurophysiology—findings that reflect the conceptual framework explicated in the first part of this book—provide the relevant empirical data for answering once and for all the Molyneux question.[1]

Molyneux, in a famous letter to Locke, had entertained the question of what it might be like for a blind man to gain sight; his question specifically asks what one sense modality, touch, adds to another, sight—whether previous tactile sensations inform first perception in the visual modality.

Suppose a man born *blind*, and now adult, and taught by his *touch* to distinguish between a cube and a sphere of the same metal, and nighly of the same bigness, so as to tell, when he felt one and the other, which is the cube, which the sphere. Suppose then the cube and sphere placed on a table, and the blind man be made to see: *quaere*, whether *by his sight, before he touched them*, he could now distinguish and tell which is the globe, which the cube?[2]

Molyneux's question at first glance looks deceptively simple, but it raises many interrelated and complex issues. Indeed, commentators have pointed out that Molyneux actually poses several questions, and there have been some philosophically

---

[1] My optimism for the proposed solution is in stark contrast to a claim made by Marjolein Degenaar in the most recent historical account of the Molyneux question. For reasons that I'll discuss later, Degenaar (1996: 132) suggests that the question cannot be answered.

[2] William Molyneux, quoted by John Locke (1694: 186). The citation of Molyneux's correspondence first occurred in the second edition of Locke's *Essay* (1694: pt. II. ch. 9, s. 8). Molyneux originally posed the question to Locke in a letter written in 1688 in response to the publication of a French *Abrégé* of Locke's soon to be published (1690) *Essay.*

heated debates about what Molyneux actually meant. Some have suggested that he was asking about the perception of distance, an issue that he clearly did raise in his first letter to Locke in 1688. Others have understood him to be asking whether spatial perception is confined to touch, or whether vision also allows for a genuine perception of space. In this context, questions about the difference between tactile objects and visual objects have exercised the minds of philosophers from Berkeley to Merleau-Ponty and Gareth Evans. For these reasons it is important that I identify at the outset the philosophical issues I want to investigate.

My intention is to pursue what Evans (1985: 382) called the 'background theories of perception' that inform answers to the Molyneux problem. Specifically, I want to identify the precise principles that best account for certain aspects of perceptual experience. To what extent is it correct to say that experience educates perception; to what extent does perception operate intermodally, so that education of one sense modality is also education of another? Answers to these questions will have a direct consequence for how we think of spatial perception, the embodied nature of our access to the world, and many of the other issues associated with the Molyneux question, issues that still reflect the divide between nativists and empiricists.

On the one hand, a negative answer to the question usually implies a theory of perception in which access to a meaningful external world is not direct but mediated in a process that necessitates an acquired capacity to synthesize sensations belonging to different sense modalities. Such a capacity is acquired through experience, although, as we will see, the concept of experience is itself open to various interpretations. On the other hand, positive answers to the Molyneux question may imply a more immediate perceptual access to the world on the basis of an innate intermodal system in which different sense modalities are already in communication.[3] In this case the concept of an innate system is also open to various interpretations. Thus the Molyneux problem is directed in part at questions about the respective contributions of nature and experience to perceptual experience.

First Perception

What is perception in its very first instance, without the contribution of previous sense experience, without being informed by established conceptual schemas, without the influences of habit, custom, language, and so forth? This question asks about *first* perception, ontogenetically the earliest instance of perception, which, for obvious reasons, is an extremely difficult state to describe or characterize. In some sense the state of first perception would be one of a pure embodied perception, without the bias of prolonged mental experience, or cultural and social influences. Thought experiments provide one avenue for the philosophical

---

[3] This is the case with Evans (1985), as we'll see, but not so with the positive answers given by Leibniz (1765), or J. J. Thomson (1974).

investigation of this notion, and in the history of empiricist philosophy there have been several famous ones that explore the question of what first perception must be like. Condillac (1754), for instance, imagines what it would be like for a statue, bereft of sensation, to awake in one modality of sensation at a time. The empiricist hope expressed in such a project is to return to first perception by stripping away the multimodal complexity of adult perception—reducing it to its barest minimum within one sense modality. I will try to make clear why the concept of Condillac's statue ignores the complexities that are implicit in embodied perception, and cannot do justice to the problems he wanted to address.

In the wake of Locke's *Essay*, discussions between Condillac (1746) and Diderot (1749) make it clear that Condillac's statue is a heuristic place-holder for both the newborn infant and the congenitally blind subject of Molyneux's question.[4] Although Molyneux himself posed his question as a thought experiment, philosophers and psychologists soon found empirical instances of congenitally blind patients who through surgical operations were given sight. I will refer to these as Molyneux patients.[5]

In Locke's view, nature contributes less than experience does to the production of coherent perception. First perception, which is no more than unorganized and meaningless sensation, can hardly be called perception at all. Perception needs to be educated by experience. For Locke, *experience* means the frequent and repeated sensation that leads to the formation of habit or custom, and which shapes judgment, which in turn, alters and improves perception. (For convenience, I will refer to this concept of experience as 'Lockean experience'.) If, for example, bare sensation presents the adult perceiver with a pure phenomenal appearance of limited adumbrations, experience in the form of 'habitual custom' fills in to complete the perceptual content. The empiricist thus maintains that one must *learn* to perceive; perception is not delivered as an innate power; uneducated or first perception cannot deliver a meaningful world.

Furthermore, on this empiricist model, first perception is always modality-specific. Experience in one sense modality is not sufficient to educate different sense modalities. As a result, Locke agrees with the negative answer of his friend Molyneux: No, the newly sighted man would not be able to discriminate, i.e. recognize, by vision alone, which was the globe and which the cube. Locke explains that the blind man, 'at first sight', would not be able with certainty to recognize by vision the globe or the cube, because of the difference and the lack of natural connection between touch and vision. Because tactile space is different from visual space, the two sense modalities do not naturally communicate, and experience in one does not translate into experience in the other. How the one relates to the other can only be learned through experience of both. Locke (1694: 187) accordingly

---

[4] Molyneux's question and variations of it still motivate thought experiments not unlike those posed in terms of Condillac's statue. See Eilan (1993) for a recent example.

[5] On the empirical side, operations to correct congenital blindness were reported as early as 1709; Cheselden reported a case in 1728 which was commented on by Diderot, Buffon, and Condillac. See Morgan (1977: 16 ff.) and Degenaar (1996: 53 ff.).

suggests that we must consider how much the perceiving subject 'may be beholden to experience, improvement, and acquired notions'.

The principle that experience enters into and shapes perception is also clearly expressed in the responses to the Molyneux problem made by Berkeley (1709), Condillac (1746), Diderot (1749), and in the twentieth century by neuropsychologists such as Donald Hebb (1949) and philosophers such as Merleau-Ponty (1962). Their negative answers appear to be reconfirmed by the empirical cases that show that Molyneux patients in fact, at first sight, cannot visually recognize objects that previously were experienced by touch alone.[6] In unexceptional cases of perception in the normal adult the senses obviously communicate with each other to produce a unified spatial experience. In the initial visual perception for the Molyneux patient, however, 'everything is at first confused and apparently in motion. Discrimination between coloured surfaces and the correct apprehension of movement do not come until later, when the subject has learned "what it is to see" . . . ' (Merleau-Ponty 1962: 223). It thus appears that the empirical cases of congenitally blind subjects who gain vision, exceptional though they are, help to show the importance and necessity of Lockean experience for the perceptual process. Such empirical studies furthermore suggest that first perception is modality-specific: for the Molyneux patient what is confused in vision is not confused in touch. This indicates that, in terms of development, unified perception is not something that blooms forth automatically in an instantaneous production, but that we have to learn perception and that our senses have to learn to communicate.

Let me summarize in three propositions what I understand to be the important principles of the empiricist reasoning on this issue.

1. *The development of coherent perception depends on Lockean experience.* At first, perception is confused; one needs to learn to perceive. In Molyneux patients the confusion of first perception means that colors are not contained by definite shapes, and everything seems to be in motion.

2. *Sense modalities do not naturally communicate.* Sense modalities are heterogeneous and have their own unique spatial and structural features.[7] They do not function intermodally; they learn to communicate with one another (usually on an amodal level) only as the result of Lockean experience. Part of the learning of perception involves learning to integrate these different systems on some perceptual or conceptual level.

3. *Lockean experience in one sense modality does not educate other sense modalities.* The Molyneux problem receives a negative answer because experience in the modality of touch is not sufficient for learning to perceive in the modality of vision.

---

[6] See von Ackroyd, Humphrey, and Warrington (1974); Gregory and Wallace (1963); Hebb (1949); von Senden (1932). Von Senden provides a comprehensive summary of cases up to 1930. Morgan (1977) surveys the empirical literature to the mid-1970s.

[7] The spatial and temporal differences between the tactile and visual modalities are clearly summarized by Martin (1992); Merleau-Ponty (1962: 222–5) and Morgan (1977: 200).

These three principles and the concept of Lockean experience provide a framework for the traditional empiricist background theory of perception. In the following sections I will argue that principles (2) and (3) have been overturned by recent discoveries in developmental psychology, and that this requires that we rethink the first principle, along with the concepts of experience and first perception that form its basis.

The Developmental Context

Historically, answers to the Molyneux question have been related to the issue of first perception in the newborn. Thus, for example, Diderot (1749: 52) contends that there is no doubt 'that vision must be very imperfect in an infant that opens its eyes for the first time, or in a blind person just after his operation'.[8] Unsurprisingly, the same three empiricist principles are often reflected in discussions of the developmental issues. Recent discoveries in developmental psychology, however, challenge the traditional empiricist theory of perception in a way that can clarify the concept of experience at stake in its formulation, and generate new principles. To see this we need to transpose the principles expressed in (1)–(3) from the context of adult perception in tactile and visual modalities to the context of developmental studies that involve tactile, visual, and proprioceptive modalities.

In the developmental context the question might be framed in this way: Where do we find in the life of an infant the emergence of coherent perception? To put the question in this way, however, is already to grant too much to the traditional empiricist model. The notion of an emergence of perception already implies that experience for the newborn infant is an inchoate, incoherent, and uncoordinated mass of sensations out of which coherent perception develops. This is nicely attested to in William James's (1890) famous phrase describing the infant's experience as 'a blooming, buzzing confusion'.[9] This idea, which reflects principle (1), is clearly expressed in the traditional view that exteroceptive perception appears relatively late in the developing infant.

As we know from our previous considerations (Ch. 3), developmental theorists until recently believed that experience begins by being interoceptive, and that the newborn is without external perceptual ability. On this view, James's 'blooming, buzzing confusion' persists until between the third and sixth month of postnatal life when the interoceptive and exteroceptive domains begin to collaborate—a collaboration that is not found at the beginning of life. Recall that one reason

---

[8] Just before his discussion of Molyneux's letter, Locke himself considered the developmental context, expressing his belief that fetuses may already exercise 'their senses about objects that affect them in the womb' (1694: 184). But, according to Locke, prenatal sense experience remains short of organized perception and, according to his examples, confined to bodily sensations such as hunger and warmth.

[9] James suggests that infants 'must go through a long education of the eye and ear before they can perceive the realities which adults perceive. *Every perception is an acquired perception*' (1890: ii. 78).

cited for this lack of organized exteroceptive perception involves the absence of a developed body schema. Thus psychologists such as Wallon and philosophers such as Merleau-Ponty regard a developed postural schema as a necessary require-ment for coherent perception. For someone like Merleau-Ponty, this idea is com-pletely consistent with the notion that perception is embodied. Perception is disorganized at this stage precisely because it is infected by the disorganization of the body.

On the empiricist model, the neonate's experience is confused; the infant has not yet learned to perceive. Moreover, reflecting the second principle (*sense modalities do not naturally communicate*), the reason for this confusion is that the infant has not yet learned to integrate the proprioceptively defined spatiality of its own body with the visual information it receives from the environment. Proprioceptive space involves an intra-bodily spatial framework; the organization of visual space involves an egocentric spatial framework. The development and integration of these two frameworks occur only with prolonged motor and sense experience. Intermodal communication or collaboration, important for the establishment of a mature perception, has not yet been established between proprioception and vision, or between proprioception and touch. Proprioceptive organization, as Merleau-Ponty indicates, is established first, prior to, and as a necessary condition for, exteroceptive perception. Reflecting the third empiricist principle (*Lockean experience in one sense modality does not educate other sense modalities*), however, proprioceptive organization alone is not a sufficient condition for organized visual or tactile perception—that is, proprioceptive experience does not inform visual or tactile sense modalities.[10]

Still, the neonate does not seem to be in the same special circumstance of the Molyneux patient. For example, the Molyneux patient already has extended experi-ence in the tactile domain and in other non-visual sense modalities. Nonetheless, as we have seen, the question of neonate imitation involves the issue of intermodal translation and does so in a way similar to the case of the Molyneux patient.[11] The recent developmental research on neonate imitation clearly challenges the empiricist principles that underpin the traditional view. Let us consider again an unfortunate infant who is taken directly from the birth process and, having under-gone ten minutes of the usual medical procedures and tests, is at this early age made to participate in a psychological experiment. A person visually presents to the newborn a facial gesture—for example, a tongue protrusion or a mouth opening.

---

[10] Although Merleau-Ponty (1962, 1964) often criticizes empiricist theories of perception, in his analysis of perceptual development in the infant and in his discussion of first visual perception in subjects who had been congenitally blind, he is led to the empiricist view by the empirical studies that he consults. It is clear, however, that he struggles with these ideas and that he thinks experience itself moves both infant and Molyneux patient toward his own phenomenological conception of intermodal perception.

[11] Meltzoff (1993) suggests that the imitation problem is quite analogous to the Molyneux problem, and he poses it in terms close to Molyneux's original question: 'Suppose a blind man can perform simple body movements, such as mouth opening and closing; he can identify the movements when he produces them and can produce them on demand. Suppose then that an actor is placed before the blind man and the blind man is made to see. The actor silently opens his mouth. Can the newly-sighted man, without being allowed to touch the actor, imitate the actor's gesture by opening his own mouth?' (p. 220).

The question is: Can the infant imitate the facial gesture? To do so the infant is required to translate its experience from one sense modality, vision (indeed, something very close to its first vision), into another, proprioception.

We would expect those who answer Molyneux's question in the negative, for reasons outlined by the three empiricist principles, to respond in a similar way to the question about the possibility of neonate imitation. And we are not disappointed. Indeed, the traditional answers to these two questions, as well as to the question of aplasic phantoms, are quite consistent. As we have seen before (in Ch. 3), Piaget, consistent with a negative answer to the Molyneux question, maintains that sense modalities initially represent heterogeneous spaces which the infant must gradually learn to synthesize. This would mean that imitation in the neonate is impossible since it could occur only on the basis of a highly organized proprioceptive experience. The infant would require proprioceptive access to its own face in order to be able to find the proper anatomical parts (for example, the mouth, the tongue, the lips) to use in the imitation process, and it would have to know how to move them. Furthermore, the infant would require an organized visual experience to be able to discern the gesture of the other's face, and seemingly would have to make the connection between these two sense modalities on some intellectual level. Thus, according to Piaget (and most other classical theorists of development), imitation is not possible prior to 8–12 months of age.[12] Accordingly, the newborn is caught up in a complete confusion: it does not yet have an organized proprioceptive experience of its own body (for example, it would not know where its mouth is or what to do with its tongue); it cannot visually perceive the face of the other person; and thus it certainly cannot imitate visually presented gestures.

As we have seen, however, newborn infants seemingly take issue with this traditional answer. Previously cited studies by Meltzoff and Moore, and others, show that neonates less than an hour old can in fact imitate facial gestures and even hand movements, that young infants imitate facial gestures after a delay of as much as 24 hours, and that infants improve their gestural performance over time (Meltzoff and Moore 1977, 1994). For reasons outlined earlier, it is also clear that neonatal imitation is not a matter of reflex behavior.

Both neonatal imitation and the issues surrounding the Molyneux question involve the concept of intermodal perception. To move us closer to the terms of the Molyneux problem, consider the following study.

Meltzoff and Borton (1979) evaluated tactile-visual cross-modal perception in thirty-two infants (average age of 29 days). Two pacifiers with quite different shapes were used—one is shaped like a sphere, the other a sphere with nubs (Fig. 7.1). Pacifiers were hidden from the infant's sight prior to slipping one of them into the infant's mouth. Half the infants were given the sphere, and the other half received the nubbed pacifier. They were allowed to suck on them for 90 seconds, during which time most infants engaged in tactile exploration with the tongue, 'furrowing

---

[12] Piaget (1962: 45). Concerning the heterogeneous spaces of different sense modalities, see Piaget (1954: 130) and Piaget and Inhelder (1969: 15). 。

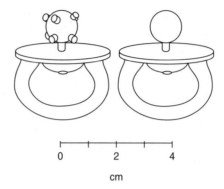

0   2   4

cm

FIG. 7.1.   Objects used in tactile-visual matching study. *Source*: Meltzoff and Borton (1979: 403).

their brows, as if the tactual exploration of the novel object was of some interest' (Meltzoff 1993: 223). The infants were then shown the two objects side by side. In the context of such experiments object recognition is often measured by how long the infant stares at a particular object within a fixed period. The results of this experiment showed that the infants did look significantly longer at the shape they had felt. Of the thirty-two infants tested, twenty-four visually fixated for a mean percentage of 71.8 per cent of the time on the shape matching the one they had explored in the tactile modality—figures greatly above chance. (See Streri and Gentaz 2003 for similar results.)

Meltzoff (1993: 224) concluded that very young infants 'register the same information about the shape of the object even if it is picked up through two different modalities, touch and vision'. Together with the intermodal communication between vision and proprioception found in the case of neonate imitation, with the results of other experiments that demonstrate intermodal communication between vision and hearing (Kuhl and Meltzoff 1984, 1992), and with many other experiments on intermodal perception, this conclusion is consistent with the general thesis that first perception is already shaped by an innate capacity, a built-in mechanism for intermodal communication among sense modalities. These experiments also make it clear that coherent perception that is *not* educated by experience (at least postnatal Lockean experience) occurs from the very beginning of our postnatal life.

What implications do these studies have for the background theory of perception, and more specifically for answering the Molyneux question? We clearly need to revise the three traditional empiricist principles in the light of the developmental context.

1'. *Relatively organized perception is possible from birth. It does not require Lockean experience as a necessary condition.* First perception is *not* confused sensation. The body is already organized by an innate body schema, and this organization is carried through to perception. Without Lockean experience, in a first instance, perception is *not* a blooming, buzzing confusion. Having said that, there is still an important sense in which experience in and beyond first perception does educate later perception in a self-organizing fashion. Moreover, there is also a sense in which experience, expanded to include prenatal experience, and understood to have a physical effect on the experiencing body, informs first perception. We return to these points below.

2'. *Sense modalities do communicate naturally. Perception is intermodal from the very start. First perception already operates in an intermodal fashion.* The perceiving subject does not have to learn to integrate different systems, because they are already innately integrated. Although separate sense modalities can be said to have their own unique spatial and structural features, they communicate intermodally in an egocentric spatial framework that is fully integrated from the beginning with a proprioceptive intra-bodily spatial framework (Ch. 6).

3'. *Experience in one sense modality does educate other sense modalities.* In the case of neonate imitation vision directly educates proprioception. In the experiment conducted by Meltzoff and Borton (1979) the tactile modality directly informed vision. Perception in one sense modality is, in certain respects, sufficient experience for the recognition of objects in another modality.

Answering the Molyneux Question

The reformulated principles seem clearly to contradict the traditional empiricist theory of perception. The latter is associated with and stands as the background theory of perception for the negative answer to the Molyneux problem. The empiricist theory extends further, of course. Most theorists who discuss the Molyneux problem generalize their conclusions concerning the role of Lockean experience in the education of perception, and the heterogeneity among sense modalities, to apply across all instances of human perception, including first perception in infancy. In other words, Molyneux patients are not exceptions or counterexamples to the original principles; they count as evidence in support of them. In contrast, neonates who imitate facial gestures would count as counterexamples. The recent developmental studies show clearly that the empiricist propositions (1)–(3) fail to describe first perception in the case of the neonate. This suggests, at the very least, that theorists from Locke to Hebb have been too quick to generalize.

On the other hand, if we generalize the principles expressed in (1')–(3') we are led to affirm an innate connection between touch and vision. This would seem to imply, as Gareth Evans suggests, a positive rather than a negative answer to the Molyneux problem.[13] Could this be right?

---

[13] Evans (1985) outlines six possible positions on the Molyneux question (see his chart, p. 381). He fails to mention that this nativist 'yes' position was actually held by William Porterfield, a Scottish philosopher who denied Berkeley's theory that custom and experience created the connections between sense

Since the time that Cheselden published, in 1728, his empirical account of a cataract operation in a patient blind from birth or from infancy, and his observations concerning the patient's visual perception, theorists as early as Berkeley (1733) have cited cases of recovery from congenital blindness as support for the negative answer to the Molyneux question.[14] After such operations patients are unable to distinguish between objects. Some patients, with the assistance or tutoring of touch, go on to learn visually to distinguish objects; others give up the difficult education of the visual sense, ignore their imperfect vision, and return to the life of a blind person. In the face of this empirical evidence, is it possible to maintain a positive answer?

The problem is that the empirical studies of Molyneux patients are plagued by ambiguities. These are well rehearsed in the literature from La Mettrie (1745) to Oliver Sacks (1995) and involve uncertainties about the timing of onset of blindness, the degree of blindness in cases of cataract, and the confused experience of the patient after the operation. The uncertainties about the empirical data create uncertainties with regard to the negative answer to the Molyneux question. Gareth Evans, in an attempt to overcome such uncertainties, suggests an experiment that would clarify the issue. Evans suggests that by means of direct electrical stimulation of the visual cortex, a pattern of experienced light flashes (phosphenes) in the shape of a square or circle could be caused in a patient with congenital blindness. If this were possible, could one not settle the matter once and for all?[15] Evans argues that under such circumstances the patient would indeed be able to tell the difference between a circle and a square. His reasons for this positive answer to the Molyneux question involve his concept of embodied action in an egocentrically organized behavioral environment; that is, his reasons are somewhat different but not necessarily inconsistent with the evidence from neonatal imitation cited above.[16]

modalities. In its place he suggested 'an original, connate and immutable Law, to which our minds have been subjected from the Time they were first united to our Bodies' (1759: ii. 414). On this basis he gave an affirmative answer to the Molyneux question. For discussion of Porterfield, see Davis (1960: 392–408). For a more contemporary expression of this position, see Eilan (1993).

[14] Others who followed Berkeley's lead include Robert Smith (1738), Voltaire (1738), for whom learning to see was similar to learning to read, and, in Holland, Petrus Camper (1746). See Degenaar (1996) for discussion.

[15] Dobelle (2000), in fact, has developed an artificial vision system that completely bypasses non-functional retinas by feeding a signal directly to the blind subject's cortex. Activation of the system causes the subject to experience flashes (phosphenes) as in the surrounding space. The spatial structure of these flashes preserves the spatial structure of the videoed edges. In effect, this technology instantiates Evans's suggestion. Unfortunately, for several reasons, it has so far not settled the matter. So far the implant technology has not been perfected, and the procedure has not been tested on congenitally blind subjects (see Jacomuzzi, Kobau, and Bruno 2003 for summary). Whether this procedure will settle the matter in the future will depend on the precise nature of the implanted device. As will be made clear in the following, if the device is designed to stimulate the subject's visual cortex directly (as is currently the case) then it is likely to undermine Evans's positive answer to the Molyneux question. If, in contrast, the implant were designed to act in place of the visual cortex (i.e. as an artificial visual cortex), and all the right connections could be made, then, I will argue, it would likely support a positive response.

[16] Evans (1985: 392–3) writes: 'To have the visual experience of four points of light arranged in a square amounts to no more than being in a complex informational state which embodies information about the egocentric location of those lights. . . . Now we are assuming that the subject has been able to

Now despite the fact that I think the evidence from neonate imitation, and Evans's conception of embodied action are in fact consistent with the reformulated principles of perception (1′)–(3′), I want to disagree with Evans's conclusion and argue in favor of a negative answer to the Molyneux question. This negative answer depends, however, on a particular interpretation of the question, which I will call the *empirical question*. If we take this question to mean: 'Will the Molyneux patient visually be able to distinguish the objects as such?', then the answer, I argue, is 'no'. On a different interpretation of the question, which I will call the 'in-principle question' and will consider below, the answer may be different. Here, on the stated interpretation of the empirical question, I want to argue that Locke, Berkeley, Condillac, Diderot, Merleau-Ponty, Hebb, and others are right to say: *No*, the newly sighted person would not be able to discriminate, by vision alone, which was the globe and which the cube. I think they base their answers on the wrong reasons, however, and more generally they are led to (or led by) the wrong principles of perception. To develop and maintain the correct version of the negative answer, however, I need to provide some reasoned explanation of the evidence from the eye operations. After all, what I take to be the most secure empirical data, the evidence from neonate imitation and other experiments on intermodal perception, point to a positive answer for the Molyneux question. The evidence from cataract and corneal operations, which supposedly supports the negative answer, remains ambiguous. Evans's suggestion about cortical stimulation has not been tried with congenitally blind subjects, but I think he is wrong about what it would show if that were done.

Locke and the empiricists correctly give the negative answer, but for the wrong reasons.[17] To see this one needs to formulate a completely different and specifically empirical explanation for the negative answer to the Molyneux problem. The solution is to be found in the neurophysiology of vision. Once understood it is easy to see that a negative answer to the Molyneux question is not inconsistent with the reformulated propositions (1′)–(3′), or with the experience of the neonate, but is an explainable exception to the principles that normally govern intermodal perception. In effect, the reasons why the negative answer to Molyneux's question can be consistent with the reformulated propositions rather than explained by the empiricist propositions (1)–(3) are to be found in the way the body works, and specifically on the subpersonal, neurophysiological level of explanation.[18]

form simultaneous perceptual representations of the locations of tactually perceived objects, and this means that he has been in a complex informational state of just this kind before.... [And] if receipt of such information was sufficient to prompt application of the concept *square* in the tactual case, it is not clear why it should not do so in the visual space.'

[17] My intention is not to suggest, however, that these thinkers agree completely in their reasoning. Park (1969), for example, outlines the differences between Locke and Berkeley on this issue (also see Berman 1999 for discussion). Davis (1960), citing eighteenth-century commentators, notes differences between Molyneux, Locke, and Berkeley, and between Locke and Condillac. In general, however, all these philosophers accepted propositions (1)–(3).

[18] Locke (1694: 26–7) had discounted neurophysiological explanations from the very start: 'I shall not at present meddle with the physical consideration of the mind; or trouble myself to examine wherein its essence consists; or by what motions of our spirits or alterations of our bodies we come to have any

As we noted in discussing (1'), even if first perception in the newborn is already somewhat organized, continued experience (in the Lockean sense) does educate later perception in a self-organizing fashion. The difference between the first empiricist principle (1) and the reformulated one (1'), however, depends on how we conceive of experience more generally, its effects, and its timing. Although it would be difficult to deny that postnatal Lockean experience educates and fine-tunes perception, we can deny that the development over time of postnatal visual experience is a necessary condition for relatively clear visual perception. The neonate sees well enough to imitate facial gestures immediately upon birth (given some moments for its eyes to adjust to light).

It may be helpful to clarify just what the visual capacities of the newborn human are. Atkinson and Braddick (1989) and Slater (1989) indicate that newborn vision involves the following characteristics:

- sufficient acuity to resolve details at close range;
- contrast sensitivity great enough for the perception of spatial patterns;
- cortical activity and control (and not just subcortical functionality);
- overt control of attention and selection of objects by means of eye movements;
- preference for some objects over others (e.g. moving objects rather than stationary objects; three-dimensional rather than two-dimensional objects; high-contrast rather than low-contrast stimuli; patterns with curved rather than straight lines);
- active searching for visual stimulation;
- ability to habituate to one stimulus and show preference for novel stimuli;
- activation of visual memory—the possibility of habituation in neonates demonstrates a very short-term visual memory (Slater 1989), but more durable memories have been demonstrated in 2-day-old babies who can retain a memory of the mother's face over a minimum of 5 minutes (Bushnell and Sai 1987).
- sensitivity to motion parallax—when the infant moves its head, nearer parts of a viewed three-dimensional object appear to move more than farther parts.

sensation by our organs.... These are speculations which, however curious or entertaining, I shall decline, as lying out of my way in the design I am now upon.' Diderot (1749: 53–4), however, did suggest that part of the answer must involve the physical mechanism, and specifically in the context of recovery following the eye operation. 'One might reply that it would take all the time necessary for the humours of the eye to arrange themselves appropriately; for the cornea to take up the convex shape necessary to vision; for the pupil to acquire its characteristic dilation and contraction; for the elements of the retina to acquire the proper sensitivity to light; for the lens to exercise the forward and backward movements that it is believed to make; for the muscles to fulfill their functions; for the optic nerves to transmit the sensation; for the entire eye to make the necessary preparations, and for all the parts of which it is composed to act together in the production of that miniature which is so indispensable when it comes to showing that the eye educates itself.' Diderot nonetheless goes on to say that if all of this were accomplished (and how long it would take he was not sure—it might take weeks after the operation or happen almost immediately) then the Molyneux patient would still not be able to recognize the cube or sphere by vision alone within a time-frame that would satisfy the Molyneux question. That is, it would still take some time to educate the visual sense. For a discussion of the significance of Diderot's views on this, see Pacherie (1997) and Sejten (1999).

Neonates are capable of discriminating between different geometrical shapes, such as triangles, squares, and circles (Landau, Gleitman, and Spelke 1981; Slater 1989; Slater and Morison 1985a; Slater, Morison, and Rose 1983). Their vision is also characterized by shape constancy, that is, across changes in orientation or slant neonates are capable of recognizing the real shape of an object (Slater and Morison 1985b). Neonate vision also shows feature constancy, that is, the ability to recognize invariant features of an object across certain varying features, such as moving versus stable objects (Slater 1989).

Qualifications need to be made on all of these aspects. Visual acuity in the newborn is approximately 30 times poorer than in adults, but is still sufficient for some degree of pattern recognition (ibid.). Further, the neonate's vision is limited in terms of distance—visual attention is not usually directed to objects more than three feet away unless they are moving (ibid.). Neonate vision is not fully binocular (Atkinson and Braddick 1989), and cortical control is far from fully developed. Nonetheless, it is clear that neonate vision is *already educated* to some degree.

To complete the explanation, however, one needs to look on the neuronal level. To ascertain whether there is an education process required for first perception one needs to look at neuronal development, and it is here that we can find the definitive answer to the Molyneux question. The established view on neuronal development from birth onward begins with a statement about the initial condition: the patterns of interconnection of human cortical cells are at first sparse (Fig. 7.2a) compared to patterns in the adult (Fig. 7.2b; see Atkinson and Braddick 1989; Shatz 1992). If this is the case, behavioral evidence tells us that there is nonetheless, in the visual cortex, a sufficient neuronal structure in place that allows the newborn to see as specified above. More recent neurological evidence strongly supports this view. It suggests that the visual cortex of the newborn may be more developed than first thought. Indeed it may be much closer to the adult brain in regard to the structure of the ocular dominance columns, groups of nerve cells in the visual cortex that respond to input from one eye or the other (Crowley and Katz 2000). Regardless of the initial condition, however, it is important to consider what happens as the result of subsequent experience, or the lack of subsequent experience.

If we interpret the evidence following the established view of sparse neuronal development in the initial condition, then continued visual experience after birth is necessary for the proper and continued development of neurons in the visual cortex. Animal experiments, conducted by Hubel and Wiesel (1963), suggest that there is a *critical period* of three to twelve weeks in early infancy in which visual experience is necessary for the proper formation of ocular dominance columns in the visual cortex (Barlow 1975; Frégnac and Imbert 1984; Hubel and Wiesel 1963; Shatz 1990, 1992; Sillito 1987; Wiesel and Hubel 1963a, b). Thus, childhood cataracts, if not removed prior to or early in the critical period, lead to visual deficiencies that remain even after they are removed. On the alternative reading, specifying the initial condition as already neurally well developed, deprivation of experience through the critical period would cause degeneration of that initial structure. As demonstrated experimentally, neurons degenerate in animals deprived of vision

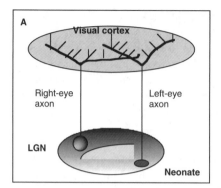
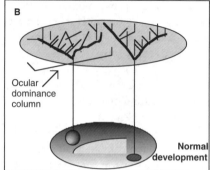
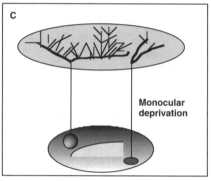

FIG. 7.2.   Neuronal development of projections from the lateral geniculate nucleus (LGN) in the ocular dominance columns of the visual cortex. A. Newborn; B. Normal development; C. Development in the case of monocular deprivation. *Source*: Based on Shatz (1992).

or raised in the dark (Fig. 7.2c; for a recent experiment on this, see White, Coppola, and Fitzpatrick 2001). On either interpretation, under the circumstances of congenital blindness, the specialized nerve cells responsible for the visual perception of shape and spatial orientation are negatively affected (Blakemore and Cooper 1973; Hubel and Wiesel 1963; Mitchell *et al.* 1973; Wiesel 1982).

Neuronal development is the continuation of a process that begins *in utero*,[19] a process that, by the time of birth, has sufficiently progressed to prepare the neonate for first visual perception. The first visual perception is not something that must wait for further Lockean experience, the prolonged and continued sensory stimulation assumed by the empiricists. If, however, that first perception does not take place, if, for example, the infant is born blind, then, lacking visual experience, not only will the proper neuronal development not happen, but the

[19] See Shatz (1990). Neuronal development begins *in utero* and continues throughout infancy. Synaptic connections in the human visual cortex are rapidly increased to excess quantities up to around the eighth postnatal month and then reduced (by approximately 40%) to normal levels over the first three years (Huttenlocher *et al.* 1982).

neuronal state in place at the time of birth will deteriorate. As a result, the functioning of later vision, as in the Molyneux patient, will be limited and quite different, not only from the normal adult, but also from the newborn infant. In neurophysiological terms, the neonate is not equivalent to the Molyneux patient.[20]

The fact of neuronal deterioration or transformation in the visual cortex of the congenitally blind person would foil Evans's proposed direct cortical stimulation experiment. Even if the visual cortex is electrically stimulated, as Evans proposes, the subject would not be able to experience the phosphenic square or circle because the neuronal substrate is not intact.[21] Neuronal changes in cortical areas responsible for vision rule out a positive answer to the Molyneux question on the empirical interpretation of that question we have been considering.

Degenaar (1996: 132) suggests that the Molyneux question cannot be answered precisely because of such neuronal changes. 'We have not answered Molyneux's question—and, indeed, we think that it cannot be answered because congenitally blind people cannot be made to see once their critical period is passed.' First, it is not quite right to say that a Molyneux patient would not be able to see. The empirical studies indicate that they do see, and that some of them go on to make their vision more precise, eventually discriminating colors and, in some cases, shapes. The amazing plasticity of the brain is not entirely one-way.[22] Nonetheless,

---

[20] Morgan (1977: 198) notes that 'Locke assumed purely hypothetically that all the sensory equipment of the congenitally blind person would remain intact, and ready to function at the first instant of vision . . .' Sacks (1995: 127) compares the Molyneux patient with the infant in some regards, but goes on to suggest a clear neurological difference: 'one would suspect that the tactile (and auditory) parts of the cortex are enlarged in the blind and may even extend into what is normally the visual cortex. What remains of the visual cortex, without visual stimulation, may be largely undeveloped. It seems likely that such a differentiation of cerebral development would follow the early loss of a sense and the compensatory enhancement of other senses . . . the newly sighted are not on the same starting line, neurologically speaking, as babies, whose cerebral cortex is equipotential—equally ready to adapt to any form of perception' (p. 140).

[21] Functional imaging studies of people blind from an early age reveal that their primary visual cortex has actually changed to accommodate an enhancement of the tactile sense. For example, the visual cortex in such blind subjects can be activated by Braille reading and other tactile discrimination tasks. Other studies have shown that visual cortical areas can be activated by somatosensory input in blind subjects but not subjects with sight. See Cohen et al. (1997).

[22] Morgan (1977) comes very close to this neurophysiological answer, but in the end discounts it for the following reason. Although visual deprivation during the critical period in infancy does result in permanent damage to the visual cortex, behavioral studies show that in such cases animals can still recover visuo-motor abilities. Morgan views this as an unresolved conflict between neurophysiological and behavioral results (pp. 185 ff.). I see no conflict here. Plasticity on the neurophysiological level can easily account for a limited degree of behavioral recovery. Thus, the fact that some Molyneux patients do improve the interaction between tactile and visual modalities over time does not necessarily require the establishment of completely normal neuronal development in the visual cortex; rather, adult brains seem quite able to find ways around such deficiencies. See e.g. Kaas (1991). Indeed, Morgan's own references to sensory substitution studies (Bach-y-Rita's TVSS experiments) confirm the brain's plasticity in this regard. It is notable that although the relevant data on neonate imitation start to appear only in the year his book is published, he does cite an important study on cross-modal transfer in 1-year-olds (Bryant et al. 1972). According to Morgan, however, this simply confirms that we have 'general ideas' very early in life (p. 192), not that perception is truly intermodal. For some qualifications on the idea that plasticity is not just one-way, especially in regard to cross-modal plasticity, see Lee et al. (2001).

the facts involving critical periods and neuronal deterioration, I would argue, indicate a definitive negative answer to the empirical Molyneux question.

Degenaar, however, interprets the Molyneux question in a different way, that is, as the *in-principle question*. It may be clear at this point that the empirical question we have been considering—'Will the Molyneux patient visually be able to distinguish the objects as such?'—means something like, 'Will the patient be able to "see" the shapes in question and thus be in a position to be able to make a "judgment" about what they are?' And the answer is 'No'. One could, however, go on to insist as follows: 'Yes, but *what if* the Molyneux patient *could see* the shapes in question? Could he at that point recognize the cube and the sphere?'[23] I think this in-principle question is what Degenaar and Evans have in mind, and it is certainly closer to what Molyneux himself was asking. In some regard, however, this form of the question begs the empirical question. But we could make it work by specifying a hypothetical subject. This subject

1. has been blind from birth, but
2. has suffered no neuronal deterioration in the visual cortex,
3. has learned to discriminate a cube from a sphere by touch, and
4. is either given sight or, following Evans's suggestion, is subject to direct cortical stimulation.

Absent the neuronal deterioration, I think that it would be correct to say that this hypothetical subject (who is not equivalent to the Molyneux patient) would indeed be able to distinguish and recognize the cube and the sphere. This positive answer to the 'in-principle' question, an answer based on the reformulated principles of perception, is quite consistent with the negative answer to the empirical question, an answer based on the empirical facts. On either interpretation, however, in contrast to Degenaar's claim, we arrive at a reasoned answer, to wit, 'Yes and no'. In effect, for empirical reasons having to do with the state of the subject's cortex, but not for principled reasons, the answer to the Molyneux question, understood as an empirical question, is 'No'. The answer to the in-principle question, however, given the reformulated principles, is 'Yes'.

The hypothesis that explains the negative experience of the Molyneux patient, and still remains consistent with the reformulated propositions (1')–(3'), is that there are significant differences in both visual performance and neuronal structures between (*a*) the newborn, (*b*) the normally sighted adult, (*c*) the hypothetical subject, and (*d*) the Molyneux patient. The latter would be as neurophysiologically different from either (*a*) or (*b*) or (*c*), as the experimentally altered case in which an animal is deprived of sight from birth is neurologically different from the visual cortex of the neonate or the normally sighted adult.

---

[23] Putting the question this way suggests an interesting experiment which, to my knowledge, has not been tried. Neuropsychologists now distinguish between vision for recognition and vision for motor control and action. Even if the Molyneux patient is unable visually to recognize the difference between the cube and the sphere, is it possible that their grasp, informed by vision, can differentiate between them? One would be able to tell from the shape of their hand as they reached to grasp the object.

This makes Locke and the empiricists correct in their negative response to the Molyneux question, understood as the empirical question, but wrong with respect to their reasons. Perhaps more importantly, it makes them wrong in their negative response if they were addressing the in-principle question. That the Molyneux patient is visually unsuccessful is not explained on the empiricist model—expressed in principles (1)–(3)—but by the empirical fact that neuronal structures do not develop properly for vision in the Molyneux patient. In contrast, first perception in the newborn is already intermodally organized; the neonate is innately prepared (by prenatal cortical development) to perceive a world coordinated across a variety of sense modalities.

Let me add one historical note before considering the implications this answer has for the principles of perception. The answer I have proposed here is based on recent scientific research in developmental psychology and neuroscience. It would be difficult to come to this precise answer without the resources of those scientific studies. Difficult, but clearly not impossible. One thinker, not usually considered in contexts of epistemology or psychology, came to exactly this answer around 1750. He advanced this solution tentatively and somewhat speculatively because he did not have the exact science he needed. Still, his suggestion was based in part on his own observations of infants and newborn animals. Adam Smith wrote, commenting on the Molyneux patient described by Cheselden,

But though it may have been altogether by the slow paces of observation and experience that this young gentleman acquired the knowledge of the connection between visible and tangible objects; we cannot from thence with certainty infer, that young children have not some *instinctive perception* of the same kind. In [the patient] this instinctive power, not having been exerted at *the proper season*, may, from disuse, have gone gradually to decay, and at last have been completely obliterated. Or, perhaps, (what seems likewise very possible) some feeble and unobserved remains of it may have somewhat facilitated his acquisition of what he might otherwise have found it much more difficult to acquire.   (1795: 161, emphasis added)

He came to the notion of an 'instinctive power' in children through his own observations. It seemed beyond reasonable doubt that numerous kinds of newborn animals were from birth able to integrate movement, touch, and vision. Because of the natural dependency of human children on others, he reasoned, they may not require such instinctive powers. Yet, Smith writes, children

appear at so very early a period to know the distance, the shape, and magnitude of the different tangible objects which are [visually] presented to them, that I am disposed to believe that even they may have some instinctive perception of this kind; though possibly in a much weaker degree than the greater part of other animals. A child that is scarcely a month old, stretches out its hands to feel any little play-thing that is presented to it. (p. 163)

As indicated by his distinction between tactile objects and visual objects, Smith accepted much of Berkeley's theory of vision. He nonetheless believed that there was a natural affinity between touch and vision immediately apparent in the behavior of infants, but open to 'decay' if not used 'in the proper season' (the neuronal deterioration and critical periods of today's neuroscience). If Smith had taken these ideas further he may have recognized their implications for a more general theory of perception.

New Principles of Perception

Developmental studies demonstrate that perception is intermodal from the start. This is not an intellectual accomplishment that we acquire after much practice, but an innate feature of our embodied existence. On that basis we have reason to reject the traditional empiricist principles (2) and (3), which claim neither connection nor mutual education between sense modalities. Such connections are already at work in the body of the newborn. Principles (2') and (3') bring us closer to the truth. Perception is intermodal from the very start, and one sense modality can educate another.

The first empiricist principle, that experience educates perception, remains viable in two ways. First, it still makes sense to say that Lockean experience is required for the continued maintenance or development of perception beyond the neonatal state. By including neurophysiological development in our explanation, we have a good conception of why and how experience works to sustain and perhaps to fine-tune perceptual mechanisms beyond the occurrence of first perception. In this sense (1) and (1') can be seen as consistent parts of a more general account. We might combine them in the following way:

(1") *Although relatively organized exteroceptive perception is possible from birth, the continued maintenance and development of perception depends on experience, understood as the exercise of perceptual mechanisms.*

This seems clearly justified by both developmental and neurological studies.

Second, it is also the case that *prenatal* neurological development requires experience. Although a good deal of neurological development is genetically coded and organizes itself in pre-designed circuits, some of that development requires sensory and motor input (Prechtl 1984; Shatz 1990, 1992). In the development of auditory and proprioceptive capability, for example, prenatal neurological development depends upon prenatal auditory stimulation and movement.[24] The required prenatal experience, however, is not a form of Lockean experience, which may involve the perception of full-fledged objects, but a more simple sense experience directed at partial aspects of objects, or 'proto-objects'—determinate

---

[24] I purposely leave out the word 'respectively' since the fetal response to auditory stimulation is often a movement; and fetal movement is often accompanied by intra-uterine sound. First perception in several of the non-visual modalities is at least partially established prior to birth and in a fashion that might be called synesthetic, or at least intermodal. In this regard continuity exists between prenatal and postnatal intermodal perception. In postnatal experience a turn of the head or the body involves a reorganization of the auditory field as much as of the visual field.

and bounded segments of the perceptual field.[25] Thus, the newborn infant may in fact recognize and prefer its mother's voice on the basis of its prenatal experience of the tone or pitch of that voice.[26] In the case of proprioception fetal movement provides the late-term fetus with a bodily sense that is already quite developed at birth. Indeed, the logic of the traditional view that suggests that exteroceptive perception necessitates a developed postural schema seems correct. But this occurs much earlier than the traditional view would allow. Precisely because some aspects of a proprioceptive body schema develop prenatally, a neonate arrives ready to imitate the movements of others, something that would be impossible without proprioception.

Given the lack of prenatal visual experience, the visual system might be said to be even more innate, in the sense of following a more genetically controlled development, with less dependence on experience than touch or proprioception. Even the visual system, however, which is quite developed at birth, may benefit from some limited prenatal stimulation for its proper neurological development. Thus the late-term fetus is sensitive to light. Bright light directed on the lower abdomen of the mother in the third trimester, for instance, elicits fetal eye blinks (Birnholz 1988).

To speak of prenatal experience as a requirement for neurological development is to extend and deepen the notion of experience beyond the complex sense experience described by Locke. If this fuller concept of experience, extended to include prenatal experience, and deepened to account for its effect on neural structures, suggests that the newborn infant is not a *tabula rasa*, it does not fully contradict the empiricist claim that experience educates perception. Even Locke was willing to allow for prenatal experience (see n. 8). But he was not ready to treat seriously the scope or import of such experience, nor was he prepared to entertain its relation to the physical basis of perception. In this context the concept of innateness is not a philosophical threat to the concept of experience, but a necessary complement. That which is innate can mean literally whatever we have prior to birth. On that definition perceptual capacity and experience itself can be considered innate. On an alternative definition we might consider the genetic code to be innate. Even here we must say that to a great extent the proper development of that which is innate (the genetically designed neuronal structure) depends on experience. In such contexts, the distinction between nature and experience cannot be drawn so sharply.

This expanded concept of experience, which includes an account of its effects on neurological development, its intermodal nature, and its complex relation to first perception suggests a revised set of perceptual principles, and provides a consistent

[25] The notion of a 'proto-object' is based on Bermúdez's definition of 'object*'—'a bounded segment of the perceived array' (1998: 100)—which can be perceived non-conceptually.

[26] Fetal responsiveness to sound is well documented. In response to auditory stimuli, as early as 24 weeks gestational age, the fetal heart rate changes; and after 25 weeks the fetus responds by blinking its eyes or moving its limbs. Cortical response to such stimuli has been demonstrated in premature infants between 24 and 29 weeks gestational age. The fetus shows preference for some sounds (such as the mother's voice) rather than others (DeCasper and Spence 1986; Fifer and Moon 1988).

explanation of both neonatal imitation and a complex and double answer to Molyneux's question. At the same time it supports an externalist and embodied account of perception. The traditional negative answers to the Molyneux question usually implied a theory of perception in which access to a meaningful external world is not direct but mediated in a process that necessitates an acquired capacity to synthesize sensations belonging to different sense modalities in a process of intellectual abstraction. On this view, much of what we perceive is internally constructed, a production of the apprehending mind that shapes sensory data and goes beyond the primary qualities of the objects perceived. The double answer that I have outlined above, however, is quite consistent with the idea of a more immediate perceptual access to the world on the basis of an innate intermodal system in which different sense modalities are already in communication. Perception is less the result of an internal processing of sense information, and more the result of an interaction between the body and its environment.

8

Complex Structures and Common Dynamics of Self-Awareness

IF the behavior of young infants can be characterized as involving a primitive form of self-awareness (Ch. 3), one might suspect that self-awareness and our capacity for self-reference are quite simple and robust in their basic structures. In this chapter I want to explore a variety of issues that pertain to the structure of self-awareness and the capacity for self-reference. These considerations will demonstrate just how complex and fragile these phenomena are. Although their complexity is for the most part hidden away within the normal range of motor and cognitive behaviors, it is nonetheless possible to discover the details of such structures in various pathological cases where self-awareness and self-reference break down. For example, in certain positive symptoms of schizophrenia specific aspects of self-awareness are disrupted. These symptoms include delusions of control in regard to bodily movements, thought insertion, and auditory hallucinations. In this chapter my intention is to sort out these aspects, and to explore their underlying mechanisms. The structures that we discover here are quite ubiquitous; they characterize not only movement organized by body-schematic processes, but human experience more generally.

In this chapter we will be led to another important qualification to be made in regard to the concepts of body schema and body image. These concepts have been thought to be too static, and inadequate for capturing the dynamic processes that characterize experience at both phenomenological and neurological levels (Kinsbourne 2002; Sheets-Johnstone 2003; also see Jeannerod and Gallagher 2002). The following discussion of schizophrenia, however, will reveal certain features of embodied experience that can only be described as dynamic, and as involving a body-schema system best understood in terms of its temporal structure.

The Dynamics of Agency and Ownership in Motor Action

Pre-reflective self-awareness may include a *sense of agency* (a sense of being the initiator or source of a movement, action, or thought) and a *sense of ownership* (a sense that it is I who am experiencing the movement or thought).[1] As we

---

[1] See Ch. 2. The phenomenological distinction between sense of ownership and sense of agency correlates with the distinction made by Graham and Stephens (1994) between 'attributions of subjectivity' and 'attributions of agency'. Graham and Stephens explain these attributions, however, to be the

previously noted, in the normal phenomenology of voluntary or willed action the sense of agency and the sense of ownership coincide and are indistinguishable. When I intentionally reach for a cup and say that this is *my* action, I mean both that this action is the movement of my own body and that I caused it to happen. When I think about the cup, I don't discriminate between the fact that this thinking is occurring in my stream of consciousness, and that the thinking was initiated by me. In the case of *involuntary* movement, however, it is quite possible to distinguish between the sense of agency and the sense of ownership. I may acknowledge ownership of a movement—for example, I have a sense that I am the one who is moving or is being moved. I can thus self-ascribe it as my movement. I may rightly claim, however, that I am not the author of the movement, because I do not have a sense of causing or controlling the movement—I have no sense of agency for it. The agent of the movement is the person who pushed me from behind, or, for example, the physician who is manipulating my limb in a medical examination.

Likewise, in the case of involuntary *cognitive* processes, I may acknowledge that I am the one who is thinking, but claim that the thoughts are not willfully generated by me. For example, certain unbidden thoughts or memories may impinge on my consciousness, even if I do not intend for them to do so, or even if I resist them (see Frankfurt 1976; Graham and Stephens 1994). We are all familiar with melodies that stay in our heads when we would rather think of something else. In such cases, of course, we may not want to say that there is a specific agent for thinking. It is not that I think someone else is causing my thoughts or my experience. Nonetheless, my claim of ownership (my self-ascription that I am the one who is undergoing such experiences) may be consistent with my lack of a sense of agency.

Certain symptoms of schizophrenia seem to involve a disruption in the sense of agency, but not the sense of ownership, and it will be helpful for understanding these concepts to examine them in the context of this pathology. In this regard, Christopher Frith's (1992) cognitive model of schizophrenia as a disruption of basic self-monitoring processes provides a possible explanation of how the sense of agency may be subject to errors of identification. Frith's basic thesis is that the schizophrenic's hallucinatory and delusional experiences are due to a breakdown of self-monitoring. He is led to this view from observations of motor behavior in schizophrenia.

Chronic schizophrenic patients suffer from a variety of movement disorders.[2] Most relevant to our concerns, they sometimes make mistakes about the agency of

product of an introspective inference. One attributes agency to oneself, for example, on the basis of a reflective acknowledgement that one has caused the action. In contrast, I understand the senses of ownership and agency to be first-order, phenomenal aspects of experience, pre-reflectively implicit in action. In regard to movement, they are generated in the subpersonal processes of body schematic control, and specifically in the processes of motor preparation and the sensory feedback that results from the action (see Gallagher 2000a, b, forthcoming a). Thus it is important to note that *senses* of ownership and agency refer to a first-order pre-reflective self-awareness. *Attributions* of subjectivity and agency involve a higher-order, reflective introspection. For example, I would reflectively acknowledge and report that the action is in fact mine only on the basis of having a sense of agency implicit in the action.

[2] Such disorders include peculiar involuntary movements and grimaces with lips and mouth (Crow *et al.* 1982; Frith 1992; Owens, Johnstone, and Frith 1982) and the loss of synchrony between finger tap and

various bodily movements. Patients suffering from delusions of control may report that their movements are made or caused by someone or something else. Frith (p. 66) provides an example from a patient: 'The force moved my lips. I began to speak. The words were made for me.' The motor action responsible for the speech is in fact the patient's own motor action, and the patient acknowledges that they are his lips that are moved, but he makes an error of identification concerning who produced this motion. Here the sense of agency, rather than the sense of ownership, is disrupted. That is, the patient knows that they are his lips and that he speaks, but seemingly his lips were moved, and the words were generated by someone else. Another example provided by Mellor (1970: 17) makes this clear: 'A 29 year old shorthand typist described her actions as follows: "When I reach my hand for the comb it is my hand and arm which move, and my fingers pick up the pen [*sic*], but I don't control them" ' (cited by Spence 1996: 82).

How can one explain this disruption in the sense of agency? The classic theory in this regard involves the notion of a hypothetical brain mechanism termed the *comparator*. Comparator models originated as ways to explain body-schematic processes responsible for motor control. When a motor command is sent to a set of muscles, a copy of that signal, the efference copy, is also sent to a comparator or self-monitoring system. Held (1961) suggested that efference copy sent to a comparator is stored there, and then compared to reafferent (proprioceptive or visual) information about the movement that is actually made. This sensory feedback, however, would arrive slightly after the fact of movement, and at best serve as verification that it was I who was moving.[3] For reasons outlined below, it is unlikely that the sense of agency is based on this sensory-feedback model (although it may be reinforced by such feedback).

This *sensory-feedback* model is consistent with ecological explanations of motor action and self-awareness. The control of motor action depends in part on proprioceptive and visual-proprioceptive feedback, and more generally on an ecological sense of one's own self-movement (Gibson 1987). If something seems to be going wrong with the action, it is quite possible to correct for it on the basis of this concurrent sense of movement.[4] Our ecological sense of moving through the world is rich and complex in the sense that it involves not only pre-reflective proprioceptive awareness and working memory, but also a non-observational and pre-reflective

---

rhythmic auditory stimuli (Manschreck 1986). Schizophrenics sometime suffer from poverty of action, often manifested in poverty of speech, and this may involve a problem with self-generated action (Frith 1992).

[3] This verificationist explanation is clearly put by Campbell (1999a: 612) '[I]n the cases in which we do have a sense of agency, in which the movement performed is felt to be your own, what grounds that sense of agency is match at the relevant comparator between the efferent copy and the sensory feedback you have about the movement. What explains the feeling that it is you who moved your arm is that at the comparator, an efferent copy was received of the instruction to move your arm which matches the movement you perceive.'

[4] Concurrency here is defined as falling within the same specious present, rather than as an absolute simultaneity. Here it is a matter of hundreds of milliseconds.

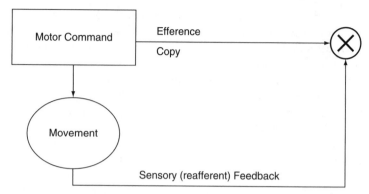

FIG. 8.1.   Sensory-feedback comparator.

differentiation between self and non-self, and a sense of one's own capacities for action (see Chs. 3 and 4).

There is a second control mechanism involved in the normal control of movement, however, and this can also be interpreted in terms of a comparator model. This comparator mechanism is understood to be part of a premotor system operating *prior to* the actual execution of movement and *prior to* sensory feedback. This 'forward' motor control, which does not depend on sensory feedback, not only helps to generate the action, but it is likely responsible for generating a conscious sense of agency for action (Georgieff and Jeannerod 1998; Jeannerod 1994). The forward comparator monitors the efference copy of the motor command as correctly or incorrectly matching motor *intentions* and makes automatic corrections to movement prior to any sensory feedback (see Fig. 8.2). This *forward comparator model* is consistent with evidence for an anticipatory, pre-action aspect of motor action. Pre-action neuronal processes, which serve part of automatic body schematic control, anticipate the actual motor performance and provide an online sense of agency that complements the ecological sense of self-movement. In one's immediate phenomenology during action, agency is not represented as separate from the action, but is an intrinsic property of action itself, experienced as a perspectival source (Marcel 2003). Experimental research on normal subjects supports the idea that such agentive awareness of action is based on motor processes that precede action and that translate intention into movement, rather than on actual feedback from movement or from peripheral effort associated with such movement.[5] The content of the experience of voluntary action, then, includes a sense of agency for the action, generated in processes that lie between intention and performance.

---

[5] Fourneret and Jeannerod (1998); Marcel (2003). Research that correlates initial awareness of action to recordings of the lateralized readiness potential and with transcranial magnetic stimulation of the supplementary motor area, strongly indicates that one's initial awareness of a spontaneous voluntary action is based on anticipatory or pre-movement motor commands relating to relevant effectors (Haggard and Eimer 1999; Haggard and Magno 1999).

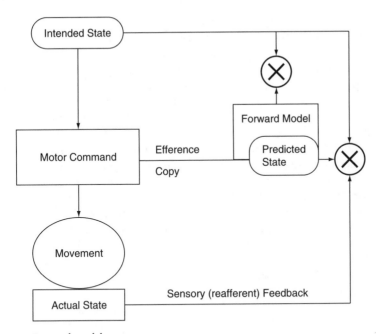

FIG. 8.2.   Forward model.

Schizophrenics have problems with the forward monitoring of movement, but not with motor control based on sensory feedback. In one experimental situation, non-schizophrenic subjects are required to use a joystick to follow a target on a computer screen. The experimenter can introduce an apparent directional bias into the subject's response, and subjects are able to use either visual feedback or the pre-action, more automatic process to correct their movement. In one situation, to correct for the apparent mistake the subject depends on visual perception of her hand (vision tends to override proprioception in such cases). When subjects see an error they correct it. If visual perception of the hand is unavailable, however, the normal subject makes a quicker and smoother correction using, presumably, the forward control mechanism. Schizophrenic patients, however, have a problem monitoring their own motor intentions at this body-schematic level (Malenka *et al.* 1982). Like normal subjects they correct the error when visual feedback of their hand is provided, but, unlike normal subjects, they often fail to correct the error when deprived of visual feedback (Frith and Done 1988). These findings are consistent with controlled studies that show abnormal pre-movement brain potentials in schizophrenia, which Singh and his colleagues associate with elements of a neural network involving supplementary motor, premotor, and prefrontal cortexes (Singh *et al.* 1992).[6]

---

[6] For more on the involvement of the prefrontal cortex and its complex interrelations with other cortical areas, see Goldman-Rakic and Selemon (1997). For the role of the supplementary motor area in the anticipation and preparation of action, see Passingham (1996) and Tanji and Shima (1994).

In schizophrenic delusions of control there is a loss of a sense of agency, but not a loss of a sense of ownership. The schizophrenic feels that he is not the agent of his own actions, and that he is under the influence of others—other persons or things seem to be moving his body. In some regards, this experience is similar to involuntary action. That is, when someone does control my movement (giving me a push, for instance), I know that it is my body that is moving, but I do not have a sense of agency for the movement. Indeed, I would attribute the agency to the person who pushed me.

The lack of a sense of agency makes good sense in the case of normal involuntary action where a subject does not intend the action; there would be no pre-action preparation, no intention registered at the comparator. On the model proposed by C. D. Frith (1992), the loss of a sense of agency in delusions of control is explained as a problem with efference copy in the central monitor, some kind of dysfunction of the forward, pre-action aspect of the body-schema system. Something goes wrong with the efference copy or with the forward comparator mechanism. As we see from the experiments, the schizophrenic is still able to correct movement errors if sensory feedback is available. Likewise, in the case of involuntary action, the ecological sensory-feedback system still seems to do its job, providing a sense that I am moving (Gibson 1987). This suggests that the distinction between ecological, sensory-feedback control and pre-action, forward control corresponds to the distinction between sense of ownership and sense of agency, respectively. That is, both in the schizophrenic's delusions of control and in the normal experience of involuntary action, the ecological sensory feedback system tells the subject that it is he who is moving or being moved (providing a sense of ownership for the movement). Absent efference copy at the forward comparator, or absent any pre-action preparatory processes at the neurological level, however, the body-schematic system will fail to register a sense of agency, a sense that it is the subject himself who is the willful generator of the movement.[7]

From Embodied Movement to Cognition

Can something like this model of motor control be applied to cognition? C. D. Frith (1992) thinks so (see Blakemore *et al.* (2000) for a good summary). Let's take a closer

---

[7] Marcel points out that often in schizophrenia, as well as in Tourette's syndrome and obsessive-compulsive disorder, an action is itself experienced as owned, but the source of the action, an intention or command, is disowned. Indeed, stimulation of the central thalamic nucleus produces hand movements, and although subjects have no idea why they did them, the actions themselves are not disowned (Hécaen *et al.* 1949). Having an intention, or having a sense of agency, is not crucial to having a sense of ownership for movement (Gallagher and Marcel 1999; Marcel 2003). The forward model is not the only neuronal-level candidate for generating the sense of agency. Following the distinction between sense of ownership and sense of agency (Gallagher 2000a), a number of researchers have been searching for the neuronal correlates for the sense of agency for embodied action, with some consensus forming around the contrastive functions of the right inferior parietal cortex and the anterior insula bilaterally (see discussion below).

look at the specifics of his model. His conception of the monitoring system in terms of subpersonal comparator mechanisms derives from an explanation of visuo-motor coordination. The visual system can distinguish between movements on the retina that are due to movements in the world, and movements on the retina that are due to movements of the perceiver's own body. In the latter case stability of the visual image is achieved by the motor system sending efference copy 'to some monitoring system at the same time as a message is sent to the eye muscles' (C. D. Frith 1992: 74). The efference copy alerts the visual system to compensate for self-generated or self-initiated movement. Frith refers to this as a monitoring of *intentions to move* (pp. 74, 81). To have an intention to move would surely signify something voluntary, or as Frith says, 'self-initiated' (p. 43). His analysis focuses precisely on such self-generated or willed action. Our considerations of motor action indicate that for the normal subject the sense of ownership for action and the sense of agency coincide in the case of willed action. The schizophrenic, however, may experience a loss of the sense of agency when in fact he is the agent, and, as we have seen, this can be explained by a failure of the forward model.

As Frith points out, this sort of self-monitoring mechanism is traditionally used in explaining motor, perceptual, and linguistic behavior (e.g. Sperry 1950; von Holst and Mittelstaedt 1950). Following Feinberg (1978), however, he postulates a similar mechanism for cognition—specifically, for thought and inner speech. He suggests that defects in such mechanisms can explain hallucination and delusion in the case of schizophrenia. Phenomena such as thought insertion, hearing voices, perceiving one's own acts as alien, etc., suggest that something has gone wrong with the central monitoring mechanism.

Thought insertion, for example, might be explained thus: 'Thinking, like all our actions, is normally accompanied by a sense of effort and deliberate choice as we move from one thought to the next. If we found ourselves thinking without any awareness of the sense of effort that reflects central monitoring, we might well experience these thoughts as alien and, thus, being inserted into our minds' (C. D. Frith 1992: 81). Frith's model assumes not only that thinking is a kind of action, but that, as in the case of a motor action, we experience an effortful intention. The intention to think, according to Frith, is the element that bestows a sense of 'mineness' on the thought, or perhaps more precisely we should say, a sense of agency for the thought. If the cognitive system is like the motor system then efference copy of the generation of thought (originating, let's say, in some thought-generating mechanism, or TGM) is sent to a feedback comparator, which also registers the occurrence of the actual thought. The efference copy also goes to a forward comparator, and there is a quick match between what was intended and what was generated (Fig. 8.3). So if efference copy is somehow blocked from reaching the forward comparator, thought occurs which seems not to be intended by the subject. If efference copy is blocked or goes astray, or is not properly generated, thinking still occurs, but it is not registered as under my control—it appears to be an alien or inserted thought. There is no match between intention and thinking.

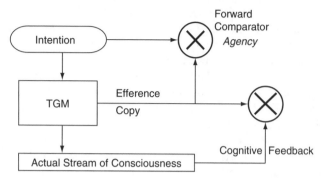

FIG. 8.3.   Cognitive comparators. Match at the forward comparator identifies thought intended.

Some Phenomenological Problems with Christopher Frith's Model

Conscious Intention

Several aspects of Frith's model are phenomenologically problematic. A first set of problems pertains to Frith's characterization of the intention to think. In the case of thinking or conscious experience, what role does something like an 'intention to think' or efference copy play? It is difficult to conceive of an intention to think prior to thinking itself, unless it is entirely a conscious preparation, as when I might decide to sit down and start thinking about this issue. In that case, however, the intention to think is itself a thinking, and an infinite regress begins to loom: do I require an intention to think in order to intend to think? Frith (1992: 86) speaks of a *conscious* feeling of effort for a willed intention to think, and he equates this with a *conscious* monitoring of efference copy. Frith's analysis relies, not just on an intention to act (move or think), but an *awareness* of the intention to act, and he defines this awareness as a case of 'metarepresentation'. Metarepresentation is a second-order reflective consciousness, 'the ability to reflect upon how we represent the world and our thoughts'. This is part of what it means to monitor our actions and, he claims, it is precisely what is missing or disrupted in the schizophrenic's experience.

Surely, however, most cases of normal thinking are neither prefaced by conscious intentions to think, nor followed by an introspective metarepresentation.[8] In the

---

[8] Kinsbourne (1995: 214) suggests, with regard to intentions to move, that such intentions do not persist long enough to be included in awareness, and that the movement itself 'rapidly supervenes and supplants the intention'. Stephens and Graham (2000) consider this issue, but not in relation to Frith's analysis. Rather they discuss an objection raised by Akins and Dennett against Hoffman's (1986) account of alien voices. Akins and Dennett (1986: 517) suggest that the idea of having an intention to think leads to a 'never-beginning regress of intentions to form thoughts'. Stephens and Graham point out, however, that Hoffman's account concerns only the kind of thought that might be called inner speech, and just as we might accept the idea that someone may have an intention to say something, it is not so odd to accept the idea that someone may have an intention to say something in inner speech. They agree, however, that

normal phenomenology, at least in the large majority of cases, there is not first an intention and then a thinking, nor thinking plus a concurrent but separate awareness of intention to think. Even in the case of intentional action it is not clear that there is always an intention to act, at least in the sense of a distinct psychological state (Anscombe 1983).

Campbell (1999a) suggests, in contrast to Frith's characterization, that efference copy is not itself available to consciousness. On his view, efference copy is part of a *subpersonal* and non-conscious process that generates an awareness of effort as thought itself is generated. As a first attempt to get the phenomenology of this model right, let us say that as thoughts are generated by the TGM (and I suppose this can happen in any number of ways) efference copy is normally sent to a comparator. Such processes, however, are subpersonal processes that subtend the thinking process. That is, following Campbell's suggestion, whatever there is of intention to think or efference copy are moved underground; they do not make an appearance in the subject's actual phenomenal experience. Ultimately they are to be cashed out in terms of neuroscience rather than phenomenology.

Unbidden Thoughts

What Frith calls 'intention to think', then, may be part of a subpersonal, non-conscious process, which, when it works properly, generates a sense of agency for our thoughts. Does the disruption of this process, however, explain the phenomenology of inserted thoughts? As with movement, it is not always the case that my thinking is characterized as something I intend. There are unbidden thoughts that, as Frankfurt (1976: 240) puts it, 'strike us unexpectedly out of the blue; and thoughts that run willy-nilly through our heads'. I may just find myself thinking of something. I may just find, without a conscious act of recollection, particular memories coming to the fore, invading or disrupting my thoughts with elements of my past that may or may not be relevant to my present circumstance. Is there any kind of intention to think in such cases, or when, for example, someone suddenly starts shouting instructions at me and causes me to start thinking?

In such cases, of course, I retain a sense of ownership, a first-person sense which tells me that it is I who am experiencing the thoughts. Similar to the case of movement, a preliminary or preparatory non-conscious intention to think, if necessary for a sense of agency, seems unnecessary to guarantee a sense of ownership—a realization that I am the one who is thinking, or having the thoughts. Yet, in cases of unbidden thoughts, without an intention to think, and without a sense of agency for generating the thoughts, I do not attribute my thoughts to someone else.[9] Importantly, this means that the problems with the intention to

not all intentional thinking could be described as inner speech, and that the idea that there is an intention to think in every case would be unacceptable.

[9] Of course it is possible to attribute thoughts in my mind to someone else, but in a very ordinary way—for example, in listening closely to a speaker, one might say that the speaker's thoughts are being inserted into one's mind.

think and efference copy are not doing all the work that Frith would like them to do in the case of schizophrenia. The absence of an intention to think, and hence, the lack of match at the comparator level do not explain anything more than a relatively normal lack of a sense of agency. It does not explain the misattribution of thought to another agent, or why some thought might seem inserted for the schizophrenic.[10] At best, in the absence of an intention to think we have unbidden thoughts, but not inserted thoughts.

Redundancy of Efference Copy

A more basic question: what purpose could *efference copy* have in the realm of thinking? In the case of the visuo-motor system, efference copy serves a pragmatic, control function rather than a verificational one. In effect, the motor system informs the visual and vestibular systems to make adjustments, with very practical effects—for example, stability of the visual field, postural balance, and so forth. The function of efference copy is to inform the visual and vestibular systems that the organism, rather than the world, is moving. Even in the case where the motor system is simply updating and correcting itself, the purpose of efference copy is for motor control. Its purpose is not to verify (simply for the record?) that movement is taking place.[11] Nor is it *primarily* an information stream that discriminates between intended movement and non-intended movement. Its purpose is rather to instruct the motor or sensory system to make important adjustments. Is there anything like this happening in the thinking process?

One can certainly distinguish different cognitive systems—memory systems, perceptual systems, and so on. But we are not talking of efference copy playing a communicative role among these systems. It does not seem to be a communication between two different systems, unless, of course, one creates an extra system and calls it the comparator or central monitor. On the Feinberg–Frith model, consciousness seems to be sending *itself* messages. Thus Campbell (1999a: 616) suggests, following Feinberg, that efference copy has the primary function of keeping thoughts on track, checking 'that the thoughts you actually execute form coherent trains of thought'. To keep thoughts coherent and on track, however, could only mean to keep them on a semantic track, that is, on a certain track of meaning or on a line of logical reasoning. It is odd, however, to assign this task to a subpersonal, non-semantic mechanism when, simply put, we are consciously aware of our thoughts and can keep track of them, and keep them on track, at a conscious, and specifically pre-reflective, first-order, phenomenal level. Simply put, when I think, I consciously think. So the question is whether one really needs a subpersonal comparator (Campbell) or anything like an observational metarepresentation (Frith) to verify that I myself am doing the thinking.

---

[10] Stephens and Graham (2000) point this out in their critique of Frith's model. Yet they fail to give an adequate account of this misattribution in their own account (see Gallagher 2004).

[11] This is very much in contrast to the idea that efference copy performs a verificational role (Campbell 1999a; Held 1961).

Campbell has argued that Frith's model provides the most parsimonious explan-ation of the sense of agency for cognition.[12] Yet Frith's model would make the normal sense of agency for thinking the work of a separate mechanism—a comparator. Is this necessary in a system that already involves consciousness? The matching process at the comparator would supposedly involve a curious and confusing mix of conscious and non-conscious elements. If we follow Campbell rather than Frith, efference copy is not something of which we are conscious; the other element of the match, however—the stream of thought itself—is already a matter of consciousness. Supposedly the *outcome* of the match, the sense of agency, must also be conscious in some way—a conscious sense that I am the one who is generating the thoughts. One might suppose, however, that the verifying match in the subpersonal comparator would not be conscious (otherwise there would have to be a consciousness of something that remains non-conscious—efference copy).

Hyperreflection

Despite its subconscious status, Campbell describes the comparator process as involving a form of introspection: 'it is the match between the thought detected by *introspection*, and the content of the efferent copy picked up by the comparator, that is responsible for the sense of ownership of the thought'.[13] Campbell's use of the term 'introspection' in this context is, I think, relatively innocuous. He is following a tradition that uses the term to mean something like an immediate reflexive access ('from the inside'), which allows one to report ongoing experience, rather than anything like a full-fledged act of reflective introspection.[14] Frith, however, invokes the notion of metarepresentation, as a full-fledged higher-order act of reflection. But a metarepresentational introspection again threatens infinite regress; I would have to ask, Is this my metarepresentation? Metarepresentational introspection is itself a thinking process and my intention to metarepresent would have to generate its own efference copy, to be matched up on top of the original

[12] 'On reflection, it also seems that this is not just one possible theory; it is the simplest theory which has any prospect of explaining the sense of agency, and we ought to work from it, introducing complications only as necessary' (Campbell 1999a: 612).

[13] Campbell (1999b)—emphasis added. He also states: 'You have knowledge of the content of the thought only through introspection. The content of the efferent copy is not itself conscious. But it is match at the monitor between the thought of which you have introspective knowledge and the efferent copy that is responsible for the sense of being the agent of that thought. It is a disturbance in that mechanism that is responsible for the schizophrenic finding that he is introspectively aware of a thought without having the sense of being the agent of that thought.'

[14] This use of the term can be found in Shoemaker (1986). Although Shoemaker begins by discussing Hume's reflective-introspective search for the self he criticizes the perceptual model of introspection as an 'inner sense' that would take primary consciousness as an object, or that would involve an identification of self. He is not committed to regarding introspection as a separate act of reflective consciousness. Shoemaker's notion of introspection is clearly stated by Cassam (1995: 315): 'introspective awareness, properly so called, is a form of awareness that serves as the basis for making first-person statements in which the first-person pronoun is used as subject. First-person statements in which "I" is used in this way are those that, in Shoemaker's terminology, are immune to error through misidentification relative to the first-person pronoun.'

match. It would be an extra level of consciousness added to the comparator's verification process. Again, in the case of thinking, which is already conscious, it seems to me that either the metarepresentation or the comparator's match (or both) is (are) redundant.

Not only does the requirement of metarepresentational verification not seem phenomenologically parsimonious in normal thought processes, it runs counter to some clinical accounts. Some theorists suggest, in contrast to Frith's notion that there is a *failure or lack* of metarepresentation (central monitoring) in schizophrenia, that there may be *too much* of it in schizophrenia. In principle, at least, it seems possible for metarepresentation to go wrong in at least two ways. First, as Frith emphasizes, it can fail in such a way that the schizophrenic can be left without the ability to monitor his own experience. Second, however, as Sass (1998) suggests, metarepresentation can become hyperreflective, and as a result, the schizophrenic can over-monitor aspects of his own experience. The failure of self-monitoring may be that there is too much of it going on (Sass 1998; Zahavi and Parnas 1998).[15] It is also possible that the disruption of metarepresentation can be selectively Frithian and Sassian. As a result of a failure to monitor certain aspects of his experience the schizophrenic may hyperreflect about what is absent from or odd about his experience. A schizophrenic may have great difficulties with attention, not because of a complete lack of attention, but because he is attending in a high degree to certain aspects of his experience that are different. To develop this suggestion, however, we need to think of this failure of monitoring, not on the Frithian model, as a failure of metarepresentation, but as a failure of some aspect of pre-reflective self-awareness (see below).

Temporality and the Episodic Nature of Positive Symptoms

A further set of problems with Frith's model involves its static nature. Frith takes no account of the temporal flow-structure of thought. To be clear, Frith may very well understand that the subpersonal comparator mechanisms involve issues of timing (for example, when does efference copy arrive at the comparator relative to registration of the conscious thought; or when precisely does the comparator do its job?).[16] What he does not account for, however, is the temporal structure of the thinking itself, which is part of the input to the central monitor.

---

[15] 'What happens here [in the case of the schizophrenic] is that the *ipseity*, the normally tacit or unnoticed "myness" of the experience, which is a precondition or a medium of any natural, spontaneous and absorbed intentionality, is deranged, and becomes an object of introspective intentionality' (Zahavi and Parnas 1998: 700).

[16] Georgieff and Jeannerod (1998), referring to the same kind of comparator model in the context of explaining motor action, describe it in implicitly temporal terms. Efference copy is said to create an 'anticipation for the consequences of the action'. Their description raises a number of issues that need to be explored: does efference copy reach the comparator prior to the registration of the motor action so that there is a real basis for anticipation; or does it reach the comparator simultaneously with the registration of the motor action, so that a simultaneous matching occurs? Spence (1996) raises a slightly different set of issues involving timing.

It is quite possible to incorporate temporality into Frith's model (see below) and I think to do so would help to address another serious objection that can been raised against it. If, in the case of schizophrenia, one of these comparator mechanisms goes wrong or is put out of operation, why do not all thoughts seem alien?[17] If either the TGM fails to generate efference copy or the central monitor fails to register efference copy, how do we explain that these mechanisms do seem to work normally sometimes, since not all the schizophrenic's thoughts are experienced as inserted thoughts? I will refer to this as *the problem of the selective or episodic nature of positive symptoms*. Selectivity involves the fact that when a particular thought seems inserted, there are other aspects of conscious experience that necessarily do not seem inserted. Either simultaneously with, or immediately after, the thought that seems inserted, there is the sense or feeling or realization that it is inserted. But this sense or feeling or realization does not itself feel inserted. That is, the subject, in recognizing a thought as inserted, does not claim that his recognition of this fact is inserted. He is rather speaking 'in his own voice' when he complains about the inserted thought. That this is the case is clear, not only from empirical reports by patients, but by logical necessity. The subject's complaint that various thoughts are inserted depends on a necessary contrast between thoughts that seem inserted and those that do not seem inserted—and at a minimum, the thoughts that constitute the subject's complaint cannot seem inserted. If all thoughts were experienced as inserted by others, the subject would not be able to complain in his own voice. He would not maintain a sufficient sense of ownership for his cognitive life, or a sense of cognitive 'space' by which to define an insertion. The selectivity problem cannot be explained by a failure of a comparator, since such a failure should also affect the sense of recognition that the thought is inserted. A theory that would credit a higher-order cognitive process (a metarepresentation, or an evaluative introspective judgment) runs into the same problem. It would need to explain why a higher-order cognition that fails to generate a sense of agency for a particular thought or experience is itself experienced as self-agentive. Why is it that a subject can have a sense of agency for one thought, but not for the other? Quite obviously the phenomenology here needs to constrain the cognitive explanation.

The Problem of Specificity

A further problem for Frith's model involves the specificity of positive symptoms. In this regard, in clinically described cases of thought insertion, specific kinds of thought contents, but not all kinds, appear to be thought inserted. It is not simply

---

[17] This objection was raised by Louis Sass at the NEH institute on Mind, Self, and Psychopathology, Cornell University, 1998. One can see this problem in Frith's (1992: 93) description of the neurophysiology associated with the positive symptoms of schizophrenia. 'Positive symptoms occur because the brain structures responsible for willed actions no longer send corollary discharges to the posterior parts of the brain concerned with perception. This would be caused by disconnections between these brain regions.' One would need to explain why these disconnections are manifested only in some and not all instances.

that in experiences of thought insertion patients occasionally experience thoughts coming into their minds from an outside source. Rather, their experiences are very specific, and are sometimes associated with specific others. For example, a schizophrenic may report that thoughts are being inserted by a particular person, and that they are always about a specified topic. In auditory hallucination the voice always seems to say the same sort of thing. Such specificity phenomena seem to have a semantic and experiential consistency and complexity that cannot be adequately explained by the disruption of subpersonal mechanisms alone.

Global Problems

A more general problem with Frith's analysis concerns the global and heterogeneous nature of schizophrenia and its various symptoms. Schizophrenics have problems, not only with movement and self-reference, but also, among other things, with working memory, episodic and autobiographical memory, and narrative construction (Gallagher 2003c). Is it possible to reduce all these problems to one central difficulty with self-monitoring, or to one comparator mechanism that is neurologically ill-defined? If the subject experiences both delusions of control and inserted thoughts, does this mean that two separate comparators—one in the motor system and one in the conscious thought system—malfunction independently? Or is the implication that one comparator covers both movement and thought? Or is something more global involved? At best Frith proposes similar mechanisms for motor action and cognition, but does not clarify how they might be related, or whether the embodied processes of motor control and cognition are connected.

Desynchronization and Subpersonal Explanation

My aim is not to solve all the problems that I have outlined above. I do want to suggest, however, that we can begin to address some of these problems by clarifying how embodied movement and cognition share some of the same temporal (dynamic) structures. My focus in the remainder of this chapter will be on considerations about the temporal nature of experience and how an understanding of the common temporal structures of both body-schematic and cognitive processes offers a way to address several of the problems involved in Frith's account. My more general aim is to show that this common structure means that embodiment is reflected in all aspects of experience.

A better account of delusions of control and of thought insertion can be had by making Frith's model less static, that is, by adding an explicit account of the temporal structure of experience. I want to pursue two strategies in this regard. On the first strategy, I will stay with Frith's model and, by introducing some considerations about temporality, try to work out a solution to the problem of the episodic nature of positive symptoms. On the second strategy, however, I suggest that even this enhanced model fails, and that an alternative account that involves a different model of temporality would be more successful.

Following the first strategy, the various cognitive processes described in Frith's model must involve time. That is, if we view the thought process to involve a Jamesian stream of thinking, then the underlying cognitive mechanisms would have to take into account the temporal flow structure of that stream. So in a temporally enhanced Frithian model, the stream of thought would have to be in sync with the streams of efference copy and other signals representing intention and thought generation, in order properly to match up at the comparators. If for some reason the signal streams go out of and then back into sync, then *some* thoughts will seem alien (as in the case of thought insertion) and others will not. One possible answer to the episodic nature of thought insertion, then, involves the idea that *on occasion* information streams go out of sync and there is a failure to match. One way this might happen is if one of the mechanisms occasionally sputters, and in the mode of sputtering, either the streams go out of sync, or the signals are not properly generated, or the comparators do not properly register one or other of the signals (see Fig. 8.4). To be more specific, however, if the TGM sputters, then it would seem plausible that both the generated thought and the efference copy would suffer the effects of the sputtering, and there would still be a synchrony between them. Further, the schizophrenic's phenomenology, if we think of it as being somewhat isomorphic with the mechanism of thought generation, does not seem to indicate anything about the thought stream that would suggest sputtering, other than the variation in the sense of agency. It is not a sputtering thought, but a relatively lucid and intelligible thought that seems inserted. If it is not the TGM that sputters, then the problem would seem to be with the signal representing the intention, or some problem in the forward comparator. These alternatives would leave the thought intact, but, lacking a match with efference copy at the comparator, it would be experienced without a sense of agency, and thus as inserted.

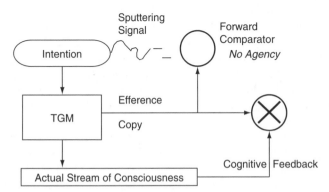

FIG. 8.4.   Sputtering mechanism. No match at the forward comparator results in the experience of inserted thoughts.

Whether a sputtering mechanism can account for a desynchronization or not, it is quite possible that one stream simply slows down relative to the other one. There is good evidence that neuronal processes (information processing) may slow down in circumstances of brain injury, and under the influence of alcohol and/or various drugs. Many times these neurophysiological distortions are accompanied by distortions in the experience of time—distortions not unlike those experienced by schizophrenics (see Pöppel 1994; Pöppel, von Cramon, and Blackmund 1975). Quite relevant to the phenomenon of hearing voices, there is evidence to suggest that auditory centers are susceptible to such slowing, on the order of over three times difference from normal (Pöppel 1994). Slowing of such processes, if, for example, they affected one sense modality more than others, or affected specific and strategic neuronal functions, could easily cause a form of 'temporal diplopia' (p. 192) in which efference copy comes to be out of joint with the conscious stream. This discrepancy might also explain the breakdown in experienced continuity suffered in some schizophrenics (Pöppel 1994: 199).

The effects of such subpersonal distortions, however, even if they only occasionally caused the disruption synchrony, would have to involve a relatively sophisticated sputtering or neurophysiological slowing in order to account for the actual phenomenology of the schizophrenic. The selectivity problem of the episodic nature of positive symptoms is complicated by the specificity problem. It is not simply that in thought insertion patients occasionally experience thoughts coming into their minds from an outside source, but in terms of content, their experiences are very specific and are often associated with specific others. Schizophrenics may experience a certain semantic consistency amid the agentive inconsistency of their inserted thoughts. That is, inserted thoughts often seem to be of a similar mind-set. This semantic and experiential consistency cannot be adequately accounted for by a disruption of subpersonal processes.

For example, a schizophrenic will report that a particular person inserts certain thoughts, and that they are always about a specified topic, or that the voice always seems to say the same sort of thing. Frith gives the following example: 'Thoughts are put into my mind like "Kill God". It's just like my mind working, but it isn't. They come from this chap, Chris. They're his thoughts' (1992: 66). Some patients feel controlled by other people, or even by machines (see e.g. Bovet and Parnas 1993). Part of the explanation, then, would seem to depend on the intentional content of the thought, and not simply on a subpersonal disruption of efference copy. If subpersonal malfunctions, or predispositions to such malfunctions, are part of the explanation, then we might have to think of intentional content as a possible trigger that would disrupt such functions.

Thus, a subpersonal explanation does not entirely resolve the specificity or selectivity problems, which may in fact have their proximate cause on the level of personal/semantic/intentional content. What kind of personal-level events could trigger a subpersonal desynchronization? There is good evidence and there are good arguments to show that intentional content has an effect on the temporal structure of experience (Friedman 1990; Gallagher 1998; James 1890). Temporal structure is not purely formal. Experience speeds up or slows down according to *what* we are experiencing. Consider, for example, the ordinary experience of how time passes when we are with different people. In some cases time passes too quickly, in other cases too slowly. Complicate this picture with emotion and/or the unconscious (whatever you take that to be). If boredom can slow the system down, and enjoyment and interest speed it up, perhaps anxiety or some such emotion can cause a desynchronization in the system. Would it not be possible that in some schizophrenics, in the presence of certain significant individuals, or in certain kinds of situations, or confronted with certain objects, or on the occasion of an unbidden thought, an unruly emotion, for example anxiety or fear, might trigger (unconsciously) a disruption in predisposed cognitive mechanisms? The result would be a desynchronization brought on by an emotion that prenoetically shades and shapes cognitive processes. The force of the emotion would be cashed out in terms of embodiment. It would involve neurophysiological and autonomic changes, caused by changes in the intentional content of experience.[18] Just in such cases or similar circumstances, frequently linked to an emotional encounter, a schizophrenic subject would then (but not always) experience thought insertion. This kind of explanation would address both the selectivity and specificity problems. One unresolved difficulty with this proposal, however, is the fact that although some schizophrenic patients present with dysphoric mood (depressed, anxious, irritable, or angry mood), in most cases they demonstrate flattened emotional patterns, that is, flat affect rather than a state of emotional upset. I return to this issue in my considerations of an alternative model.

An alternative model is motivated because even the enhanced Frithian model still involves a number of the other unresolved problems: the uncertain status of an intention to think, the redundancy of efference copy in a system that involves conscious thought, the uncertain role of metarepresentation, the fact that the model does not explain misattribution of agency, and the other global problems. Although there is no question of explaining all the complex aspects of schizophrenia, there is an alternative model that addresses many of the problems just mentioned.

An Alternative Model: The Ubiquitous Temporal Structure of Experience

To develop an alternative model it will be helpful to return briefly to the context of motor action. There we distinguished a sense of ownership from a sense of agency, and we suggested that this same distinction could be worked out in the context of

---

[18] See Ch. 6. Gerrans (1999), and the work of Young (1999) and Damasio (1994) provide some indication of how to think of affect as crossing personal and subpersonal levels.

cognition. In terms of underlying mechanisms, we distinguished two basic models in regard to motor action:

1. an ecological, sensory-feedback model that delivers a sense of ownership for action;
2. an *anticipatory* pre-action or forward model that delivers a sense of agency for action.

I note two things in regard to these body-schematic systems. First, both the experiential aspects of intentional motor action, the sense of ownership and the sense of agency, are normally experienced as *intrinsic* to the action. They are phenomenologically indistinguishable properties of the acting itself. Second, the pre-action system is *anticipatory*. Alain Berthoz in his recent work on movement, makes much of the ubiquity of such anticipatory mechanisms in the sensory-motor systems. Anticipation is 'an essential characteristic of their functioning', and serves our capacity to reorganize our actions in line with events that are yet to happen (Berthoz 2000: 25). Georgieff and Jeannerod (1998) also emphasize this anticipatory character of motor control: efference copy is said to create an 'anticipation for the consequences of the action'. Neurological and behavioral evidence suggests that the sense of agency for action, which goes awry in pathological symptoms such as delusions of control, is not based on a *post factum* sensory-feedback match occurring subsequent to the action or thought, even if we consider this a concurrent confirmation implicit to action, and as enhancing the sense of agency. Rather, the sense of agency is generated in a control function (the forward model) that anticipates action (see Jeannerod 2001; MacKay 1966; Wolpert, Ghahramani, and Jordan 1995).

As we have indicated, efference copy may indeed play an important practical (control) role in the case of visuo-motor systems, but it is not clear what role it would play in the stream of thought. Alternative and more parsimonious explanations for a sense of agency that is *intrinsic* to thought, and for the loss of the sense of agency in schizophrenic thought insertion, can be advanced by employing a phenomenological model of the retentional-protentional structure of consciousness. Starting with an analysis of this temporal structure developed by Husserl (1991), one can develop a phenomenologically based cognitive model. Husserl finds phenomenological evidence for what he calls 'retentions' and 'protentions' as structural features of consciousness. As part of a cognitive model, these structures may be regarded as prenoetic operations that generate the flow-structure of consciousness and are related in some general way to working memory. They constitute the pre-reflective structure of consciousness. My conscious experience includes a pre-reflective sense of what I have just been thinking (or perceiving, or remembering, etc.) and a pre-reflective sense that this thinking (perceiving, remembering, etc.) will continue in either a determinate or indeterminate way. This phenomenological temporal sense is based on retentional and protentional processes that ultimately need to be cashed out in terms of neurological processes. Although such suggestions go beyond Husserl's phenomenological analysis in the direction of neuroscience, they follow the same logic of time-consciousness that he outlines.

I will explicate in a brief and relatively rough manner Husserl's phenomenology of time-consciousness. I can do this most expeditiously by referring to a diagram (Fig. 8.5). This diagram, and Husserl's theory, not only explain how the perception of temporal objects, such as a melody, is possible, given an *enduring* act of consciousness, they also explain how consciousness unifies *itself* across time.[19] The horizontal line ABCD represents a temporal object such as a melody of several notes. The vertical lines represent abstract momentary phases of an enduring act of consciousness. Each phase is structured by three functions:

- *primal impression* (pi), which allows for the consciousness of an object (a musical note, for example) that is simultaneous with the current phase of consciousness;
- *retention* (r), which retains previous phases of consciousness and their intentional content;
- *protention* (p), which anticipates experience that is just about to happen.

In the now-phase there is a retentioning (r_3) of the previous phase of consciousness. Of course the just-past phase includes its own retentioning of the prior phase. This means that there is a retentional continuum—$r_3(r_2(r_1))$, and so forth—that stretches back over prior experience. The continuity involved in retention has two aspects. The first provides for the intentional unification of consciousness itself since retention is the retention of previous phases of consciousness. Husserl characterizes this as the longitudinal intentionality (*Längsintentionalität*) of retention. But since the prior phases of consciousness contain their respective primal impressions of the previously sounded notes, there is also established a continuity of the experienced

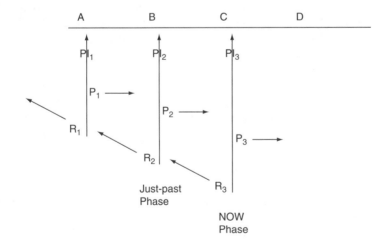

FIG. 8.5.   Husserlian model of time-consciousness.

[19] A more detailed account can be found in Husserl (1991). For an extended analysis of Husserl's model and its similarities and differences from James's and Broad's notion of the specious present, see Gallagher (1998).

object. Husserl (1991: 85) calls this the 'transverse intentionality' (*Querintentionalität*) of retention.

The example of speaking or listening to a sentence may help to clarify some things. Consider the beginning of a sentence: 'I often think that Julia . . . ' When in uttering this sentence I reach the word 'Julia' I am no longer saying the previous words, but I still retain a sense of what I have just said. For a sentence to be meaningful, for a speaker or listener, the sense of the earlier words must be kept in mind in some fashion when I am uttering the later words. *Retention*, or what cognitive scientists call working memory, keeps the intentional sense of the words available even after the words are no longer sounded. Built into this retentional (longitudinal) function is the sense that *I* am the one who has just said these words. The words do not become part of a free-floating anonymity, nor do they seem to belong to someone else; they remain, for me, part of the sentence that *I* am in the process of uttering, because they remain part of my stream of consciousness. In addition, at the moment that I am uttering 'Julia', I have some anticipatory sense of where the sentence is going, or at the very least, that the sentence is heading to some kind of ending. This sense of knowing where the sentence (the thought) is heading, even if not completely definite, seems essential to the experience I have of speaking in a meaningful way. It helps to provide a sense that I am speaking in a sentential fashion, and not speaking a meaningless set of phrases. Indeed, one might say that this working anticipation helps me to keep my utterances sentential and on track.

Protentioning provides consciousness with an intentional sense that something more will happen. Although Husserl provides an exhaustive explication of retention, he says very little of protention, except that it is like retention in the direction of the future. Husserl does point out that the protentional aspect of consciousness allows for the experience of surprise. If I am listening to a favorite melody, there is some sense of what is to come, a primal expectation of the notes to follow, and the best indication of this is that if someone hits the wrong note, I am surprised or disappointed. If a person fails to complete a sentence, I experience a sense of incompleteness. This kind of perceptual disappointment is based on a lack of fulfillment of that primal expectation that Husserl calls protention. In some sense we might speak here of a failure to match my anticipation with what actually happens. The content of protention is not always completely determinate, however. Indeed, to the extent that the future itself is indeterminate, the content of protention may approach the most general sense of 'something (without specification) has to happen next'.

Husserl's analysis of protention does not go much further. As we saw above, however, in his analysis of retention he suggests that there is a double intentionality—one aspect of which is directed at the content of experience and another at consciousness itself. This double intentionality involves a structure that is similar to the Gibsonian notion of an ecological self-awareness.[20] That is, I am not only aware

---

[20] It would be difficult to explicate the similarities and differences between Gibsonian psychology and Husserlian phenomenology on such points. Gibson (1987: 418) himself was inclined to think of his ecological model as applying to thinking as well as to perceptual and motor functions. 'Awareness of the

of the melody, I am implicitly self-aware of being aware of the melody—to put it in its adverbial form, I am *consciously* aware of the melody (see Thomasson 2000).

My experience of the passage of a melody is at the same time a non-observational, pre-reflective awareness of my own flowing experience. This retentional self-awareness delivers a sense that this thinking process is *mine*—that *I* am the one who is listening to the melody or uttering the sentence. Without meaning to suggest any other kind of symmetry, is there not something like a double intentionality involved in protention as well? That is, my anticipatory sense of the next note of the melody, or of where the sentence is heading, or that I will continue to think, is also, implicitly, an anticipatory sense that these will be experiences *for me*, or that *I* will be the one listening, speaking, or thinking. In effect, protention also has what Husserl calls a longitudinal aspect—it involves a projective sense, not only of what is about to happen, but of what *I* am about to do or experience.

In the normal case the sense of agency with respect to my own thought comes not retrospectively, as if I had to stop to think whether I am really the one who is thinking (this in contrast to Frith's metarepresentation). Rather, it is a sense that is built into thinking itself. It is part of the very structure of consciousness. The fact that it is not retrospective, or a matter of verification, suggests that it is not initially a matter of the retentional aspect of this structure. Rather, following the clues from our considerations of motor action, I want to suggest that the *protentional* mechanism underlies the sense of agency for thought, or more precisely, that protention is a necessary but not a sufficient condition for the sense of agency. The function of *retention*, on the other hand, is, in part, to provide a sense of ownership for thought.

Consider first that thought may be generated by the subject in a willed and controlled fashion. Problem solving, thinking through a set of instructions, and narrating a story are good examples. I may intend to solve a problem and to do so by following precise steps in a known procedure. I have a sense of where I am going in the procedure, and I push the thinking process along from one step to another in a controlled manner. When I follow a set of instructions, or when I tell a story (perhaps just to myself), I have the same sense that I am promoting my thinking along a path that is, or is becoming, relatively well defined. In such cases, the protentional aspect of consciousness operates to give me a sense of where the thinking process is going *in its very making*, that is, as it is being generated and developed. It provides a sense that the thinking process is being generated in my

---

persisting and changing environment (perception) is concurrent with the persisting and changing self (proprioception in my extended use of the term). This includes the body and its parts and all its activities from locomotion to thought, without any distinction between the activities called "mental" and those called "physical" '. If we try to look beyond the different starting points involved in these models, there is one important structural difference. For Gibson, the proprioceptive awareness of the changing self comes about only on the basis of awareness of the changing environment. In these terms, I would be aware of my own flowing experience only as a result of being aware of the changing environment. For Husserl, retention of the past phase of the objective content (transverse intentionality) is possible only on the basis of retention of past phases of consciousness itself (longitudinal intentionality). Translated to Gibsonian terminology, proprioceptive awareness is the basis for the experience of a coherent objectivity.

own stream of consciousness and, to some degree, under my control. Consider what would happen if I had no protentional anticipation of what was to come. In that case I would be left to the mercy of chance and constantly surprised.

A second kind of thinking, however, may be more passive. Unbidden thoughts, memories, fantasies, and so forth, may invade our current stream of consciousness. These are thoughts for which we may have no sense of agency. Still, in such cases, we have a sense that these thoughts are coming from ourselves, rather than from some alien source. Not only do they appear to be part of my stream of consciousness, but, despite the fact that I am not willing them, and may even be resisting them, they still seem to be generated within my own cognitive experience. Protention, in such cases, may be operating perfectly well, providing a sense of where these thoughts are coming from and where they are heading, as they are being passively generated, even within the framework of an unwanted memory or an unwelcome fantasy. Protention may also function to provide a sense of *not knowing* where we are heading, that is, providing a sense of uncertainty, or indeterminacy with respect to where such thoughts will lead. For even though I do not intend such thoughts, nor have a sense of where they are heading, I do feel that they are leading somewhere, and I still have a sense that they are originating and developing within my stream of consciousness. Protention provides some kind of expectancy for them, even if it is completely indeterminate.

What would happen, however, if, just in such cases of unbidden thoughts, the protentional function itself failed? Thinking would continue to happen, but there would be neither a sense of agency, nor a sense that these thoughts were being passively generated in my cognitive system, even though they were appearing in my stream of consciousness. I would be unready for such thoughts. They would appear as if from nowhere, and their occurrence would be sudden and unexpected. I would be able to make sense of them only in their retentional train, in retrospect, but not as something self-generated. Protention normally puts me in the forefront of my thoughts and allows me to take them up as my own product, as they develop. Lacking protention, thoughts would seem to impose themselves on me.

Consider listening to a partial sentence uttered by someone else. 'I often think that Laura ... ' Normally, protention, and the context, allow me to make sense of the sentence as it is being uttered. I might even be tempted to complete the sentence because I know what the person is going to say. Or, even if I do not know what the person is going to say, I could quickly organize a reasonable end to the sentence—as people often do when someone seems unable to find the right words to finish the thought. But consider a case in which I am caught completely by surprise, as when someone close by, but out of sight, suddenly yells 'Surprise!' In this case, there is no anticipation of the event, even of the most indeterminate kind. The event passes before I realize it is happening. In listening to someone form a sentence, I have a sense of how it is being formed; but in the case of the sudden shout, I catch onto it only as it comes into retention. Absent a properly directed protention, the sudden and quickly formed event is *already made* by the time I come to grasp it. Over the course of a second or two, however, an adjustment of attention will bring this event and whatever follows into its proper framework; I regain a sense of where the voice is coming from and its significance, and my experience is quickly put back on track.

A similar surprise effect may be had, however, if, instead of an external event catching the protentional function off guard, something goes wrong with the protentional mechanism itself. Imagine my surprise if it was I who yelled 'Surprise', without any expectation on my part of doing so. Or, if in the case of an unbidden thought for which I have no sense of agency, something goes wrong with the normal anticipatory sense of what my own thinking will be, the result will be a sense that the thought is not being generated by me.[21] Thought generation, like any experience, is normally protentional. Without protention, thought continues, but it appears already made, not generated by me, appearing suddenly, already formulated as it enters into retention. It is a thought that is neither intended nor anticipated; it will seem to be a thought in my stream of consciousness, but not a thought generated by me. In some way I am not open to it; I am not projected or absorbed into it; it feels alien and less than transparent to me.

Indeed, this may also be the case with intended thoughts for which I would normally have a sense of agency. Without protention, whatever intention I may have, whatever sense I would have of where my thoughts will be going, or whatever sense I have of where *I* will be going with them, or where I *will* them to go, is disrupted. My non-observational, pre-reflective sense of agency for my own thinking, which is normally based on anticipatory aspects of experience, will be deferred by the lack of protention. That is, my intention will register experientially only after the fact (as it is captured in retention). In this case, I experience thoughts that seem not to be generated by me but seem to have anticipated what I wanted to think. A schizophrenic patient will sometimes report that another person seems to know what she is thinking before she actually thinks it. The thought seems to match up with her own intention, but it still seems to her that she is not the agentive cause of the thought.[22]

Thus, *without protention*, in cases both of intended thought and of unintended thinking, thinking will occur within the stream of consciousness that is not experienced *in the making*, but is nonetheless captured by a retentional structure that continues to function and, in its longitudinal function, to provide a sense of ownership for that stream. I will experience what is actually my own thinking, as thinking that is not generated by me, a thinking that is *already made* or preformed for me, as if I were a receptor of thought. It is only then, on the basis of this first-order experience of alien thought, that a metarepresentational element might be

---

[21] Something along this same line happens when one is falling asleep. Both protentional and retentional mechanisms seem to close down. Consider what happens to comprehension when one is falling asleep while reading. In dreaming too, one does not have a good sense of what will happen next, or a good sense of what has been happening. Memory for dream content is limited because retention dissipates too quickly to register in episodic memory.

[22] Spence (1996: 82) cites a case that he interprets in this way. He indicates, however, that this kind of experience resembles something that is more frequently found in anarchic hand syndrome, that is, in cases where a subject loses control over a limb.

initiated in the patient, a reflective introspection that is likely to become the hyperreflection characteristic of schizophrenic experience, motivated by something gone wrong with the flow of consciousness. In metarepresentation the patient may start to ascribe the thought to some particular force or individual and report that it has been inserted.[23]

We can see good evidence for the breakdown of the protentional function in schizophrenia in an experiment carried out by Frith and Done (1988). It had been demonstrated that a randomly occurring tone elicits a relatively large response in EEG, but that if the tone is self-generated, for example by pushing a button, the EEG response will be of much smaller amplitude (Shafer and Marcus 1973). In the latter case, the protentional anticipation of the tone, linked to the subject's own agency, obviously diminishes the evoked response. Frith and Done tested schizophrenic patients with positive symptoms using the same paradigm. They verified that for 80 per cent of these subjects the evoked responses to self-generated tones were similar in amplitude to the evoked responses to randomly occurring tones. That is, compared to controls, the relatively high EEG response for self-generated tones suggests that the schizophrenic patients did not expect the tone, despite their own agency in its production.[24]

A breakdown in the protentional function is also consistent with the schizophrenic's experience of time. Minkowski, who describes schizophrenia as involving 'acts without concern for tomorrow', 'fixed acts', 'short-circuit acts', and 'purposeless acts', quotes one of his patients: 'There is an absolute fixity around me. I have even less mobility for the future than I have for the present and the past. There is a kind of routine in me which does not allow me to envisage the future. The creative power in me is abolished. I see the future as a repetition of the past' (1933: 277).[25]

Empirical studies show that schizophrenics experience difficulties in indexing events in time, and these difficulties are positively correlated to inner–outer confusions (manifested in symptoms such as auditory hallucinations, feelings of being

---

[23] Spence (1996: 81) suggests that thought insertion involves two elements: first, alienation from one's own thoughts; second, 'a delusional elaboration' which seeks to explain the former. The delusional elaboration takes place at the metarepresentational level and follows the initial alienation that has already occurred at the level of pre-reflexive consciousness. This is consistent with the view developed by Parnas (2000) and Sass (2000). The second, but not the first, element is consistent with Stephens and Graham (2000). The first, but not necessarily the second, is consistent with Gallagher (2004).

[24] A similar result was found by Posada *et al.* (2001). They showed their subjects colors appearing on a computer screen in a fixed temporal order. The subjects were able to learn the sequence of colors easily, by watching and repeating the color names verbally. During the learning process they were instructed to press a key each time a given color appeared on the screen. As a subject learnt the order, the time to press the key sharply decreased so that after a certain time, the key was pressed in anticipation *before* the color was shown. Schizophrenic patients were able to learn the sequence normally, but in contrast to a normal control group, they proved to be impaired in using their explicit knowledge to produce anticipatory responses. Differences were not due to differences in reaction times.

[25] This explanation may also account for the perseverative repetitious responses that are often found in schizophrenic patients. A failed protentional mechanism may explain difficulty in generating spontaneous actions, a negative symptom in schizophrenia, as well as difficulties in performing self-directed search (see Frith 1992: 48).

influenced, delusional perceptions, and so forth), problems that involve distinguishing between self and non-self (Melges 1982; Melges and Freeman 1977). Other studies suggest that future time-perspective is curtailed in schizophrenia (Dilling and Rabin 1967; Wallace 1956). Schizophrenics have difficulty planning and initiating action (Levin 1984) and problems with temporal organization (DePue, Dubicki, and McCarthy 1975; Klonoff, Fibiger, and Hutton 1970). Bovet and Parnas (1993: 584) describe these problems in general terms as an 'impairment of self-temporalization' and they are certainly symptoms we might expect if the protentional mechanism malfunctions. It is suggestive, and perhaps important, that Singh and his colleagues have linked these temporalization problems with the same neurological dysfunctions involved in the schizophrenic's voluntary movement (Singh *et al.* 1992; also see Graybiel 1997).

The temporal structure that is shared by consciousness, cognition, and action is evidenced in the precise timing that is covertly present in coordinated movement and consciousness of that movement. If I am asked to tap my foot simultaneously with movement of my finger, the two movements are experienced as precisely simultaneous, when in fact the foot moves slightly before the finger in objective time. This temporal discrepancy in movement accommodates the extra time it takes for proprioceptive signals from the foot to reach the brain (Jacques Paillard, private correspondence). If this precise timing were disrupted to a significant degree, it is likely that the subject would experience the self-generated movement as alien.

Consider a report made by Cole, Sacks, and Waterman (2000). They explain how during an experiment with robotic arms at NASA's Houston Space Center they were led to misidentify the robotic arms as parts of their own body. It is to be noted that Jonathan Cole and Oliver Sacks both have normal proprioception; Ian Waterman, as we know from Ch. 3, does not.

The robot's arms have joints which move like human arms and three fingers on each hand. The arms are viewed by the human subject through a virtual reality set placed over the eyes, with robot cameras set in the robot's head, so that one views the robot arms from a similar viewpoint as one views one's own arms. No direct vision of one's own body is possible, as one sits across the room from the robot. A series of sensors are placed on one's own arms which in turn control the robot arms' movement. Then when one moves, the robot's arms move similarly, after a short delay.

Then one sees and controls the robot's moving arms, without receiving any peripheral feedback from them, (but [for JC and OS] having one's own peripheral feedback from one's unseen arms). We transferred tools from one hand to another, picked up an egg and tied knots. After a few minutes we all became at home with the feeling of being in the robot. Making a movement and seeing it successful led to a strong sense of embodiment within the robot arms and body. This was manifest when one of us thought that he had better be careful for if he dropped a wrench it would land on his leg. Only the robot arms had been seen and moved, but the perception was that one's body was in the robot. This feeling was present in able-bodied people who have tried the robot and in a subject [IW] with a large fibre sensory neuropathy without the sensations of movement/position sense or light touch below the neck. (Cole, Sacks, and Waterman 2000: 167)

Cole, Sacks, and Waterman note the existence of a short delay between motor command and robotic movement. The question is, how long could that delay become before the sense of agency breaks down?

To answer this, and to see the importance of timing to the sense of agency, consider a different set of experiments. Jesper Brøsted Sørensen, a psychologist at the University of Copenhagen, asked me to help test an 'alien hand' experiment that he designed (see Sørensen 2005). The apparatus he was using was actually a very old one, originally used by Nielsen (1963) (see Fig. 8.6). As the subject in the experiment I look through a scope to see a piece of paper on which I am going to draw a straight vertical line from point A to point B. Through the scope, however, I cannot see point A, although I can see point B and the space between A and B. Point A is visible to me only before looking into the scope, and I set the point of my pen at A prior to the start of the test. I wear a glove on my right hand, which is the hand with which I am going to draw. The task is very simple and I perform it without difficulty on the first three trials. On the fourth and subsequent trials, however, something goes wrong. My hand veers off to the right and draws a line that misses point B by about 10 degrees. Not only do I see my hand veer off to the right, but the proprioceptive feel is as if my hand is being pulled to the right, against my will. It turns out that this is an illusion in which vision distorts proprioceptive awareness. The experimental apparatus allows the experimenter to play some tricks on the subject. Jesper, invisible to me on the other side of the apparatus, has the matching glove on his left hand and is drawing a line 10 degrees to the left of a different point B. A mirror set at 45 degrees has been shifted in such a way that when I look through the scope I actually see Jesper's hand drawing his line. Both my vision and my proprioception are fooled.[26]

The illusion concerns self-awareness of self-generated action. Throughout the experiment, my sense of ownership and sense of agency for the action remained intact, despite the feeling that some force was pulling my hand off course. Deprati et al. (1997), however, using a similar design, showed that at a discrepancy of above 10–15 degrees normal subjects start to suspect that the hand they see really isn't their own. For schizophrenics, the divergence has to approach 30 degrees. In those cases where movements of the alien hand were close to identical to the subjects, non-schizophrenic subjects were unable to tell that it was not their hand 30 per cent of the time; but for schizophrenics who suffered from delusions of control, the percentage was closer to 80. But what happens if, instead of a spatial discrepancy, we introduce a temporal discrepancy? An experiment conducted by Franck et al. (2001), based on Nielsen's (1963) original paradigm, introduces a time delay. In cases where

[26] Vision is the primary component of this illusion. If, as I started to draw my line I also closed my eyes, proprioception on its own would tell me that I was drawing a straight line toward point B. And in fact, I would be drawing a straight line toward point B. With my eyes open, however, proprioception works intermodally with vision, and vision controls. Vision tells me that I am veering towards the right, and on that basis I attempt to correct, trying to keep my hand moving towards the target. As a result, the line that I actually draw goes to the left of point B. The proprioceptive sense of my arm being pulled or forced to the right is generated by my effort to correct the line in opposition to what visually continues to be a veering toward the right.

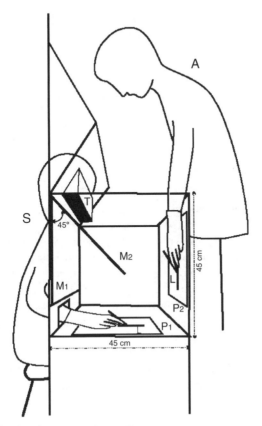

Fɪɢ. 8.6.   The alien hand apparatus. *Source:* Sørensen 2005.

normal (non-psychotic) subjects see a computer image of their action at delays up to 150 msec. they judge the observed action to be their own. When the delay is over 150 msec., however, they start to judge the action not to be their own.[27]

This suggests that in non-schizophrenic experience the protentional anticipation of self-generated movement, and the sense of self-agency, start to dissipate in discrepancies that extend beyond 150 msec. Although I still know that I have moved (I retain a sense of ownership for my action), outside this temporal window what I anticipate as the result of my initiation of action is left unfulfilled; the

---

[27] Schizophrenic subjects, however, don't make that judgment until closer to a delay of 300 msecs. The interpretation of these results is complicated, however, by a number of factors, as noted by the authors— including the fact that the subjects were on medication, and that schizophrenics have difficulty in perceiving slight temporal differences. As we have seen, in some cases, schizophrenics who suffer from delusions of influence seem unable to anticipate the results of their own action (Frith and Done 1988). As a result, patients sometimes attribute their own actions to others ('underattribution'). In other cases their sense of self-agency seems to extend beyond the protentional frame (Franck *et al.* 2001). This results in 'overattribution' in which patients self-attribute the actions of others.

action that is in fact generated by me fails to register within the protentional frame as the one that I generated, and it seems alien to me. If we introduce a delay on this order of magnitude into the NASA experiments with robotic arms, it is likely to produce that same sense of alienation. As Cole, Sacks, and Waterman (2000) suggest, our senses of self-agency and ownership are fragile structures. This fragility reflects the more general frailty of the temporal structures of self-awareness outlined here.

Emotion and Intersubjectivity

This alternative, phenomenologically guided account begins with evidence about the structure of experience, but also lends itself to the explication of subpersonal mechanisms and brain processes that may be responsible for that structure (see the following section). If the episodic nature of positive symptoms, and the specificity problem, require something more than a subpersonal account, however, we need to re-examine the idea that there is a personal-level trigger for this disruption of the temporal structure of experience. So again we must ask what could cause the malfunction of protentional mechanisms that would lead to schizophrenic symptoms? One suggestion, outlined above, is that content has an effect on the temporal structure of experience. Affective content, that is, experiential content that generates prenoetic emotional effects, complicates both the phenomenological and neurological pictures. So again, it is quite possible that in schizophrenia, unruly emotions such as anxiety or fear might trigger a disruption in cognitive mechanisms, specifically a disruption of protention. This may happen in the presence of certain significant individuals, or in a certain kind of situation, or confronted with a certain object, or in rehearsing certain thoughts. In those cases or similar circumstances, and in line with the episodic and selective nature of positive symptoms, a subject would then (but not always) experience thought insertion or similar loss in the sense of agency. It is also possible that this disruption of the protentional function could cause a looping effect that would reinforce the affective trigger. Without protention, for example, it is quite possible that patients would experience the world as being invasive, 'on top of them', too close, etc., which are, in fact, experiences reported by schizophrenics.

Schizophrenic patients manifesting these symptoms do not always appear to be emotionally upset, although in some cases they do. Here I think it is important to distinguish between overt emotional states that may be the result of positive symptoms, and prenoetic disruptions of affective experience that may not always manifest themselves in emotional attitudes. Examples of the former can be found in patients who suffer and report terror (Eilan 2000) or anguish (Sass 2000) as a result of their delusions or their inability to cope with reality. Instances of prenoetic disruptions may lead to just such emotional manifestations, or, in complete contrast, to flattened affect (traditionally classified as a negative symptom). For understanding the possibility of a breakdown of protentional structure, the idea of a prenoetic disruption of affect is important.

The retentional-protentional structure of consciousness (specifically in its longitudinal aspect) is constitutive of self-identity within the changing flow of consciousness; it generates the basic sense of *auto-affection* or *ipseity* (Parnas 2000; Sass and Parnas 2003). This is the feeling of identity, of being the perspectival origin of one's own experience, which is a basic component of the experienced differentiation of self from non-self. This feeling is an 'affective tonality' that is implicit to the structure of the stream of experience.[28] We might say that there is *something it feels like* to be me; something that is sometimes set askew, as when I'm sick I might say that I don't quite feel myself today. This includes the sense that *I am the one who is experiencing*, explicated in terms of my senses of ownership and agency. As Depraz (1994: 75) describes it, in auto-affection, 'I am affected before knowing that I am affected. It is in that sense that affect can be said to be primordial.' This affective tonality is tacit in the sense that I am not usually or explicitly aware of it. Rather, I notice it when it is not there. A short-term disruption motivates reflection on this normally tacit dimension; in the case of the schizophrenic, it can motivate hyper-reflection (Sass 2000).

Some illness, some trauma, some personal-level event may trigger the original disruption of auto-affective protentional functions—functions that in some people, in terms of their neurological underpinnings, may be genetically or developmentally predisposed to disruption. This original disruption may be further reinforced by subsequent emotional reactions. The various positive symptoms are not affectively neutral (even if the content of thought is not overtly emotionally charged), but are characterized by specific affective dispositions, which in some cases involve a lack of or alienation from affect. Such symptoms may lead to hyperreflective behavior, to the fragmentation of meaning, to transformations of intentionality, to a lack of attunement with the world, to abnormal feelings of saliency, or to negative symptoms such as flattened affect.

If the protentional mechanism is essentially linked to affective tonality, and if affective tonality is, as Varela suggests, 'a major boundary and initial condition for neurodynamics' more generally (Varela 1999*a*, *b*), then a disruption of protention is likely to involve widespread cognitive and emotional problems of the sort found in schizophrenia.[29] As Parnas (2000: 122) indicates, any disturbance in this tacit, auto-affective dimension of ipseity 'is likely to have subtle but broadly reverberating effects; such disturbances must necessarily upset the balance and shake the foundations of both self and world'. Let's add to this, not only self and world, but self and other.

---

[28] This analysis links up closely to Francisco Varela's explication of protention in terms of a primordial affective tonality. Following Husserl (also see Depraz 1994, 1998), Varela (1999*a*, *b*) bestows on protention the function of providing a felt tension or readiness for action. See Gallagher and Varela (2002).

[29] The emotional problems include incongruity of affect, and flat affect (athymia) (DSM-III-R). Bovet and Parnas (1993) summarize a number of premorbid characteristics of schizophrenia patients, which include difficulties in interpersonal relations, anxiety, neophobia, and defective emotional rapport.

Through all this the one thing that has not been explained is why in schizophrenic symptoms of delusions of control and thought insertion the subject misattributes agency to someone else. The idea that problems with protention can reflect or contribute to problems with the integration of information in the nervous system (and in the next section I suggest that this is the case on a global dynamic scale) and that this can lead to problems with recognizing self-agency, is perfectly consistent with a number of recent brain imaging studies (some conducted by Frith) that attempt to track down the neural correlates of the sense of agency.

Here I will mention one theoretical model that is based on a promising and ongoing empirical research project. This model is usually referred to as the 'Who' system (Georgieff and Jeannerod 1998). Overlapping brain areas, or 'shared representations', in the motor, premotor, and prefrontal cortexes are activated in the following conditions: during motor action, during the observation of another's motor action, and during the imaginative enactment (conscious simulation) of my own or another's motor action. That is, the same neuronal areas are activated when I engage in intentional action and when I see or imagine such action performed by another person. In itself the model of shared representations suggests that there is occasion for a confusion concerning who is doing the action. Jeannerod and his colleagues point out, however, that the distinction between my own action and the action of the other may depend on the non-overlapping areas of this neural matrix. On this model the sense of agency would be generated in those brain areas that are activated when I engage in intentional action but are not activated when I see or imagine someone else similarly engaged, and vice versa. A number of recent studies have fleshed out this model.

Neuroimaging experiments by Farrer and Frith (2002), for example, have shown contrasting activation in the right inferior parietal cortex for perception of action caused by others, and in the anterior insula bilaterally when action is experienced as caused by oneself. Such activation is consistent with the idea that actions performed by others are perceptually mapped in allocentric coordinates (Jeannerod 1999). Farrer and Frith (2002: 601) note that 'there is strong physiological evidence that the inferior parietal cortex [involves this] kind of [allocentric mapping] . . . to generate representations of body movements [by others] in allocentric coordinates'. In contrast, the anterior insula involves information that is specified in egocentric spatial coordinates. Specifically, the anterior insula involves the integration of various kinds of self-specifying signals generated in self-movement: proprioceptive, visual, and auditory ecological information about movement, and the efference copy (or corollary discharge) associated with motor commands that control movement. It is likely, as Farrer and Frith conclude, that a 'close correspondence between all these signals helps to give us a sense of agency' (p. 602).[30]

[30] Studies by Farrer et al. (2003) support this conclusion. Note that in the experiments mentioned here the authors have adopted the same concept I have defined above as the sense of agency, and as outlined in my 2000 paper in Trends in Cognitive Sciences (Gallagher 2000a). Other empirical studies consistent with the findings mentioned here have also used this definition (see e.g. Blakemore et al. 2000; Chaminade and Decety 2002; Fourneret et al. 2001; Jeannerod 2003; Ruby and Decety 2001; van den Bos and Jeannerod 2002; Vogeley et al. 2001; Vogeley and Fink 2003).

It is also likely that protentional problems in schizophrenia could disrupt the integration of these signals. We also know that in schizophrenic patients the feeling of alien control during a movement task has been associated with an increased activity in the right inferior parietal lobe (Spence *et al.* 1997). Accordingly, if for the schizophrenic some neurological component (the 'Who' model) responsible for the differentiation between self and other has been disrupted, then it is quite possible that some sense of *alterity* is already implicit in his first-order phenomenal experience. In this case, the attribution of agency to another is not the result of a metarepresentational confabulation that would read into first-order experience something that is not there. Rather, the misattribution of the action or thought to another is a genuine report of what is truly experienced in the pathology.

The Common Structure of Embodied Action and Cognition

The alternative to the Frithian account that I have outlined here requires no mechanisms over and above those that account for the temporal structure of consciousness itself. One does not need to postulate the additional system of a central monitor—self-monitoring is built into consciousness as the longitudinal aspects of the retentional–protentional structure. I do not need a separate stream of efferent copy to verify that I am the one who is thinking; the sense of ownership is already included in the original stream of consciousness. The 'intention to think' is not something separate from thinking itself; it is included in the very structure of thought. The schizophrenic does not discover alien thoughts by means of a metarepresentational introspection; rather he has an immediate, non-observational sense that something is wrong, a first-order phenomenal-level experience that motivates and results in the hyperreflective effects of metarepresentation.

A more complete story about the failure of protention needs to include a subpersonal and neuroscientific account. In terms of traditional cognitive science, the task would be to identify a certain set of subpersonal mechanisms and to cash them out in terms of specific neurological functions. This approach would be partially consistent with Frith's attempt to identify the cognitive mechanisms responsible for the positive symptoms of schizophrenia. That is, one would attempt to identify specific dysfunctions or disconnections in brain structures responsible for integration of signals, or delivery of efference copy to relevant parts of the brain. Affect, however, has a deeply rooted biological basis; affective tonality or disposition may be tied to more global neuronal dispositions, or abnormal levels of neuro-transmitters such as dopamine.[31] Affective attunement can be entirely reordered,

---

[31] Parnas indicates that basic auto-affectivity 'is on a biological level, heavily dependent on the evolution of capacities for intra-modal binding of disparate Gestalt features, as well as on the capacities for inter-modal sensory and sensori-motor integrations. Intact intracortical and cortico-cortical connectivity is a necessary condition for such developments' (2000: 143 n. 28). For recent work on the relation between hyperdopaminergic states and hyperreflective, aberrant degrees of saliency for one's own experience and environmental events, see Kapur (2003).

leaving a subject specifically indisposed for experience or action by neuronal events and changes in the balance of neurotransmitters. If, as Varela suggests, affective tonality is, 'a major boundary and initial condition for neurodynamics', then on the neurological level, the sort of mechanism that underlies protention is more appropriately thought of in terms of widely distributed and dynamical processes than in terms of localized functions (Gallagher and Varela 2001; Varela 1999a). This also appears to be in line with the fact that schizophrenia involves global, widespread cognitive and emotional problems. As a result, the conceptual framework for thinking about the neurological mechanisms responsible for symptoms of schizophrenia is likely to be quite different from one focused on such concepts as comparator, central monitor, efference copy, etc. It is likely to involve a more pervasive function such as working memory. A disruption of information-processing in the neuronal mechanisms that underpin working memory could be responsible for the disruption of temporal structures.

It also follows that there is a certain ubiquity to the temporal structure we are here considering. Schizophrenic patients feel alienated not just from thought and action; they also feel alienated from affects, from their own body and skin, from their own saliva, from their own name, etc. (Louis Sass, private correspondence). It seems unlikely that all these phenomena can be explained by problems involving local failures of efference copy—problems that may in fact be secondary to a more global or structural dysfunction. The more general fact is that the temporal, auto-affective structure that shapes cognitive experience also shapes embodied action.[32] In the first place, if part of what is at stake in self-generated action is precisely a *sense* or experience of agency, it is likely that the protentional–retentional structure has a role to play in the conscious registration of that sense of agency for movement, or in its failure, for example, in delusions of control. More than this, however, motor action itself, in its prenoetic body-schematic performance, has the same tacit and auto-affective structure that involves the retention of previous postures, and the anticipation of future action.[33]

In his original definition, Head noted that the body schema is retentional in that it dynamically organizes sensory-motor feedback in such a way that the final sensation of position is 'charged with a relation to something that has happened before' (Head 1920: 606). He uses the metaphor of a taximeter, which computes and registers movement as it goes. Merleau-Ponty (1968: 173) borrows this metaphor from Head and associates it with temporality—movement is organized prenoetically according to the 'time of the body, taximeter time of the corporeal schema'. And this includes a retentional component: 'At each successive instant of a movement, the preceding instant is not lost sight of. It is, as it were, dovetailed into the present.... [Movement draws] together, on the basis of one's present position,

---

[32] Merleau-Ponty recognizes the auto-affective aspect as essential to the body schema: 'The corporeal schema would not be a *schema* if it were not this contact of self with self...' (1968: 255).

[33] Again, more pervasively, across both motor and cognitive functions that pertain to action, Jeannerod points out the involvement of the prefrontal cortex, which is associated with working memory and anticipation (Jeannerod 2001).

the succession of previous positions, which envelop each other' (Merleau-Ponty 1962: 140).

This retentional component is important to keep in view. With the recent emphasis on forward models in the neuroscience of movement the role of reafferent sensory feedback seems to be reduced. But it is essential that reafferent information about current posture be represented in motor preparation. One can say that reafferent signals are not actually present in the forward representation of action (see e.g. Jeannerod 2001) only if one regards that representation as part of a static model, and ignores previous movement. Clearly, specifications about the current posture of the body, which is the result of the just previous movement, must be included in the representation for a movement that I am just about to effect.[34]

We have also seen good examples of anticipatory or prospective control of movement. The mouth of the newborn anticipates the hand; the grasp of a reaching hand tacitly anticipates the shape of the object to be grasped, according to the specific intentional action involved. Empirical research has shown that protentional or prospective processes are pervasive in low-level sensorimotor actions. Eye-tracking involves moment-to-moment anticipations concerning the trajectory of the target. Reaching for an object involves feed-forward components that allow last-minute adjustments if the object is moved. Since these prospective processes are present even in infants, the 'conclusion that [anticipatory or protentional processes] are immanent in virtually everything we think or do seems inescapable' (Haith 1993: 237).

The emphasis placed on anticipatory aspects of motor control by neuroscientists (Berthoz 2000; Georgieff and Jeannerod 1998; Jeannerod 2001) has served as a good clue to the alternative model we have now formulated. This alternative model points to the common temporal structure of embodied movement, action, and cognition—a structure that breaks down in cases of schizophrenia. We see the disruption of this auto-affective, temporal structure reflected in the cognitive symptoms of thought insertion and delusions of control, leading to loss of a sense of agency for thought and action. But we also see it in the loss of automatic skills, in the disruption of the smooth flow of motor activity, and in symptoms that involve abnormal somatic sensations (see Sass 2000).

In the same way that cognitive disruptions can lead to an introspective hyper-reflection that exasperates and complicates the symptomatology of schizophrenia, somatic and motor problems lead to a hyperreflection that brings to the forefront those prenoetic processes that normally remain in the background. As Sass (2000: 167) suggests, such hyperreflection can generate a body image that exaggerates proprioceptive and kinesthetic sensations, and interferes with the normal functioning of the normally tacit body schema.

---

[34] The importance of dynamical models with respect to body schematic processes has been made clear to me by Francisco Varela and Marc Jeannerod (see Gallagher and Varela 2002; Jeannerod and Gallagher 2001). Given the temporal nature of the body schema as outlined by Head and Merleau-Ponty, the traditional view of these things may not be as static as Jeannerod, Kinsbourne (2001), and Sheets-Johnstone (2003) think. They nonetheless offer an important criticism by emphasizing a more dynamic view in regard to embodied experience.

9

The Interactive Practice of Mind

IN psychology, philosophy of mind, and recently in the neurosciences, studies of how one person understands and interrelates with another person have been conducted under the heading *theory of mind*. Discussions of theory of mind are dominated by two main approaches: theory theory and simulation theory. The major tenets of theory theory are based on well-designed scientific experiments that show that children develop an understanding of other minds around the age of 4. One version of theory theory claims that this understanding is based on an innately specified, domain-specific mechanism designed for 'reading' other minds (Baron-Cohen 1995; Leslie 1991). An alternative version claims that the child attains this ability through a course of development in which the child tests its social environment and gradually learns about people (Gopnik and Meltzoff 1997). Common to both versions of theory theory is the idea that children attain their understanding of other minds by implicitly employing a theoretical stance. This stance involves postulating the existence of mental states in others and using such postulations to explain and predict another person's behavior. In the earliest level of development, the 4- to 5-year-old child's theory of mind involves 'first-order belief attribution' in which she distinguishes her own belief from someone else's belief. The next level involves 'second-order belief attribution', the ability to 'think about another person's thoughts about a third person's thoughts about an objective event' (Baron-Cohen 1989: 288). Normal children between the ages of 6 and 7 years are able to achieve the second level. The few autistic children who attain the earliest level do so late, and they fail to attain the second level.

The second approach, simulation theory, argues that one does not *theorize* about the other person but uses one's own mental experience as an internal model for the other mind (e.g. Goldman 1989; Gordon 1986, 1995a; and Heal 1986, 1998a, b). To understand the other person, I simulate the thoughts or feelings that I would experience *if I were in the situation of the other*. I emulate what must be going through the other person's mind; or I create in my own mind pretend beliefs, desires, or strategies that I use to understand the other's behavior. My source for these simulations is not a theory that I have. Rather, I have a real model of the mind at my immediate disposal, that is, I have *my own mind*, and I can use it to generate and run simulations. I simply run through the sequence or pattern of behavior or decision-making that I would engage in if I were faced with the situation in question. I do it 'off line', however. That is, my imaginary rehearsal does not lead to actualizing the behavior on my part. Finally, I attribute this pattern to the other person who is actually in that situation. According to simulation theory, this process may remain unconscious, with only an awareness of the resulting understanding or prediction. The process itself, nonetheless, is structured as an internal, representational simulation (Gordon 1986).

Across both approaches one can distinguish two specific kinds of claims. First, *developmental claims* involve the timing and order of development, the importance and balance of innate mechanisms versus experience, and so forth. In this regard, the experimental and neurological evidence used to support such claims is impressive. I will nonetheless suggest that it is possible to raise questions about certain background assumptions that shape experimental design and that lead to the interpretation of data as supportive of certain aspects of theory of mind. Second, *pragmatic claims* concern the scope of the applicability of theory of mind.[1] Pragmatic claims may be strong or weak. Some theorists (e.g. Baron-Cohen 1995; Leslie 2000; Tooby and Cosmides 1995) make a very strong pragmatic claim, namely, that, once formed, theory of mind is our primary and pervasive means for understanding other persons. It is not clear, however, that the experimental evidence used to support the developmental claims counts as evidence to support the strong pragmatic claim. Although I will question the interpretation of the science that informs the developmental claims, my main target is the strong pragmatic claim, that ordinarily and for the most part theory of mind forms the basis for our understanding of others.

To make clear what the strong pragmatic claim for theory of mind entails, let me review several of its various formulations. Recently, in an extensive conversation with Paul Ricœur, the neuroscientist Jean-Pierre Changeux proposed that one's relations to others depend on a 'cognitive device' that allows for the representation of the others' mental states, 'their sufferings, plans of action, [and] intentions'. He specifically cites experiments that support the concept of a theory of mind, and he maintains that it is just this type of mechanism that allows humans to acquire a system of moral values and aesthetic preferences (Changeux and Ricœur 2000: 154–7). Two important researchers of this cognitive mechanism, Tooby and Cosmides (1995: p. xvii), suggest that 'humans everywhere interpret the behavior of others in ... mentalistic terms because we all come equipped with a "theory of mind" module (ToMM) that is compelled to interpret others this way, with mentalistic terms as its natural language'. Baron-Cohen (1995: 3) writes: 'it is hard for us to make sense of behavior in any other way than via the mentalistic (or "intentional") framework'. And quoting Dan Sperber he continues: 'attribution of mental states is to humans as echolocation is to the bat'. It is our natural way of understanding the social environment' (p. 4). Uta and Christopher Frith (1999) maintain that mental state attribution plays a major role in all social interactions, a conclusion echoed by Alan Leslie (2000). He defines ToMM as a specialized component of social intelligence, but claims that it is necessarily involved 'whenever

---

[1] These specific claims aside, the distinction between developmental aspects and pragmatic aspects of theory of mind is mirrored in recent research suggesting that the development of theory of mind may depend on normal language development (Astington and Jenkins 1999) but that near-perfect performance on theory of mind tasks does not depend on normal language functioning (Varley and Siegal 2000).

an agent's behavior is attended', for example, 'in conversations and other real-time social interactions' (p. 1236).[2]

In this chapter my intention is not simply to criticize the approaches of theory theory and simulation theory. I will offer an alternative proposal—I'll refer to it as 'interaction theory'—consistent with the framework developed in previous chapters. The understanding of the other person is primarily neither theoretical nor based on an internal simulation. It is a form of embodied practice. In explicating this idea I do not want to deny that we do develop capacities for both theoretical interpretation and simulation, and that in certain cases we do understand others by enacting just such theoretical attitudes or simulations. Such instances are rare, however, relative to the majority of our interactions. Theory theory and simulation theory at best explain a very narrow and specialized set of cognitive processes that we sometimes use to relate to others. On this basis, one could justify a weaker pragmatic claim for theory of mind. But neither theoretical nor simulation strategies constitute the primary way in which we relate to, interact with, or understand others. Furthermore, in those cases where we do use theoretical and simulation strategies, these strategies are already shaped by a more primary embodied practice.

What Does Phenomenology Say about Theory of Mind?

I will start with a critical review of the two major theory of mind approaches. There are significant differences between theory theorists and simulation theorists, as well as between nativist and non-nativist accounts of theory theory. There are also disagreements among both simulationists and theory theorists on the question of implicit versus explicit processes. I do not mean simply to brush over these differences. They will motivate a variety of qualifications on the points that I will outline here. These qualifications notwithstanding, and although all the following

---

[2] Strong claims such as these can be found in too many places to list, but several others are worth noting. Currie and Sterelny (2000: 145) write: 'mind-reading and the capacity to negotiate the social world are not the same thing, but the former seems to be necessary for the latter. . . . our basic grip on the social world depends on our being able to see our fellows as motivated by beliefs and desires we sometimes share and sometimes do not'. Frith and Happé (1999: 2) propose that mind-reading 'appears to be a prerequisite for normal social interaction: in everyday life we make sense of each other's behaviour by appeal to a belief-desire psychology'. Wellman (1993: 31–2) maintains that children at age 4 begin to 'see people as living their lives within a world of mental content that determines how they behave in the world of real objects and acts', they construe 'people's real-world actions as inevitably filtered through representations of the world rather than linked to the world directly'. Karmiloff-Smith (1992: 117) writes: 'young children are spontaneous psychologists. They are interested in how the mind can have thoughts and theories and in how representations mediate between the mind and the world. In order to engage in human interaction . . . to understand their intentions/beliefs/desires, to interpret their statements/gestures/actions . . . each of us relies on . . . a folk theory that enables us to ascribe mental states to ourselves.' And according to Malle (2002, and see 2001): 'Theory of mind arguably underlies all conscious and unconscious cognition of human behavior, thus resembling a system of Kantian categories of social perception—i.e., the concepts by which people grasp social reality.' I thank Matthew Ratcliff for several of these citations.

critical points do not apply to every representative of these richly diverse positions, they do apply to a large part of the literature on theory of mind.

A common and basic assumption implicit to theory of mind accounts is that to know another person is to know that person's mind, and this means to know their beliefs, desires, or intentional states. I will refer to this as the *mentalistic supposition*.

> *The mentalistic supposition:* The problem of intersubjectivity is precisely the problem of other *minds*. That is, the problem is to explain how we can access the minds of others.

According to this supposition, this is a problem of access because other minds are hidden away, closed in, behind the overt behavior that we can see. This seems to be a Cartesian supposition about the very nature of what we call 'the mind'. The mind is conceived as an inner realm, in contrast to behavior, which is external and observable, and which borrows its intentionality from the mental states that control it. Both theory theory and simulation theory set the problem as one of gaining access to other minds, and their explanations of social cognition are framed in precisely these terms.

Furthermore, theory of mind suggests that we use our knowledge of another person's mind to *explain* or *predict* the other person's behavior. Since, according to theory of mind, we have no direct access to another person's intentional states, we either postulate what their beliefs or desires are on the basis of a set of causal-explanatory laws (theory theory) or we project the results of certain simulation routines. For example, Karmiloff-Smith (1992: 138) contends that theory of mind 'involves inferences based on unobservables (mental states, such as belief), a coherent set of explanations and causal links between mental states and behavior which are predictive of future actions'. There is no requirement that such theorizing or simulating be conscious or explicit. We may learn to engage in such interpretation to the point that it becomes habitual and transparent.

The mentalistic supposition implies that an explicit recognition of another person's beliefs, desires, or intentional states is clearly conceptual; and that an implicit recognition is informed by such conceptual knowledge. One requires a concept of belief or desire before one can attribute such things to another person. To discover a belief as an intentional state even in myself requires that I take up a second-order reflective stance and recognize that my cognitive action can be classified as a belief. Indeed, explicitly to recognize that I myself 'have a mind' is already something of a theoretical postulate. This is not to deny that I might have something like a direct access to my own experience, or that this experience can be characterized as self-conscious. I can easily say, for example, 'I feel very good about planning my trip.' But to say that this experience of feeling good is in fact a *feeling*, and that this feeling depends on a *belief* that I will actually take the trip, requires something like a reflective detachment from my phenomenal experience, and the positing of a feeling (or belief) as a feeling (or as a belief). It would involve a further postulation that such feelings and beliefs are in some fashion part of what it means to have a mind. This kind of metacognitive theorizing is always possible for the adult human, but for the most part I would suggest that, in practice, this is not the way we think of ourselves—unless we are practicing philosophical meditations of the sort Descartes practiced.

For some theorists of mind (e.g. Carruthers and Smith 1996; Frith and Happé 1999; Gopnik 1993), even to know our own mind we need to take this conceptual, theoretical attitude toward our own experience, and they discount the idea that we have something like a direct access to our own experience (see Zahavi and Parnas 2003 for a phenomenological critique of this idea). And since we certainly have no direct access to other people, to understand them we must take just such a theoretical attitude. In order to understand that the other person feels very good about planning her trip, I can only hypothesize that she has a certain set of feelings and beliefs that normally go along with a situation like that. One's theory depends upon and is complicated, however, by what one knows of such situations. We know that some people do not have good feelings about planning trips; they actually get stressed out. Sometimes they may even say 'I don't believe that I'm actually going!' Clearly if I am to take a theoretical stance toward what the other person is experiencing, I need to interpret her behavior on the basis of what I see and hear, and on the basis of what I know of such things. What I know of such things, however, is not easily summarized. Part of what I know includes some kind of pre-theoretical knowledge that I get through being raised in a social environment. If I were forced to formalize the rule that guided my theoretical stance, it would likely include aspects of pre-theoretical knowledge. Consider the following formulation. 'When someone is planning a trip and she says something like "I don't believe that I am actually going," with intonations that signal exasperation, she really means that she does believe that she is going and she is not enjoying the planning process.' An exasperated intonation, however, is not something that I gain through a theoretical explanation; rather, I know what an exasperated intonation is by means of perceptual experience.

Do we react to the exasperation in a person's voice by appealing (implicitly or explicitly) to a theory? It seems possible to describe it in this way in cases where the situation is not typical, or when, perhaps, the behavior of the other person is out of character or out of context, or when we don't know the person, or in cases where we are talking with someone else about a third person. When we do not know the person we may need to run through certain possibilities and perhaps engage in a process of interpretation from a distance, much as a historian might attempt to understand a historical figure—forming a hypothesis on the basis of evidence.[3] Even in cases where we know (or think we know) a person very well, we may express puzzlement about their behavior. In discussing a friend's behavior with someone who doesn't know her as well, we may come to devise a theory about why she is acting in a certain way. It seems very possible to describe such cases in terms of a theory of mind. Is this a good description of our ordinary interactions with others?

---

[3] Davies and Stone (1998) consider certain limitations of historical analysis based on simulation, citing Collingwood's claim that historical understanding can be achieved by the re-enactment of the historical character's thought.

Simulation theory claims that it is not. It is not clear that we represent, explicitly or implicitly, the sorts of rules (causal-explanatory laws) that would summarize what we know of human situations and that would operate as the bases for a theoretical understanding of the other person. Indeed, we find it difficult even to formulate such rules, and this seems odd if we actually use them all the time (Goldman 1989). Furthermore, at least on the developmental version of theory theory, there is no way to account for the fact that children as young as 3 or 4 years putatively develop the very same theory (a common folk psychology). Theory formation in general usually leads to a diversification of theory (Carruthers 1996; Goldman 1989).

Do we, then, simulate the other person's belief? Again, this process itself may remain implicit, with only an awareness of the resulting prediction. The process itself, nonetheless, is structured as an internal, representational simulation (Gordon 1986). The simulation model involves something more like a practiced skill than a theoretical stance. Indeed, there is some suggestion that the result of simulation is not so much a mental model of the other's mind as a motor adjustment in my own system that allows me insight into the other person's behavior (Gordon, unpublished MS, cited in Stich and Nichols 1992; Grezes and Decety 2001). On the other hand, various descriptions of simulation invoke the idea of predicting behavior on the basis of hypothetical beliefs and desires that are fed into a cognitive decision-making system (see Carruthers 1996 for a description of an approach that combines theory and simulation along this line). The result of this process is to project or attribute relevant intentional states to the mind of the other person. Like theory theory, simulation theory understands the other person as a collection of such mental states, and often understands the simulation itself as a mental state.

In the situation of talking with someone else about a third person, it seems possible to describe our attitude toward the person under discussion as theoretical or as involving a simulation of the other person's mental states. But does the same description capture the dynamics of our interaction with our interlocutor? That is, in a second-person conversational situation, although we may indeed tacitly follow certain rules of conversation, our process of interpretation does not seem to involve a detached or abstract, third-person quest for causal explanation. Nor does it seem to be a theory-driven interpretation that takes the other person's words as evidence for a mental state standing behind what he has just said. Even if we are trying to read 'between the lines' and we reach the conclusion that the person we are conversing with believes the wrong thing concerning the other person, our understanding of this is poorly described as resulting from formulating a theoretical hypothesis or running a simulation routine about what he believes. We do not posit a theoretical entity called a belief and attribute it to him. We do not interact with him by conceiving of his mind as a set of *cogitationes* closed up in immanence (Merleau-Ponty 1962: 353).

Both theory theory and simulation theory conceive of communicative inter-action between two people as a process that takes place between two Cartesian minds. It assumes that one's understanding involves a retreat into a realm of *theoria* or *simulacra*, into a set of internal mental operations that come to be expressed (externalized) in speech, gesture, or action. If, in contrast, we think of communicative interaction as being accomplished in the very action of communication, in the expressive movement of speech, gesture, and the interaction itself,[4] then the idea that the understanding of another person involves an attempt to theorize about an unseen belief, or to 'mind-read', is problematic.

This phenomenologically based criticism is subject to an objection that is often raised at this point. Is an appeal to phenomenology in this context justified? Theory theorists and simulation theorists often claim that the employment of a theory or simulation routine is unconscious and that what we experience or seemingly experience is not a good guide for what is really going on in such cases (e.g. Goldman and Gallese 2000). On this account we should think of the theory or simulation routine as somehow programmed into the very structure of our experience of others. If that is the case and our engagement in a theory or simulation procedure is not always explicit or conscious, does this mean that our phenomenology is simply wrong?

In principle, phenomenology would not be able to say whether a subpersonal cognitive routine is operative; but it would be able to say whether my normal experience of the other person is best characterized as *explanation* and *prediction*, the kind of interpretations that both theory theory and simulation theory posit. I suggest that what phenomenology tells us is that explanation and prediction are specialized and relatively rare modes of understanding others, and that something like evaluative understanding about what someone means or about how I should respond in any particular situation best characterize most of our interactions. Phenomenology tells us that our primary and usual way of being in the world is pragmatic interaction (characterized by action, involvement, and interaction based on environmental and contextual factors), rather than mentalistic or conceptual contemplation (characterized as explanation or prediction based on mental contents).[5]

Phenomenology cannot tell us whether our response to the exasperation in a person's voice involves an implicit (subconscious) theory or simulation routine. But a careful and methodical phenomenology[6] should be able to tell us whether, when

---

[4] In contrast to someone like Merleau-Ponty (1962), who conceives of thought as being accomplished in speech, Baron-Cohen (1995: 29), defending theory theory, endorses a traditional Augustinian view of language: 'language functions principally as a "printout" of the contents of the mind'. It follows that 'in decoding speech we go way beyond the words we hear or read, to hypothesize about the speaker's mental states' (p. 27).

[5] Heidegger (1968) emphasizes the primacy of our pragmatic interactions with the world. Our primary encounter with things in the world is not as objects to contemplate, but as things that we are already using. Only when something goes wrong do we start to treat them as things that need explanation. For Heidegger and several other phenomenologists like Gurwitsch (1931/1978), our primary encounters with others are in these pragmatic contexts. This is directly related to secondary intersubjectivity, discussed below.

[6] In contrast to non-methodical introspection. This qualification is meant to head off the standard reply that introspective reports are notoriously suspect guides to what subjects are doing even at the conscious level, since they are infected (as it were) by folk theories. A methodological phenomenology

we hear the exasperated voice, our usual response involves formulating an explanation, or predicting what the person will do next. Our encounters with others are in fact not normally occasions for theorizing or simulating if such non-conscious procedures are cashed out phenomenologically as explaining or predicting on the basis of postulated mental states. Rather, pragmatic interaction and evaluative understanding take up most of our effort. Only when second-person pragmatic interactions or our evaluative attempts to understand break down do we resort to the more specialized practices of third-person explanation and prediction.

The distinction between explanation and evaluation is an important one to make in this context. In our everyday and ordinary encounters we rarely look for causal-mentalistic explanations for people's actions. Rather than being occasions for explanation, our encounters are primarily occasions for interactions and evaluations. My action, or the action of another, may be motivated in part by the fact that the situation is just such that this is the action that is called for. In such cases, an action is not caused by a well-formed mental state, but is motivated by some aspect of the situation, as I experience and evaluate it.

One way to understand what I mean by evaluation is to reframe a distinction made by Perner (1991) in his explication of theory theory. He distinguishes between 'situation theory' employed by 3-year-olds, prior to attaining a theory of mind, and 'representational theory' or theory of mind. According to Perner, 3-year-olds employ some aspect of the environment plus some understanding of desire, but are unable to comprehend the concept of the other's belief. One should note, however, that the environment, or the situation, is not something that the child, or the adult, objectively confronts as an outside observer. The notion of situation should be understood to include the experiencing subject (that is, oneself) and the action of that subject. Our involvement in a situation is not as a third-person observer developing a situation theory, as if we were not part of the situation ourselves. Our interaction with another human being is not equivalent to a detached observation (or explanation) of what that person is doing. The notion of evaluation signifies an embedded cognitive practice that relies on certain pre-theoretical embodied capabilities that 3-year-olds have already developed to understand intersubjective situations. Even to the extent that evaluation becomes reflective, it is more like an 'embedded reflection' on possible actions (Gallagher and Marcel 1999) than a detached consideration of mental states. Rather than drawing up a theory about a particular situation, or taking an objective, observational stance toward the other person, we have the capacity for measuring it up in pragmatic terms. This capacity does not disappear when the child reaches the age of 4, but rather is enhanced by further experience.[7]

would include a bracketing of just such folk theories, folk psychology, theories about theory of mind, etc. This is referred to as the phenomenological reduction of the sort practiced by Husserl, and its aim is to attend to experience as it happens.

[7] Perner (1991) goes on to suggest that theory of mind doesn't actually replace situation theory. It simply amends it to cover problem cases. Even as adults, 'we stay situation theorists at heart. We resort to a representational theory only when we need to.' Barresi and Moore (1996) also argue that the more

Consider the following example that Baron-Cohen (1995: 28) cites from Pinker (1994):

Woman: I'm leaving you.
Man: Who is he?

Overhearing this bit of discussion, the task, according to Baron-Cohen, is to explain why the man utters this phrase. The explanation is offered: 'the man must have thought [formed a belief] that the woman was leaving him for another man'. A certain thought or belief causes the man to say what he says. And what causes the thought? Perhaps some cognitive schema that associates this scenario with the influence of a third party (the other man). If indeed an explanation is needed, this may be a good folk-psychological one, but the question to start with is whether, upon overhearing this bit of conversation, we would be motivated *to explain it* rather than to comprehend it in an evaluative way. From our perspective, as interlopers who are listening in, the thought expressed in the man's words does not have the status of a belief in his head; the thought (and most likely, an emotional overtone) is already given to us in the words and we have no need to posit a belief over and above them. Would we not already have a pre-theoretical understanding of what was meant, and, instead of formulating an explanation, would we not be taking some stance or action—choosing sides or perhaps moving as far away as we could to give the couple some privacy? And in reality, the man himself may have no such discrete belief. He may have blurted out the question as a question that had never before dawned on him, because he saw something like shame or defiance in the woman's eyes.

Theory of mind conceptualizes beliefs and other intentional states as discretely representational. There are good reasons, however, to view beliefs as dispositions that are sometimes ambiguous even from the perspective of the believer. To have a belief is not to have an all-or-nothing mental representation, but to have some more-or-less-complete set of dispositions to act and to experience in certain ways. Dispositions are actualized, not only in overt behavior, including verbal behavior, but also in phenomenal experience.[8] Thus, given a particular context, one may have

primary processes of social understanding are not replaced by the more mentalistic ones, but that the more primary ones continue to function. Gordon (1995b), however, in a gloss on Perner, suggests that what passes as situation theory in adult behavior is really a sophistication in simulating and attributing beliefs and intentions which becomes manifest only when there is a problem. The sophistication of our simulation abilities, he contends, simply makes it seem as if we are not simulating. Yet Gordon does suggest that prior to the development of simulation abilities, the mental, in some sense, 'is already "out there" in the environment, though not yet conceptualized as mental'. I will argue that a good part of the mental stays 'out there' and does not end up hidden away. It becomes embedded in our embodied and communicative practices.

[8] The dispositional theory of belief as found in Ryle and Wittgenstein, is appealing in this context. When dispositions are activated, however, there is something it is like to believe or to act on belief. This view, which Eric Schwitzgebel (2002) calls a 'phenomenal, dispositional account of belief', clearly does not involve a reductionist type of behaviorism, as one finds in the usual interpretation of Ryle (1949). Schwitzgebel's excellent account, framed in a purely analytic exposition, is quite consistent with phenomenological accounts found in theorists such as Merleau-Ponty. For its implications in the developmental context see Schwitzgebel (1999a, b).

a disposition to feel upset or to perceive things as grating, depending on a variety of circumstances. For our understanding of other people, I am suggesting that we rarely need to go beyond contextualized overt behaviors (actions, gestures, speech-acts, etc.). We are rarely required to postulate an idealized and abstract mental belief standing behind these behaviors in order to grasp the disposition that is overtly constituted and expressed in the contextualized behavior. In certain contextualized interactions, I need go no further than the person's gestures or emotional expressions to gain my understanding of how it is with that person.

Those who defend theory of mind might reply that even if our relations with others phenomenologically *seem* to be pragmatically interactive, they are, in fact, implicitly matters of theorizing or simulating. Even if we are aware of only direct evaluative responses, such responses may be the result of busy subpersonal mechanisms that have the structure of theory or simulation. In this case, controlled experimentation (rather than phenomenology) is the only way to investigate such cognitive mechanisms.

To push this idea further, and to make it clear, theorists of mind might claim not only that the process is unconscious but also that the *product* is often unconscious, that is, that we make unconscious predictions and perhaps even unconsciously explain things (if by 'explanation' we just mean discovering causes).[9] If so, the idea of using phenomenology to discover how we interact with others loses its bite. Even if we don't find explanation and prediction in (most of) our phenomenology, we still might be explaining and predicting, theorizing or simulating at an unconscious level.

To this I offer two responses. The second is perhaps the more important, but the first is a matter of vocabulary, terminology, or perhaps description. If in fact, on the non-conscious or subpersonal level, there is some ongoing process that might be described in terms of discovering causes, why call this 'explanation' (likewise, if it is something like a natural inference, why use the term 'theory')? Explanation (or theory) seems to mean (even in our everyday psychology) a process that involves reflective consciousness. The term 'prediction' also seems to me to describe a reflective conscious act (something much more than a pre-reflective anticipation that is part of the structure of experience). It sounds odd, for example, to say that the motor system has developed a theory (or a prediction or an explanation), that allows it to anticipate where a particular movement will end up. 'Explanation' and 'prediction' are personal-level terms.

Terminology aside, however, my second point is about evidence. What evidence could be offered to support the idea that an explanation or prediction is taking place on the subpersonal, non-conscious level? I suppose that to show that some subpersonal process is a process of explanation, one would have to show, at the very least, that this process is a process of inferring causes. Obviously, neurons are firing at a subpersonal level, but how we get from neurons to inference-making is not clear. Although it seems possible to go the other way, that is, in some cases to go

---

[9] My thanks to Eric Schwitzgebel for raising this point in private correspondence.

from a description of experience to the claim that we are making non-conscious inferences, one would have to provide a description of what that experience is. But if the theorist of mind did offer a description of that experience, their own rejection of the validity of what phenomenology can show would undermine their claim. As a result, everything would depend on the results found in controlled experimentation. Thus, we clearly need to examine the scientific evidence in support of this claim.

The Science of Other Minds

Both theory theory and simulation theory claim the support of good science. Theory theory appeals to classic false-belief tests in developmental psychology for its justification. Simulation theory has recently received support from neuroscience. If one is going to challenge either of these approaches, it is important to consider the scientific evidence. I cannot review all the scientific evidence for either of these approaches here, but I will look at a representative sampling and try to indicate certain limitations in the empirical data consistent with my remarks in the previous section.

False-Belief Experiments

In the 'standard' false belief task a subject is asked about the thoughts and actions of another person or character who lacks certain information that the subject has. For example, the subject knows that a candy box actually contains pencils. Someone else who doesn't know that the box contains pencils (this could be a puppet or a real person) enters the room. The question that is posed to the subject is 'What will the other person say is in the candy box?' Four-year-olds generally answer correctly that the other person will think that there are candies in the box. A 3-year-old is unable to see that the other person may falsely believe that there are candies in the box. So 3-year-olds answer that the other person will say there are pencils in the box (see e.g. Perner, Leekam, and Wimmer 1987). False belief tests can be made more or less complicated.

In a series of experiments often cited in support of theory theory, Heinz Wimmer and Josef Perner (1983) investigated a subject's competence in representing another person's belief when that belief differs from what the subject knows to be true.

In four experiments children between the ages of 3 and 9 were divided into three groups: 3–4-year-olds, 4–6-year-olds, and 6–9-year-olds. Each child was told stories that involved, first, a cooperative situation and then a competitive situation. For example, a kid named Maxi puts a piece of chocolate in a blue cupboard and then goes out to play. While he is gone, and without his knowledge, the chocolate is moved into a green cupboard. In the cooperative version of the story Maxi, upon returning, cooperates with another character in obtaining the chocolate. In the competitive version Maxi is in competition with an antagonist. All stories are told up to the point where the main characters look for the hidden object. At this time, each subject is asked to indicate (*a*) where the chocolate actually is located (the reality question), (*b*) where Maxi would look for the chocolate (the belief question), and (*c*) where Maxi would tell the other character to look.

All age groups were able to answer the reality question correctly. Answers to the other questions generally varied in relation to the age of the subjects. When asked where Maxi would look for the object (the belief question) most of the 4–5-year-olds chose the green cupboard incorrectly. However, most of the 6–9-year-olds chose the blue cupboard, correctly, despite the fact that the object was really in the green cupboard. When asked, in the competitive version, where Maxi would say the object was hidden, most of the subjects who answered correctly on the belief question were able to create a deceitful utterance required for the competitive versions of the stories. These subjects understood that Maxi would deceive his competitor purposely. Most of the same subjects were also able to create a truthful utterance for the cooperative versions of the stories.

Why were the youngest subjects unable to correctly ascribe a wrong belief to Maxi? A second experiment was designed to answer this question. The same stories were used as in the previous experiment, but with several modifications. A memory question (Do you remember where Maxi put the chocolate?) was asked when the subject answered incorrectly to the belief question. Also, subjects were reminded of what Maxi did before he went outside before being asked the belief question. The results showed an improvement of the 5–6-year-olds in their responses to the belief question. The 3–4-year-olds were unable correctly to ascribe a wrong belief even with the modifications.

Wimmer and Perner concluded from these and several other experiments that children age 6 and above are able to cope with representational complexities. children of 4–6 have the ability to represent wrong beliefs, but are sensitive to modifications in the task. Few in the 3–4-year-old group are able to represent false beliefs or another person's absence of knowledge. Most children who are able to represent false beliefs are also able to construct deceitful utterances. Children between the ages of 4 and 6 are able to demonstrate inferential skills.

These experiments, and many others based on the same experimental paradigm (see e.g. Baron-Cohen, Leslie, and Frith 1985), are often cited as evidence for the development of a theory of mind at around 4 years of age. As Stich and Nichols (1992) point out, however, theory theory, as well as simulation theory, are compatible with, but do not necessarily entail, the Maxi experiments (see Gordon 1995b). So these experiments cannot be used to support one approach over another. Others argue that subjects who fail false-belief tests do not necessarily fail them because they lack a theory of mind. It may be that the intellectual processing involved in the testing is simply too complicated.[10] Furthermore, the false-belief paradigm does not

---

[10] Leslie and Thaiss (1992) show that when photographs are used to represent mental states, 4-year-olds do worse than their performance on the standard false-belief tests. If it were a matter of picturing mental states as representations, the 4-year-old should do equally well on the photograph test

capture all there is to say about children's abilities to understand others. Bloom and German (2000), who generally support a theory approach, cite various presupposed capabilities already developed prior to age 4. They conclude, rightly, that the false-belief test is 'an ingenious, but very difficult task that taps one aspect of people's understanding of the minds of others' (p. B30).

The fact that these experiments are designed to test one aspect of how people understand the minds of others is both their strength and their weakness. The experiments clearly show that something new happens at age 4, and that what happens is somewhat consistent with certain assumptions that are shared by both theory theory and simulation theory. The experiments are designed to test whether children at certain ages have acquired an ability to explain or predict the behavior of others. But, as I suggested above, explaining and predicting are very specialized cognitive abilities, and do not capture the fuller picture of how we understand other people.[11]

Two other important limitations of false-belief tests in relation to theory of mind should be pointed out. First, subjects are asked to predict the behavior of others with whom they are *not* interacting. Based on a *third-person* observation, the child is asked to predict what the other person will do. If *second-person* interaction is the primary and ordinary way of encountering the other person, and I suggest that it is, then we cannot be certain that results based on third-person observation truly characterize our understanding of others. In this respect, it is simply not valid to use the results of these experiments to characterize second-person ('I–you') interaction, or to appeal to this evidence as justification for what I have called the strong pragmatic claim for theory of mind.[12] It is interesting to note that in the 3-year-old subject's second-person interaction with the experimenter, the subject does not seem to have difficulty understanding the experimenter in the way that she seems to misunderstand the third person about whom she is asked. It is not at all clear that direct interaction in a second-person relationship can be captured by activities in the category of third-person observation.

Second, false-belief experiments, like the one conducted by Wimmer and Perner, are designed to test a conscious, metarepresentational process. That is, in such

---

(see Leslie 2000). Three-year-olds fail both the photograph tests (in which false-beliefs are not at stake) and the false-belief tests, suggesting not that children have problems with beliefs *per se*, but with the complexity of the problems (Bloom and German 2000). Furthermore, Siegal and Beattie (1991) and Surian and Leslie (1999) have shown that 3-year-olds are capable of passing false-belief tests if the wording of the questions is modified. This suggests that 'normally developing children's performance on false-belief problems is limited by processing resources rather than by inability to represent belief states in others' (Leslie 2000: 1242). Bloom and German (2000) and Barresi and Moore (1996) present similar arguments.

[11] Stich and Nichols (1992) suggest concerning these experiments, 'the explanation of the data offered by the experimenters is one that presupposes the correctness of the theory-theory'. One could further suggest that the kinds of questions that are asked, and the kinds of answers that are sought in these experiments, are framed by theory of mind's contention that explanation and prediction are primary ways of interpreting other's minds.

[12] For more on the concept of second-person interaction, and its irreducibility to first-person and/or third-person perspectives, see Gomez (1996) and Reddy (1996).

experiments, the subjects are not only provided the task of explaining or predicting, but they are asked to perform these tasks consciously, and in a reflective manner. The science of false-belief tests does not provide any evidence for the claim that theory of mind processes are implicit or subpersonal. The experimental design does not address the issue of how theory of mind mechanisms function non-consciously. In this regard the science simply cannot count against the phenomenology.

Thus, there are at least three factors that limit the conclusions that can be drawn from such experiments for theory of mind, and especially for the pragmatic claim that theory of mind characterizes all our interpersonal interactions.

1. The experiments explicitly test for the specialized cognitive activities of explaining and predicting.
2. The experiments involve third-person perspectives rather than second-person interactions.
3. The experiments involve conscious processes and do not address theory-of-mind mechanisms that operate non-consciously.

It might seem that the following experiment could address the second limitation. In Wimmer, Hogrefe, and Sodian (1988), two children face each other and each one answers questions about what they know or about what the other child knows concerning the contents of a box into which one of them has looked. Children of 3 and 4 years of age answer correctly about their own knowledge, but incorrectly about the other child's knowledge, even when they see that the other child has looked into the box. Although this seems closer to second-person interaction, the children are not really interacting on the cognitive level that is being tested. That is, the questions are posed by the experimenter (with whom the children *are* interacting), but they call for third-person explanation or prediction of the other person with whom they are not interacting.

A theory-theory interpretation of this experiment is that these children use different mental processes to assess what they themselves know as opposed to what the other child knows. To answer about their own knowledge the children use an 'answer check procedure'. 'They simply check to see whether they have an answer to the embedded question in their knowledge base, and if they do they respond affirmatively' (Stich and Nichols 1992). According to this account they do not know that they know the contents of the box until they find a belief or piece of knowledge in their own cognitive system. To say that they know what is in the box, it is not enough to have looked inside the box; they also have to look inside their own minds. They have to 'check' with themselves in something like a metarepresentative introspection (Leslie 1988).

It seems more likely, and much more parsimonious, however, that their answer about what they know is based simply on looking inside the box rather than looking inside their own mind. The child looks inside the box and is then asked whether she knows what is in the box. Her positive answer is based on the fact that she just saw what was inside the box, rather than on an introspective discovery of a belief about the contents of the box (see Gordon 1995b). Her knowledge, one might say, is already in her action. As Gareth Evans (1982) pointed out, if a subject is asked 'Do you believe that p?' the subject does not start searching in her mind for the *belief that p*. Rather, she straightforwardly considers whether p is or is not the case. When a child does not know what is in the box, her failure to acknowledge that another child, who has looked inside the box, does know would be surprising only to someone who would expect her to think theoretically, in terms of intentional states abstracted from her own actions. What is not surprising, however, is that the subject has no problem understanding the question put to her by the experimenter with whom she is interacting. Nor is there any indication that she is surprised by the possibility that someone else may or may not have knowledge.

Children aged 4–5 years of age have progressed to the point of having the ability to tell correctly what another child who has seen the transfer of a piece of candy from one box to another knows about the contents of the second box. In this part of the experiment, however, both children (the subject and the other) have seen the transfer together. But the same age group fails to understand that in certain circumstances the other child, without visual knowledge, might know the same fact by inference. Again, this would be surprising only if the subject understood the other child in terms of having abstract mental states. The same experiments show that a 6-year-old child is capable of precisely this realization and has thus attained some advanced part of a theory of mind. Yet to show that a child attains a theory of mind at some specific point in development, such that they can consciously explain or predict what someone with whom they are not interacting knows, is not to demonstrate that the child's primary understanding of others is based on theory of mind capabilities. These same children, we would assume, were able to play together and communicate prior to learning that knowledge and beliefs can be caused by inference as well as by direct perceptual access.

Mirror Neurons: Who, Where, and When

A different sort of scientific evidence has recently been cited in support of simulation theory, namely, the specific operations of mirror neurons or shared neural representations (see Ch. 8). The proposal is that these operations constitute an internal simulation of another person's behavior. Since mirror neurons or shared representations respond *both* when a particular motor action is performed by the subject *and* when the subject observes the same goal-directed action performed by another individual, they constitute an intermodal link between the visual perception of action or dynamic expression, and the first-person, *intra*subjective, proprioceptive sense of one's own capabilities.

Simulation theorists suggest that mirror neurons help us to translate our visual perception of the other person's behavior into a mental plan of that behavior in ourselves, thus enabling an explanation or prediction of the other person's thoughts or actions. Mirror neurons facilitate the creation of pretend ('off-line') actions (motor images) that correspond to the visually perceived actions of others (Gallese and Goldman 1998). Mirror neurons, of course, are part of the motor system, so the 'plan' that is generated is a motoric one. This, it is argued, at least prefigures (or is a primitive kind of) mental simulation, and as such it supports simulation theory rather than theory theory. 'The point is that [mirror neuron] activity is not mere theoretical inference. It creates in the observer a state that matches that of the target [person]' (Gallese and Goldman 1998: 498).

This approach addresses some of the limitations found in the false-belief experiments. First, the activation of mirror neurons can be thought to be most appropriately the result of specific *second-person* interactions, although they also operate in third-person perspectives on how others interact.[13] Second, studies of mirror neurons are clearly studies of *non-conscious*, automatic processes that may or may not be experienced at a conscious level, although they surely shape conscious behavior. Nonetheless, the process thought to prefigure a more mature simulation routine is still described in a fashion similar to the theory-theory approach, as resulting in the specialized cognitive activities of explaining, predicting, and 'retrodicting'. Indeed, only by describing the activity as involving a representational 'plan' (Goldman and Gallese [2000] reject the idea of a non-representational intentionality) can simulation theorists claim that mirror neuron activity prefigures the more developed representational processes involved in explaining and predicting.

The implication of this representationalist view is that my own first-person model mediates my understanding of another person's behavior. Goldman and Gallese (2000: 256) suggest that mirror neurons rely on an 'internal representation of goals, emotions, body states and the like to map the same states in other individuals'. Consider two possible interpretations of this idea. One interpretation is that the internal representation is literally a re-presentation, or copy, of the originally perceived action. In other words, two things are happening: I *perceive* an action, and I *simulate* it in terms of my own possibilities. In this case, simulation is secondary to and distinguishable from perception. On the second interpretation, since mirror neurons involve extremely good examples of intermodal perception (translating vision into proprioceptive and body schematic registrations), the most parsimonious simulationist account is that when we perceive another person's actions, that perception registers in the mirror system as already a first-person model of what such actions would be if they were the perceiver's own actions.[14]

---

[13] Third-person perspectives are often employed in experimental situations. That is, the observation of the other person is conducted in a detached rather than interactive setting. This difference is usually ignored. For example, Ruby and Decety (2001) use the term 'third-person simulation' to signify the motor simulation of another person's action (in contrast to 'first-person simulation' of one's own action), without considering whether interactive observation might be different from detached observation, or for that matter whether the simulation of another's action could itself take the form of egocentric simulation (that is, I simulate the other's action as if it were my own) or allocentric simulation (I simulate the other's action as if it were her action performed where she is). See Gallagher (2003a) for discussion.

[14] Frederique de Vignemont (2004) has recently proposed a third possibility. Mirror neurons may encode intentional action by default in strictly neutral terms—neither in first- nor third-person perspectives. Whether the action registers as such, it then requires specification as to whether it is my action or someone else's action. This is accomplished by non-overlapping brain areas connected with the 'Who' system—e.g. the right inferior parietal cortex for third-person perspective, and the anterior insula for

On either interpretation, however, the subject seemingly reads off the meaning of the other, not directly from the other's actions, but from the internal simulation of *the subject's own* 'as if' actions. This view suggests that the subject who understands the other person is not interacting with the other person so much as interacting with an internally simulated model of himself, pretending to be the other person. In effect, in contrast to the eclipse of second-person interaction by third-person observation in false-belief tests, here second-person interaction is reduced to a first-person internal activity.

Not only is this interpretation not phenomenologically parsimonious, at the level of explaining or predicting the other person's behavior, it is also not clear that the neurological picture supports it. We may be able to see this by considering some of the brain-scan experiments that were done in connection with the 'Who' system and shared representations discussed in Ch. 8 (Georgieff and Jeannerod 1998, and various other studies). These studies use the terminology of simulation theory. Subjects are asked to simulate their own first-person movements or the movements of others in a third-person perspective. In this case, simulation means mental simulation—an explicit imaginative enaction of the movement—consciously imagining oneself or the other doing the action. The neuronal representations responsible for explicit action simulation are in large part the same neuronal representations that are activated in the case of observing action and in performing action (Blakemore and Decety 2001; Grezes and Decety 2001). In the experimental situation when I am asked to observe or to simulate an action performed by someone else, imaging results show significant overlap for observation and simulation in the supplementary motor area (SMA), the dorsal premotor cortex, the supramarginal gyrus, and the superior parietal lobe.

Of course to distinguish the simulation from the observation, the subject's mental simulation in these experiments cannot happen simultaneously with an occurrent observation of another's action. It seems reasonable to assume that some of the same brain areas that are activated in the conscious imaginative enaction of mental simulation would be the same areas activated in the more covert, subpersonal simulation. In the observation mode the specified brain areas are activated. However, there is no evidence in the observation mode for a secondary activation of the overlapping areas that would count as a subpersonal simulation over and above the original activation generated by the observation. In other words, if I observe another person perform action X, then there is activation in the relevant brain areas that corresponds to my perception of that action. In opposition to the first interpretation of simulation theory outlined above, which claims that simulation is an extra step over and above the perception of an action, there is no evidence that there is something like a second activation of those same areas that would correspond to an internal copy or simulation of action X. The neurological underpinnings of what could count as a simulation are part and parcel of the activation

first-person perspective, as discussed in the previous chapter. For the simulationist this offers the possibility that the simulation is carried out in neutral terms and then applied to the right person.

that corresponds to the original perception. The point is that there is no evidence that perception and simulation are two separate processes. Rather, one could say, in effect, perception of action is already an understanding of the action; there is no extra step involved that could count as a separate simulation routine.

One might object that there is certainly an articulated process involved in the observation of the other's action. There is the visual perception that involves processing in the visual cortex, and there is an additional activation of the shared representation areas in the frontal and parietal cortexes. This may be a definitional problem about where to draw the line between perception and other cognitive processes. Where in the brain does perception end and some other process begin? The 'Where' question, in this sense, is not easily answerable—nor is the 'When' question. Perception is not a momentary event. Even if we conceive it as a very short visual glance, if it attains semantic significance it will take some small amount of time. One might register this in temporal frameworks of working memory or the retentionally-protentionally constituted specious present. It is not clear, however, that we can even ask the question about how long a perception lasts, or how short is the shortest possible perception. Brain processes may be measured in msecs, but perceptual experience involves experienced time.

If simulation is not separate from perception, this may or may not support the second interpretation—namely, that the perception of another person's action registers as already a first-person model of what that action would be if it were the perceiver's own action. But if perception already has a simulation structure, it is not clear why one needs an 'internal' model at all. The required model *is* the action of the other, and it is already being perceived. Why would one need to 'read off' the meaning of an action on an internal 'as if' model, indirectly, when one is observing that very action performed by the other? On this non-simulationist view, mirror neurons and shared representations are not primarily the mediators of simulation but are the enactment of direct intersubjective perception.

There is growing consensus that mirror neurons and the related brain areas that are activated for self-movement and perception of another person's movement play an important role in neonate imitation and the infant's ability to perceive intentions (Blakemore and Decety 2001; Chaminade, Meltzoff, and Decety 2002; and Decety *et al.* 2002; Gallagher 2001b). To imitate a facial gesture that it sees, however, the infant has no need to simulate the gesture internally. It is already simulating it on its own face. Its own body is already in communication with the other's body at prenoetic and perceptual levels that are sufficient for intersubjective interaction.

Interaction and Intersubjectivity

There is good scientific evidence to support the developmental claim that around the age of 4 children come to recognize that others are capable of having beliefs different from their own. Prior to this, however, the basis for human interaction and for understanding others has already been laid down by certain embodied practices—practices that are emotional, sensory-motor, perceptual, and non-conceptual. I want to suggest that these embodied practices constitute our primary access for understanding others, and continue to do so in large measure even after we attain theory of mind abilities. Development that is specific to theory of mind happens within a wider framework of interpersonal pragmatics, which can be characterized as *second-person* embodied interactions with other persons perceived as others.

The basic claim that I will defend is that in most intersubjective situations we have a direct understanding of another person's intentions because their intentions are explicitly expressed in their embodied actions, and mirrored in our own capabilities for action. For the most part this understanding does not require the postulation of some belief or desire that is hidden away in the other person's mind, since what we might reflectively or abstractly call their belief or desire is expressed directly in their behavior. The evidence to support this claim overlaps to some extent with evidence that has been cited for both theory theory and simulation theory. I will review and reinterpret this evidence first, and then go on to discuss evidence that suggests that theory theory and simulation theory are unable to capture the full range of second-person interactions.

Many who argue for the theory or simulation approach acknowledge that for either a theoretical stance or a simulation routine to get off the ground some understanding of the context and behavior of the other person must be had first. Otherwise I would have nothing to simulate or to theorize about. This suggests that before I can develop a theory of mind I must already have an understanding of the other person and his/her experience—including an understanding of the other as the subject of intentional action. Prior to the possibility of knowing another person's mind in either a theoretical or simulation mode, one already requires

1. an understanding of what it means to be an experiencing subject;
2. an understanding that certain kinds of entities (but not others) in the environment are indeed such subjects;
3. an understanding that in some ways these entities are similar to and in other ways different from oneself; and
4. a specific pre-theoretical knowledge about how people behave in particular contexts.

One way to summarize these pre-theoretical conditions is to say, following a formulation suggested by Bruner and Kalmar (1998) concerning our understanding of the self, that the understanding of others in terms of their mental states requires a 'massively hermeneutic' background. This suggests that there is much going on in our understanding of others, in excess of and prior to the acquisition of theoretical and/or simulation capabilities. How do we get this background understanding? Some theorists answer this question by pointing to capabilities in infants and young children that they consider 'precursors' of theory of mind (Baron-Cohen 1995; Gopnik and Meltzoff 1997; Meltzoff 1995, 2002; Nadel and Butterworth 1999).

In contrast, I take these capabilities as clues for an alternative approach to the issue of how we understand other people.

Primary Intersubjectivity

Pre-theoretical (non-conceptual) capabilities for understanding others already exist in very young children. Children, prior to the age of 3, already have a sense of what it means to be an experiencing subject; that certain kinds of entities (but not others) in the environment are indeed such subjects; and that in some way these entities are similar to and in other ways different from themselves. This sense of others is already implicit, at least in a primitive way, in the behavior of the newborn. We see evidence for it in instances of neonate imitation. As we have seen (Ch. 3), neonate imitation depends not only on a distinction between self and non-self, and a proprioceptive sense of one's own body, but also on the recognition that the other is in fact of the same sort as oneself (Bermúdez 1996; Gallagher 1996; Gallagher and Meltzoff 1996). Infants are able to distinguish between inanimate objects and people (agents), and can respond in a distinctive way to human faces and human bodies, that is, in a way that they do not respond to other objects (see S. C. Johnson 2000; S. C. Johnson et al. 1998; Legerstee 1991; Meltzoff 1995). Following Meltzoff and Moore (1977, 1994), we have seen that from birth, actions of the infant and the perceived actions of others are coded in the same 'language', in a cross-modal system that is directly attuned to the actions and gestures of other humans. In the case of imitated facial gestures, one does not require an intermediate theory or simulation to translate between one's proprioceptive experience of one's face and the visual perception of the other's face. The translation is already accomplished at the level of an innate body schema that integrates sensory and motor systems. There is, in this case, a common bodily intentionality that is shared across the perceiving subject and the perceived other. As Gopnik and Meltzoff (1997: 129) indicate, 'we innately map the visually perceived motions of others onto our own kinesthetic sensations'.[15]

Should we interpret this intermodal and intersubjective mapping as a primitive form of theorizing or an 'initial theory' of action? Gopnik and Meltzoff (p. 130) answer in the affirmative. They suggest that infants form a 'plan', an internal representation of what they will do, and then they 'recognize the relationship between their plan to produce the action and the action they perceive in others'. On this view, this is the beginning of an inference-like operation that is eventually promoted into a theoretical attitude. But is the motor plan equivalent to a mental state? They suggest it is, although not a very sophisticated mental state. But if, in this case, we ask what a mental state is, it seems to be nothing other than a certain

---

[15] This idea is reminiscent of Husserl's (1973) analysis of the link between kinesthetic experience and perception. On the neurological level it is also supported by the recent research on mirror neurons and shared activation patterns for self-movement and perception of movement. Petit (1999) points out the relation between Husserl's analysis and the results of research on mirror neurons. Here we seem to have good agreement between phenomenology, neuroscience, and developmental psychology.

disposition of the body to act intentionally, plus the phenomenal sense of what it is like to do the action. Certainly it does not have the status of an ideational event that intervenes to mediate vision and proprioception. Intermodal experience is characterized as phenomenologically transparent. That is, the sensory-motor process does not require an internal copy (a mental simulation) that the infant consults in order to know what to do. Neonates, as we have noted, perfect their imitative actions. They improve the match between their gesture and the perceived gesture. They therefore register the difference between themselves and the other. But to do this they need no internal plan to consult, since they have a visual model right in front of them, namely, the face of the other, as well as a proprioceptive model, namely, the gesture that is taking shape on their own face. Even in those cases where the infant has cause to remember the presented gesture in order to imitate it after a delay (see Meltzoff and Moore 1994), it is difficult to construe a sensory-motor memory as a theory of action.

Accordingly, the body schema does not function as an 'abstract representation', as sometimes claimed (Gopnik and Meltzoff 1997: 133). If, as Meltzoff himself proposes, the body schema is an innate system designed for motor control, it seems more appropriate to understand it as a set of pragmatic (action-oriented) capabilities embodied in the developing nervous system. In the human infant this system accounts for the possibility of recognizing and imitating other humans.

To the capabilities implicit in neonate imitation, we need to add a number of other early interactive capabilities that constitute what Trevarthen (1979) has called 'primary intersubjectivity'. Although these aspects of behavior are sometimes enlisted in the cause of theory theory (see Baron-Cohen 1995: 55; Gopnik and Meltzoff 1997: 131), it is quite possible to understand them as supporting a more immediate, less theoretical (non-mentalistic) mode of interaction. Baron-Cohen (1995), for example, proposes two mechanisms as necessary, but not sufficient, components of a theory of mind mechanism. The first he terms the 'intentionality detector' (ID). He considers this to be an innate capability that allows the infant to read 'mental states in behavior' (p. 32). The ID allows the infant to interpret bodily movement as goal-directed intentional movement. Notably this is possible without the intervention of theory or simulation, which, all evidence indicates, are more sophisticated abilities that develop later. In effect, the infant is capable of perceiving other persons as agents. On the one hand, this mechanism may not be specific enough to limit the attribution of agency to just humans (see Scholl and Tremoulet 2000). On the other hand, combined with other capabilities, such as imitation of human gestures and eye-tracking (see below), ID is quickly honed to serve intersubjective interpretation. The understanding of others fostered by ID, however, does not require advanced cognitive abilities. It is perceptual, and as Scholl and Tremoulet (2000: 299) suggest, 'fast, automatic, irresistible and highly stimulus-driven'.

The second mechanism proposed by Baron-Cohen is what he terms the 'eye-direction detector' (EDD). EDD allows the infant to recognize where another person is looking. Obviously, this mechanism is more specific than ID since it is linked to the perception of eyes and faces. It allows the infant to see (1) that the other person is looking in a certain direction, and (2) that the other person sees what she is looking at. Does EDD involve an inference in moving from step (1) to step (2)? Baron-Cohen (1995: 43) suggests that an inference is necessary to understand that the other person actually sees what she is looking at. Specifically, he points out that the infant experiences its own vision as contingent on opening versus closing its eyes. His suggestion is more in line with simulation theory: 'from very early on, infants presumably distinguish seeing from not-seeing. . . . Although this knowledge is initially based on the infant's own experience, it could be generalized to an Agent by analogy with the Self'. But, if we take this situation beyond the simple eyes open/eyes closed contrast, one could ask, how does seeing differ from looking? Of course *by virtue of experience* we may come to discover that someone can be looking in a certain direction and not seeing something that is located in that direction. I sometimes look, but don't see. But that is something we learn by experience rather than a default mode of EDD. *On the face of it*, that is, at a primary (default) level of experience, from the perspective of the child who is observing the event, there does not seem to be an extra step between looking at something and seeing it.[16]

There are many more intention-signaling behaviors that infants and young children are capable of perceiving. In addition to the eyes, it is likely that various movements of the head, the mouth, the hands, and more general body movements are perceived as meaningful or goal-directed. Such perceptions are important for a non-mentalistic (pre-theoretical) understanding of the intentions and dispositions of other persons as well as for social reinforcement (see review by Allison, Puce, and McCarthy 2000), and they are operative by the end of the first year (Baldwin 1993; S. C. Johnson 2000; S. C. Johnson *et al.* 1998). In effect, this kind of perception-based understanding is a form of 'body-reading' rather than mind-reading. In seeing the actions and expressive movements of the other person, one already sees their meaning; no inference to a hidden set of mental states (beliefs, desires, etc.) is necessary.

There is also evidence for affective and temporal coordination between the gestures and expressions of the infant and those of the other persons with whom they interact. Infants 'vocalize and gesture in a way that seems "tuned" [affectively and temporally] to the vocalizations and gestures of the other person' (Gopnik and Meltzoff 1997: 131). At 5–7 months infants are able to detect correspondences between visual and auditory information that specify the expression of emotions (Walker 1982). Importantly, the perception of emotion in the movement of others is a perception of an embodied comportment, rather than a theory or simulation of an emotional state. Moore, Hobson, and Lee (1997) have demonstrated the emotional nature of human movement using actors with point-lights attached to various body

---

[16] Baron-Cohen (1995), who carefully provides evidence for the other aspects of EDD, does not provide evidence for there being an inference between looking and seeing at this age. Also see Meltzoff and Brooks (2001).

joints.[17] Non-autistic subjects view the abstractly outlined, but clearly embodied, movement of the actors in a darkened room and are able to identify the emotion that is being represented. As early as 5 months of age infants show preferential attentiveness to human shape and movement in such displays (Bertenthal, Proffitt, and Cutting 1984). The emotional states of others are not, in primary experience, mental attributes that we have to infer. One perceives the emotion in the movement and expression of the other's body and especially in the face.[18]

Secondary Intersubjectivity

Baron-Cohen makes it clear that ID and EDD separately or together are sufficient to enable the child to recognize dyadic relations between the other and the self, or between the other and the world. The child can understand that the other person *wants* food or *intends* to open the door; that the other can *see* him (the child) or is *looking at* the door. These are basic intentional relations. Of course children do not simply observe others, they interact with others, and in doing so they develop a further capability which Baron-Cohen terms the 'shared attention mechanism' (SAM). Behavior representative of joint attention begins to develop around 9–14 months. The child alternates between monitoring the gaze of the other and what the other is gazing at, checking to verify that they are continuing to look at the same thing. This marks the beginnings of what Trevarthen terms 'secondary intersubjectivity'.

Trevarthen shows that around the age of 1 year, infants go beyond the person-to-person immediacy of primary intersubjectivity, and enter into contexts of shared attention—shared situations—in which they learn what things mean and what they are for (see Trevarthen and Hubley 1978). Peter Hobson nicely summarizes this notion of secondary intersubjectivity. 'The defining feature of secondary intersubjectivity is that an object or event can become a focus *between* people. Objects and events can be communicated about. . . . the infant's interactions with another person begin to have reference to the things that surround them' (Hobson 2002: 62). Children do not simply observe others; they are not passive observers. Rather they interact with others, and in doing so they develop further capabilities in the contexts of those interactions.

---

[17] The subjects in Moore, Hobson, and Lee (1997) were older children classified in three groups as normal, autistic, and non-autistic mentally retarded. The results demonstrated that the autistic children had relatively more difficulty in recognizing (or simply failed to recognize) emotional attitudes (see below for more on autism).

[18] Hobson (1993) provides a strong argument along this line. He cites Merleau-Ponty (1964), who notes the 'simple fact that I live in the facial expressions of the other, as I feel him living in mine' (p. 146). One could also cite Scheler (1954): 'For we certainly believe ourselves to be directly acquainted with another person's joy in his laughter, with his sorrow and pain in his tears, with his shame in his blushing, with his entreaty in his outstretched hands. . . . And with the tenor of this thoughts in the sound of his words. If anyone tells me that this is not "perception", for it cannot be so, in view of the fact that a perception is simply a "complex of physical sensations" . . . I would beg him to turn aside from such questionable theories and address himself to the phenomenological facts.' Also see Cole (1998, 1999) on the importance of the face in such contexts.

Further evidence for early, non-mentalistic interpretation of the intentional actions of others can be found in numerous studies. Baldwin and colleagues have shown that infants at 10–11 months are able to parse some kinds of continuous action according to intentional boundaries (Baldwin and Baird 2001; Baldwin et al. 2001). Children of 15–18 months can comprehend what another person intends to do. They are able to re-enact to completion the goal-directed behavior that an observed subject does not complete (Meltzoff 1995; Meltzoff and Brooks 2001). Quite obviously ID provides an understanding of what an intentional state is; in the first place, however, another's intentional state is not a private mental state, but simply the other's action or the state of a perceived body.

The child also learns to point around this same time. Phillips, Baron-Cohen, and Rutter (1992) show that infants between 9 and 18 months look to the eyes of the other person to help interpret the meaning of an ambiguous event. In such interactions, well before the development of a theory of mind mechanism, the child looks to the body and the expressive movement of the other to discern the intention of the person or to find the pragmatic meaning of some object. In this kind of second-person interaction 2-year-olds are even capable of recognizing pretend behavior, for example the mother pretending the banana is a telephone (Leslie 1994).

This understanding is non-mentalistic in the same sense that our understanding of our own intentional actions is non-mentalistic. As I've suggested in previous chapters, when questioned about what we are doing, we do not interpret our own actions (e.g. getting a drink or greeting a friend) on either an abstract, physiological level ('I am activating a certain group of muscles'), or in terms of a mentalistic performance ('I am acting on a belief that I'm thirsty, or that this is a familiar human being capable of communication'). Rather, quite naturally, we understand our own actions on the highest pragmatic level possible. I tend to understand my actions at just that pragmatic, intentional (goal-oriented) level, ignoring possible subpersonal or lower-level descriptions, and also ignoring ideational or mentalistic interpretations. Likewise, the interpretation of the actions of others occurs at that same pragmatic (intentional) level. We interpret their actions in terms of their goals and intentions set in contextualized situations, rather than abstractly in terms of either their muscular performance or their beliefs.

Do such interpretations, even in the adult, depend on inference? Baldwin and Baird (2001) argue that inference is required to sort out which one of many possible interpretations is correct. They cite an example proposed by John Searle.

If I am going for a walk to Hyde Park, there are any number of things that are happening in the course of my walk, but their descriptions do not describe my intentional actions, because in acting what I am doing depends in large part on what I think I am doing. So for example, I am also moving in the general direction of Patagonia, shaking the hair on my head up and down, wearing out my shoes and moving a lot of air molecules. However, none of these other descriptions seems to get at what is essential about this action, as the action it is.

(Searle 1984: 58)

According to Baldwin and Baird, to work out the right interpretation of Searle's action we need much more information about him and human behavior, and on that basis we proceed to make an inferential judgment about his intentions. But clearly, given the situation, Patagonia, the simple physical facts of bouncing hair and foot-wear, and molecular movement simply do not enter into my interpretation, even as possibilities, unless I start to make abstract, theoretical inferences. Rather, if I see John Searle walking toward Hyde Park, I'm likely to say, 'There's John Searle out for a walk.' Or, 'That guy is heading for the park.' The other interpretations simply do not come up, unless I start making large and abstract inferences. Since I don't see John Searle every day, I may in fact start to wonder what his further intentions are—is he going to philosophize in the park? But if I were seriously to pursue this question I would have to take action—follow him, stop and ask him, ask someone else who might know, etc. Without such action my inferences would be blind.

Given the capabilities that are available under the title of primary and secondary intersubjectivity, I propose what is, in relation to theory theory or simulation theory, a revised, and in some sense enhanced or extended *developmental claim*. Before we are in a position to form a theory about someone, or to simulate what the other person believes or desires, we already have specific pre-theoretical knowledge about how people behave in particular contexts. We are able to get this kind of knowledge precisely through the various capabilities that characterize primary and secondary intersubjectivity, including imitation, intentionality detection, eye-tracking, the per-ception of meaning and emotion in movement and posture, and the understanding of intentional or goal-related movements in pragmatic contexts. This kind of knowledge is the 'massively hermeneutic' background required for the more con-ceptual accomplishments of mentalistic interpretation. It derives from embodied practices in second-person interactions with others long before we reach the age of theoretical reason. As a result, before we are in a position to explain or predict the behavior of others, to mentalize or mind-read, to theorize or simulate, we are already in a position to interact with and to understand others in terms of their gestures, intentions, and emotions, and in terms of what they see, what they do or pretend to do with objects, and how they act toward ourselves and others in the pragmatically contextualized activities of everyday life.

This expanded developmental claim undermines the strong pragmatic claim made for theory of mind, and supports a strong pragmatic claim for interaction theory. Primary embodied intersubjectivity is not primary simply in developmental terms. Rather it remains primary across all face-to-face intersubjective experiences, and it subtends the occasional and relatively rare intersubjective practices of explaining or predicting what other people believe, desire, or intend in the practice of their own minds.

Autism, Central Coherence, and Interaction Theory

Theory of mind has provided an important framework for understanding autism. It is one of the most widely discussed approaches to explaining the cognitive and behavioral aspects of this developmental disorder (e.g. Baron-Cohen 1995; Baron-Cohen, Leslie, and Frith 1985; Frith and Happé 1999). Autistic children clearly demonstrate impairment of certain social abilities, and especially inadequate development in the mentalistic understanding of others. Proponents of theory of mind link these social impairments to delayed development of the cognitive abilities associated with the theory of mind mechanism. Experiments in support of this view are based on the standard false belief tasks, comparing the performance of normal and Down syndrome children to the performance of autistic children. The results are quite dramatic. Baron-Cohen (1989) shows that autistic children, more advanced in mental age than normal, and Down syndrome children who pass the test are unable to recognize the significance of false belief. Leslie and Frith (1988) suggest that autistic children are specifically impaired in their capacity for metarepresentation, and this in turn impedes their formulation of a theory of mind. To the extent that metarepresentation is also necessary for pretense, this view is also consistent with impairments in pretend play in autistic subjects.

This is a bare bones and oversimplified version of the theory of mind account, but I think it captures its essential features. Even ignoring the problems that we have considered in the previous sections, it is generally acknowledged that there are some significant 'internal' problems or limitations in this account of autism. They are internal in the sense that they are problems that appear when one accepts the general terms of the theory of mind account. For example, if theory of mind is to be an account that captures the definitive nature of autism, it is problematic that a significant percentage of autistic individuals are capable of passing false belief and other 'theory of mind' tests. Happé (1995), for example, points out that the range of autistic children who pass such tests varies across different studies from 15 to 60 per cent (Reed and Paterson 1990, and Prior, Dahlstrom, and Squires 1990, respectively). This suggests that some autistic subjects seemingly do possess a theory of mind. Another problem involves the fact that although the theory of mind approach is capable of addressing some of the major cognitive symptoms of autism, especially those involving social cognition and communication, it is unable to explain other symptoms, most of them non-social symptoms, characteristically found in many autistic individuals, for example: restricted range of interest, obsessive concern for sameness, preoccupation with objects or parts of objects, high cognitive ability for rote memory, echolalia, non-semantic form perception, and a variety of sensory and motor behaviors such as oversensitivity to stimuli and repetitious and odd movements (see Happé 1995: 113 ff.).

To the extent that these non-social symptoms of autism show the limits of theory of mind accounts, they also show the limits of interaction theory, or any theory that focuses on just the social aspects, to explain all there is to explain in autism. We need to face up to this fact by developing an account of the social symptoms that is not inconsistent with a broader account that would explain the non-social symptoms. In this concluding section I want to map out a general account in which the problem of specialized cognitive functions related to theory of mind appears at the end of a long line of effects that are more basic and start with disruptions in some basic sensory-motor processes.

Unfortunately, there is still no consensus about what happens in the brain of the autistic subject. Recent research on apoptosis (the natural pruning of the excess of neuronal cells with which we are born) suggests that the normal timing of this process is disrupted in the autistic brain (see e.g. Courchesne, Carper, and Akshoomoff 2003; Fatemi and Halt 2001; Fatemi et al. 2001; Margolis, Chuang, and Post 1994). If that is the case, it is likely that many and diverse neurological problems affecting many different parts of the brain, and different kinds of dynamic processing in the brain, could result. It is not surprising, then, to find abnormalities in the neuronal processes that underlie face recognition (the fusiform gyrus (Pierce et al. 2001)), emotion perception (amygdala and limbic system (Bachevalier 2000; Bauman and Kemper 1994)), and many other sensory, motor, and cognitive problems that can result from a variety of brain abnormalities. Since the neurological picture remains unclear, however, we need to look to behavioral indicators to find the first clues about autism.

A variety of basic sensory-motor problems exist in autistic children between ages 3 and 10 years (see Damasio and Maurer 1978; Vilensky et al. 1981) and even before that in infants who are later diagnosed as autistic. Teitelbaum et al. (1998) studied videos of infants who were diagnosed as autistic around age 3 years. Movement disturbances were observed in all the infants as early as age 4–6 months, and in some from birth. These include problems in lying, righting, sitting, crawling, and walking, as well as abnormal mouth shapes. They involve delayed development, as well as abnormal motor patterns, for example, asymmetries or unusual sequencing in crawling and walking.

Just these kinds of sensory-motor processes have been shown to be important in explaining some basic aspects of social cognition. Here the evidence that a subject's understanding of another person's actions and intentions depends to some extent on a mirrored reverberation in the subject's own motor system is relevant. The neurology of 'shared representations' for intersubjective perception (Georgieff and Jeannerod 1998) suggests that problems with our own motor or body-schematic system could significantly interfere with our capacities for understanding others. Accordingly, it is possible that developmental problems involving sensory-motor processes may have an effect on the capabilities that make up primary intersubjectivity, and therefore the autistic child's ability to understand the actions and intentions of others.[19]

Importantly, however, the disrupted development of these sensory-motor processes may contribute not only to deficiencies in primary intersubjectivity, but are likely to offer some explanation of the other sensory-motor symptoms of autism:

---

[19] Much more work is needed in this regard. An easy objection to this idea is that there are many individuals with severe sensory-motor problems who do not show autistic symptoms in regard to social development. We could imagine, however, that some specific, early-developed sensory-motor problems may interfere with capacities to interact with others, while other sensory-motor problems may not. So it would be important to find out more about the nature of these problems—more, at least, than the study of videotapes may reveal.

oversensitivity to stimuli, repetitive and odd movements, and, possibly, echolalia. In addition, studies that focus on the perception of emotion show that autistic children do not understand the embodied behavior of other persons in the same way that normal children would. Autistic children have difficulties in perceiving the bodily expression of emotion in others, and in imitating certain stylistic aspects of actions performed by others, especially those stylistic aspects indicative of emotional state (Moore, Hobson, and Lee 1997). They also have problems in understanding the other person as a self-oriented agent (Hobson and Lee 1999). Some autistic children, for example, attempt to perform an imitative action within the spatial framework of the experimenter's body rather than their own, and thus demonstrate a sensory-motor confusion between egocentric and allocentric spatial frameworks.[20]

There are, however, other cognitive problems in autism. Uta Frith (1989) and Francesca Happé (1995) have developed a proposal meant to supplement the theory of mind approach, since the latter leaves many symptoms unexplained. Frith (1989) suggested that autism involves an imbalance in the integration of information, and specifically in integrating parts and wholes. She refers to this as a problem with 'central coherence'. Perception and understanding are normally shaped by gestalt principles. In autism these gestalt principles seem to break down. Happé emphasizes the idea that autistic cognition focuses on parts rather than on the broader contexts that provide meaning for the parts. Autistic subjects thus have difficulty seeing things in their context; they treat them as non-contextualized, in an impoverished or abstract way. Happé cites a clinical example: 'A clinician testing a bright autistic boy presented him with a toy bed, and asked the child to name the parts. The child correctly labeled the bed, mattress and quilt. The clinician then pointed to the pillow and asked, "And what is this?" The boy replied, "It's a piece of ravioli" ' (Happé 1995: 117). Indeed, the pillow did resemble a piece of ravioli, out of context, but ordinarily one would see it as a pillow in the context of the bed.

This problem of central coherence permeates autistic cognition and can generate a variety of symptoms and test results, including what might be regarded as positive effects (unusual talents for remembering word-strings or unrelated items, echoing nonsense, sorting faces by accessories, recognizing faces upside down) and negative effects (unusual weakness for remembering sentences and related items, sorting faces by emotion, recognizing upright faces). Problems with central coherence also affect perceptual experience. In contrast to normal test subjects, for example, autistic children are better able to find embedded figures in complex backgrounds— for them, the background context does not interfere with their search abilities, as it does for non-autistic subjects.

---

[20] This is a tentative conclusion based on reviewing videotape of the Hobson and Lee experiments. The autistic child does not represent his own body in the action of the other. This would also interfere with any attempt at simulation. In such cases, it is as if the autistic child's mirror neurons are not working properly (see Gallagher 2001b). Ohta (1987) notes a pattern of 'partial imitation' of manual gestures in a significant proportion of autistic subjects. For example, subjects positioned face-to-face with the model produced gestures that reversed the orientation of the hands. Barresi and Moore (1996) suggest that such problems can be caused by a failure of intermodal integration of first-person (proprioceptive) information and third-person (visual) information. In the failed imitation, third-person, visual information predominates.

If we characterize these gestalt problems of central coherence to be problems that involve understanding context, then it is clear that such problems may interfere with the capabilities that make up secondary intersubjectivity—intersubjective capabilities that depend on understanding others and interacting with them *in contexts*—contexts that are pragmatic, but also social. Seeing another person move in a certain way could mean many different things if it is done outside any particular context. Imagine, for example, that you see my right arm, with open hand, drop through the air, but nothing else that would provide the context for what it means, then it could mean many different things. It might be part of a gesture that means 'hello' or 'goodbye'; it might mean 'get out of here'; it might be that I intend to make an important point by bringing my hand down hard on the desk in front of me. Without the context, my intention is simply not clear to anyone who would be watching me, or trying to interact with me.

Problems with central coherence can contribute to an explanation of other non-social problems as well. Specifically, we would expect someone with a central coherence problem to manifest certain non-social symptoms found in autistic subjects: restricted range of interest, obsessive concern for sameness, preoccupation with objects or parts of objects, high cognitive ability for rote memory, and non-semantic form perception.

Theorists of mind might suggest that there may be a connection between central coherence and metarepresentation, so that a deficit that affects central coherence may affect the capacity for metarepresentation, which is seemingly important for attaining a theory of mind. Happé (p. 124) notes, however, that one can find weakness in central coherence even in autistic subjects who pass theory of mind tasks. This loosens the tie between central coherence and theory of mind.

Metarepresentation involves taking a view on oneself as if upon another person, and on some accounts it develops only as an internalization of an already established social interaction. With respect to autism, however, the etiological order is not clear. Rather than understanding a deficit in metarepresentation as the cause of problems in social interaction, it seems just as feasible to understand a deficit in metarepresentation as the result of more primary problems in social interaction. Furthermore, there is good evidence to suggest that in autism the deficiency in social interaction is not confined to cognitive dimensions. In some limited respects the autistic's cognitive understanding of others can be at age level. For example, the autistic child may be able to say correctly that the other person does not know that a sought-for object is in a particular location. In spite of that understanding, the same child will predict that the person in question will look for it there—an incorrect response to the false belief task. Leslie and Frith (1988) explain this as based on the independence between understanding that the other has limited knowledge, and the understanding of false belief—in effect, a difference between knowing two different cognitive states. An alternative explanation might be that it is a difference between knowing that the other person has limited knowledge (a cognitive state) and knowing how the other person will act. Understanding action may require just those kinds of shared sensory-motor representations of the other's body that interaction theory predicts may be problematic in the autistic individual.

To see the difference between a theory of mind approach, supplemented with considerations of central coherence, and a fuller account that includes interaction theory, we can compare two diagrams (Figs. 9.1 and 9.2). Figure 9.1 shows the idea that problems of central coherence may interfere with the functioning of meta-representation, and sketches what Happé terms the 'exciting suggestion' that there may be two possible cognitive deficits that underlie autism. But this simply ignores the evidence for other more basic and non-cognitive problems.

If, instead, we consider the effects that both sensory-motor problems and problems of central coherence may have on primary and secondary intersubjectivity, as well as their connections to the non-social symptoms, we could develop a fuller theory as represented in Fig. 9.2.

Here we see that sensory-motor problems may lead to symptoms that are both social (in primary intersubjectivity) and non-social. Problems with central coherence may also lead to symptoms that are both social (including problems in both primary and secondary subjectivity) and non-social. We may also ask whether there is any connection between sensory-motor problems and the problems with central coherence. In general I have been arguing that there are good reasons to think that body-schematic processes are closely related to perceptual and cognitive abilities, but the precise nature of the autistic sensory-motor problems needs to be studied further before any clear answer can be given in regard to their relations to either central coherence or primary intersubjectivity.

The status of theory of mind in this account of autism is left open. In contrast to an autistic deficiency in theory of mind, as argued by theory of mind proponents, high-functioning autistic individuals may actually employ theorizing strategies as a way to compensate for the loss in the capacities of primary and secondary inter-subjectivity. If they are not able to perceive the intentions or emotions in the other person's bodily comportment, they may resort to a purely intellectual mentalizing to develop hypotheses about what motivates others to do what they do. Pursuing this suggestion, Zahavi and Parnas (2003) cite accounts of strategies used by high-functioning autistic individuals. A high-functioning autistic person such as Temple

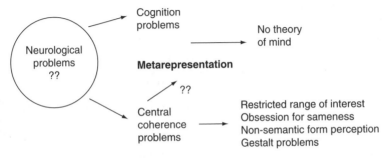

FIG. 9.1. Theory-theory account of autism.

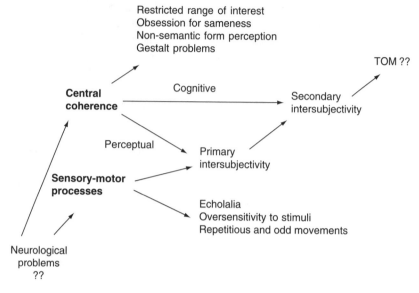

Restricted range of interest
Obsession for sameness
Non-semantic form perception
Gestalt problems

TOM ??

Central coherence

Cognitive

Secondary intersubjectivity

Perceptual

Primary intersubjectivity

Sensory-motor processes

Echolalia
Oversensitivity to stimuli
Repetitive and odd movements

Neurological problems ??

FIG. 9.2.   A more comprehensive account of autistic symptoms.

Grandin, for example, uses a variety of strategies to make up for a loss of a natural intersubjectivity. She reads about people, and observes them, in an attempt to arrive at the various principles that would explain and predict their actions in what she describes as 'a strictly logical process'. As Zahavi and Parnas suggest, 'Grandin's compensatory way of understanding others perfectly resembles how *normal* intersubjective understanding is portrayed by the proponents of the theory-theory' (pp. 67–8). She decodes emotional behavior. As Oliver Sacks explains, she lacks an 'implicit knowledge of social conventions and codes'. 'This implicit knowledge, which every normal person accumulates and generates throughout life on the basis of experience and encounters with others, Temple seems to be largely devoid of. Lacking it, she has instead to "compute" others' intentions and states of mind, to try to make algorithmic, explicit, what for the rest of us is second nature' (Sacks 1995: 258).[21] Perhaps, however, it is something more basic than a *second* nature, to the extent that primary intersubjectivity may come along for most of us as part of our innate genetic endowment as humans.

[21] Another high-functioning autistic person, Jared Blackburn, puts it this way: 'Those Autistic people who are very intelligent may learn to model other people in a more analytical way, however, as part of adapting to society. For those who are skilled in this, it may become very accurate, and make a few Autistic people seem to have exceptional insight into people. However, even for them there is a social disability, because this accuracy is at a great cost in terms of speed and efficiency, and is maybe virtually useless in practical situations (which involve 'real-time' interaction and fast interpretation and response). Thus, given time I may be able to analyze someone in various ways, and seem to get good results, but may not pick-up on certain aspects of an interaction until I am obsessing over it hours or days later. So in practical situations, I have impaired social cognition, with problematic results, while I may seem to have good insights into people at other times' (Blackburn *et al.* 2000).

10

Before You Know It

THE body sets the stage for action. Perhaps the claim should be a stronger one. Your body is already acting 'before you know it'. Certainly there is evidence that indicates that one's body anticipates one's conscious experience. I reach to pick up a glass. Before I am aware of it—if I ever do become explicitly aware of it—my hand shapes itself in the best way possible for purposes of picking up the glass. If I had reached for some differently shaped object, I would find that my hand had already shaped itself accordingly. This is a general rule followed by the sensory-motor body. It anticipates its encounters in both instrumental and expressive contexts. Even in my encounters with others, prenoetically, before I know it, I seem to have a sense of how it is with them.

As we saw in previous chapters, the sense of ownership for action depends on sensory feedback from proprioceptive, visual, and tactile sources. It is generated as the action is taking place. The sense of agency, however, is based, in part, on pre-motor processes that happen just prior to the action. In this regard the sense of agency seems to depend on neurological events that we do not control, and that, if they fail, lead to a sense that my body is being passively moved, or in the case of schizophrenic symptoms, that someone else is causing me to do the action against my will. This has led some theorists to suggest that our *sense* of free will is just that, a sense or feeling produced by the brain to accompany certain actions, but really an unessential accessory to action, an illusion (e.g. Wegner 2002). To the long-standing philosophical debate about free will and determinism, recent neurological evidence has been added on the side of determinism. It might seem that much of what I have reviewed in this book—certain innate capacities, the anticipatory aspects of movement, perception, etc.—would lend support to that position. This is the final issue that I want to examine.

Agency and Free Will

Consider the extensively discussed experiments conducted by Benjamin Libet (1985, 1992, 1996; Libet *et al.* 1983). Libet has shown that motor action itself, and the sense of agency that comes along with it, depend on neurological events that we do not control, and that happen before our conscious decision. In Libet's experiments an array of surface electrodes are attached to the scalp to monitor brain activity. He asked subjects with their hands on a table-top to flick their wrists whenever they want to. The time course of brain activity leading up to the movement lasts from

500–1,000 msecs (0.5 to 1 sec). Just before the flick, there is 50 msec of activity in the motor nerves descending from motor cortex to the wrist. But this is preceded by several hundred (up to 800) msecs of brain activity known as the readiness potential (RP). To ascertain when subjects were first aware of their decision to move their wrists, Libet designed a large clock that allowed subjects to report fractions of a second. Using the clock, subjects were asked to indicate when they decided to move their wrist, or were first aware of the urge to do so. The results of this experiment indicated that on average, 350 msecs before you are conscious of deciding (or having an urge) to move, your brain is already working on the motor processes that will result in the movement. Before you know it, the readiness potential is already underway, and you are preparing to move. Thus, voluntary acts are 'initiated by unconscious cerebral processes before conscious intention appears' (Libet 1985). The brain seemingly decides and then enacts its decisions in a non-conscious fashion, on a subpersonal level, but also inventively tricks us into thinking that we consciously decide matters and that our actions are personal events. Is free will nothing more than the false sense or impression of free will?

This is just the kind of evidence that some theorists appeal to in order to make the case against free will. 'The initiation of the freely voluntary act appears to begin in the brain unconsciously, well before the person consciously knows he wants to act. Is there, then, any role for conscious will in the performance of a voluntary act?' (Libet 1999: 51). Libet (1985, 2003) himself answers in the positive: we can still save free will—because there is still approximately 150 msecs of brain activity left after we are conscious of our decision, and before we move. So, he suggests, we have time consciously to veto the movement.

I will argue that the attempt to frame the question of free will in terms of these subpersonal, prenoetic processes—either to dismiss it or to save it—is misguided for at least two reasons. First, free will cannot be squeezed into time-frames of 150–350 msecs; free will is a longer-term phenomenon that depends on consciousness, and in this respect the sense of agency is more than just an accessory. Second, the notion of free will does not apply primarily to abstract motor processes that make up intentional actions—rather it applies to intentional actions themselves, described at the highest pragmatic level of description. Let me clarify these two points.

First, in regard to time-frame, anyone who wants to talk about free will has to consider that decisions are not confined to the spur of the moment—and specifically, they are not momentary (and to the extent that they are, they may not be as free as we think). There is a distinction between fast, automatic reflex action and slower voluntary action. Let's consider an example. At time T a snake moves in the grass next to my feet. T + 150 msecs, before I know there is anything there, the amygdala in my brain is activated, and before I know why, at T + 200 msecs—and without a sense of agency—I jump and move several yards away. Once I become aware of what is happening (at T + 1,000 msecs), my next move is not of the same sort. At T + 4,000 msecs I recognize the snake as harmless and at T + 5,000 msecs decide to catch it. At T + 5,150 msecs I take a step back and *voluntarily* reach for the snake.

Now in some sense my choice to reach for the snake is momentary. At some point in time (T + 4,900 msecs) I had not decided to catch the snake; msecs later I had decided. But what goes into this decision involves awareness of what has just happened plus recognition of the snake as harmless. At T + 5,150 msecs I take a step back and reach for the snake. One could focus on this movement and say: at T + 4,650 msecs, unbeknownst to me, processes in my brain were already under-way to prepare for my reaching action, before I had even decided to catch the snake—therefore, what seemed to be my decision was actually predetermined by my brain. But this ignores the context defined by the larger time-frame—which involves previous movement and a conscious recognition of the snake. But now consider that it could easily happen that things don't go as fast as I've portrayed, and that, waiting for the opportune moment, I don't actually reach for the snake until 10 seconds after my decision to catch it. Even if Libet would say that an extra decision would have to be made to initiate the reach precisely at that time, isn't that decision already under the control of the initial decision? The voluntary act, in this case—and I would suggest, in most cases—is spread out over a larger time-frame than the experimental milliseconds.

All of these processes (reflex and voluntary) depend on a very basic biological function found in all living organisms: the feedback loop. In nature, even feedback loops that are purely automatic require time. Feedback loops that involve conscious deliberation require an extended duration equivalent to a specious present—that is, a duration that is stretched out over at least several seconds, and is experienced as such. If, as in some cases of schizophrenia, this duration is closed down due to a phenomenal foreshortening of the protentional future (see Ch. 8), then not only is our sense of agency disrupted or non-existent, our free will is also subverted. As in the normal circumstances of involuntary movement, the sense and reality of free will disappears. Importantly, given a slightly extended time-frame and our ability to react consciously to the involuntary forces, some degree of freedom is restored.

I want to suggest that the temporal framework for the exercise of free will is, at a minimum, the temporal framework that allows for the process to be informed by consciousness. Once events of conscious deliberation are included in the behavioral feedback loop certain things in the environment begin to matter to the agent. Meaning and interpretation come into the picture. Conscious interpretation intro-duces a temporally extended 'looping effect' (Hacking 1995). The conscious delib-eration of the agent, which involves memory and knowledge—cognitive schemas (about snakes)—rather than being epiphenomenal, has real effects on behavior. The reason that reaching for the snake is not a reflex or involuntary action is that my conscious interpretation of the situation has an effect. To the extent that consciousness enters into the ongoing production of action, and contributes to the production of further action, *even if significant aspects of this production take place non-consciously*, our actions are intentional.

This issue of time-frame also tells us something about the proper level of description relevant to free will. In this respect, and in contrast to Libet's experi-ments, the question of free will is not about bodily movements, but about intentional actions. The kinds of actions that we freely decide are not the sort of bodily movements described by Libet's experiments. Consider once again that intentional actions are normally characterized on the highest pragmatic level possible. If I am reaching to catch the snake and you stop and ask what I'm doing, which one of the following descriptions is the most appropriate?

I am activating my neurons.
I am flexing my muscles.
I am moving my arm.
I am reaching and grasping.
I am trying to catch the snake.

I hope you agree that it is the last one listed. For the kind of misdirection that is generated when one attempts to use the vocabulary of volition in relation to activations and activities not at the level of intentional action, consider the question which, as Max Velmans (2002: 8) points out, completely misses the point. 'One is not conscious of one's own brain/body processing. So how could there be conscious control of such processing?'

Voluntary actions are not about neurons, muscles, body parts, or even movement—all of which play some part in what is happening, and for the most part, nonconsciously—but all such processes are carried along by (and are intentional because of) my decision to catch the snake (or to participate in an experiment, etc.)—that is, by what is best described on a personal level as my intentional action. My free choice is not about neurons, muscles, or bodily movement; it's not 'a mediating executive mental process, which somehow puts the bodily parts into action' (Zhu 2003: 64); and such motor acts are not the 'prototype' of free action. Rather, free will is about my purposive actions, which are best described in terms of intentions rather than neurons, muscles, reachings, etc. In this regard, such extra-conscious aspects of body-schematic control are like the vehicle to the volitional content. Just as we don't say that the neurons that generate visual red are themselves red, likewise, we shouldn't say that the bodily movements that carry my freely chosen intentional action are themselves freely chosen, at least in any direct sense. I don't choose to take a drink and then, in addition, choose to extend my arm and shape my grasp . . . nor vice versa. I can *say*, in a derivative fashion, that in taking a drink I am freely extending my arm, etc., but only in the same way that I might say that the neurons activated when I see red are the 'red neurons'—I don't mean that the neurons are *actually* red, nor do I mean that the reach and grasp, the muscle extension, the neuronal activity are freely chosen *per se*. The questioner cited by Velmans, however, thinks that consciousness, if it is to generate free actions, should be filled with vehicles rather than content: if consciousness controls my action, then I should be conscious of my bodily movements; if consciousness controls my actions, then I should be conscious of the neurons that must be activated for movement—and if I am not conscious of such things, then consciousness does not have volitional control over my action. This would be a severe involution of embodied conscious experience.

It might be argued that if components involved in a feedback process are completely limited to non-conscious brain events, the loop may be completely reflex or deterministic—and I would agree. But one might then try to take this argument further and claim that brain events and body-schematic mechanisms that work on a prenoetic level may simply be irrelevant to free will. I do not think this is correct. Indeed, for two closely related reasons, such non-conscious embodied processes, including the kind of neurological events described by Libet, are essential to a free will that is specifically human. First, as we have shown in previous chapters, body-schematic mechanisms support intentional action and are structured and regulated by relevant intentional goals. I want to grant, with Anscombe (1957), that these levels of operation are intentional, even if they are not intentional actions. These embodied mechanisms enable the exercise of free will. Second, precisely to the extent that we are not required to consciously deliberate about bodily movement or such things as autonomic processes, our deliberation can be directed at the more meaningful level of intentional action. In some limited ways, the loss of a body schema and the disruption of automatic processes, rob a person of a degree of freedom.[1]

What we call free will, however, cannot be conceived as something *purely* subpersonal, or as something instantaneous, an event that takes place in a knife-edge moment located between being undecided and being decided. If that were the case it would completely dissipate in the milliseconds between brain events and our conscious awareness. Free will involves temporally extended feedback or looping effects that are transformed and enhanced by the introduction of deliberative consciousness. This means that the conscious sense of agency, even if it starts out as an accessory experience generated by the brain, is itself a real force that counts in the formation of our future action. It contributes to the freedom of action, and bestows responsibility on the agent.

Daniel Dennett (2003a) has addressed these issues in his recent work *Freedom Evolves*. On his view, the processes that constitute free will need not be conscious and need not depend on conscious decision. Indeed, the unconscious processes that precede conscious decision in Libet's experiments, are part of the system that he calls the person. Although free will does not depend on consciousness, he does insist that it requires an extended time-frame.

Once you distribute the work done . . . in both space and time in the brain, you have to distribute the moral agency around as well. You are not out of the loop, you *are* the loop. You

---

[1] Here I disagree with Anscombe, who writes: 'My actions are mostly physical movements; if these physical movements are physically predetermined by processes I do not control, then my freedom is perfectly illusory' (1981: 146). Anscombe doesn't think that free will is illusory, since she thinks that in some sense there is a truth to physical indeterminism. But I would say that my actions are *not simply* physical (i.e. bodily) movements, although they depend on physical movements. And in some sense I do not control the processes of those movements in the sense that I would have a decision or choice to make in regard to how my grasp is shaped when I reach for the snake rather than for a drink. One could say, however, that I indirectly control motor processes in so far as those processes are subservient to the intentional actions that I do choose.

are that large. You are not an extentionless point. What you do and what you are *incorporates* all these things that happen and is not something separate from them.   (Dennett 2003a: 242)

In response to the position that I have outlined above, Dennett gives and takes. He writes:

One commentator on Libet who gets close is Sean [*sic*] Gallagher: 'I think that this problem can be solved as long as we do not think of free will as a momentary act. Once we understand that deliberation and decision are processes that are spread out over time, even, in some cases, very short amounts of time, then there is plenty of room for conscious components that are more than accessories after the fact' (Gallagher 1998). But, then he goes on to say that if the feedback is all unconscious, it will be 'deterministic' but if it is conscious, it won't be. Cartesian thinking dies hard.   (Dennett 2003a: 242 n. 3)[2]

I don't disagree with Dennett concerning the role played by nonconscious elements, except that I think we are even larger than he thinks—we are not just what happens in our brains. The 'loop' extends through and is limited by our bodily capabilities, into the surrounding environment, which is social as well as physical, and feeds back through our conscious experience into the decisions we make.

Non-conscious embodied processes, including the kind of neurological events described by Libet, and distributed by Dennett, are, as I have indicated, essential to a free will that is specifically human. All such relevant processes are structured and regulated by my intentional goals as much as they also limit and enable my action. When I decide to reach for the snake or for a drink all the appropriate physical movements fall into place. These embodied mechanisms thus enable the exercise of free will. And to the extent that we are not required consciously to deliberate about bodily movement and autonomic processes, our deliberation can be directed at the more meaningful level of intentional action.

If, however, we think of free will and intentional action as *solely* the product of these infra-intentional events (or of feedback that is *all* unconscious), or as possible for something only as large as a brain in a vat, or as conducted by a committee of 'mindless robots' (Dennett 2003a: 2), we fail to recognize the true size of the system that we are. There is much more to say about what enters into the system and into the looping effects to show that free will is neither magical nor absolute. Free decisions do not occur by chance or randomly. The relevant opposite of determinism here is not arbitrary chance. Our deliberations or 'considerations' do not occur by accident, nor do they introduce a degree of indeterminism, if we mean that to be chance (Dennett 1978). Nor is free will something that will be settled by quantum theories—the idea that indeterminism at the quantum level allows for some measure of freedom. As Anscombe (1981: 145) writes:

---

[2] Dennett's misspelling of my name in his text, but correct spelling of it in his list of references, seems quite consistent with his 'multiple drafts' theory of consciousness (Dennett 1991). Also the reference he makes to Gallagher (1998) is to my afterword to Gazzaniga and Gallagher (1998). Merleau-Ponty's (1987: 11) response to what today amounts to an accusation, but to him was a question—*Are you a Cartesian?*—was this: 'The question does not make much sense, since those who reject this or that in Descartes do so only in terms of reasons which owe much to Descartes.'

It was natural that when physics went indeterministic, some thinkers should have seized on this indeterminism as being just what was wanted for defending the freedom of the will. They received severe criticism on two counts: one, that this 'mere hap' is the very last thing to be invoked as the physical correlate of 'man's ethical behaviour'; the other, that quantum laws predict statistics of events when situations are repeated; interference with these, by the *will's* determining individual events which the laws of nature leave undetermined, would be as much a violation of natural law as would have been interference which falsified a deterministic mechanical law.

Let's assume that by default the physical system that makes up the human is deterministic—in the sense that it is determined by the various inputs and forces that act upon it and such processes follow and are explainable by physical laws. But the system is open in so far as the body is affected by environmental (both physical and social) factors and has selective memory and the possibility of consciousness. The inputs to the system are neither mechanistically received nor one-way. The system is open in the sense that the system itself contributes to how these inputs are shaped, and how they are delivered (how they become conscious) already dressed up with meaning. Certain things in the environment are taken as affordances, but an affordance is not a pure objective fact; it is defined only relative to the system that is designed to take advantage of certain things in the environment. This openness is not arbitrary; it has definite limitations—e.g. I can't decide to fly. Some softer limitations are imposed by social practices. These limitations introduce biases into the system. The inputs to the system, however, are not decided in advance, and the complexity of the system is such that one cannot predict or determine precisely what the outcome will be. This is not simply because we do not yet understand the complexity—'Give us a hundred years and we will know with precision how the brain works.' Rather, it may turn out that in a hundred years we will be able to say more precisely how complexity can generate unpredictable (but not arbitrary) results.

In this complex interaction conscious decision-making—the taking up of intentions—the interpretations of what we experience—can shift the system and alter the biases, can create new biases that in the long run add up to 'character'—which in turn may determine future responses. So, what is 'in the loop' is not just the non-conscious processes happening in our brain, but the larger system of body-environment-intersubjectivity. Dennett is right to say that you are not out of the loop. But the loop isn't just you. It's larger than you. It's you as you interact with the things and with other people in the world. And it is only in those larger contexts that the issue of free will is at stake.

Redrawing the Map

The studies that I have pursued in this book are part of an attempt to develop a vocabulary, which is to say, a discursive or explanatory framework, that helps us to understand *how* the body shapes the mind. This vocabulary is meant to hit its target at a behavioral level that is close to our ordinary human experience. At the same time, on one side, it is meant to remain open to empirical scientific explanation, especially from the perspectives of developmental psychology and neuroscience, and, on the other side, to remain true to a phenomenological description of experience. As an attempt to redefine the terrain, to redraw, or perhaps to erase the boundaries between body and mind, the vocabulary of embodiment is thus intended to serve as an integrative remapping of the other two more abstract levels of description.

The rough discursive framework proposed in Table 10.1 is oversimplified and overly static, but it suggests that one cannot go directly from cognitive neuroscience to phenomenology. The standard computational, representational, or functionalist models of the mind, no matter how complex they become, remain oversimplified because they start without considering the prenoetic effects of embodiment. Nor is it possible to go in the other direction, directly from phenomenology to neurological accounts. To look for isomorphic correlations of phenomenal structure in neuronal processes is to leave out of account the dynamic contributions of the environmentally constrained body-in-action. The idea, however, is not to block the route between the neuroscience of brain functions and the phenomenology of mind, but to recognize that there are no short cuts that can bypass the effects of embodiment.

Here is a partial list of some of the relevant and scientifically supported facts that we have considered in previous chapters. Each of them raises questions about traditional ways of understanding experience, and complicates the cognitive and phenomenological cartography in a way that forces us to consider the contributions of embodiment.

- Neonates are capable of imitating facial gestures from the first minutes after birth.
- Phantom limbs exist in some subjects who suffer from congenital absence of limbs.

TABLE 10.1.   *Three vocabularies*

Subpersonal vocabulary	Vocabulary of embodiment	Mentalistic vocabulary
Neurons	Prenoetic processes	Consciousness
Neurotransmitters	Body image	Beliefs
Action potentials	Body schema	Desires
Computations	Proprioception	Intentional states
Networks	Ecological experience	Noetic acts
Dynamical processes	Intermodal perception	Noematic correlates
Representations	Movements	Theoretical stances
Cognitive mechanisms	Action and action types	Simulations
	Ownership	
	Agency	

- Some unilateral neglect patients use their neglected limbs to perform intentional actions.
- Subjects who lack proprioception can control their movements using visual perception and cognitive effort.
- With neither proprioception nor vision, deafferented subjects are still able to gesture in a close to normal manner.
- Subjects who are congenitally blind use gestures when in conversation with other blind subjects.
- Senses communicate intermodally, and they inform movement in a direct way.
- Intentional action normally generates an implicit sense of ownership that can be distinguished from an implicit sense of agency for action.
- Phenomenally, the visual shape and size of an object varies according to distance from the subject; pragmatically (as an object I can grasp or manipulate), it remains invariant in shape and size.
- The visual observation of an object automatically evokes the most suitable motor program required for interaction with it.
- The same neuronal patterns in the premotor cortex are activated both when a subject performs a specific action and when the subject observes someone else perform the action.
- Before children attain a theory of mind, they already have an embodied understanding of other people.

In all these aspects of experience, and *before you know it*, the body is working to shape the mind. In order to find a viable interpretation of experience, a viable science of cognition that is consistent with these facts, requires that we begin to redraw the map that guides our understanding of how precisely embodiment contributes to human experience.

As a first step in this practice of conceptual cartography, I proposed a clear distinction between two concepts that are frequently confused in the psychological literature: body image and body schema. To make this conceptual distinction, however, is not to draw a clear line on the behavioral level. Nor is the distinction meant to push the body image over to the mentalistic side or to relegate the body schema to neurophysiology. Rather, there is a behavioral complexity to be acknowledged in any account of these phenomena that tries to map out their ontogenesis, their neurophysiological underpinnings, and the various pathologies that their failure may entail.

The body image cannot be relegated to the mentalistic side. It is, as we first defined it, a system of perceptions, beliefs, and emotional attitudes pertaining to one's own body. Such intentional states concerning one's body, however, are not reducible to a set of explicit and discrete propositions. The visual perception of my own body is not reducible to the statement: 'I see my body', since what I see is already operating in my seeing and in the constitution of the 'I' who sees. My experience of seeing my body is already conditioned not only by what I believe about my body, and how I feel about it, but also by my physical posture, my nutritional state, my health, my degree of fatigue, and so forth. The perception of my body already speaks about certain dispositions that I have toward it (my beliefs and attitudes toward my body are just such dispositions to act in regard to it) as well as certain dispositions that my body has toward the world. The latter set of dispositions can be characterized in terms of a body schema (a posture, a sense of balance, a certain control of my movement) and other prenoetic (autonomic and visceral) aspects of embodiment. The body schema, however, is not reducible to a purely neurophysiological explanation of motor control, since the way my body moves is in support of my pragmatic intentions and in response to environmental features that either afford or prevent my action, or make it difficult. In the same way, my gestures are not reducible to body-schematic processes that are purely instrumental, but are generated in the service of communicative or cognitive processes. These conclusions are supported by empirical studies, and they make sense out of our own normal phenomenological observations.

The explanatory framework outlined in these terms also takes us some distance in accounting for pathologies, such as unilateral neglect, deafferentation, and phantoms in cases of congenital absence of limb. We learned, however, that we need to go beyond the limited conceptual distinctions between body image and body schema to get a more adequate account of these and other pathologies such as schizophrenia and autism, and other diverse phenomena such as neonate imitation, expressive movement, and intersubjective perception.

By considering the capacity for gesture in deafferented subjects, for example, we discovered that there is more to be explained about *expressive* movement than can be captured by the body image/body schema distinction, or the details of motor processing. If instrumental and locomotive movements are normally dependent on body-schematic control, or in the case of deafferentation, on control by body image, expressive movement, which characterizes gesture, as well as imitation of gesture (including neonate imitation), involves something more.

Two facts about expressive movement can be stated with surety. First, even if it is not reducible to terms of motoric processing, expressive movement, in so far as it is movement, is necessarily embodied—enabled and at the same time constrained in specific ways by the structure and performance possibilities of the motor system. Although Merleau-Ponty suggests that language transcends embodiment, one cannot take this idea too far. Topokinetic properties of expressive movement (and this includes, for example, movement required to perform or respond to music) still necessarily depend to some degree on body-schematic functions in the normal case (and on body image in the case of deafferentation). Second, expressive movement is necessarily intersubjective and for that reason, despite the conceptual distinction, we can see a direct relation between instrumental and expressive movement. Indeed, in some cases, there is no distinction between instrumental and expressive movement. The movement of my eyes to gain a better view of things, or the movement of my hand toward the cup, may for my purposes be purely instrumental in nature. But I may do it with style; and certainly for an observer, the very same movements can be expressive whether I intend them to be or not. At a minimum they express my interests and intentions, and perhaps, in the style of such movement, my emotions, and these are things that even infants can perceive. Furthermore, movement that is explicitly expressive may serve instrumental purposes. When my daughters want something from me they get it by expressing the importance of their request with their eyes—and they know it works in most cases. Indeed, only in the setting of intersubjectivity, which is the ubiquitous setting of human behavior, and which is less than ubiquitous in other species, can movement be expressive. As I have tried to indicate in previous chapters, this has important philosophical implications concerning human nature.

The study of expressive movement can be taken much further. Developmentally, of course, it relates directly to what we have said about primary and secondary intersubjectivity. This brings us back to neonate imitation, a movement that is expressive and intersubjective from the very beginning—and that is the case even if it is nothing more than the effect of motor priming, since it happens only between the infant and another human. We are capable of moving expressively and of directly perceiving the expressive movements of others. The infant of 18 months can already see the unfulfilled intentions of the other person. Before the infant knows what such intentions could possibly signify on any sort of theoretical or conceptual level, she is already informed by the pragmatic know-how of what those intentions are, framed in terms of her own possibilities. In turn, such an embodied know-how helps to expand further the initial capacities that define the infant's behavior, leading to further development of the body schema, more sophisticated and dynamical intersubjective reverberations between motor systems, the social development of the body image—and all along, the infant's humanity and personal sense of self.

The enhancement of one's own body image and sense of self, therefore, is an intersubjective accomplishment in so far as I see my own possibilities in the behaviors of others. The beginning of this development can be traced to the perception the infant has of the other. The human infant attends to human movement more than to anything else. The intentions of the other person, and the embodied possibilities of the interacting infant, can be directly read in the face and the actions of the other. No intermediate simulation or extra knowledge is required because the infant comes equipped with a body schema and with the proprioception, intermodal transducers, mirror neurons, and many other neurological mechanisms genetically coded for the expressive intersubjective movement that is human interaction.

I hope that I have furthered the realization that nothing about human experience remains untouched by human embodiment: from the basic perceptual and emotional processes that are already at work in infancy, to a sophisticated interaction with other people; from the acquisition and creative use of language, to higher cognitive faculties involving judgment and metaphor; from the exercise of free will in intentional action, to the creation of cultural artifacts that provide for further human affordances. Thus the Aristotelian insight that the human soul is an expression of the human body finds significant verification in contemporary scientific studies of human experience. Before you know it, your body makes you human, and sets you on a course in which your human nature is expressed in intentional action and in interaction with others.

References

Ackroyd, C., Humphrey, N. K., and Warrington, E. K. 1974. Lasting effects of early blindness: A case study. *Quarterly Journal of Experimental Psychology*, 26: 114–24.

Adame, D. D., Radell, S. A., Johnson, T. C., and Cole, S. P. 1991. Physical fitness, body image, and locus of control in college women dancers and nondancers. *Perceptual and Motor Skills*, 72: 91–5.

Aglioti, S., Bonazzi, A., and Cortese, F. 1994. Phantom lower limb as a perceptual marker of neural plasticity in the mature human brain. *Proceedings of the Royal Society of London*, 255: 273–8.

Aglioti, S., Cortese, F., and Franchini, C. 1994. Rapid sensory remapping in the adult brain as inferred from phantom breast perception. *Neuroreport*, 5: 473–6.

Akins, K. A., and Dennett, D. 1986. Who may I say is calling? *Behavioral and Brain Sciences*, 9: 517–18.

Allebeck, P., Hallberg, D., and Espmark, S. 1976. Body image—an apparatus for measuring disturbances in estimation of size and shape. *Journal of Psychosomatic Research*, 20: 583–9.

Allison, T., Puce, Q., and McCarthy, G. 2000. Social perception from visual cues: Role of the STS region. *Trends in Cognitive Sciences*, 4 (7): 267–78.

Allot, R. 1992. The motor theory of language: Origin and function. In J. Wind *et al.* (eds.), *Language Origin: A Multidisciplinary Approach*. Dordrecht: Kluwer.

Anscombe, G. E. M. 1957. *Intention*. Oxford: Blackwell.

—— 1981. Causality and determination. In G. E. M. Anscombe. *The Collected Philosophical Papers*, ii (pp. 133–47). Oxford: Oxford University Press.

—— 1983. The causation of action. In L. Ginet and S. Shoemaker (eds.), *Knowledge and Mind* (pp. 174–90). Oxford: Oxford University Press.

Arbib, M. A. 1985. Schemas for the temporal organization of behavior. *Human Neurobiology*, 4: 63–7.

—— and Hesse, M. B. 1986. *The Construction of Reality*. Cambridge: Cambridge University Press.

Assaiante, C., Amblard, G., and Carblanc, A. 1988. Peripheral vision and dynamic equilibrium control in five to twelve year old children. In B. Amblard, A. Berthoz, and F. Clarac (eds.), *Posture and Gait: Development, Adaptation and Modulation* (pp. 75–82). Amsterdam: Excerpta Medica.

Astington, J. W., and Jenkins, J. M. 1999. A longitudinal study of the relation between language and theory-of-mind development. *Developmental Psychology*, 35: 1311–20.

Atkinson, J., and Braddick, O. 1989. Development of basic visual functions. In A. Slater and G. Bremner (eds.), *Infant Development* (pp. 7–41). Hillsdale, NJ: Erlbaum.

Bachevalier, J. 2000. The amygdala, social cognition, and autism. In J. P. Aggleton (ed.), *The Amygdala: A Functional Analysis* (pp. 509–43). Oxford: Oxford University Press.

Bailey, A. A., and Moersch, F. P. 1941. Phantom limb. *The Canadian Medical Association Journal*, 45: 37–42.

Baldwin, D. A., and Baird, J. A. 2001. Discerning intentions in dynamic human action. *Trends in Cognitive Sciences*, 5 (4): 171–8.

Baldwin, D. A., Baird, J. A., Saylor, M. M., and Clark, M. A. 2001. Infants parse dynamic action. *Child Development*, 72 (3): 708–17.

Barbaras, R. 1999. *Le désir et la distance*. Paris: J. Vrin.

—— 2000. Perception and movement: The end of the metaphysical approach. In F. Evans and L. Lawlor (eds.), *Chiasms: Merleau-Ponty's Notion of Flesh*. Albany: State University of New York Press.

Barlow, H. 1975. Visual experience and cortical development. *Nature*, 258: 199–204.

Baron-Cohen, S. 1989. The autistic child's theory of mind: A case of specific developmental delay. *Journal of Child Psychology and Psychiatry*, 30: 285–98.

—— 1995. *Mindblindness: An Essay on Autism and Theory of Mind*. Cambridge, Mass.: MIT.

—— Leslie, A., and Frith, U. 1985. Does the autistic child have a theory of mind? *Cognition*, 21: 37–46.

Barresi, J., and Moore, C. 1996. Intentional relations and social understanding. *Behavioral and Brain Sciences*, 19 (1): 107–54.

Bauermeister, M. 1964. The effect of body tilt on apparent verticality, apparent body position and their relation. *Journal of Experimental Psychology*, 67: 142–7.

Bauman, M. L., and Kemper, T. L. 1994. *The Neurobiology of Autism*. Baltimore: Johns Hopkins University Press.

Bellugi, U., and Klima, E. S. 1997. Language, spatial cognition, and the brain. In M. Ito, Y. Miyashita, and E. T. Rolls (eds.), *Cognition, Computation, and Consciousness* (pp. 177–88). Oxford: Oxford University Press.

Berkeley, G. 1709. *A New Theory of Vision*. London: Everyman's Library, 1910.

—— 1733. *The Theory of Vision Vindicated and Explained*. London: J. Tonson; repr. in G. Berkeley, *Philosophical Works, Including the Works on Vision*. London: Everyman's Library, 1975.

Berlucchi, G., and Aglioti, S. 1997. The body in the brain: Neural bases of corporeal awareness. *Trends in Neuroscience*, 20: 560–4.

Berman, D. 1999. *Berkeley*. New York: Routledge.

Bermúdez, J. L. 1995. Transcendental arguments and psychology: The example of O'Shaughnessy on intentional action. *Metaphilosophy*, 26: 379–401.

—— 1996. The moral significance of birth. *Ethics*, 106: 378–403.

—— 1998. *The Paradox of Self-Consciousness*. Cambridge, Mass.: MIT.

—— Marcel, A., and Eilan, N. 1995. *The Body and the Self*. Cambridge, Mass.: MIT.

Bernett, M. E., Cole, J. D., McLellan, D. L., and Sedgwick, E. M. 1989. Gait analysis in a subject without proprioception below the neck. *Journal of Physiology*, 417: 102.

Bertenthal, B. I., and Campos, J. J. 1990. A systems approach to the organizing effects of self-produced locomotion during infancy. *Advances in Infancy Research*, 6: 1–60.

—— —— and Kermoian, R. 1994. An epigenetic perspective on the development of self-produced locomotion and its consequences. *Current Directions in Psychological Science*, 3: 140–5.

—— Proffitt, D. R., and Cutting, J. E. 1984. Infant sensitivity to figural coherence in biomechanical motions. *Journal of Experimental Child Psychology*, 37: 213–30.

Berthoz, A. 2000. *The Brain's Sense of Movement*. Cambridge, Mass.: Harvard University Press.

Biocca, F. 1997. The cyborg's dilemma: Progressive embodiment in virtual environments. In J. Marsh, C. Nehaniv, and B. Gorayska (eds.), *Proceedings of the Second International*

Conference on Cognitive Technology (pp. 12–27). 25–8 August 1997, Aizu, Japan (http://www.ascusc.org/jcmc/vol3/issue2/biocca2.html).

Birnholz, J. C. 1988. On observing the human fetus. In W. P. Smotherman and Scott R. Robinson (eds.), *Behavior of the Fetus* (pp. 47–60). Caldwell, NJ: Telford.

Blackburn, J., Gottschewski, K., George, E., and Niki, L. 2000. A discussion about theory of mind: From an autistic perspective. Proceedings of *Autism Europe's 6th International Congress*, Glasgow, 19–21 May 2000 (http://www.autistics.org/library/AE2000-ToM.html).

Blakemore, C., and Cooper, G. F. 1973. Development of the brain depends upon the visual experience. *Vision Research*, 13: 535–58.

Blakemore, S-J., and Decety, J. 2001. From the perception of action to the understanding of intention. *Nature Reviews: Neuroscience*, 2: 561–7.

—— Smith, J., Steel, R., Johnstone, E., and Frith, C. D. 2000. The perception of self-produced sensory stimuli in patients with auditory hallucinations and passivity experiences: Evidence for a breakdown in self-monitoring. *Psychological Medicine*, 30: 1131–9.

Blass, E. M., Fillion, T. J., Rochat, P., Hoffemeyer, L. B., and Metzger, M. A. 1989. Sensorimotor and motivational determinants of hand mouth coordination in 1–3 day old human infants. *Developmental Psychology*, 25: 963–75.

Bloom, P., and German, T. P. 2000. Two reasons to abandon the false belief task as a test of theory of mind. *Cognition*, 77: B25–B31.

Blouin, J., Gauthier, G. M., Vercher, J-L., and Cole, J. 1996. The relative contribution of retinal and extraretinal signals in determining the accuracy of reaching movements in normal subjects and a deafferented patient. *Experimental Brain Research*, 109: 148–53.

Boden, M. 1982. Implications of language studies for human nature. In T. W. Simon and R. J. Scholes (eds.), *Language, Mind and Brain* (pp. 129–43). Hillsdale, NJ: Erlbaum.

Bonnier, P. 1905. L'Aschematie. *Revue Neurologie*, 13: 604–9.

Bordo, S. 1993. *Unbearable Weight: Feminism, Western Culture, and the Body.* Berkeley: University of California Press.

Bovet, P., and Parnas, J. 1993. Schizophrenic delusions: A phenomenological approach. *Schizophrenia Bulletin*, 19: 579–97.

Brandt, T. 1988. Sensory function and posture. In B. Amblard, A. Berthoz, and F. Clarac (eds.), *Posture and Gait: Development, Adaptation and Modulation* (pp. 127–36). Amsterdam: Excerpta Medica.

Browder, J., and Gallagher, J. P. 1948. Dorsal cordotomy for painful phantom limb. *Annals of Surgery*, 128: 456–69.

Brown, T. 1820. *Lectures on the Philosophy of the Human Mind*. Edinburgh: Bell & Bradfute.

Brugger, P., *et al.* 2000. Beyond re-membering: Phantom sensations of congenitally absent limbs. *Proceedings of the National Academy of Science, USA*, 97 (11): 6167–72.

Bruner, J., and Kalmar, D. A. 1998. Narrative and metanarrative in the construction of self. In M. Ferrari and R. J. Sternberg (eds.), *Self-Awareness: Its Nature and Development* (pp. 308–31). New York: Guilford.

Bryant, P. E., Jones, P., Claxton, V., and Perkins, G. M. 1972. Recognition of shapes across modalities by infants. *Nature (London)*, 240: 303–4.

Bushnell, E. W., and Boudreau, J. P. 1993. Motor development and the mind: The potential role of motor abilities as a determination of aspects of perceptual development. *Child Development*, 64: 1005–21.

Bushnell, I. W. R., and Sai, F. 1987. Neonatal recognition of the mother's face. University of Glasgow Report, 87/1.

Butterworth, G. 1995. An ecological perspective on the origins of self. In J. Bermúdez, A. Marcel, and N. Eilan (eds.), *The Body and the Self* (pp. 87–107). Cambridge, Mass.: MIT.

—— and Hicks, L. 1977. Visual proprioception and postural stability in infancy: A developmental study. *Perception*, 6: 255–62.

—— and Hopkins, B. 1977. Visual proprioception and postural stability in infancy: A developmental study. *Perception*, 6: 255–62.

—— —— 1988. Hand-mouth coordination in the newborn baby. *British Journal of Developmental Psychology*, 6: 303–14.

—— and Pope, M. 1983. Les Origines de la proprioception visuelle chez le nourisson. In S. de Schonen (ed.), *Le Development dans la première année* (pp. 107–27). Paris: Presses Universitaires de France.

Buytendijk, F. J. J. 1974. *Prolegomena to an Anthropological Physiology*, trans. A. I. Orr. Pittsburgh: Duquesne University Press.

Cacioppo, J. T., Sandman, C. A., and Walker, B. B. 1978. The effects of operant heart rate conditioning on cognitive elaboration and attitude change. *Psychophysiology*, 15: 330–8.

Calden, G., Lundy, R. M., and Schlafer R. J. 1959. Sex differences in body concepts. *Journal of Consulting Psychology*, 23: 378.

Campbell, J. 1994. *Past, Space, and Self*. Cambridge, Mass.: MIT.

—— 1995. The body image and self-consciousness. In J. Bermúdez, A. Marcel, and N. Eilan (eds.), *The Body and the Self* (pp. 29–42). Cambridge, Mass.: MIT.

—— 1999a. Schizophrenia, the space of reasons and thinking as a motor process. *The Monist*, 82 (4): 609–25.

—— 1999b. Immunity to error through misidentification and the meaning of a referring term. *Philosophical Topics*, 26: 89–104.

Camper, P. 1746. *Dissertatio optica de visu/Optical Dissertation on Vision*, trans. G. ten Doesschate. Niewkoop: B. de Graaf, 1962.

Campos, J. J., Bertenthal, B. I., and Kermoian, R. 1992. Early experience and emotional development: The emergence of wariness of heights. *Psychological Science*, 3: 61–4.

Carmichael, S. T., and Price, J. L. 1995. Sensory and premotor connections of the orbital and medial prefrontal cortex of macaque monkeys. *The Journal of Comparative Neurology*, 363: 642–64.

Carruthers, P. 1996. Simulation and self-knowledge: A defense of theory-theory. In P. Carruthers and P. K. Smith (eds.), *Theories of Theories of Mind* (pp. 22–38). Cambridge: Cambridge University Press.

—— and Smith, P. K. 1996. Introduction. In P. Carruthers and P. K. Smith (eds.), *Theories of Theories of Mind*. Cambridge: Cambridge University Press.

Casaer, P. 1979. Postural behaviour in newborn infants. *Clinics in Developmental Medicine*, 72. London: Heinemann Medical.

Cash, T. F., and Brown, T. A. 1987. Body image in anorexia nervosa and bulimia nervosa: A review of the literature, *Behavior Modification*, 11: 487–521.

Cassam, Q. 1995. Introspection and bodily self-ascription. In J. Bermúdez, A. Marcel, and N. Eilan (eds.), *The Body and the Self* (pp. 311–36). Cambridge, Mass.: MIT.

Cassirer, E. 1951. *The Philosophy of the Enlightenment*. Princeton: Princeton University Press.

Chaminade, T., and Decety, J. 2002. Leader or follower? Involvement of the inferior parietal lobule in agency. *Neuroreport*, 13 (1528): 1975–8.

—— Meltzoff, A. N., and Decety, J. 2002. Does the end justify the means? A PET exploration of the mechanisms involved in human imitation. *NeuroImage*, 15: 318–28.

Changeux, P., and Ricœur, P. 2000. *What Makes us Think?* trans. M. B. DeBevoise. Princeton: Princeton University Press.

Cheselden, W. 1728. An account of some observations made by a young gentleman, who was born blind, or lost his sight so early, that he had no remembrance of ever having seen, and was couch'd between 13 and 14 years of age. *Philosophical Transactions of the Royal Society of London*, 35 (402): 447–50.

Chiel, H. J., and Beer, R. D. 1997. The brain has a body: Adaptive behavior emerges from interactions of nervous system, body and environment. *Trends in Neurosciences*, 20: 553–7.

Clark, A. 1997. *Being There: Putting Brain, Body, and World Together Again*. Cambridge, Mass.: MIT.

Clark, D. F. 1984. Body image and motor skills in normal and subnormal subjects. *International Journal of Rehabilitation Research*, 7: 207–8.

Cohen, L. G., et al. 1997. Functional relevance of cross-modal plasticity in blind humans. *Nature*, 389 (11 Sept.): 180–3.

Cole, J. 1995. *Pride and a Daily Marathon*. Cambridge, Mass.: MIT; originally London: Duckworth, 1991.

—— 1998. *About Face*. Cambridge, Mass.: MIT.

—— 1999. On being faceless: Selfhood and facial embodiment. In S. Gallagher and J. Shear (eds.), *Models of the Self* (pp. 301–18). Exeter: Imprint Academic.

—— 2004. *Still Lives: Narratives of Spinal Cord Injury*. Cambridge, Mass.: MIT.

—— and Katifi, H. A. 1991. Evoked potentials in a subject with a large fibre peripheral neuropathy. *Electroencephalography and Clinical Neurophysiology*, 80: 103–7.

—— and Paillard, J. 1995. Living without touch and peripheral information about body position and movement: Studies upon deafferented subjects. In J. Bermúdez, A. Marcel, and N. Eilan (eds.), *The Body and the Self* (pp. 245–66). Cambridge, Mass.: MIT.

—— and Sedgwick, E. M. 1992. The perceptions of force and of movement in a man without large myelinated sensory afferents below the neck. *Journal of Physiology*, 449: 503–15.

—— Gallagher, S., and McNeill, D. 2002. Gesture following deafferentation: A phenomenologically informed experimental study. *Phenomenology and the Cognitive Sciences*, 1 (1): 49–67.

—— —— —— Duncan S., Furuyama, N., and McCullough, K-E. 1998. Gestures after total deafferentation of the bodily and spatial senses. In S. Santi et al. (eds.), *Oralité et gestualité: Communication multi-modale, interaction* (pp. 65–9). Paris: L'Harmattan.

—— Merton, W. L., Barrett, G., Katifi, H. A., and Treede, R-D. 1995. Evoked potentials in a subject with a large fibre sensory neuropathy below the neck. *Canadian Journal of Physiology and Pharmacology*, 73: 234–45.

—— —— Sacks, O., and Waterman. I. 2000. On the immunity principle: A view from a robot. *Trends in Cognitive Sciences*, 4 (5): 167.

Condillac, É. B. de 1746. *Essai sur l' origine des connaissances humaines*. Two volumes. Paris.

—— 1754. *Treatise on the Sensations*, trans. G. Carr. Los Angeles: University of Southern California School of Philosophy, 1930.

Corina, D., Kritchevsky, M., and Bellugi, U. 1996. Visual language processing and unilateral neglect: Evidence from American Sign Language. *Cognitive Neuropsychology*, 13: 321–56.

Coslett, H. B. 1998. Evidence for a disturbance of the body schema in neglect. *Brain and Cognition*, 37: 527–44.

Courchesne, E., Carper, R., and Akshoomoff, N. 2003. Evidence of brain overgrowth in the first year of life in autism. *Journal of the American Medical Association*, 290: 337–44.

Crook, J. 1987. The nature of conscious awareness. In C. Blakemore and S. Greenfield (eds.), *Mindwaves: Thoughts on Intelligence, Identity, and Consciousness* (pp. 383–402). Oxford: Basil Blackwell.

Crow, T. J., Cross, A. J., Johnstone, E. C., Owen, F., Owens, D. G. C., and Waddington, J. L. 1982. Abnormal involuntary movements in schizophrenia: Are they related to the disease process or its treatment? Are they associated with changes in dopamine receptors? *Journal of Clinical Psychopharmacology*, 2: 336–40.

Crowley, J. C., and Katz, L. C. 2000. Early development of ocular dominance columns. *Science*, 290 (17 Nov.): 1321–4.

Cumming, W. J. K. 1988. The neurobiology of the body schema. *British Journal of Psychiatry*, 153 (suppl. 2): 7–11.

Currie, G., and Sterelny, K. 2000. How to think about the modularity of mind-reading. *Philosophical Quarterly*, 50: 145–60.

Damasio, A. R. 1994. *Descartes' Error: Emotion, Reason, and the Human Brain*. New York: G. P. Putnam.

—— 1999. *The Feeling of What Happens: Body and Emotion in the Making of Consciousness*. New York: Harcourt Brace and Co.

Damasio, A. R., and Maurer, R. G. 1978. A neurological model for childhood autism. *Archives of Neurology*, 35: 777–86.

Daprati, E., Franck, N., Georgieff, N., Proust, J., Pacherie, E., Dalery, J., and Jeannerod, M. 1997. Looking for the agent: An investigation into consciousness of action and self-consciousness in schizophrenic patients. *Cognition*, 65: 71–86.

Dasch, C. S. 1978. Relation of dance skills to body cathexis and locus of control orientation. *Perceptual and Motor Skills*, 46: 465–6.

Davies, M., and Stone, T. 1998. Folk psychology and mental simulation. In A. O'Hear (ed.), *Contemporary Issues in the Philosophy of Mind*. Royal Institute of Philosophy, Suppl. 42. Cambridge: Cambridge University Press.

Davis, C., and Cowles, M. 1991. Body image and exercise: A study of relationships and comparisons between physically active men and women. *Sex Roles*, 25: 33–44.

Davis, J. W. 1960. The Molyneux Problem. *Journal of the History of Ideas*, 21: 392–408.

DeCasper, A. J., and Spence, M. J. 1986. Prenatal maternal speech influences newborns' perception of speech sounds. *Infant Behavior and Development*, 91: 37–150.

Decety, J., and Sommerville, J. A. 2003. Shared representations between self and other: A social cognitive neuroscience view. *Trends in Cognitive Sciences*, 7 (12): 527–33.

Decety, J., Chaminade, T., Grèzes, J., and Meltzoff, A. N. 2002. A PET exploration of the mechanisms involved in imitation. *NeuroImage*, 15: 265–72.

Degenaar, M. 1996. *Molyneux's Problem: Three Centuries of Discussion on the Perception of Forms*, trans. M. J. Collins. Dordrecht/Boston: Kluwer.

della Sala, S., Marchetti, C., and Spinnler, H. 1994. The anarchic hand: A fronto-mesial sign. In F. Boller and J. Grafman (eds.), *Handbook of Neuropsychology*, ix. New York: Elsevier.

Dennett, D. 1976. Conditions of personhood. In A. Rorty (ed.), *The Identities of Persons* (pp. 175–96). Berkeley: University of California Press.

—— 1978. *Brainstorms: Philosophic Essays on Mind and Psychology*. Montgomery, Vt.: Bradford Books.

—— 1981. Where am I? In D. R. Hofstadter and D. C. Dennett, *The Mind's I: Fantasies and Reflections on Mind and Soul* (pp. 217–29). New York: Basic Books.

—— 1991. *Consciousness Explained*. Boston: Little, Brown.

—— 2003a. *Freedom Evolves.* New York: Viking.

—— 2003b. Who's on first? Heterophenomenology explained. *Journal of Consciousness Studies,* 10 (9–10): 19–30.

Denny-Brown, D., Meyer, J. S., and Horenstein, S. 1952. The significance of perceptual rivalry resulting from parietal lesion. *Brain,* 75: 433–71.

Depraz, N. 1994. Temporalité et affection dans les manuscrits tardifs sur la temporalité (1929–1935) de Husserl. *Alter,* 2: 63–86.

—— 1998. Can I anticipate myself? Self-affection and temporality. In D. Zahavi (ed.), *Self-awareness, Temporality, and Alterity* (pp. 83–97). Dordrect: Kluwer Academic.

DePue, R. A., Dubicki, M. D., and McCarthy, T. 1975. Differential recovery of intellectual, associational, and psychophysiological functioning in withdrawal and active schizophrenics. *Journal of Abnormal Psychology,* 84: 325–30.

De Renzi, E. 1991. Spatial disorders. In M. Swash and J. Oxbury (eds.), *Clinical Neurology,* i (pp. 44–53). Edinburgh: Churchill Livingstone.

de Vignemont, F. 2004. The co-consciousness hypothesis. *Phenomenology and the Cognitive Sciences,* 3 (1): 114–32.

de Vries, J. I. P., Visser, G. H. A., and Prechtl, H. F. R. 1982. The emergence of fetal behaviour: I. Qualitative aspects. *Early Human Development,* 7: 301–22.

—— —— —— 1984. Fetal motility in the first half of pregnancy. In H. F. R. Prechtl (ed.), *Continuity of Neural Functions from Prenatal to Postnatal Life* (pp. 46–64). London: Spastics International Medical Publications.

Descartes, R. 1641. *Meditations Concerning First Philosophy,* trans. L. J. Lafleur. Indianapolis: Bobbs-Merrill, 1960.

Diderot, D. 1749. Letter on the blind. In M. J. Morgan (trans), *Molyneux's Question: Vision, Touch and the Philosophy of Perception* (pp. 31–58). Cambridge: Cambridge University Press, 1977.

Dilling, C., and Rabin, A. 1967. Temporal experience in depressive states and schizophrenia. *Journal of Consulting Psychology,* 31: 604–8.

Di Pellegrino, G., Fadiga, L., Fogassi, L., Gallese, V., and Rizzolatti G. 1992. Understanding motor events: A neurophysiological study. *Experimental Brain Research,* 91: 176–80.

Dobelle, W. H. 2000. Artificial vision for the blind by connecting a television camera to the visual cortex. *ASIAO Journal,* 46: 3–9.

Edelman, G. 1992. *Bright Air, Brilliant Fire.* New York: Basic Books.

Eilan, N. 1993. Molyneux's question and the idea of an external world. In N. Eilan, R. McCarthy, and B. Brewer (eds.), *Spatial Representation: Problems in Philosophy and Psychology* (pp. 236–55). Oxford: Blackwell.

—— 2000. On understanding schizophrenia. In D. Zahavi (ed.), *Exploring the Self* (pp. 97–113). Amsterdam: John Benjamins.

Evans, G. 1982. *The Varieties of Reference,* ed. J. McDowell. Oxford: Oxford University Press.

—— 1985. *Collected Papers.* Oxford: Clarendon Press.

Fadiga, L., Fogassi, L. Pavesi, G., and Rizzolatti, G. 1995. Motor facilitation during action observation: A magnetic stimulation study. *Journal of Neurophysiology,* 73: 2608–11.

Farrer, C., and Frith, C. D. 2002. Experiencing oneself vs. another person as being the cause of an action: The neural correlates of the experience of agency. *NeuroImage,* 15: 596–603.

—— Franck, N., Georgieff, N., Frith, C. D., Decety, J., and Jeannerod, M. 2003. Modulating the experience of agency: A positron emission tomography study. *NeuroImage,* 18: 324–33.

Fatemi, S. H., and Halt, A. R. 2001. Altered levels of Bcl2 and p53 proteins in parietal cortex reflect deranged apoptotic regulation in autism. *Synapse*, 42 (4): 281–4.

—— —— Stary, J. M., Realmuto, G. M., and Jalali-Mousavi, M. 2001. Reduction in anti-apoptotic protein Bcl-2 in autistic cerebellum. *Neuroreport*, 12 (5): 929–33.

Feinberg, I. 1978. Efference copy and corollary discharge: Implications for thinking and its disorders. *Schizophrenia Bulletin*, 4: 636–40.

Feldman, J. F., and Brody, N. 1978. Non-elicited newborn behaviours in relation to state and prandial condition. *Merrill-Palmer Quarterly*, 24: 79–84.

Feldman, M. M. 1975. The body image and object relations: Exploration of a method utilizing repertory grid techniques. *British Journal of Medical Psychology*, 48: 317–32.

Fichte, J. G. 1794. *The Science of Knowledge*, ed. P. Heath and J. Lachs. Cambridge: Cambridge University Press, 1982.

Field, T. M., Woodson, R., Greenburg, R., and Cohen, D. 1982. Discrimination and imitation of facial expression by neonates. *Science*, 218: 179–81.

Fifer, W. P., and Moon, C. 1988. Auditory experience in the fetus. In W. P. Smotherman and S. R. Robinson (eds.), *Behavior of the Fetus* (pp. 175–88). Caldwell, NJ: Telford.

Fisher, S. 1964. Sex differences in body perception. *Psychological Monographs*, 78: 1–22.

—— 1970. *Body Experience in Fantasy and Behavior*. New York: Appleton-Century-Crofts.

—— 1972. Body image. In D. Sills (ed.), *International Encyclopedia of the Social Sciences*, ii. New York: Collier-Macmillan; repr. in T. Polhemus (ed.), *The Body Reader: Social Aspects of the Human Body* (pp. 115–21). New York: Pantheon Books, 1978.

—— 1976. Body perception upon awakening. *Perceptual and Motor Skills*, 43: 275–8.

—— 1978. Body experience before and after surgery. *Perceptual and Motor Skills*, 46: 699–702.

—— and Abercrombie, J. 1958. The relationship of body image distortions to body reactivity gradients. *Journal of Personality*, 28: 320–9.

—— and Cleveland, S. E. 1957. An approach to physiological reactivity in terms of a body-image schema. *Psychological Review*, 64: 26–37.

—— —— 1958. *Body Image and Personality*. Princeton, NJ: D. van Nostrand.

—— Greenberg, R. G., and Reihman, J. 1984. Body perception and somatic discomfort in relation to right vs. left-handedness. *Cortex*, 20: 285–94.

Flower, M. J. 1985. Neuromaturation of the human fetus. *Journal of Medicine and Philosophy*, 10: 237–51.

Fogassi, L. *et al.* 1996. Coding of peripersonal space in inferior premotor cortex (area f4). *Journal of Neurophysiology*, 76: 141–57.

Forget, R., and Lamarre, Y. 1995. Postural adjustments associated with different unloadings of the forearm: Effects of proprioceptive and cutaneous afferent deprivation. *Canadian Journal of Physiology and Pharmacology*, 73: 285–94.

Fourneret, P., and Jeannerod, M. 1998. Limited conscious monitoring of motor performance in normal subjects, *Neuropsychologia*, 36: 1133–40.

—— Franck, N., Slachevsky, A. *et al.* 2001. Self-monitoring in schizophrenia revisited. *Neuroreport*, 12 (6): 1203–8.

Franck, N., Farrer, C., Georgieff, N., Marie-Cardine, M., Daléry, J., d'Amato, T., and Jeannerod, M. 2001. Defective recognition of one's own actions in patients with schizophrenia. *American Journal of Psychiatry*, 158: 454–9.

Frankfurt, H. 1971. Freedom of the will and the concept of a person. *Journal of Philosophy*, 68: 5–20.

—— 1976. Identification and externality. In A. O. Rorty (ed.), *The Identities of Persons* (pp. 239–51). Berkeley: University of California Press.

Freeman, R. J., Thomas, C. D., Solyom, L. and Hunter, M. A. 1984. A modified video camera for measuring body image distortion: Technical description and reliability. *Psychological Medicine*, 14: 411–16.

Frégnac, Y., and Imbert, M. 1984. Development of neuronal selectivity in primary visual cortex of cat. *Physiological Reviews*, 64: 325–434.

Friedman, W. 1990. *About Time: Inventing the Fourth Dimension*. Cambridge, Mass.: MIT.

Frith, C. D. 1992. *The Cognitive Neuropsychology of Schizophrenia*. Hillsdale, NJ: Erlbaum.

—— and Done, D. J. 1988. Towards a neuropsychology of schizophrenia. *British Journal of Psychiatry*, 153: 437–43.

—— and Frith, U. 1999. Interacting minds—a biological basis. *Science*, 286: 1692–5.

Frith, U. 1989. *Autism: Explaining the Enigma*. Oxford: Basil Blackwell.

—— and Happé, F. 1994. Autism: Beyond 'Theory of Mind'. *Cognition*, 50: 115–32.

—— —— 1999. Theory of mind and self-consciousness: What is it like to be autistic? *Mind and Language*, 14 (1): 1–22

Gallagher, S. 1986a. Hyletic experience and the lived body. *Husserl Studies*, 3: 131–66.

—— 1986b. Body image and body schema: A conceptual clarification. *Journal of Mind and Behavior*, 7: 541–54.

—— 1995. Body schema and intentionality. In J. Bermúdez, N. Eilan, and A. Marcel (eds.), *The Body and the Self* (pp. 225–44). Cambridge, Mass.: MIT.

—— 1996. The moral significance of primitive self-consciousness. *Ethics*, 107: 129–40.

—— 1997. Mutual enlightenment: Recent phenomenology in cognitive science. *Journal of Consciousness Studies*, 4 (3): 195–214.

—— 1998. *The Inordinance of Time*. Evanston, Ill.: Northwestern University Press.

—— 2000a. Philosophical conceptions of the self: Implications for cognitive science. *Trends in Cognitive Sciences*, 4 (1): 14–21.

—— 2000b. Self-reference and schizophrenia: A cognitive model of immunity to error through misidentification. In D. Zahavi (ed.), *Exploring the Self: Philosophical and Psychopathological Perspectives on Self-Experience* (pp. 203–39). Amsterdam and Philadelphia: John Benjamins.

—— 2001a. The practice of mind: Theory, simulation, or interaction? *Journal of Consciousness Studies*, 8 (5–7): 83–107.

—— 2001b. Emotion and intersubjective perception: A speculative account. In A. Kazniak (ed.), *Emotions, Qualia and Consciousness* (pp. 95–100). Cambridge, Mass.: MIT; Naples: Instituto Italiano per gli Studi Filosofici.

—— 2001c. Dimensions of embodiment: Body image and body schema in medical contexts. In K. Toombs (ed.), *Handbook in the Philosophy of Medicine*, i. *Phenomenology and Medicine* (pp. 147–75). Dordrecht: Kluwer Academic.

—— 2001d. Book review of K. Wider, *The Bodily Nature of Consciousness*, in *Mind*, 110 (438): 577–82.

—— 2003a. Phenomenology and experimental design. *Journal of Consciousness Studies*, 10 (9–10): 85–99.

—— 2003b. Bodily self-awareness and object-perception. *Theoria et Historia Scientiarum: International Journal for Interdisciplinary Studies*, 7 (1): 53–68.

—— 2003c. Self-narrative in schizophrenia. In A. S. David and T. Kircher (eds.), *The Self in Neuroscience and Psychiatry* (pp. 336–57). Cambridge: Cambridge University Press.

Gallagher, S. 2004. Neurocognitive models of schizophrenia: A phenomenological critique. *Psychopathology*, 37(1): 8–19.

—— (forthcoming *a*). Sense of agency and higher-order cognition: Levels of explanation for schizophrenia. *Cognitive Semiotics*, 18.

—— (forthcoming *b*). Fantasies and perspectives in the science of consciousness. *Intellectica: Revue de l'Association pour la Recherche Cognitive*.

—— (forthcoming *c*). Phenomenological contributions to a theory of social cognition (The Aron Gurwitsch Memorial Lecture 2003). *Husserl Studies*.

—— and Cole, J. 1995. Body schema and body image in a deafferented subject. *Journal of Mind and Behavior*, 16: 369–90.

—— and Marcel, A. J. 1999. The self in contextualized action. *Journal of Consciousness Studies*, 6 (4): 4–30.

—— and Meltzoff, A. 1996. The earliest sense of self and others: Merleau-Ponty and recent developmental studies. *Philosophical Psychology*, 9: 213–36.

—— and Varela, F. 2001. Redrawing the map and resetting the time: Phenomenology and the cognitive sciences. In S. Crowell, L. Embree, and S. J. Julian (eds.), *The Reach of Reflection: The Future of Phenomenology* (pp. 17–45). ElectronPress (http://www.electronpress.com/reach.asp). Also (forthcoming) *Canadian Journal of Philosophy* (2004).

—— Butterworth, G., Lew, A., and Cole, J. 1998. Hand-mouth coordination, congenital absence of limb, and evidence for innate body schemas. *Brain and Cognition*, 38: 53–65.

—— Cole, J., and McNeill, D. 2001. The language-thought-hand system. In C. Cave, I. Guaitella, and S. Santi (eds.), *Oralité et gestualité: Interactions et comportements multimodaux dans la communication* (pp. 420–4). Paris: L'Harmattan.

—— —— —— 2002. Social cognition and the primacy of movement revisited. *Trends in Cognitive Sciences*, 6 (4): 155–6.

Gallese, V. 1998. Mirror neurons: From grasping to language. Paper presented at Tucson III Conference: Towards a Science of Consciousness (Tucson 1998).

—— 2000. The acting subject: Towards the neural basis of social cognition. In T. Metzinger (ed.), *Neural Correlates of Consciousness: Empirical and Conceptual Questions* (pp. 325–33). Cambridge, Mass.: MIT.

—— and Goldman, A. 1998. Mirror neurons and the simulation theory of mind-reading. *Trends in Cognitive Sciences*, 2: 493–501.

—— Fadiga, L., Fogassi L., and Rizzolatti, G. 1996. Action recognition in the premotor cortex. *Brain*, 119: 593–609.

Gardner, R. M., and Moncrieff, C. 1988. Body image distortion in anorexics as a non-sensory phenomenon: A signal detection approach. *Journal of Clinical Psychology*, 44: 101–7.

—— Martinez, R., Espinoza, T., and Gallegos, V. 1988. Distortion of body image in the obese: A sensory phenomena [*sic*]. *Psychological Medicine*, 18: 633–41.

—— Morrell, J. A., Watson, D. N., and Sandoval, S. L. 1989. Subjective equality and just noticeable differences in body-size judgments by obese persons. *Perceptual and Motor Skills*, 69: 595–604.

Garner D. M., and Garfinkel, P. E. 1981. Body image in anorexia nervosa: Measurement, theory, and clinical implications. *International Journal of Psychiatry in Medicine*, 11: 263–84.

—— —— Stacer, H. C., and Moldofsky, H. 1976. Body image disturbances in anorexia nervosa and obesity. *Psychosomatic Medicine*, 38: 327–36.

Garraghty, P. E., and Kaas, J. H. 1991. Functional reorganization in adult monkey thalamus after peripheral nerve injury. *Neuroreport*, 2: 747–50.

Gazzaniga, M. 1998. *The Mind's Past*. Berkeley: University of California Press.

—— and Gallagher, S. 1998. A neuronal Platonist: An interview with Michael Gazzaniga (includes introduction and postscript), *Journal of Consciousness Studies*, 5: 706–17.

Gellhorn, E. 1943. *Autonomic Regulations: Their Significance for Physiology, Psychology, and Neuropsychiatry*. New York: Interscience Publications.

Georgieff, N., and Jeannerod, M. 1998. Beyond consciousness of external events: A 'Who' system for consciousness of action and self-consciousness. *Consciousness and Cognition*, 7: 465–77.

Gerrans, P. 1999. Delusional misidentification as subpersonal disintegration. *The Monist*, 82 (4): 590–608.

Gerstmann, J. 1927. Agnosie und isolierte Agraphie: ein neues Syndrom, *Zeitschrift für Neurologie*, 108: 152–77.

—— 1942. Problems of imperception of disease and of impaired body territories with organic lesions. *Archives of Neurology and Psychiatry*, 48: 890–912.

Gibson, J. J. 1966. *The Senses Considered as Perceptual Systems*. Boston: Houghton-Mifflin.

—— 1979. *The Ecological Approach to Visual Perception*. Boston: Houghton-Mifflin.

—— 1987. A note on what exists at the ecological level of reality. In E. Reed and R. Jones (eds.), *Reasons for Realism: Selected Essays of James J. Gibson* (pp. 416–18). Hillsdale, NJ: Erlbaum.

Gillon, R. 1985. *Philosophical Medical Ethics*. Chichester: John Wiley.

Glucksman, M. L., and Hirsch, J. 1973. The perception of body size. In N. Kiell (ed.), *The Psychology of Obesity*. Springfield, Ill.: Charles C. Thomas.

Goldfarb, W. 1945. Effect of psychological deprivation in infancy and subsequent stimulation. *American Journal of Psychiatry*, 102: 18–33.

Goldin-Meadow, S. 1999. The role of gesture in communication and thinking. *Trends in Cognitive Sciences*, 3: 419–29.

Goldman, A. I. 1989. Interpretation psychologized. *Mind and Language*, 4: 161–85.

—— and Gallese, V. 2000. Reply to Schulkin. *Trends in Cognitive Sciences*, 4 (7): 255–6.

Goldman-Rakic, P. S., and Selemon, L. D. 1997. Functional and anatomical aspects of prefrontal pathology in schizophrenia. *Schizophrenia Bulletin*, 23: 437–58.

Gomez, J. C. 1996. Second person intentional relations and the evolution of social understanding. *Behavioral and Brain Studies*, 19 (1): 129–30.

Gopnik, A. 1993. How we know our minds: The illusion of first-person knowledge of intentionality. *Behavioral and Brain Sciences*, 16: 1–14.

—— and Meltzoff, A. 1997. *Words, Thoughts, and Theories*. Cambridge, Mass.: MIT.

Gordon, R. M. 1986. Folk psychology as simulation. *Mind and Language*, 1: 158–71.

—— 1995a. Simulation without introspection or inference from me to you. In M. Davies and T. Stone (eds.), *Mental Simulation: Evaluations and Applications*. Oxford: Blackwell.

—— 1995b. Developing commonsense psychology: Experimental data and philosophical data, APA Eastern Division Symposium on Children's Theory of Mind, 27 December 1995 (http://www.umsl.edu/~philo/Mind_Seminar/New%20Pages/papers/Gordon/apakids9.htm).

Gorman, W. 1969. *Body Image and the Image of the Brain*. St Louis: Warren H. Green.

Grafton, S. T., Arbib, M. A., Fadiga, L., and Rizzolatti, G. 1996. Localization of grasp representations in humans by PET: 2. Observation compared with imagination. *Experimental Brain Research*, 112: 103–11.

Graham, G., and Stephens, G. L. 1994. Mind and mine. In G. Graham and G. L. Stephens (eds.), *Philosophical Psychopathology* (pp. 91–109). Cambridge, Mass.: MIT.

Graybiel, M. S. 1997. The basal ganglia and cognitive pattern generators. *Schizophrenia Bulletin*, 23: 459–69.

Graziano, M. S., and Gross, C. G. 1998. Spatial maps for the control of movement. *Current Opinion in Neurobiology*, 8: 195–201.

—— Yap, G. S., and Gross, C. G. 1994. Coding of visual space by premotor neurons. *Science*, 266: 1054–7.

Gregory, R. L., and Wallace, J. G. 1963. *Recovery from Early Blindness*. EPS Monograph No. 2. Cambridge: Heffer.

Grezes, J., and Decety, J. 2001. Functional anatomy of execution, mental simulation, observation, and verb generation of actions: A meta-analysis. *Human Brain Mapping*, 12: 1–19.

Grubb, J. D., and Reed, C. L. 2002. Trunk orientation induces neglect-like lateral biases in covert attention. *Psychological Science*, 13: 554–7.

Guillaume, P. 1943. *Psychologie*. Paris: Presses Universitaires de France.

Guldin, W. O., Akbarian, S., and Grüsser, O. J. 1992. Cortico-cortical connections and cytoarchitectonics of the primate vestibular cortex: A study in squirrel monkeys (*Saimiri sciureus*). *Journal of Comparative Neurology*, 326: 375–401.

Gurfinkel, V. S., and Levick, Yu. S. 1991. Perceptual and automatic aspects of the postural body scheme. In J. Paillard (ed.), *Brain and Space* (pp. 147–62). Oxford: Oxford University Press.

Gurwitsch, A. 1931/1978. *Human Encounters in the Social World*. Pittsburgh: Duquesne University Press.

—— 1964. *The Field of Consciousness*. Pittsburgh: Duquesne University Press.

Hacking, I. 1995. The looping effects of human kinds. In D. Sperber, D. Premack, and A. J. Premack (eds.), *Causal Cognition: A Multidisciplinary Debate* (pp. 351–83). New York: Oxford University Press.

Haggard, P., and Eimer, M. 1999. On the relation between brain potentials and the awareness of voluntary movements. *Experimental Brain Research*, 126: 128–33.

—— and Magno, E. 1999. Localising awareness of action with transcranial magnetic stimulation. *Experimental Brain Research*, 127: 102–7.

Haith, M. M. 1993. Future-oriented processes in infancy: The case of visual expectations. In C. Granrud (ed.), *Carnegie-Mellon Symposium on Visual Perception and Cognition in Infancy* (pp. 235–64). Hillsdale, NJ: Erlbaum.

Halligan, F. R., and Reznikoff, M. 1985. Personality factors and change with multiple sclerosis. *Journal of Consulting and Clinical Psychology*, 53: 547–8.

Halligan, P. M., Zeman A., and Berger, A. 1999. Phantoms in the brain: Question the assumption that the adult brain is hard wired. *British Medical Journal*, 319 (7210): 587–8.

—— Marshall, L. C., Wade, D. T., Davey, J., and Morrison, D. 1993. Thumb in cheek? Sensory reorganization and perceptual plasticity after limb amputation. *Neuroreport*, 4: 233–6.

Ham, G. L., Easton, P. S., Himburg, S. P., and Greenberg, B. 1983. Body image perceptions of children and adolescents with psychiatric disorders. *International Journal of Obesity*, 7: 321–6.

Happé, F. 1995. *Autism: An Introduction to Psychological Theory*. Cambridge: Harvard University Press.

Harris, C. S. 1965. Perceptual adaptation to inverted, reversed, and displaced vision. *Psychological Review*, 72: 419–44.

Head, H. 1920. *Studies in Neurology*, ii. London: Oxford University Press.

—— 1926. *Aphasia and Kindred Disorders of Speech*, i. Cambridge: Cambridge University Press.

—— and Holmes, G. 1911–12. Sensory disturbances from cerebral lesions, *Brain*, 34: 102–245.

Heal, J. 1986. Replication and functionalism. In J. Butterfield (ed.), *Language, Mind, and Logic* (pp. 45–59). Cambridge: Cambridge University Press.

—— 1998*a*. Co-cognition and off-line simulation: Two ways of understanding the simulation approach. *Mind and Language*, 13: 477–98.

—— 1998*b*. Understanding other minds from the inside. In A. O'Hear (ed.), *Current Issues in Philosophy of Mind*. Cambridge: Cambridge University Press.

Hebb, D. O. 1949. *The Organization of Behavior: A Neuropsychological Theory*. New York: Science Editions, 1961.

Hécaen, H., Talairach, J., David, M., and Dell, M. B. 1949. Coagulations limités du thalamus dans les algies du syndrome thalamique: résultats thérapeutiques et physiologiques. *Revue de Neurologie*, 81: 917–31.

Heidegger, M. 1968. *Being and Time*, trans. J. Macquarrie and E. Robinson. New York: Harper & Row.

Heilman, K. M., Bowers, D., Valenstein, E., and Watson, R. T. 1987. Hemispace and hemispatial neglect. In M. Jeannerod (ed.), *Neurophysiological and Neuropsychological Aspects of Spatial Neglect* (pp. 115–50). Amsterdam: North-Holland.

Held, R. 1961. Exposure-history as a factor in maintaining stability of perception and coordination. *Journal of Nervous and Mental Diseases*, 132: 26–32.

Hickok, G., Bellugi, U., and Klima, E. S. 1998. The neural organization of language: evidence from sign language aphasia. *Trends in Cognitive Sciences*, 2: 129–36.

Hobson, P. 1986. The autistic child's appraisal of expressions of emotion. *Journal of Child Psychology and Psychiatry*, 27: 321–42.

—— 1993. The emotional origins of social understanding. *Philosophical Psychology*, 6: 227–49.

—— 2002. *The Cradle of Thought*. London: Macmillan.

—— and Lee, A. 1999. Imitation and identification in autism. *Journal of Child Psychology and Psychiatry*, 40: 649–59.

Holst, E. von, and Mittelstaedt, H. 1950. Das Reafferenzprinzip (Wechselwirkungen zwischen Zentralnervensystem und Peripherie). *Naturwisenschaften*, 37: 464–76.

Hopkins, B. and Prechtl, H. F. R. 1984. A qualitative approach to the development of movements during early infancy. In H. F. R. Prechtl (ed.), *Continuity of Neural Functions from Prenatal to Postnatal Life*. Oxford: Blackwell.

Hubel, D. H., and Wiesel, T. N. 1963. Receptive fields of cells in striate cortex of very young, visually inexperienced kittens. *Journal of Neurophysiology*, 26: 994–1002.

Humphrey, T. 1964. Some correlations between the appearance of human fetal reflexes and the development of the nervous system. *Progress in Brain Research*, 4: 93–135.

Hurley, S. 1999. *Consciousness in Action*. Cambridge, Mass.: Harvard University Press.

Husserl, E. 1970. *Cartesian Meditations*, trans. D. Cairns. The Hague: Martinus Nijhoff.

—— 1973. *Ding und Raum*. Husserliana, 16. The Hague: Martinus Nijhoff.

—— 1991. *On the Phenomenology of the Consciousness of Internal Time (1893–1917)*, trans. J. Brough. Collected Works, 4. Dordrecht: Kluwer Academic.

Huttenlocher, P. R., de Courten, C., Garey, L. J., and van der Loos, H. 1982. Synaptogenesis in human visual cortex—evidence for synapse elimination during normal development, *Neuroscience Letters*, 33: 247–52.

Iacoboni, M., Woods, R. P., Mazziotta, J. C., Brass, M., Bekkering, H., and Rizzolatti, G. 1999. Cortical mechanisms of human imitation. *Science*, 286 (24 Dec.): 2526–8.

Iverson, J. M., and Goldin-Meadow, S. 1998. Why people gesture when they speak. *Nature*, 396 (19 Nov.): 228.

Iverson, J. M., and Thelen, E. 1999. Hand, mouth and brain: The dynamic emergence of speech and gesture. *Journal of Consciousness Studies*, 6 (11–12): 19–40.

Jackson, S. R., and Husain, M. 1996. Visuomotor functions of the lateral premotor cortex. *Current Opinion in Neurobiology*, 6: 788–95.

—— Newport, R., Husain, M., Harvey, M., and Hindle, J. V. 2000. Reaching movements may reveal the distorted topography of spatial representations after neglect. *Neuropsychologia*, 38 (4): 500–7.

Jacobson, E. 1970. *Modern Treatment of Tense Patients*. Springfield, Vt.: Charles C. Thomas.

Jacomuzzi, A. C., Kobau, P., and Bruno, N. 2003. Molyneux's question redux. *Phenomenology and the Cognitive Sciences*, 2 (4): 255–80.

James, W. 1890. *The Principles of Psychology*. New York: Dover, 1950.

Jaspers, K. 1972. *General Psychopathology*, trans. J. Hoenig and M. W. Hamilton. Chicago: University of Chicago Press.

Jeannerod, M. 1994. The representing brain: Neural correlates of motor intention and imagery. *Behavioral and Brain Sciences*, 17: 187–245.

—— 1997. *The Cognitive Neuroscience of Action*. Oxford: Blackwell.

—— 1999. To act or not to act: Perspectives on the representation of actions. *Quarterly Journal of Experimental Psychology*, 52A: 1–29.

—— 2001. Neural simulation of action: A unifying mechanism for motor cognition, *NeuroImage*, 14: 103–9.

—— 2003. The mechanism of self-recognition in humans. *Behavioral and Brain Research*, 142 (1–2): 1–15.

—— and Gallagher, S. (2002). From action to interaction: An interview with Marc Jeannerod. *Journal of Consciousness Studies*, 9 (1): 3–26.

Jensen, T. S., Krebs, B., Nielsen, J., and Rasmussen, P. 1984. Non-painful phantom limb phenomena in amputees: Incidence, clinical characteristics and temporal course. *Acta Neurol. Scand.*, 70: 407–14.

Johnson, M. 1987. *The Body in the Mind: The Bodily Basis of Meaning, Imagination, and Reason*. Chicago: University of Chicago Press.

Johnson, S. C. 2000. The recognition of mentalistic agents in infancy. *Trends in Cognitive Sciences*, 4: 22–8.

Johnson, S. C., *et al.* 1998. Whose gaze will infants follow? The elicitation of gaze-following in 12-month-old infants. *Developmental Science*, 1: 233–8.

Jones, E. G., and Pons, T. P. 1998. Thalamic and brainstem contributions to large scale plasticity of primate somatosensory cortex. *Science*, 282: 1121–5.

Jouen, F. 1986. La Contribution des récepteurs visuels et labyrinthiques à la détection des mouvements du corps propre chez le nourrisson. *Année Psychologique*, 86: 169–92.

—— 1988. Visual-proprioceptive control of posture in newborn infants. In G. Amblard, A. Berthoz, and F. Clarac (eds.), *Posture and Gait: Development, Adaptation, and Modulation* (pp. 13–22). Amsterdam: Excerpta Medica.

—— and Gapenne, O. 1995. Interactions between the vestibular and visual systems in the neonate. In P. Rochat (ed.), *The Self in Infancy: Theory and Research* (pp. 277–301). Amsterdam: Elsevier Science.

Kaas, J. H. 1991. Plasticity of sensory and motor maps in adult mammals. *Annual Review of Neuroscience*, 14: 137–67.

—— 2000. The reorganization of sensory and motor maps after injury in adult mammals. In M. S. Gazzaniga (ed.), *The New Cognitive Neurosciences* (pp. 223–36). Cambridge, Mass.: MIT.

Kandel, E. R., and Hawkins, R. D. 1992. The biological basis of learning and individuality. *Scientific American* (U.K.), 267 (3): 53–60.

Kapur, S. 2003. Psychosis as a state of aberrant salience: A framework linking biology, phenomenology, and pharmacology in schizophrenia. *American Journal of Psychiatry*, 160 (1): 13–23.

Karl, A., Birbaumer, N., Lutzenberger, W., Cohen, L. G., and Flor, H. 2001. Reorganization of motor and somatosensory cortex in upper extremity amputees with phantom limb pain. *The Journal of Neuroscience*, 21 (10): 3609–18.

Karmiloff-Smith, A. 1992. *Beyond Modularity: A Developmental Perspective on Cognitive Science*. Cambridge, Mass.: MIT.

Katz, J. 1993. The reality of phantom limbs. *Motivation and Emotion*, 17: 147–79.

Kelso, J. A. 1995. *Dynamic Patterns: The Self-Organization of Brain and Behavior*. Cambridge, Mass.: MIT.

Keltikangas-Jarvinen, L. 1987. Body-image disturbances ensuing from juvenile rheumatoid arthritis. *Perceptual and Motor Skills*, 64: 984.

Kermoian, R., and Campos, J. J. 1988. Locomotor experience: A facilitator of spatial cognitive development. *Child Development*, 59: 908–917.

Kew, J. J. M., Halligan, P. W., Marshall, J. C., *et al.* 1997. Abnormal access of axial vibrotactile input to deafferented somatosensory cortex in human upper limb amputees. *Journal of Neurophysiology*, 77: 2753–64.

Kinsbourne, M. 1975. The mechanisms of hemispheric control of the lateral gradient of attention. In P. M. A. Rabbitt and S. Dornic (eds.), *Attention and Performance*. London: Academic Press.

—— 1987. Mechanisms in unilateral neglect. In M. Jeannerod (ed.), *Neurophysiological and Neuropsychological Aspects of Spatial Neglect* (pp. 69–86). Amsterdam: North-Holland.

—— 1995. Awareness of one's own body: An attentional theory of its nature, development, and brain basis. In J. Bermúdez, A. Marcel, and N. Eilan (eds.), *The Body and the Self* (pp. 206–23). Cambridge, Mass.: MIT.

—— 2002. The role of imitation in body ownership and mental growth. In A. N. Meltzoff and W. Prinz (eds.), *The Imitative Mind: Development, Evolution, and Brain Bases* (pp. 311–30). Cambridge: Cambridge University Press.

Kita, S. 2000. How representational gestures help speaking. In D. McNeill (ed.), *Language and Gesture* (pp. 162–85). Cambridge: Cambridge University Press.

Klonoff, H., Fibiger, C., and Hutton, G. H. 1970. Neuropsychological pattern in chronic schizophrenia. *Journal of Nervous and Mental Disorder*, 150: 291–300.

Knecht, S., Henningsen, H., Elbert, T., Flor, H., Höhling, C., Pantev, C., Birbaumer, N., and Taub, E. 1995. Cortical reorganization in human amputees and mislocalization of painful stimuli to the phantom limb. *Neuroscience Letters*, 201: 262–4.

Kolb, L. C. 1954. *The Painful Phantom*. Springfield, Ill.: Thomas.

—— 1959. The body image in schizophrenic reaction. In A. Auerbach (ed.), *Schizophrenia: An Integrated Approach* (pp. 87–97). New York: Ronald.

Kollias, S., Brugger, P., Crelier, G. R., Regard, M-C., Hepp, M., and Valavanis, A. 1998. Cortical representation of phantom limbs in congenital tetramelia demonstrated by fMRI. *NeuroImage*, 7 (4), Part 2, Abstract.

Kuhl, P. K., and Meltzoff, A. N. 1984. The intermodal representation of speech in infants. *Infant Behavior and Development*, 7: 361–81.

—— —— 1992. The bimodal perception of speech in infancy. *Science*, 218: 1138–41.

Lackner, J. R. 1988. Some proprioceptive influences on the perceptual representation of body shape and orientation. *Brain*, 3: 281–97.

Lakoff, G. 1987. *Women, Fire, and Dangerous Things: What Categories Reveal about the Mind*. Chicago: University of Chicago Press.

—— and Johnson, M. 1980. *Metaphors We Live By*. Chicago: University of Chicago Press.

La Mettrie, J. O. de. 1745. *Histoire naturelle de l'âme*. Paris.

Landau, B., Gleitman, H., and Spelke, E. 1981. Spatial knowledge and geometric representation in a child blind from birth. *Science*, 213: 1275–7.

LeBaron, C., and Streeck, J. 2000. Gestures, knowledge, and the world. In D. McNeill (ed.), *Language and Gesture* (pp. 118–38). Cambridge: Cambridge University Press.

Lee, D. N., and Aronson, E. 1974. Visual proprioceptive control of standing in human infants. *Perception and Psychophysics*, 15: 529–32.

—— and Lishman, J. R. 1975. Visual proprioceptive control of stance. *Journal of Human Movement Studies*, 1: 87–95.

Lee, D. S., *et al.* 2001. Deafness: Cross-modal plasticity and cochlear implants, *Nature*, 409: 149–50.

Legerstee, M. 1991. The role of person and object in eliciting early imitation. *Journal of Experimental Child Psychology*, 51: 423–33.

Leibniz, G. 1765. *Nouveaux essais sur l'entendement humain*, trans. A. G. Langley. *New Essays Concerning Human Understanding* (3rd edn.). La Salle, Ill.: Open Court, 1949.

Lempert, H., and Kinsbourne, M. 1982. Effect of laterality of orientation on verbal memory. *Neuropsychologia*, 20: 211–14.

Leslie, A. 1988. Some implications of pretense for mechanisms underlying the child's theory of mind. In J. Astington, P. Harris, and D. Olson (eds.), *Developing Theories of Mind* (pp. 19–46). Cambridge: Cambridge University Press.

—— 1991. The theory of mind impairment in autism: Evidence for a modular mechanism of development? In A. Whiten (ed.), *Natural Theories of Mind: Evolution, Development and Simulation of Everyday Mindreading* (pp. 63–78). Oxford: Blackwell.

—— 1994. ToMM, ToBy, and agency: Core architecture and domain specificity. In L. Hirschfeld and S. Gelman (eds.), *Mapping the Mind: Domain Specificity in Cognition and Culture* (pp. 119–48). Cambridge: Cambridge University Press.

—— 2000. Theory of mind as a mechanism of selective attention. In M. Gazzaniga (ed.), *The New Cognitive Neurosciences* (pp. 1235–47). Cambridge, Mass.: MIT.

—— and Frith, U. 1988. Autistic children's understanding of seeing, knowing and believing. *British Journal of Developmental Psychology*, 6: 315–24.

—— and Thaiss, L. 1992. Domain specificity in conceptual development: Neuropsychological evidence from autism. *Cognition*, 43: 225–51.

Levin, S. 1984. Frontal lobe dysfunction in schizophrenia—Eye movement impairments. *Journal of Psychiatric Research*, 18: 27–55.

Lew, A., and Butterworth, G. E. 1995. Hand-mouth contact in newborn babies before and after feeding. *Developmental Psychology*, 31: 456–63.

Lhermitte, J. 1939. *L'Image de notre corps*. Paris: Nouvelle Revue Critique.

Libet, B. 1985. Unconscious cerebral initiative and the role of conscious will in voluntary action. *Behavioral and Brain Sciences*, 8: 529–66.

—— 1992. The neural time-factor in perception, volition, and free will. *Revue de Métaphysique et de Morale*, 2: 255–72.

—— 1996, Neural time factors in conscious and unconscious mental functions. In S. R. Hammeroff *et al.* (eds.), *Toward a Science of Consciousness: The First Tucson Discussions and Debates.* Cambridge, Mass.: MIT.

—— 1999. Do we have free will? *Journal of Consciousness Studies,* 6 (8–9): 47–57.

—— 2003. Can conscious experience affect brain activity? *Journal of Consciousness Studies,* 10 (12): 24–8.

—— Gleason, C. A., Wright, E. W., and Perl, D. K. 1983. Time of conscious intention to act in relation to cerebral activities (readiness potential): The unconscious initiation of a freely voluntary act. *Brain,* 102: 193–224.

Locke, J. 1690. *An Essay Concerning Human Understanding* (2nd edn. 1694.), ed. A. C. Fraser. New York: Dover, 1959.

Lockman, J. J., and Thelen, E. 1993. Developmental biodynamics: Brain, body, behavior connections. *Child Development,* 64: 953–9.

Lutchmaya, S., Baron-Cohen, S., and Raggatt, P. 2002. Foetal testosterone and vocabulary size in 18- and 24-month-old infants. *Infant Behavior and Development,* 24 (4): 418–24.

McCanne, T. R., and Sandman, C. A. 1974. Instrumental heart rate responses and visual perception: A preliminary study. *Psychophysiology,* 11: 283–7.

—— —— 1976. Operant autonomic conditioning and Rod-and-Frame Test performance. *Journal of Personality and Social Psychology,* 24: 821–9.

McEwan, M. H., Dihoff, R. E., and Brosvic, G. M. 1991. Early infant crawling experience is reflected in later motor skill development. *Perceptual and Motor Skills,* 72: 75–9.

MacKay, D. 1966. Cerebral organization and the conscious control of action. In J. C. Eccles (ed.), *Brain and Conscious Experience* (pp. 422–45). New York: Springer.

McNeill, D. 1992. *Hand and Mind: What Gestures Reveal about Thought.* Chicago: University of Chicago Press.

Mahoney, M. J. 1991. *Human Change Processes: The Scientific Foundations of Psychotherapy.* New York: Basic Books.

Malenka, R. C., Angel, R. W., Hampton, B., and Berger, P. A. 1982. Impaired central error correcting behaviour in schizophrenia. *Archives of General Psychiatry,* 39: 101–7.

Malle, B. F. 2001. The folk theory of mind: Conceptual foundations for social cognition. In R. Hassin, J. Uleman, and J. Bargh (eds.), *The New Unconscious.* New York: Oxford University Press.

—— 2002. The relation between language and theory of mind in development and evolution. In T. Givón and B. F. Malle (eds.), *The Evolution of Language out of Pre-Language* (pp. 265–84). Amsterdam: John Benjamins.

Manning, J. T. 2002. *Digit Ratio: A Pointer to Fertility, Behavior and Health.* New Brunswick, NJ: Rutgers University Press.

Manschreck, T. C. 1986. Motor abnormalities in schizophrenia. In H. A. Nasrallah and D. K. Weinberger (eds.), *Handbook of Schizophrenia,* i. *The Neurology of Schizophrenia* (pp. 65–96). Amsterdam: Elsevier.

Marbach, E. 1993. *Mental Representation and Consciousness: Toward a Phenomenological Theory of Representation and Reference.* Dordrecht: Kluwer Academic.

Marcel, A. J. 1983. Conscious and unconscious perception: An approach to the relations between phenomenal experience and perceptual processes. *Cognitive Psychology,* 15: 238–300.

—— 1992. The personal level in cognitive rehabilitation. In N. von Steinbuchel, E. Pöppel, and D. von Cramon (eds.), *Neuropsychological Rehabilitation* (pp. 155–68). Berlin: Springer.

Marcel, A. J. 2003. The sense of agency: Awareness and ownership of actions and intentions. In J. Roessler and N. Eilan (eds.), *Agency and Self-Awareness* (pp. 48–93). Oxford: Oxford University Press.

Margolis, R. L., Chuang, D. M., Post, R. M. 1994. Programmed cell death: Implications for neuropsychiatric disorders. *Biological Psychiatry*, 35 (12): 946–56.

Marivita, A. and Iriki, A. 2004. Tools for the body (schema). *Trends in Cognitive Sciences*, 8 (2): 79–86.

Martin, M. 1992. Sight and touch. In T. Crane (ed.), *The Contents of Experience: Essays on Perception* (pp. 196–215). Cambridge: Cambridge University Press.

Martinez-Conde, S., Macknik, S. L., and Hubel, D. H. 2000. Microsaccadic eye movements and firing of single cells in the striate cortex of macaque monkeys. *Nature Neuroscience*, 3 (3): 251–8.

Mason, R. E. 1961. *Internal Perception and Bodily Functioning*. New York: International Universities Press.

Maturana, H. R., and Varela, F. G. 1987. *The Tree of Knowledge: The Biological Roots of Human Understanding*. Boston: Shambhala.

Medin, D. L., and Wattenmaker, W. D. 1987. Category cohesiveness, theories, and cognitive archeology. In U. Neisser (ed.), *Concepts and Conceptual Development: Ecological and Intellectual Factors in Categorization* (pp. 25–62). Cambridge: Cambridge University Press.

Meijsing, M. (2003). Phantoms and movements, or, are we really just our brains? *Theoria et Historia Scientiarum*, 7 (1): 93–118.

Melges, F. T. 1982. *Time and the Inner Future: A Temporal Approach to Psychiatric Disorders*. New York: Wiley.

—— and Freeman, A. M. 1977. Temporal disorganization and inner-outer confusion in acute mental illness. *American Journal of Psychiatry*, 134: 874–7.

Mellor, C. S. 1970. First rank symptoms of schizophrenia. *British Journal of Psychiatry*, 117: 15–23.

Meltzoff, A. 1988a. Infant imitation and memory: Nine-month-olds in immediate and deferred tests. *Child Development*, 59: 217–25.

—— 1988b. Infant imitation after a 1-week delay: Long-term memory for novel acts and multiple stimuli. *Developmental Psychology*, 24: 470–6.

—— 1990a. Foundations for developing a concept of self: The role of imitation in relating self to other and the value of social mirroring, social modeling, and self practice in infancy. In D. Cicchetti and M. Beeghly (eds.), *The Self in Transition: Infancy to Childhood* (pp. 139–64). Chicago: University of Chicago Press.

—— 1990b. Towards a developmental cognitive science: The implications of cross-modal matching and imitation for the development of representation and memory in infancy. *Annals of the New York Academy of Sciences (The Development and Neural Bases of Higher Cognitive Functions)*, 608: 1–31.

—— 1993. Molyneux's babies: Cross-modal perception, imitation, and the mind of the preverbal infant. In N. Eilan, R. McCarthy, and B. Brewer (eds.), *Spatial Representation: Problems in Philosophy and Psychology* (pp. 219–35). Oxford: Basil Blackwell.

—— 1995. Understanding the intentions of others: Re-enactment of intended acts by 18-month-old children. *Developmental Psychology*, 31: 838–50.

—— 2002. Elements of a developmental theory of imitation. In A. N. Melzoff and W. Prinz (eds.), *The Imitative Mind: Development, Evolution, and Brain Bases* (pp. 19–41). Cambridge: Cambridge University Press.

—— and Borton, R. W. 1979. Intermodal matching by human neonates. *Nature*, 282: 403–4.

—— and Brooks, R. 2001. 'Like Me' as a building block for understanding other minds: Bodily acts, attention, and intention. In B. F. Malle *et al.* (eds.), *Intentions and Intentionality: Foundations of Social Cognition* (pp. 171–91). Cambridge, Mass.: MIT.

—— and Gopnik, A. 1993. The role of imitation in understanding persons and developing a theory of mind. In S. Baron-Cohen, H. Tager-Flusberg, and D. Cohen (eds.), *Understanding Other Minds: Perspectives from Autism* (pp. 335–66). New York: Oxford University Press.

—— and Moore, M. K. 1977. Imitation of facial and manual gestures by human neonates. *Science*, 198: 75–8.

—— —— 1983. Newborn infants imitate adult facial gestures. *Child Development*, 54: 702–9.

—— —— 1989. Imitation in newborn infants: Exploring the range of gestures imitated and the underlying mechanisms. *Developmental Psychology*, 25: 954–62.

—— —— 1994. Imitation, memory, and the representation of persons, *Infant Behavior and Development*, 17: 83–99.

—— —— 1995. Infants' understanding of people and things: From body imitation to folk psychology. In J. Bermúdez, A. Marcel, and N. Eilan (eds.), *The Body and the Self* (pp. 43–69). Cambridge, Mass.: MIT.

—— —— 1997. Explaining facial imitation: A theoretical model, *Early Development and Parenting*, 6: 179–92.

Melzack, R. 1989. Phantom limbs, the self and the brain. *Canadian Psychology*, 30: 1–16.

—— 1990. Phantom limbs and the concept of a neuromatrix. *Trends in Neuroscience*, 13: 88–92.

Merleau-Ponty, M. 1945. *Phénomenologie de la perception*. Paris: Gallimard.

—— 1962. *Phenomenology of Perception*, trans. C. Smith. London: Routledge & Kegan Paul.

—— 1964. *The Primacy of Perception*, trans. W. Cobb. Evanston: Northwestern University Press.

—— 1968. *The Visible and the Invisible* trans. A. Lingis. Evanston: Northwestern University Press.

—— 1987. *Signs* trans. R. C. McCleary. Evanston: Northwestern University Press.

Merzenich, M. M., and Kaas, J. H. 1980. Principles of organization of sensory-perceptual systems in mammals. *Progress in Psychobiology and Physiological Psychology*, 9: 1–42.

Meuse, S. 1996. Phantoms, lost limbs, and the limits of the body-self. In M. O'Donovan-Anderson (ed.), *The Incorporated Self: Interdisciplinary Perspectives on Embodiment* (pp. 47–64). Lanham: Rowman & Littlefield.

Milner, D. 1998. Unconscious visual processing for action: Neuropsychological evidence. Paper presented at *Towards a Science of Consciousness*, Third Conference, Tucson, 27 April 1998.

Minkowski, E. 1933. *Lived Time: Phenomenological and Psychological Studies*, trans. N. Metzel. Evanston: Northwestern University Press, 1970.

Mitchell, D. E., Freeman, R. D., Millodot, M., and Haegerstrom, G. 1973. Meridional amblyopia: Evidence for modification of the human visual system by early visual experience. *Visual Research*, 13: 535–58.

Moore, D. G., Hobson, R. P., and Lee, A. 1997. Components of person perception: An investigation with autistic, non-autistic retarded and typically developing children and adolescents. *British Journal of Developmental Psychology*, 15: 401–23.

Morgan, M. 1977. *Molyneux's Question: Vision, Touch and the Philosophy of Perception*. Cambridge: Cambridge University Press.

Munk, H. 1890. *Über die Functionen der Grosshirnrinde*. Berlin: Hirschwald.

Murata, A., Fadiga, L., Fogassi, L., Gallese, V., Raos, V., and Rizzolatti, G. 1997. Object representation in the ventral premotor cortex (Area F5) of the monkey. *Journal of Neurophysiology*, 78: 2226–30.

Müri, R. M., Schnyder, H., Brugger, P., Hepp-Reymond, M-C., and Regard, M. 1998. Transcranial magnetic stimulation (TMS) mapping in a patient with phantoms of congenitally absent limbs. Poster presentation, *Schweizerische Gesellschaft für Klinische Neurophysiologie*, Zurich, 13 June 1998.

Myers, G. 1967. Self and body-image. In J. Edie (ed.), *Phenomenology in America* (pp. 147–60). Chicago: Quadrangle Books.

Nadel, J., and Butterworth, G. 1999. *Imitation in Infancy*. Cambridge: Cambridge University Press.

Neisser, U. 1976. *Cognition and Reality: Principles and Implications of Cognitive Psychology*. New York: W. H. Freeman.

—— (ed.). 1987. *Concepts and Conceptual Development: Ecological and Intellectual Factors in Categorization*. Cambridge: Cambridge University Press.

—— 1988. Five kinds of self-knowledge. *Philosophical Psychology*, 1: 35–59.

—— 1991. Two perceptually given aspects of the self and their development. *Developmental Review*, 11: 197–209.

Nielsen, T. I. 1963. Volition: A new experimental approach. *Scandinavian Journal of Psychology*, 4: 225–30.

Ogden, J. A. 1996. *Fractured Minds: A Case-Study Approach to Clinical Neuropsychology*. Oxford: Oxford University Press.

Ohta, M. 1987. Cognitive disorders of infantile autism: A study employing the WISC, spatial relationship conceptualization, and gesture imitation. *Journal of Autism and Developmental Disorders*, 17: 45–62.

Ojemann, G. A. 1984. Common cortical and thalamic mechanisms for language and motor functions. *American Journal of Physiology*, 246 (Regulatory Integrative and Comparative Physiology, 15): R901–R903.

Ojemann, J. G., and Silbergeld, D. L. 1995. Cortical stimulation mapping of phantom limb rolandic cortex. *Journal of Neurosurgery*, 82: 641–4.

Olson, E. T. 1997. *The Human Animal: Personal Identity without Psychology*. Oxford: Oxford University Press.

O'Rahilly, R., and Müller, F. 1994. *The Embryonic Human Brain*. New York: Wiley-Liss.

O'Shaughnessy, B. 1980. *The Will: A Dual Aspect Theory*. Cambridge: Cambridge University Press.

—— 1995. Proprioception and the body image. In J. Bermúdez, A. Marcel, and N. Eilan (eds.), *The Body and the Self* (pp. 175–203). Cambridge, Mass.: MIT.

Owens, D. G. C., Johnstone, E. C., and Frith, C. D. 1982. Spontaneous involuntary disorders of movement. *Archives of General Psychiatry*, 39: 452–61.

Pacherie, E. 1997. Du problème de Molyneux au problème de Bach-y-Rita. In J. Proust (ed.), *Perception et Intermodalité, Approches actuelles du Problème de Molyneux* (pp. 255–93). Paris: PUF.

Paillard, J. 1991a. Motor and representational framing of space. In J. Paillard (ed.), *Brain and Space* (pp. 163–82). Oxford: Oxford University Press.

—— 1991b. Knowing where and knowing how to get there. In J. Paillard (ed.), *Brain and Space* (pp. 461–81). Oxford: Oxford University Press.

—— 1997. Divided body schema and body image in peripherally and centrally deafferented patients. In V. S. Gurfinkel and Yu. S. Levik (eds.), *Brain and Movement*. Moscow: Institute for Information Transmission Problems RAS.

—— 1999. Body schema and body image: A double dissociation in deafferented patients. In G. N. Gantchev, S. Mori, and J. Massion (eds.), *Motor Control, Today and Tomorrow* (pp. 197–214). Sofia: Bulgarian Academy of Sciences, Academic Publishing House.

—— 2000. The neurobiological roots of rational thinking. In H. Cruse *et al.* (eds.), *Prerational Intelligence: Adaptive Behavior and Intelligent Systems Without Symbols and Logic*, i (pp. 343–55). Dordrecht: Kluwer Academic.

—— Michel, F., and Stelmach, G. 1983. Localization without content: A tactile analogue of blind sight. *Archives of Neurology*, 40: 548–51.

Panksepp, J. 1998. The periconscious substrates of consciousness: Affective states and the evolutionary origins of the self. *Journal of Consciousness Studies*, 5 (5/6): 566–82.

Park, D. 1969. Locke and Berkeley on the Molyneux problem. *Journal of the History of Ideas*, 30: 253–360.

Parnas, J. 2000. The self and intentionality in the pre-psychotic stages of schizophrenia. In D. Zahavi (ed.), *Exploring the Self* (pp. 115–47). Amsterdam: John Benjamins.

Parsons, L. M. 1990. Body image. In M. W. Eysenck (ed.), *The Blackwell Dictionary of Cognitive Psychology* (pp. 46–7). Oxford: Blackwell Reference.

Passingham, R. E. 1996. Functional specialization of the supplementary motor area in monkeys and humans. In H. O. Lüders (ed.), *Advances in Neurology*, 70 (pp. 105–16). Philadelphia: Lippincott-Raven.

Perner, J. 1991. *Understanding the Representational Mind*. Cambridge, Mass.: MIT.

—— Leekam, S. R., and Wimmer, H. 1987. Three-year olds' difficulty with false belief: The case for a conceptual deficit. *British Journal of Developmental Psychology*, 5: 125–37.

Petit, J-L. 1999. Constitution by movement: Husserl in light of recent neurobiological findings. In J. Petitot *et al.* (eds.), *Naturalizing Phenomenology: Issues in Contemporary Phenomenology and Cognitive Science* (pp. 220–44). Stanford: Stanford University Press.

Petitot, J., Varela, F., Pachoud, B., and Roy, J-M. (eds.) 1999. *Naturalizing Phenomenology: Issues in Contemporary Phenomenology and Cognitive Science*. Stanford: Stanford University Press.

Petty, R. E., and Cacioppo, J. T. 1977. Forewarning, cognitive responding and resistance to persuasion. *Journal of Personality and Social Psychology*, 35: 645–55.

Phillips, C. 1985. *Movements of the Hand*. Liverpool, Sherrington Lectures, XVII.

Phillips, W., Baron-Cohen, S., and Rutter, M. 1992. The role of eye-contact in the detection of goals: Evidence from normal toddlers, and children with autism or mental handicap. *Development and Psychopathology*, 4: 375–83.

Piaget, J. 1954. *The Construction of Reality in the Child*. New York: Basic Books.

—— 1962. *Play, Dreams, and Imitation in Childhood*. New York, Norton.

—— 1971. *Biology and Knowledge: An Essay on the Relations between Organic Regulations and Cognitive Processes*. Chicago: University of Chicago Press.

—— and Inhelder, B. 1969. *The Psychology of the Child*. New York: Basic Books.

Pick, A. 1915*a*. Störung der Orientierung am eigenen Körper: Beitrag zur Lehre vom Bewusstsein des eigenen Körpers, *Psychologische Forschung*, 1: 303–18.

—— 1915*b*. Zur Pathologie des Bewusstseins vom eigenen Korper: Ein Beitrag aus der Kriegsmedizin, *Neurologisches Centralblatt*, 34: 257–65.

Pierce, K., Muller, R. A., Ambrose, J., Allen, G., and Courchesne, E. 2001. Face processing occurs outside the fusiform 'face area' in autism: Evidence from functional MRI. *Brain*, 124 (Pt. 10): 2059–73.

Pinker, S. 1994. *The Language Instinct*. Baltimore: Penguin.

Plugge, H. 1967. *Der Mensch und sein Leib*. In S. Spicker (ed.), *The Philosophy of the Body* (pp. 293–311). Chicago: Quadrangle, 1970.

Poeck, K. 1963. Zur Psychophysiologie der Phantomerlebnisse. *Nervenarzt*, 34: 241–56.

—— 1964. Phantoms following amputation in early childhood and in congenital absence of limbs. *Cortex*, 1: 269–75.

—— and Orgass, B. 1971. The concept of the body schema: A critical review and some experimental results. *Cortex*, 7: 254–77.

Pons, T. P., Garraghty, P. E., Ommaya, A. K., Kaas, J. H., Taub, E., and Mishkin, M. 1991. Massive cortical reorganization after sensory deafferentation in adult macaques. *Science*, 252: 1857–60.

Pöppel, E. 1994. Temporal mechanisms in perception. *International Review of Neurobiology*, 37: 185–202.

—— von Cramon, D., and Blackmund, H. 1975. Eccentricity-specific dissociation of visual functions in patients with lesions of the central visual pathways. *Nature (London)*, 256: 489–90.

Porterfield, W. 1759. *A Treatise on the Eye: The Manner and Phaenomena of Vision*, 2 vols. Edinburgh.

Posada, A., Franck, N., Georgieff, N., and Jeannerod, M. 2001. Anticipating incoming events: An impaired cognitive process in schizophrenia. *Cognition*, 81: 209–25.

Powers, P. S., Schulman, R. G., Gleghorn, A. A., and Prange, M. E. 1987. Perceptual and cognitive abnormalities in bulimia. *American Journal of Psychiatry*, 144: 1456–60.

Prechtl, H. F. R. 1984. Continuity and change in early neural development. In H. R. R. Prechtl (ed.), *Continuity of Neural Functions from Prenatal to Postnatal Life* (pp. 1–15). Oxford: Blackwell Scientific/Spastics International.

—— and Hopkins, B. 1986. Developmental transformations of spontaneous movements in early infancy. *Early Human Development*, 14: 233–83.

Preuss, T. M., Stepniewska, I., and Kaas, J. H. 1996. Movement representation in the dorsal and ventral premotor areas of owl monkeys: A microstimulation study. *The Journal of Comparative Neurology*, 371: 649–76.

Pribram, K. H. 1999. Brain and the composition of conscious experience. *Journal of Consciousness Studies*, 6 (5): 19–42.

Prior, M. R., Dahlstrom, B., and Squires, T. L. 1990. Autistic children's knowledge of thinking and feeling states in other people. *Journal of Child Psychology and Psychiatry*, 31: 587–601.

Rakic, P. 1995. Corticogenesis in human and nonhuman primates. In M. S. Gazzaniga (ed.), *The Cognitive Neurosciences* (pp. 127–45). Cambridge, Mass.: MIT.

Ramachandran, V. S., and Blakeslee, S. 1998. *Phantoms in the Brain: Probing the Mysteries of the Human Mind*. New York: William Morrow.

—— and Hirstein, W. 1998. The perception of phantom limbs. *Brain*, 121: 1603–30.

—— and Rogers-Ramachandran, D. 1996. Synaesthesia in phantom limbs induced with mirrors. *Proceedings of the Royal Society of London*, 263: 377–86.

—— —— and Cobb, S. 1995. Touching the phantom limb. *Nature*, 377: 489–90.

—— —— and Stewart, M. 1992. Perceptual correlates of massive cortical reorganization. *Science*, 258: 1159–60.

Ratcliffe, M. 2004. Interpreting delusions. *Phenomenology and the Cognitive Sciences*, 3 (1): 24–48.

Reddy, V. 1996. Omitting the second person in social understanding. *Behavioral and Brain Sciences*, 19 (1): 140–1.

Reed, T., and Paterson, C. 1990. A comparative study of autistic subjects' performance at two levels of visual and cognitive perspective taking. *Journal of Autism and Developmental Disorders*, 29: 555–68.

Riva, G. 1994. What is body image? *European Commission VREPAR Virtual Body Project* (http://www.ehto.org/ht_projects/vrepar/whatbody.htm).

—— 1995. Virtual reality in the assessment and treatment of body image. Paper presented at the Center for Disabilities 1995 Virtual Reality Conference (http://www.csun.edu/cod/95virt/0015.html).

Rizzolatti, G., Fogassi, L., and Gallese, V. 2000. Cortical mechanisms subserving object grasping and action recognition: A new view on the cortical motor functions. In M. S. Gazzaniga (ed.), *The New Cognitive Neurosciences* (pp. 539–52). Cambridge, Mass.: MIT.

—— Fadiga, L., Gallese, V., and Fogassi, L. 1996. Premotor cortex and the recognition of motor actions. *Cognitive Brain Research*, 3: 131–41.

—— —— Matelli, M., Bettinardi, V., Paulesu, E., Perani, D., and Fazio, G. 1996. Localization of grasp representations in humans by PET: 1. Observation compared with imagination. *Experimental Brain Research*, 111: 246–52.

Rochat, P. 2002. Ego function of early imitation. In A. N. Meltzoff and W. Prinz (eds.), *The Imitative Mind: Development, Evolution, and Brain Bases* (pp. 85–97). Cambridge: Cambridge University Press.

—— Blass, E. M., and Hoffemeyer, L. B. 1988. Oropharyngeal control of hand-mouth coordination in newborn infants. *Developmental Psychology*, 24: 459–63.

Rock, I., and Harris, C. S. 1967. Vision and touch. *Scientific American*, 216 (5): 96–104.

Roll, J-P., and Roll, R. 1988. From eye to foot: A proprioceptive chain involved in postural control. In G. Amblard, A. Berthoz, and F. Clarac (eds.), *Posture and Gait: Development, Adaptation, and Modulation* (pp. 155–64). Amsterdam: Excerpta Medica.

—— —— and Velay, J-L. 1991. Proprioception as a link between body space and extra-personal space. In J. Paillard (ed.), *Brain and Space* (pp. 112–32). Oxford: Oxford University Press.

Rosenbaum, D. A., Vaughan, J., Jorgensen, M. J., Barns, H. J., and Stewart, E. 1993. Plans for object manipulation. In D. E. Meyer and S. Kornblum (eds.), *Attention and Performance XIV: Synergies in Experimental Psychology, Artificial Intelligence, and Cognitive Neuroscience*. Cambridge, Mass.: MIT.

Rosenfield, I. 1992. *The Strange, Familiar, and Forgotten: An Anatomy of Consciousness*. New York: Alfred A. Knopf/Vintage Books.

Rossetti, Y., Rode, G., Pisella, L. *et al.* 1998. Prism adaptation to a rightward optical deviation rehabilitates left hemispatial neglect. *Nature*, 395 (10 Sept.): 166–9.

Rothwell, J. C., Thompson, P. D., Day, B. L., Dick, J. P. R., Kachi, T., Cowman, J. M. A., and Marsden, C. D. 1987. Motor cortex stimulation in man. 1. General characteristics of the EMG responses in different muscles. *Brain*, 110: 173–90.

Ruby, P., and Decety, J. 2001. Effect of subjective perspective taking during simulation of action: A PET investigation of agency. *Nature Neuroscience*, 4 (5): 546–50.

Ruggieri, V., Milizia, M., Sabatini, N., and Tosi, M. T. 1983. Body perception in relation to muscular tone at rest and tactile sensitivity to tickle. *Perceptual and Motor Skills*, 56: 799–806.

Russell, J. 1996. *Agency: Its Role in Mental Development*. Hove: Lawrence Erlbaum.

Ryle, G. 1949. *The Concept of Mind*. New York: Barnes & Noble.

Saadah, E. S. M., and Melzack, R. 1994. Phantom limb experiences in congenital limb-deficient adults. *Cortex*, 30: 479–85.

Sabatini, N., Ruggieri, V., and Milizia, M. 1984. Barrier and penetration scores in relation to some objective and subjective somesthetic measures. *Perceptual and Motor Skills*, 59: 195–202.

Sacks, O. 1985. *The Man who Mistook his Wife for a Hat and Other Clinical Tales*. New York: Summit Books.

—— 1995. *An Anthropologist on Mars*. New York: Alfred A. Knopf.

Sandman, C. A. 1986. Cardiac afferent influences on consciousness. In R. J. Davidson, G. E. Schwartz, and D. Shapiro (eds.), *Consciousness and Self-Regulation: Advances in Research and Theory*, i. (pp. 55–85). New York: Plenum.

Sarnat, H. B. 1992. *Cerebral Dysgenesis: Embryology and Clinical Expression*. Oxford: Oxford University Press.

Sartre, J-P. 1956. *Being and Nothingness: An Essay on Phenomenological Ontology*, trans. H. E. Barnes. New York: Philosophical Library.

Sass, L. 1998. Schizophrenia, self-consciousness and the modern mind. *Journal of Consciousness Studies*, 5: 543–65.

—— 2000. Schizophrenia, self-experience, and the so-called negative symptoms. In D. Zahavi (ed.), *Exploring the Self* (pp. 149–82). Amsterdam: John Benjamins.

—— and Parnas, J. 2003. Schizophrenia, consciousness, and the self. *Schizophrenia Bulletin*, 29 (3): 427–44.

Scatena, P. 1990. Phantom representations of congenitally absent limbs, *Perceptual and Motor Skills*, 70: 1227–32.

Schacter, D. L., Reiman, E., Curran, T., Sheng Yun, L., Bandy, D., McDermott, K. B., and Roediger, H. L. (1996). Neuroanatomical correlates of veridical and illusory recognition memory: Evidence from positron emission tomography. *Neuron*, 17: 1–20.

Scheerer, E. 1984. Motor theories of cognitive structure: A historical review. In W. Prinz and A. F. Sanders (eds.), *Cognition and Motor Processes* (pp. 77–97). Berlin: Springer.

Scheler, M. 1954. *The Nature of Sympathy*, trans. Peter Heath. London: Routledge & K. Paul. (Original: 1912/1973. *Wesen und Formen der Sympathie*. Berne: Francke).

Schilder, P. 1923. *Das Körperschema*. Berlin: Springer.

—— 1935. *The Image and Appearance of the Human Body*. London: Kegan, Paul, Trench, Trubner; New York: International University Press, 1950.

Scholl, B. J., and Tremoulet, P. D. 2000. Perceptual causality and animacy. *Trends in Cognitive Sciences*, 4 (8): 299–309.

Schutz, A. 1932. *Der sinnhafte Aufbau der sozialen Welt: eine Einleitung in die verstehende Soziologie*. Vienna: J. Springer.

—— 1966. *Collected Papers*, iii. *Studies in Phenomenological Philosophy*, ed. I. Schutz and A. Gurwitsch. The Hague: Martinus Nijhoff.

Schwitzgebel, E. 1999a. Children's theories and the drive to explain. *Science and Education*, 8: 457–88.

—— 1999b. Gradual belief change in children. *Human Development*, 42: 283–96.

—— 2002. A phenomenal, dispositional account of belief. *Nous*, 36: 249–75.

Searle, J. 1983. *Intentionality: An Essay in the Philosophy of Mind*. Cambridge: Cambridge University Press.

—— *Minds, Brains, and Science*. Cambridge, Mass.: Harvard University Press.

Sejten, A. E. 1999. *Diderot ou le défi esthétique*. Paris: J. Vrin.

Senden, M. von. 1932. *Space and Sight: The Perception of Space and Shape in the Congenitally Blind Before and After Operation*, trans. P. Heath. Glencoe, Ill. Free Press, 1962.

Shafer, E. W. P., and Marcus, M. M. 1973. Self-stimulation alters human sensory brain responses. *Science*, 181: 175–7.

Shatz, C. J. 1990. Impulse activity and the patterning of connections during CNS development. *Neuron*, 5: 745–56.

—— 1992. The developing brain, *Scientific American* (U.K.) 267 (3): 35–41.

Sheets-Johnstone, M. 1990. *The Roots of Thinking*. Philadelphia: Temple University Press.

—— 1998. Consciousness: A Natural History, *Journal of Consciousness Studies*, 5 (3): 260–94.

—— 1999a. *The Primacy of Movement*. Amsterdam: John Benjamins.

—— 1999b. Emotion and movement: A beginning empirical-phenomenological analysis of their relationship. *Journal of Consciousness Studies*, 6 (11–12): 259–77.

—— 2003. Kinaesthetic memory. *Theoria et Historia Scientiarum*, 7 (1): 69–92.

Sherrington, C. 1953. *Man on His Nature*, 2nd edn. New York: Doubleday.

Shoemaker, S. 1984. *Identity, Cause, and Mind*. Cambridge: Cambridge University Press.

—— 1986. Introspection and the self. In P. A. French, T. E. Vehling, and H. K. Wettstein (eds.), *Studies in the Philosophy of Mind. Midwest Studies in Philosophy*, 10: 101–20.

—— 1994. Self-knowledge and 'inner sense'. *Philosophy and Phenomenological Research*, 54: 249–314.

—— 1999. Self, body, and coincidence. *Proceedings of the Aristotelian Society*, Suppl. 73: 287–306.

Shontz, F. C. 1969. *Perceptual and Cognitive Aspects of Body Experience*. New York: Academic Press.

—— 1974. Body image and its disorders. *International Journal of Psychiatry in Medicine*, 5: 461–72.

Siegal, M., and Beattie, K. 1991. Where to look for children's knowledge of false beliefs. *Cognition*, 38: 1–12.

Sillito, A. M. 1987. Visual system: Environmental influences. In R. L. Gregory (ed.), *The Oxford Companion to the Mind*. Oxford: Oxford University Press.

Simmel, M. L. 1958. The conditions of occurrence of phantom limbs. *Proceedings of the American Philosophical Society*, 102: 492–500.

—— 1961. The absence of phantoms for congenitally missing limbs. *American Journal of Psychology*, 74: 467–70.

—— 1962. Phantoms—experiences following amputation in childhood. *Journal of Neurology, Neurosurgery and Psychiatry*, 25: 69–78.

—— 1966. Developmental aspects of the body scheme. *Child Development*, 37: 83–95.

Sims, A. 1995. *Symptoms in the Mind: An Introduction to Descriptive Psychopathology*. London: W. B. Saunders.

Singer, P. 1979. *Practical Ethics*. Cambridge: Cambridge University Press.

Singh, J. R., Knight, T., Rosenlicht, N., Kotun, J. M., Beckley, D. J., and Woods, D. L. 1992. Abnormal premovement brain potentials in schizophrenia. *Schizophrenia Research*, 8: 31–41.

Skrinar, G. S., Bullen, B. A., Cheek, J. M., McArthur, J. W., and Vaughan, L. K. 1986. Effects of endurance training on body-consciousness in women. *Perceptual and Motor Skills*, 62: 483–90.

Slade, P. D. 1977. Awareness of body dimensions during pregnancy: An analogue study. *Psychological Medicine*, 7: 245–52.

Slater, A. M. 1989. Visual memory and perception in early infancy. In A. Slater and G. Bremner (eds.), *Infant Development* (pp. 43–71). Hillsdale, NJ: Erlbaum.

—— and Morison, V. 1985a. Selective adaptation cannot account for early infant habituation: A response to Dannemiller and Banks (1983). *Merrill-Palmer Quarterly of Behavior and Development*, 31: 99–103.

—— —— 1985b. Shape constancy and slant perception at birth. *Perception*, 14: 337–44.

—— —— and Rose, D. 1983. Perception of shape by the new-born baby. *British Journal of Developmental Psychology*, 1: 135–42.

Smith, A. 1795. *Essays on Philosophical Subjects*. Oxford: Clarendon Press, 1980.

Smith, R. 1738. *A Compleat System of Opticks in Four Books*. Cambridge and London: Austen & Dodsley.

Sohn, D. L. 1914. The psychic complex in congenital deformity. *New York Medical Journal*, 100: 959–61.

Sørensen, J. B. (2005). The alien-hand experiment. *Phenomenology and the Cognitive Sciences*, 4(1).

Spence, S. A. 1996. Free will in the light of neuropsychiatry. *Philosophy, Psychiatry, and Psychology*, 3: 75–90.

—— Brooks, D. J., Hirsch, S. R., Liddle, P. F., Meehan, J., and Grasby, P. M. 1997. A PET study of voluntary movement in schizophrenic patients experiencing passivity phenomena (delusions of alien control). *Brain*, 120: 1997–2011.

Sperry, R. W. 1950. Neural basis of the spontaneous optokinetic response produced by visual inversion. *Journal of Comparative and Physiological Psychology*, 43: 482–9.

—— 1952. Neurology and the mind-brain problem. *American Scientist*, 40: 291–312.

Stephens, G. L., and Graham, G. 2000. *When Self-Consciousness Breaks: Alien Voices and Inserted Thoughts*. Cambridge, Mass.: MIT.

Stich, S., and Nichols, S. 1992. Folk psychology: Simulation or tacit theory? *Mind and Language*, 7: 35–71.

Stone, T., and Young, A. 1997. Delusions and brain injury: The philosophy and psychology of belief. *Mind and Language*, 12: 327–64.

Straus, E. 1966. *Philosophical Psychology*. New York: Basic Books.

—— 1967. On anosognosia. In E. Straus and D. Griffith (eds.), *Phenomenology of Will and Action* (pp. 103–25). Pittsburgh: Duquesne University Press.

—— 1970. The phantom limb. In E. Straus and D. Griffith (eds.), *Aisthesis and Aesthetics* (pp. 130–48). Pittsburgh: Duquesne University Press.

Strawson, G. 1997. The self. *Journal of Consciousness Studies*, 4 (5/6): 405–28.

Streeck, J. 1996. How to do things with things: Objects, trovés, and symbolization. *Human Studies*, 19: 365–84.

Streri, A., and Gentaz, E. 2003. Cross-modal recognition of shape from hand to eyes in human newborns. *Somatosensory and Motor Research*, 20: 13–18.

Sumner, L. W. 1981. *Abortion and Moral Theory*. Princeton: Princeton University Press.

Surian, L., and Leslie, A. 1999. Competence and performance in false belief understanding: A comparison of autistic and three-year-old children. *British Journal of Developmental Psychology*, 17: 141–55.

Szmukler, G. 1984. Body image disturbance in anorexia nervosa. *British Journal of Psychiatry*, 144: 553.

Talmy, L. 1988. Force dynamics in language and cognition. *Cognitive Science*, 12: 49–100.

Tanji, J., and Shima, K. 1994. Role for supplementary motor area cells in planning several movements ahead. *Nature*, 371: 413–16.

Teitelbaum, P., *et al.* 1998. Movement analysis in infancy may be useful for early diagnosis of autism. *Proceedings of the National Academy of Sciences*, 95: 13982–7.

Thelen, E. 1985. Developmental origins of motor coordination: Leg movements in human infants. *Developmental Psychobiology*, 18: 760–75.

—— 1986. Threadmill-elicited stepping in seven-month-old infants. *Child Development*, 57: 1498–506.

—— 1995. Time-scale dynamics and the development of an embodied cognition. In R. F. Port and T. van Gelder (eds.), *Mind as Motion: Explorations in the Dynamics of Cognition* (pp. 69–100). Cambridge, Mass.: MIT.

—— and Fisher, D. M. 1982. Newborn stepping: An explanation for a 'disappearing reflex'. *Developmental Psychology*, 18: 760–75.

—— Ulrich, B. D., and Niles, D. 1987. Bilateral coordination in human infants: Stepping on a split-belt treadmill. *Journal of Experimental Psychology: Human Perception and Performance*, 13: 405–10.

Thomasson, A. 2000. After Brentano: A one-level theory of consciousness. *European Journal of Philosophy*, 8 (2): 194–9.

Thomson, J. J. 1974. Molyneux's question. *Journal of Philosophy*, 71: 637–50.

Tiemersma, D. 1982. Body-image and body-schema in the existential phenomenology of Merleau-Ponty. *Journal of the British Society of Phenomenology*, 13: 246–55.

—— 1989. *Body Schema and Body Image: An Interdisciplinary and Philosophical Study*. Amsterdam: Swets & Zeitlinger.

Tooby, J., and Cosmides, L. 1995. Foreword to S. Baron-Cohen, *Mindblindness: An Essay on Autism and Theory of Mind* (pp. xi–xviii). Cambridge, Mass.: MIT.

Toombs, S. K. 1988. Illness and the paradigm of lived body. *Theoretical Medicine*, 9: 201–26.

Touyz, S. W., Beumont, P. J. V., Collins, J. K., McCabe, M., and Jupp, J. 1984. Body shape perception and its disturbance in anorexia nervosa. *British Journal of Psychiatry*, 144: 167–71.

Trevarthen, C. B. 1979. Communication and cooperation in early infancy: A description of primary intersubjectivity. In M. Bullowa (ed.), *Before Speech*. Cambridge: Cambridge University Press.

—— 1986. Neuroembryology and the development of perceptual mechanisms. In F. Falkner and J. M. Tanner (eds.), *Human Growth: A Comprehensive Treatise*, 2nd edn. (pp. 301–83). New York: Plenum.

—— and Hubley, P. 1978. Secondary intersubjectivity: Confidence, confiding and acts of meaning in the first year. In A. Lock (ed.), *Action, Gesture and Symbol: The Emergence of Language* (pp. 183–229). London: Academic.

Tulving, E. 1983. *Elements of Episodic Memory*. Oxford: Clarendon Press.

Turner, M. 1991. *Reading Minds: The Study of English in the Age of Cognitive Science*. Princeton: Princeton University Press.

Uexküll, J. von 1926. *Theoretical Biology*. New York: Harcourt, Brace.

Vallar, G., Antonucci, G., Guariglia, C., and Pizzamiglio, L. 1993. Deficits of position sense, unilateral neglect and optokinetic stimulation. *Neuropsychologia*, 31: 1191–200.

van den Bos, E., and Jeannerod, M. 2002. Sense of body and sense of action both contribute to self-recognition. *Cognition*, 85 (2): 177–87.

Varela, F. J. 1996. Neurophenomenology: A methodological remedy for the hard problem. *Journal of Consciousness Studies*, 3 (4): 330–49.

—— 1999a. The specious present: A neurophenomenology of time consciousness. In J. Petitot, F. J. Varela, B. Pachoud, and J-M. Roy (eds.), *Naturalizing Phenomenology: Issues in Contemporary Phenomenology and Cognitive Science* (pp. 266–314). Stanford: Stanford University Press.

—— 1999b. Present-time consciousness. In F. J. Varela and J. Shear (eds.), *The View from Within: First-Person Approaches to the Study of Consciousness* (pp. 111–40). Exeter: Imprint Academic.

—— and Depraz, N. 2000. At the source of time: Valence and the constitutional dynamics of affect. *Arobase*, 4 (1–2): 143–66.

—— Thompson, E., and Rosch, E. 1991. *The Embodied Mind: Cognitive Science and Human Experience*. Cambridge, Mass.: MIT.

Varley, R., and Siegal, M. 2000. Evidence for cognition without grammar from causal reasoning and theory of mind in an agrammatic aphasic patient. *Current Biology*, 10: 723–6.

Velmans, M. 2002. How could conscious experiences affect brains? *Journal of Consciousness Studies*, 9 (11): 3–29.

Vercher, J-L., Gauthier, G. M., Guedon, O., Blouin, J., Cole, J., and Lamarre Y. 1996. Self-moved target eye tracking in control and deafferented subjects: Roles of arm command and proprioception in arm-eye coordination. *Journal of Neurophysiology*, 76 (2): 1133–44.

Vetter, R. J., and Weinstein, S. 1967. The history of the phantom in congenitally absent limbs. *Neuropsychologia*, 5: 335–8.

Vilensky, J. A., Damasio, A. R., and Maurer, R. G. 1981. Disturbances of motility in patients with autistic behavior: A preliminary analysis. *Archives of Neurology*, 38: 646–9.

Vogeley, K., and Fink, G. R. 2003. Neural correlates of the first-person-perspective. *Trends in Cognitive Sciences*, 7 (1): 38–42.

—— Bussfeld, P., Newen, A., *et al.* 2001. Mind reading: Neural mechanisms of theory of mind and self-perspective. *Neuroimage*, 14 (1): 170–81.

Volpe, B. T., Ledoux, J. E., and Gazzaniga, M. S. 1979. Spatially oriented movements in the absence of proprioception. *Neurology*, 29: 1309–13.

Voltaire, F. 1738. *Élémens de la philosophie de Neuton*. Amsterdam: Jacques Desbordes; repr. in *Oeuvres complètes de Voltaire*, xxviii. Paris: Antoine-Augustin Renouard, 1819.

Walker, A. S. 1982. Intermodal perception of expressive behaviors by human infants. *Journal of Experimental Child Psychology*, 33: 514–35.

Wallace, M. 1956. Future time perspectives in schizophrenia. *Journal of Abnormal and Social Psychology*, 52: 240–5.

Wann, J. P., Simon, K., Rushton, M. S., Smyth, M., and Jones, D. 1998. Virtual environments for the rehabilitation of disorders of attention and movement. In G. Riva (ed.), *Virtual Reality in Neuro-Psycho-Physiology: Cognitive, Clinical and Methodological Issues in Assessment and Rehabilitation*. Amsterdam: IOS Press (http://www.psicologia.net/pages/book1.htm).

Wapner, S., and Werner, H. 1965. An experimental approach to body perception from the organismic developmental point of view. In S. Wapner and H. Werner (eds.), *The Body Percept*. New York: Random House.

Wegner, D. 2002. *The Illusion of Conscious Will*. Cambridge, Mass.: MIT.

Weimer, W. B. 1979. A conceptual framework for cognitive psychology: Motor theories of the mind. In R. Shaw and J. Bransford (eds.), *Perceiving, Acting, and Knowing*. Hillsdale, NJ: Erlbaum.

Weinstein, S., and Sersen, E. A. 1961. Phantoms in cases of congenital absence of limbs. *Neurology*, 11: 905–11.

—— —— and Vetter, R. J. 1964. Phantoms and somatic sensation in cases of congenital aplasia. *Cortex*, 1: 276–90.

Weiss, G. 1998. *Body Images: Embodiment as Intercorporeality*. New York: Routledge.

Wellman, H. M. 1993. Early understanding of mind: The normal case. In S. Baron-Cohen, H. Tager-Flusberg, and D. J. Cohen (eds.), *Understanding Other Minds: Perspectives from Autism* (pp. 10–39). Oxford: Oxford University Press.

Wernicke, C. 1900. *Grundriss der Psychiatrie in klinischen Vorlesungen*. Leipzig: Thieme.

White, J. C., and Sweet, W. H. 1955. *Pain: Its Mechanism and Neurosurgical Control*. Springfield, Ill.: Thomas.

White, L. E., Coppola, D. M., and Fitzpatrick, D. 2001. The contribution of sensory experience to the maturation of orientation selectivity in ferret visual cortex. *Nature*, 411: 1049–52.

Wiesel, T. N. 1982. Postnatal development of the visual cortex and the influence of environment. *Nature*, 299: 583–92.

—— and Hubel, D. H. 1963a. Effects of visual deprivation on morphology and physiology of cells in the cat's lateral geniculate body. *Journal of Neurophysiology*, 26: 978–93.

—— —— 1963b. Single-cell responses in striate cortex of kittens deprived of vision in one eye. *Journal of Neurophysiology*, 26: 1003–17.

Wilf, R., Tyano, S., Munitz, H., and Wijsinbeek, H. 1983. Internal body image of the brain. *Psychotherapy and Psychosomatics*, 39: 129–35.

Wimmer, H., Hogrefe, J., and Sodian, B. 1988. A second stage in children's conception of mental life: Understanding informational access as origins of knowledge and belief. In J. Astington, P. Harris, and D. Olson (eds.), *Developing Theories of Mind* (pp. 173–92). Cambridge: Cambridge University Press.

—— and Perner, J. 1983. Beliefs about beliefs: Representation and constraining function of wrong beliefs in young children's understanding of deception. *Cognition*, 13: 103–28.

Windle, W. F. 1971. *Physiology of the Fetus*. Springfield, Ill.: Charles C. Thomas.

Winer, G. A. 1975. Children's preference for body or external object on a task requiring transposition and discrimination of right-left relations. *Perceptual and Motor Skills*, 41: 291–8.

Wolpert, D. M., Grahramani, Z., and Flanagan, J. R. 2001. Perspectives and problems in motor learning. *Trends in Cognitive Sciences*, 5: 487–94.

—— —— and Jordan, M. I. 1995. An internal model for sensorimotor integration. *Science*, 269: 1880–2.

Yamadori, A. 1997. Body awareness and its disorders. In M. Ito, Y. Miyashita, and E. T. Rolls (eds.), *Cognition, Computation, and Consciousness* (pp. 169–76). Oxford: Oxford University Press.

Yang, T. T., Gallen, C., Schwartz, B., Bloom, F. E., and Ramachandran, V. S. 1994. Sensory maps in the human brain. *Nature*, 368: 592.

Young, A. 1999. Delusions. *The Monist*, 82 (4): 571–89.

Zahavi, D. 1999. *Self-Awareness and Alterity: A Phenomenological Investigation*. Evanston: Northwestern University Press.

Zahavi, D., and Parnas, J. 1998. Phenomenal consciousness and self-awareness: A phenomenological critique of representational theory. *Journal of Consciousness Studies*, 5: 687–705.

Zahavi, D., and Parnas, J. 2003. Conceptual problems in infantile autism research: Why cognitive science needs phenomenology. *Journal of Consciousness Studies*, 10 (9–10): 53–71.

Zajac, F. E. 1993. Muscle coordination of movement: A perspective. *Journal of Biomechanics*, 26 (suppl. 1): 109–24.

Zhu, J. 2003. Reclaiming volition: An alternative interpretation of Libet's experiments. *Journal of Consciousness Studies*, 10 (11): 61–77.

Index